Master your Mind, Master your Leadership

The 7 Es: A Guidebook to Redefining Leadership for the 21st Century

By

Chandan Lal Patary

From the Author of the books, The Scrum Master Guidebook, The Product Owner Guidebook, High-Performance Team Coaching Guidebook and The Innovation Blueprint

INDIA • SINGAPORE • MALAYSIA

ISBN 979-8-89673-622-6

Also, by Chandan Lal Patary

- *THE INNOVATION BLUEPRINT*
- *101 ENTERPRISE BUSINESS TRANSFORMATION CASE STUDIES*
- *THE PRODUCT OWNER GUIDEBOOK: A PRAGMATIC REFERENCE MANUAL FOR MATURING PRODUCT COACHING*
- *A GUIDEBOOK OF COACHING HIGH-PERFORMANCE TEAM*
- *WE CAN LEAD: A GUIDEBOOK OF PERSONAL LEADERSHIP AND SELF-COACHING*
- *THE SCRUM MASTER GUIDEBOOK: A REFERENCE FOR OBTAINING MASTERY*
- *THE AGILIST'S GUIDEBOOK – A REFERENCE FOR AGILE TRANSFORMATION*
- *AND BUSINESS TRANSFORMARTION COACHING TOOLS*

About the Author

Chandan Lal Patary, lives in Bangalore, Karnataka, India, with his wife and two kids. He had commenced his career as an apprentice engineer in an Electrical Machine repairing company. He had started his software career as a Software Trainer, subsequently played various alternative roles like Test engineer, Developer, Technical Lead, Project Manager, Program Manager, Global Program Manager, Engineering Manager, and as an Agile coach for the last several years.

He has been conducting research on Organizational Development and Transformation for a decade. He is a practitioner and captures his analysis and shares his views through his writing.

His focus areas are **Organizational Transformation and Business Agility, Innovation, Strategy, Execution excellence, and** correlation **with People Leadership** and the impact of all these into Organizational growth.

He is working as an **Enterprise Agile Transformation Coach and Change Agent**.

He has **two decades** of deep experience in developing software products across various domains and has executed many large projects.

He has worked in product development for industries such as **Retail Fashion, Oil & Gas, Banking, Healthcare, Aerospace, Building**

automation, Power automation, Consumer Electronics, and Industrial automation. He has also worked on large-scale application development projects that are real-time mission critical.

He has worked with start-ups and large companies like **GE Medical Systems, Honeywell, ABB, Société Générale**, **Royal Dutch Shell, Samsung, and H&M.**

He has worked with team members of the **USA, Germany, Sweden, China, Australia, Finland, Switzerland, France, and Poland, London**, **Korea**, and **the Netherlands,** which has shaped his knowledge, personality, and skills.

He is a certified PMP since 2008 and Green Belt certified holder since 2005. He is an agile practitioner, a Certified Scrum Master since 2011, and SAFe Agilist since 2017.

He has completed a **Bachelor of Engineering** from the National Institute of Technology (National Institute of Technology–**Agartala, Tripura, India**) in Electrical Engineering-1998.

He completed a one-year **Executive General Management Program** from the Indian Institute of Management-Bangalore (IIM-B), Karnataka, India, in 2007.

He is the author of the best-selling books, **The Agilist Guidebook – A Reference for Organizational Agile Transformation (2018), The Scrum Master Guidebook – A Reference for Obtaining Mastery (2019), We Can Lead – A Guidebook of Personal Leadership and Self-Coaching (2020), A guidebook of coaching High-performance team (2021), The Product Owner Guidebook (2022), 101 Enterprise Business Transformation Case studies(2023) and Business Metamorphosis: 50 Tools to Coach Your Way to Success (2024)**

He has authored seven diverse e-books available for free download on SlideShare and has shared over **1000+ blogs** on LinkedIn.

As a speaker at various conferences, he has delivered over **20 talks** and created more than **30 presentations** covering a wide range of subjects on SlideShare.

Additionally, he has published over **50 technical** papers in numerous domestic and international journals, along with **21 papers** on Dzone.

He has earned many rewards in all the enterprises he has served for. He has received PM World Journal, 2017 Editor's Choice Awards for the paper "*Increasing Business Agility through Organizational Restructuring and Transformation*".

All the **20+** years he has worked on software product development projects and companies have taught him how to build better software while working with world-class team members.

While he was employed by the company Datex Ohmeda, he first had genuine experience creating software products (now known as GE Datex Ohmeda). He had spent seven months in Finland working with top-notch software architects. He spent more than three years developing a method for tracking the patient's vital signs in urgent situations. He has amassed excellent learning experience in software architecture and real-time system development.

His subsequent outstanding experience was gained while working as a software developer for Honeywell Aerospace's top-notch aviation software division. Many businesses, including Airbus and Boeing, had received products from him for cockpit systems. He had spent seven months working in Redmond, Seattle, at the Honeywell office. For this crucial product development, he collaborated with a large number of aerospace systems engineers and outstanding software architects. In the Honeywell plant in Seattle, he has taken flight tests with the Honeywell aircraft. For him, it was a wonderful experience! On this product, he had labored for more than three years.

His subsequent experience to a top-tier environment was with the Sweden-based ABB Power automation unit. Also, he collaborated with the team members who had developed this system many years earlier while visiting Sweden and Vasteras's office. They are an incredible team with a strong product that has been developed over time. He gained considerable understanding of Distributed Agile software product development in a mission-critical setting through this product development experience. He has spent more than three years developing this.

He has a ton of stories about how these products came to be. His life was drastically altered by the three products that he personally assisted in developing.

In addition to these initiatives, he was engaged in other management roles that provided him with a variety of opportunities to establish stronger teams for the creation of software products. He has experience working with the Honeywell HVAC system, the ABB Industrial Automation control system products, the Société Générale (SG) banking system, the Oil and Gas products in Shell, the Consumer Electronics & Mobile Products in Samsung, and the Retail Omni channel Products in H&M.

He stumbled into being a coach! The Head of Global Product Management from Finland recommended Chandan to his management while he was serving as the global program manager for one of the Industrial Automation projects that Chandan should be their agile coach. His adventure as an agile coach started at this point in January 2012. His purpose in life was to effect transformational change. He's having fun in the part, too.

Chandan is passionate about building a "**Body of Knowledge (BoK)**" for others to support and improve.

Purpose: Share the research I am carrying out with all so that they can reuse a few of my conclusions and workout the Challenges. Collectively we build up a body of knowledge (**BoK**), **KNOWLEDGE TREE – GUIDEBOOKS**

Vision: Let us share all our challenges and results associated with organization transformation **Mission**: Pursue building all the discoveries on a periodic basis to focus on these challenges and disseminate knowledge with all.

Join here to know more: **https://chandanpatary.com/**

Acknowledgments

The contributions of numerous people have influenced this book. I want to thank everyone who offered feedback, shared tales, or offered suggestions. This book was inspired by all of my friends and coworkers from both my current and past businesses. In order to write this book, I would like to thank all the Scrum masters, Agile coaches, and leaders with whom I have had contact or who I have interviewed. I'd like to thank everyone of my fans and readers on social media for leaving me comments and suggestions so I can get better.

The wonderful people I have had the pleasure of getting to know and working with contributed to this book in a truly collaborative manner. It is an honor for me to work with such supportive coworkers. They offer motivation to write more effectively and pointers for doing study.

The hundreds of team members and clients that I have had the privilege of working with and listening to, coaching, advising, and learning from have allowed me to advance in my proficiency.

I would like to thank all of my colleagues with whom I have discussed ideas and confirmed my knowledge. I appreciate the constant support and criticism from all **30,000+** of my LinkedIn contacts.

My sincere gratitude goes out to all of the prior supervisors and mentors who have molded, supported, and encouraged my professional progress over the past two decades.

I am profoundly grateful for the valuable leadership lessons I've learned from remarkable individuals throughout my journey. Each mentor and colleague have contributed uniquely to my growth, imparting insights that have shaped my leadership philosophy. From understanding the importance of empathy to navigating complex challenges with resilience, these lessons have been instrumental in my professional development. I owe a debt of gratitude to each of them for the opportunities they provided and the wisdom they shared.

A heartfelt expression of gratitude extends to my beloved wife, children, and parents, who have been unwavering pillars of support throughout my endeavors. Their encouragement, love, and understanding have played an indispensable role in my ability to overcome challenges and achieve milestones. My wife's unwavering support has been my anchor, providing the strength needed to navigate the complexities of leadership. My children's boundless enthusiasm has infused joy into my journey, reminding me of the significance of passion and purpose. Lastly, my parents' guidance and wisdom have been a constant source of inspiration, instilling in me the values that guide my leadership approach.

Completing this task was not an individual achievement but a collective effort, and I am immensely grateful for the profound impact my family has had on my personal and professional growth. Their presence has touched every aspect of my life, making this accomplishment a shared success.

Contents

Introduction:

Imagine you're a captain of a ship in the middle of a storm. The waves are unpredictable, the wind is fierce, and your crew is counting on you to guide them safely through the turmoil. Now, imagine being in a boardroom, facing an unforeseen market shift, a sudden crisis, or a breakthrough opportunity. The pressure mounts, your options are unclear, and the decisions you make could determine the future of your team, your company, or even your industry.

In both scenarios, the common denominator is the leader's ability to **adapt**—to think quickly, to shift direction with confidence, and to keep moving forward despite uncertainty. This is where **mental agility** comes into play. It's the invisible force that empowers leaders to not just manage complexity but to thrive in it. In today's world, where disruption and change seem like constant companions, the leaders who stand out are not the ones who have all the answers, but those who can think on their feet, adjust their approach, and inspire others even in the most trying moments.

Mental agility isn't just a buzzword—it's the defining quality of great leadership. It's not enough to simply be knowledgeable or experienced. The most successful leaders of the 21st century have learned to cultivate the ability to navigate the unexpected, to embrace ambiguity, and to make decisions that balance short-term needs with long-term goals. They remain calm under pressure, approach problems with fresh perspectives, and most importantly, act decisively in the face of the unknown.

But mental agility goes beyond intellectual flexibility—it is a blend of emotional resilience, creative problem-solving, and strategic foresight. It's the ability to stay open to new ideas, challenge assumptions, and manage complexity with clarity. It's what allows a leader to pivot when circumstances change and to keep pushing forward when the path ahead isn't clearly marked. Whether it's leading a global corporation through a market crash, guiding a small team through a product launch, or navigating the challenges of a startup in an ever-changing landscape, mental agility is the key to finding success in the most uncertain of times.

In the pages that follow, we will explore how mental agility is not an innate trait, but a skill—one that can be developed, honed, and refined. It's a mindset that allows you to not just survive but to thrive in the chaos of the modern world. This book is about providing you with the tools to become a more agile leader. We'll show you how to stay focused when everything around you is in flux, how to turn setbacks into opportunities, and how to maintain your clarity of vision even when the storm seems overwhelming.

Through real-world examples, actionable strategies, and a deep dive into the mindset of resilient leaders, this book will help you understand and master the art of mental agility. We'll explore how to apply this agility in different aspects of leadership—from making tough decisions to inspiring your team, from navigating disruption to fostering innovation. And above all, we'll demonstrate how these skills can transform not just your leadership style, but also the way you approach life's challenges.

Leadership in the 21st century is not about having all the answers—it's about knowing how to find them when they're needed most. It's about being able to pivot with purpose, to inspire others with confidence, and to make bold decisions even when the landscape is shifting beneath your feet. By the end of this book, you'll have a toolkit to enhance your mental agility, helping you to lead with vision, purpose, and resilience, no matter what comes your way.

So, let's begin this journey together. Let's discover how you can sharpen your mental agility to become the kind of leader who doesn't just adapt to change—but leads it.

The Science of Mental Agility

Mental agility—often referred to as cognitive flexibility—refers to the ability of the brain to adapt, shift, and adjust its thinking in response to new, changing, or unexpected situations. It's the mental skill that allows individuals to problem-solve effectively, think creatively, and maintain clarity in complex situations. While many view mental agility as an innate ability, it is, in fact, a skill that can be developed and honed through specific practices and strategies. Understanding the science behind it can illuminate why it's so important in leadership, and how anyone, regardless of background, can cultivate it.

1. Cognitive Flexibility: The Core of Mental Agility

At its core, mental agility is about cognitive flexibility. The term "cognitive flexibility" refers to the brain's ability to shift between thinking about different concepts, or to think about multiple concepts simultaneously. It is the ability to move between different tasks, solutions, or strategies without becoming stuck in one mode of thinking. In the context of leadership, cognitive flexibility is crucial because it allows leaders to adapt quickly when they face shifting goals, changing priorities, or new challenges.

The prefrontal cortex, the area of the brain responsible for decision-making, planning, and problem-solving, plays a significant role in cognitive flexibility. It enables us to adjust our responses based on new information, unexpected outcomes, or changing conditions. Leaders with high cognitive flexibility are able to approach problems from various angles, considering a range of possibilities before making a decision.

2. Neuroplasticity: The Brain's Ability to Rewire Itself

One of the most exciting aspects of mental agility is that it's not a fixed trait. Thanks to **neuroplasticity**, the brain's remarkable ability to reorganize and form new neural connections, individuals can actually improve their mental agility over time. Neuroplasticity means that the brain has the capacity to adapt to new experiences, learn from mistakes, and shift strategies when necessary. In fact, each time we practice adapting to change, managing stress, or solving problems creatively, our brain forms new connections that make these processes easier and faster in the future.

This concept is particularly important for leaders. As they encounter new challenges and complex problems, their ability to think and react quickly is shaped by their experiences. The more they engage in tasks that challenge their thinking—such as brainstorming, problem-solving, and adapting to unpredictable situations—the more their brain strengthens the neural pathways that facilitate mental agility.

3. The Role of Emotional Intelligence in Mental Agility

While mental agility often focuses on cognitive flexibility, emotional intelligence (EQ) plays an equally vital role. Emotional intelligence is the ability to recognize, understand, manage, and influence emotions—both your own and others'. Leaders with high EQ are better at managing stress, maintaining calm under pressure, and making decisions that account for both logical and emotional considerations.

For mental agility to work effectively in leadership, leaders must be able to manage their emotions in high-pressure situations. This emotional control allows them to stay objective, analyze situations clearly, and make decisions without being overwhelmed by stress or anxiety. Moreover, emotional intelligence enables leaders to connect with their teams, understand their needs, and create an environment where collaboration and adaptability are encouraged.

4. The Role of Working Memory in Mental Agility

Working memory—the ability to hold and manipulate information in your mind over short periods of time—is also a critical component of mental agility. Leaders constantly juggle multiple tasks, goals, and priorities, and the ability to hold complex information while managing multiple inputs is essential to making decisions quickly and accurately.

Working memory allows leaders to keep track of multiple variables at once, assess situations, and determine the best course of action. Leaders with a strong working memory can keep key facts and ideas at the forefront of their minds while remaining open to new information and adjusting their strategies accordingly. In short, a well-functioning working memory enables leaders to act decisively and intelligently under pressure.

5. Cognitive Bias and Mental Agility: Overcoming Traps

Another key element of mental agility is the ability to recognize and overcome **cognitive biases**. These are mental shortcuts that the brain takes to simplify decision-making, but they can sometimes lead to faulty judgments and skewed thinking. Common biases include confirmation bias (favoring information that confirms existing beliefs) and anchoring bias (relying too heavily on the first piece of information encountered).

Leaders with high mental agility can spot these biases and adjust their thinking accordingly. Instead of being anchored by initial impressions or past experiences, they are able to seek out new perspectives, question assumptions, and make decisions based on the most relevant and up-to-date information. This process of challenging cognitive biases helps leaders stay open-minded and adaptable, key traits for navigating uncertainty and complexity.

6. The Importance of Stress Management in Mental Agility

The ability to think and perform under pressure is another key component of mental agility. Stress and anxiety can cloud judgment, impair cognitive functions, and hinder decision-making. However, when managed properly, stress can also fuel creativity and enhance focus. Leaders who can regulate their stress levels can maintain mental clarity, make better decisions, and remain adaptable in the face of challenges.

Stress management techniques, such as mindfulness, deep breathing exercises, or regular physical activity, can improve a leader's ability to stay calm and focused when faced with high-pressure situations. By building resilience and managing stress, leaders can preserve their cognitive resources and continue to operate with high mental agility, even when stakes are high.

In two decades of working alongside remarkable leaders in various industries, I have observed a set of common traits that help them remain relevant in this ever-changing and complex world.

Each of these leaders possesses a strong desire to adapt and grow, even when faced with uncertainty. They embrace the idea that continuous improvement is essential for effective leadership.

To encapsulate these insights, I developed the **7E Leadership Framework**.

This framework has empowered numerous leaders to enhance their skills and become even better in their roles.

The framework focuses on seven essential elements: **Ethics, Envisioning, Endurance, Excellence, Encouragement, Enablement, and Effectiveness.**

By reflecting on these elements and assessing their maturity, individuals can identify areas for growth and expand their leadership capabilities.

As leaders engage with this framework, they find opportunities to strengthen their approach, adapt to new challenges, and inspire those around them. The journey of leadership is not just about reaching a destination; it's about the continuous evolution and commitment to excellence that shapes who they are. Embracing this journey can lead to a profound impact, not only on their teams but also on the broader organization and community.

By reflecting on these seven elements and embracing the journey of growth, leaders can stay relevant and impactful in their endeavors. This framework serves as a guide to cultivate the qualities that foster effective leadership in today's dynamic landscape.

Why Improving Leadership Mental Agility is Crucial for Today's Challenges?

Mental strength is the bedrock of effective leadership. It's the ability to remain calm under pressure, make sound decisions, and inspire others, even in the face of adversity.

Let us explore these questions?

- *How effectively can your organization adapt to change when leaders struggle to respond to market shifts or unexpected challenges?*
- *What are the risks associated with poor decision-making if leaders rely on outdated information or fail to consider new perspectives?*
- *How does a lack of mental agility contribute to stifled creativity and innovation within your teams?*
- *In what ways does a leader's inability to embrace change affect employee engagement and morale?*
- *How might ineffective communication among leader's impact team dynamics and workflows?*
- *What happens to team relationships when conflicts escalate due to a leader's limited ability to navigate complexities?*
- *How does a decline in overall performance manifest when organizations lack agile leadership in the face of challenges?*
- *What competitive disadvantages could arise if your organization cannot pivot quickly in response to changes in the market?*
- *How does the erosion of trust within teams affect collaboration and accountability when leaders fail to demonstrate mental agility?*
- *To what extent does the inability to achieve strategic objectives stem from a lack of mental agility in leadership?*

These questions can help leaders and organizations reflect on the critical importance of **mental agility in effective leadership**.

How This Book Came to Life?

The inspiration for writing this book stems from years of hands-on experience in leading transformation programs across the globe. Over the past decade, I've been fortunate to work with exceptional teams and leaders, each presenting unique challenges and opportunities for growth. My journey began with Societe Generale, collaborating with dedicated leaders from France and India, whose resilience and creativity left a lasting impression on me. Observing their leadership traits, I started documenting insights, aiming to understand what drives impactful change.

This learning expanded during my tenure with Shell, where I partnered with leaders from London, the Netherlands, and India to drive large-scale transformations. Each project deepened my understanding of how leadership adapts to complex scenarios. Similarly, at Samsung India, the fast-paced world of consumer electronics provided profound exposure to leadership in a rapidly evolving technological environment.

Currently, my work with H&M in Sweden has added new dimensions to my learning, particularly in navigating leadership transformation amid dynamic business landscapes. Each of these organizations became a laboratory where I observed, experimented, and learned how leaders can thrive amidst rapid changes and challenges in technology and business.

The book captures these insights in a coaching and storytelling format, enabling readers to reflect on their leadership styles and amplify their impact. It's designed to inspire leaders to navigate turbulence, empower their teams, and make meaningful changes, ultimately contributing to a better world for everyone.

Introducing, 7E Leadership Framework:

This **7E** leadership framework integrates **Ethics, Envisioning, Endurance, Excellence, Encouragement, Enablement, and Effectiveness** as key pillars. Each pillar supports the overall goal of effective and sustainable leadership:

1. **Ethics (Integrity, Trust, Moral Courage)** form the ethical foundation.
2. **Envisioning (Visionary, Strategic, Boldness)** provides direction.
3. **Endurance (Resilience, Adaptability, Perseverance)** ensures leaders can navigate adversity.
4. **Excellence (Discipline, Focus)** drives sustained progress and achievement.
5. **Encouragement (Influence, Collaboration)** empowers leaders to unite and inspire others.

6. **Enablement (Empowerment, Transformation)** allows leaders to foster growth and guide change.
7. **Effectiveness (Innovation, Impact)** ensures that leadership actions create positive and lasting effects.

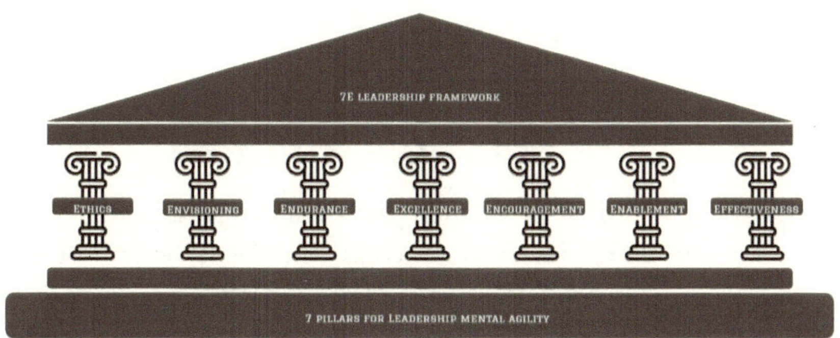

The 7E Leadership Framework stands tall on seven key pillars: **Ethics, Envisioning, Endurance, Excellence, Encouragement, Enablement, and Effectiveness**. Each pillar serves as a vital part of a leader's journey, intertwining to create a solid foundation for personal and professional growth.

Picture a leader grounded in strong **Ethics**. They navigate their decisions with integrity, earning the trust of their team. Every choice they make reflects their values, building a culture of honesty and respect. As they demonstrate moral courage, their team sees that standing up for what is right is not just encouraged but expected.

As this leader looks to the future, their ability to **Envision** inspires everyone around them. They craft a vivid picture of what success looks like and communicate it passionately. Their team feels the excitement of shared goals and rallies together, energized by a clear direction that sparks creativity and collaboration.

When faced with challenges, this leader embodies **Endurance**. They understand that setbacks are part of the journey, and rather than backing down, they face difficulties head-on. Their resilience becomes a beacon of hope, motivating the team to persevere through tough times. With each obstacle overcome, the bond within the team strengthens, fostering a spirit of unity.

Excellence is a standard they uphold. This leader encourages a commitment to quality in all endeavors, inspiring others to take pride in their work. They celebrate achievements, no matter how small, fostering an environment where everyone strives for their best. Each success builds confidence and inspires even greater efforts.

Encouragement flows freely from this leader. They recognize the potential in each team member, offering praise and support those uplifts spirits and nurtures growth. This positive reinforcement creates a space where people feel valued, igniting a desire to contribute and innovate.

Enablement is at the heart of their leadership style. By providing the tools and resources necessary for success, this leader empowers their team to take ownership of their roles. They trust their team members to make decisions, fostering a sense of autonomy that leads to higher engagement and satisfaction.

Finally, the **Effectiveness** of their leadership manifests in the impact they have. Their actions resonate beyond the immediate team, influencing the larger organization and community. The leader's dedication to these pillars cultivates a legacy of positive change that inspires others to follow suit.

As one delves into each pillar of the **7E Leadership Framework**, it becomes clear how they work in harmony. Together, they form a cohesive model that shapes leaders who inspire, uplift, and drive meaningful change in their organizations and beyond.

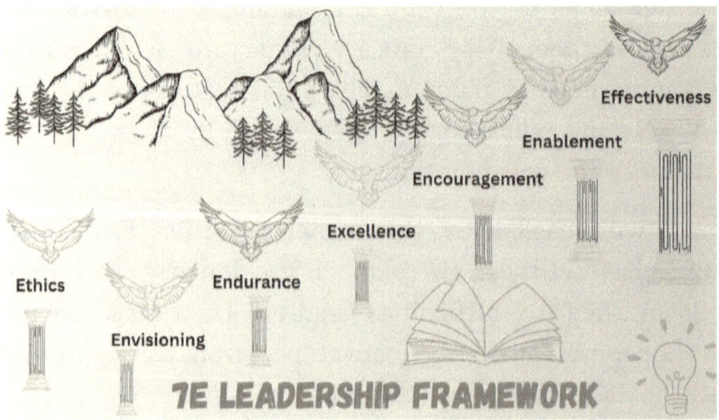

1. Ethics (Integrity, Trust, Moral Courage): **The Ethical Foundation**

Ethics are the bedrock of the leadership framework. Without a strong ethical foundation, a leader cannot build trust or inspire followership. Integrity, trust, and moral courage ensure that all other leadership actions are principled and aligned with ethical standards.

Let us Reflect on these questions.

- **Do your decisions consistently reflect the values you claim to stand for? Can you think of an example where this wasn't the case?**

  This highlights potential misalignment between stated values and actual behavior.

- **How do you react when you see unethical behavior in your organization? Do you take action or stay silent?**

  If a leader fails to address unethical behavior, it can indicate a lack of moral courage.

- **Have there been moments when you've prioritized personal gain over team or organizational ethics? How did that affect trust within your team?**

  This question probes whether the leader's actions have undermined trust.

- **When faced with pressure to compromise your principles for success, how do you respond?**

  Shows how the leader handles moral challenges under pressure.

- **Do your team members trust you to act with integrity, even when it's difficult? How do you know?**

  Trust is key, and this question asks the leader to reflect on how their team views their integrity.

Maturity in leadership comes with a deep understanding of how essential ethical principles are. With experience, leaders learn that true strength lies in making principled decisions, especially when the stakes are high. When faced with challenges, they become a source of strength for their team, proving that trust is not just given; it is earned through consistent, ethical behavior.

In every choice made, the leader cultivates an environment where team members can thrive, secure in the knowledge that they are led by someone who values integrity. This leader inspires others, not just by words but through actions that reflect unwavering ethical standards. Their journey shows that real leadership is not merely about personal success, but about nurturing trust, fostering a culture of ethical behavior, and standing firm on principles, even when it's hard.

2. **Envisioning** (Visionary, Strategic, Boldness)**: Providing Direction**

In the heart of every effective leader lies the ability to envision a brighter future. Envisioning goes beyond merely imagining; it involves creating a clear direction and purpose that guides a team or organization. A leader with a strong vision becomes a compass, steering their group toward shared goals. This vision is deeply intertwined with their core values, reflecting not only ethical priorities but also the long-term aspirations that fuel their journey.

Let us reflect on These questions.

- **Do you have a clear vision for where your team or organization should go in the next five years? If not, why?**
  - This question probes whether the leader has a well-defined long-term goal.
- **When making strategic decisions, how often do you focus on immediate issues rather than the bigger picture?**
  - This helps assess if the leader lacks strategic foresight and tends to react rather than plan ahead.
- **Do you find it difficult to inspire others to share and believe in your vision? What might be holding you back?**
  - This explores whether the leader can effectively communicate and rally others around their vision.

- **When faced with uncertainty, do you tend to play it safe or take bold actions to pursue your vision?**
  - A lack of boldness and risk-taking might indicate hesitation in driving the vision forward.
- **How adaptable are you when your original vision faces challenges? Do you revise your strategy, or do you struggle to pivot?**
  - This question uncovers whether the leader struggles with adaptability, an essential component of visionary leadership.

As a leader starts their path, they may focus on crafting a personal vision for themselves and their team. They spend time contemplating what they truly want to achieve in the next few years, drawing from their values and experiences to shape that vision. Over time, as they grow and mature, they transition from merely having a vision to being strategic and bold. They learn to inspire others, encouraging them to embrace this vision, even when faced with obstacles.

Imagine a leader who stands before their team, eyes bright with conviction, sharing a picture of the future that ignites hope and enthusiasm. They don't just talk about goals; they paint a vivid picture of success, illustrating how everyone plays a crucial role in getting there. Their words resonate, creating a sense of belonging and purpose.

In moments of uncertainty, this leader does not shy away from bold actions. They recognize that risks are part of the journey. Instead of playing it safe, they take calculated steps that might seem daunting but are necessary to pursue their vision. Their courage becomes contagious, encouraging others to step out of their comfort zones and innovate.

But envisioning isn't just about sticking to a plan; it's about adaptability. When challenges arise, a visionary leader remains flexible, willing to adjust their strategy without losing sight of their ultimate goal. They understand that the path to success is rarely linear, and they embrace changes as opportunities for growth. This adaptability inspires their team to do the same, fostering a culture of resilience and innovation.

As they reflect on their journey, they might ask themselves tough questions. Do they have a clear vision for where their team should be in five years? Are they focused on the immediate challenges, or do they keep their eyes on the larger picture? They consider how they inspire others and whether they can rally their team around their vision. When faced with uncertainty, do they leap into bold action, or do they hesitate?

Through these reflections, they deepen their understanding of what it means to be a visionary leader. They realize that it's not just about having a dream; it's about actively shaping the future and inspiring others to join them on that journey. With every step, they embody the essence of envisioning, creating a legacy that motivates others to strive for greatness.

3. Endurance (Resilience, Adaptability, Perseverance): Navigating Adversity

In the journey of leadership, endurance shines as a vital trait that helps navigate the stormy waters of adversity. Picture a leader standing firm in the face of challenges, embodying resilience as they encounter obstacles that test their resolve. This leader understands that resilience is not just about bouncing back; it's about staying the course when their vision is threatened. When setbacks strike, they don't succumb to despair. Instead, they dig deep, drawing on their core values to keep their eyes on the long-term goals, determined not to waver.

Let us reflect on these questions.

- **When faced with a major setback, do you tend to lose motivation or find it hard to stay focused on your long-term goals?**

  This question checks whether the leader struggles to maintain resilience when challenges arise.

- **How do you usually respond when your plans fail, or circumstances change unexpectedly? Do you quickly adapt or feel overwhelmed?**

  This probes the leader's adaptability and ability to pivot in the face of adversity.

- **When things get tough, how often do you question whether you should continue pursuing your vision?**

  This explores whether the leader lacks perseverance and tends to reconsider their commitment under pressure.

- **Do you find it difficult to inspire your team to stay resilient and focused when the situation is uncertain or difficult?**

  This assesses the leader's ability to not only maintain their own resilience but also influence and motivate others.

- **When dealing with prolonged challenges, do you prioritize short-term fixes over long-term solutions? Why or why not?**

  This reveals if the leader struggles with balancing immediate reactions with long-term perseverance and strategic thinking.

Imagine a moment when plans fall apart unexpectedly. While some might feel overwhelmed, this leader remains focused, adapting swiftly to the new reality. They approach each change not as a barrier but as an opportunity to pivot, their mind racing with possibilities for a new direction. They know that adaptability is key; it allows them to stay relevant in an ever-changing environment.

But endurance goes beyond personal resilience. It's also about inspiring those around them. When the team faces uncertainty, this leader steps forward with confidence, encouraging everyone to keep their spirits high. They share stories of perseverance, reminding their team that every challenge can be a steppingstone to greater achievements. Their words resonate, fostering a collective sense of determination that motivates others to push through difficulties.

Even when times get tough, this leader does not question their commitment to the vision. Instead, they remain steadfast, exhibiting a level of perseverance that reassures their team. They understand that doubts may creep in, but they refuse to let uncertainty derail their mission. They are the anchor that holds their team steady, ensuring everyone is focused on the shared goals despite the turbulence surrounding them.

In prolonged periods of hardship, this leader also understands the importance of strategic thinking. They resist the temptation to seek quick fixes, knowing that true solutions take time and effort. They balance immediate reactions with a clear vision of long-term success, guiding their team through each challenge with patience and wisdom. Their maturity shows as they transition from reacting to adversity with individual resilience to fostering an organization-wide culture of endurance and innovation.

In every challenge they face, this leader exemplifies what it means to navigate adversity with grace. They lead by example, demonstrating how resilience, adaptability, and perseverance can transform not only their own journey but also inspire others to embrace their strengths and move forward together.

4. **Excellence** (Discipline, Focus)**: Driving Progress**

In the world of leadership, excellence shines as a guiding star, illuminating the path toward progress. Imagine a leader who starts each day with a clear vision and unwavering discipline. They understand that discipline is not merely about strict rules but about maintaining focus on what truly matters. As they rise each morning, they embrace the tasks ahead, knowing that each small action contributes to a larger goal.

Let us reflect on these questions.

- **Do you find yourself often distracted by non-essential tasks, making it hard to focus on your core objectives?**
    - This checks if the leader struggles with maintaining focus on priorities.
- **How consistent are you in following through with your long-term plans, even when daily pressures arise?**
    - This probes whether the leader has the discipline to stick to their goals despite short-term distractions.
- **Do you find it challenging to maintain discipline in your team or organization, especially when facing prolonged periods of routine work?**
    - This explores if the leader can effectively extend their personal discipline to their broader team or organization.

- **How often do you review and refine your processes to ensure continuous improvement, or do you tend to stick with what's comfortable?**
  - This question evaluates the leader's focus on progress and improvement, rather than being stagnant.
- **When dealing with setbacks, do you have a structured plan to stay on track, or do you find it difficult to re-focus?**
  - This highlights whether the leader can maintain discipline and focus during challenging times, without losing sight of their vision.

When distractions arise—emails, meetings, and urgent requests—this leader remains steadfast. They recognize that the noise around them can easily pull them off course, yet they have trained themselves to prioritize their core objectives. By filtering out the non-essential, they create space for meaningful work. Each decision they make reflects a commitment to their vision, allowing them to move forward confidently.

As challenges emerge, this leader demonstrates resilience. They don't shy away from setbacks; instead, they approach them with a structured plan. When faced with obstacles, they revisit their strategies, refining their approach to ensure they stay on track. They understand that discipline is a dynamic force, not a rigid rulebook. With each setback, they learn, adapt, and grow stronger, driving progress even in difficult times.

This leader also recognizes the importance of cultivating discipline within their team. They strive to extend their focus and commitment to everyone around them. By sharing their vision and providing guidance, they inspire others to embrace the same discipline in their work. Together, they create a culture where everyone is encouraged to pursue excellence and strive for continuous improvement.

As they evolve, the leader realizes that maturity in discipline means not just personal habits but influencing the organizational processes. They engage in regular reviews, assessing what works and what doesn't, always seeking ways to improve. They understand that excellence isn't a destination; it's a journey, one that requires constant attention and adaptation.

In this journey toward excellence, the leader inspires those around them. They embody the values of focus and discipline, showing that true leadership is not just about setting a vision but about actively pursuing it with determination and grace. Their commitment to progress not only elevates their own leadership but also empowers their entire team, creating a legacy of excellence that resonates beyond their immediate influence.

5. **Encouragement** (Influence, Collaboration)**: Uniting and Inspiring Others**

In the realm of leadership, encouragement emerges as a powerful force, weaving together the threads of influence and collaboration. Imagine a leader who walks into a room filled with their team, their energy palpable. With a genuine smile and an open heart, they effortlessly draw people in. Their ability to influence others stems from the deep trust they've built over time, rooted in their core values. They understand that to inspire their team, they must first unite them around a shared vision.

Let us reflect on these questions!

- **Do you often find it difficult to get your team or peers fully aligned with your vision?**
    - This checks if the leader struggles to unite others or gain their buy-in.
- **How comfortable are you in collaborating across different teams or departments, and do you often rely on working alone?**
    - This probes whether the leader avoids collaboration or fails to foster cross-functional teamwork.
- **When trying to influence others, do you focus more on telling people what to do rather than guiding them to see the value in your ideas?**
    - This explores whether the leader uses effective influence tactics or relies on authority without building trust.

- **How frequently do you engage in active listening when working with your team, rather than just driving your own agenda?**
  - This evaluates the leader's openness to collaboration and other perspectives.
- **Do you regularly recognize and encourage your team's contributions, or do you find it hard to praise others for their role in collective success?**
  - This checks if the leader misses opportunities to inspire and motivate through encouragement.

As this leader engages with their team, they ask thoughtful questions and genuinely listen to the responses. They don't merely seek to impose their ideas; instead, they guide their team to see the value in their collective goals. This approach fosters a culture of collaboration, where every voice matters and every contribution are recognized. Instead of standing alone as the sole decision-maker, the leader encourages open dialogue, inviting ideas from all corners of the room. This collaborative spirit helps create an environment where innovation thrives, and everyone feels a sense of belonging.

The leader knows that true encouragement goes beyond just words; it's about recognizing the efforts of others. They make it a point to celebrate small victories, praising team members for their hard work and creativity. With each acknowledgment, they ignite a spark of motivation that radiates throughout the team. Their encouragement becomes a source of inspiration, energizing the group to push boundaries and achieve more than they thought possible.

As this leader matures, they begin to influence not just individuals but larger groups. They become adept at fostering collaboration across different teams and departments. They understand that leadership is not about authority but about empowering others to take ownership of their roles. By becoming a thought leader in their field, they inspire their colleagues to strive for excellence and to innovate together.

Through this journey of encouragement and influence, the leader transforms their vision into a collective mission. They create a vibrant community where everyone is committed to contributing their best. In doing so, they not only achieve their goals but also leave a lasting impact on their organization, proving that true leadership is about uniting and inspiring others to reach their full potential.

6. **Enablement** (Empowerment, Transformation)**: Fostering Growth and Change**

In the world of leadership, enablement stands as a beacon of growth and transformation. Picture a leader who understands that their role extends beyond simply managing tasks; they are committed to empowering their team members. This leader walks through the office, engaging with each person, listening intently to their ideas and aspirations. They recognize that every team member has unique potential waiting to be unleashed.

Let us reflect these questions.

- **Do you find it challenging to delegate important decisions to your team, or do you tend to retain control over most key choices?**
  - This highlights whether the leader is truly empowering others to take ownership.
- **When was the last time you actively coached a team member to take on a leadership role or a new responsibility?**
  - This checks whether the leader fosters individual growth or keeps team members in their current roles.
- **Do your team members feel empowered to innovate and offer new ideas, or do they usually wait for your direction before taking action?**
  - This reveals if the leader creates an environment that encourages initiative and innovation.
- **How comfortable are you with your team making mistakes as they take on new challenges, and how do you respond when they do?**
  - This probes whether the leader allows room for growth through learning from failures.

- **Do you often facilitate opportunities for team-wide improvement and transformation, or do you focus more on maintaining the status quo?**
  - This assesses if the leader drives organizational transformation by empowering larger groups to embrace change.

Instead of holding onto decision-making power, this leader takes a step back, allowing their team the freedom to make important choices. They embrace the challenge of delegation, understanding that true empowerment means giving others the opportunity to own their work. This approach fosters a sense of responsibility among team members, who feel valued and trusted to contribute to the vision.

One day, during a team meeting, the leader encourages a shy colleague to present an idea they've been developing. As the colleague speaks, the leader watches with pride, knowing that this moment is not just about a presentation but about nurturing growth. They often take time to coach individuals, guiding them as they take on new responsibilities. Through mentorship, they help others rise to leadership roles, creating a ripple effect of empowerment throughout the team.

In this environment, innovation flourishes. Team members feel encouraged to share their ideas, confident that their contributions matter. They are not waiting for the leader to dictate the next steps; instead, they take initiative, exploring creative solutions to challenges. The leader embraces this culture of innovation, understanding that mistakes are part of the journey. When someone stumbles while trying something new, the leader responds with support, reminding everyone that failures are simply stepping stones to learning and growth.

This leader also prioritizes opportunities for the entire team to improve and adapt. They don't just maintain the status quo; they actively seek ways to transform the organization. By facilitating workshops and discussions, they inspire collective progress and encourage everyone to embrace change. This commitment to enablement creates a dynamic environment where the team feels empowered to push boundaries and drive transformation together.

As this leader matures, they shift their focus from individual coaching to fostering a culture of empowerment within the entire organization.

They become a catalyst for change, inspiring adaptability, and resilience throughout their team. In this way, they not only cultivate growth in individuals but also help create a thriving, innovative organization ready to meet the challenges of tomorrow.

7. **Effectiveness** (Innovation, Impact): **Creating Lasting Positive Effects**

In the realm of leadership, effectiveness emerges as the ultimate goal, marked by the ability to create lasting positive change. A leader embodies core values and a clear vision, weaving these elements into their daily actions. They demonstrate resilience when faced with obstacles, maintain discipline in pursuing their goals, and inspire others through their influence. This combination not only drives their team forward but also resonates throughout the wider community.

- **Do you tend to focus on short-term wins, or do you have a long-term strategy for creating lasting impact?**
    - This helps assess if the leader is more focused on immediate results than on sustainable change and innovation.
- **How often do you encourage your team to challenge the status quo and innovate, even if it disrupts current processes?**
    - This probes whether the leader fosters an environment of innovation or sticks to conventional methods.
- **When faced with a new challenge, do you look for new, creative solutions, or do you rely on existing methods that have worked before?**
    - This reveals if the leader is committed to innovation or is resistant to change.
- **Do you measure your success by the immediate results you achieve, or by the long-term impact on your team, organization, or community?**
    - This checks if the leader's focus is on creating lasting, positive effects.

- **How much emphasis do you place on ensuring that your decisions and strategies lead to sustainable growth and transformation for your organization?**
    - This question assesses the leader's commitment to making decisions that have enduring benefits beyond their own tenure.

Imagine a leader who doesn't merely celebrate short-term wins. Instead, they look ahead, crafting a long-term strategy that prioritizes meaningful impact. In meetings, they encourage their team to think boldly, challenging the status quo and fostering an atmosphere where innovation thrives. They know that true progress often comes from questioning existing processes, allowing their team the freedom to explore new ideas, even if it means shaking things up a bit.

When new challenges arise, this leader dives deep into creative problem-solving. Rather than falling back on tried-and-true methods, they inspire their team to brainstorm innovative solutions, proving that adaptability is crucial in today's fast-paced world. They measure success not just by immediate results but by the enduring effects their actions have on their team and the community. Each decision they make is weighed against its potential for sustainable growth, reflecting their commitment to long-term transformation.

As this leader grows, they shift their focus away from personal achievements. Their aim expands to encompass the wider organizational landscape and society as a whole. They become a visionary, creating systems and practices that ensure lasting change. This leader understands that the true measure of effectiveness lies in the legacy they leave behind—a legacy built on innovation, collaboration, and a shared commitment to positive impact.

Through their journey, they inspire others to follow suit, igniting a collective desire for transformation that reverberates beyond the walls of their organization. In doing so, they prove that effective leadership is not just about achieving goals; it's about making a difference that lasts.

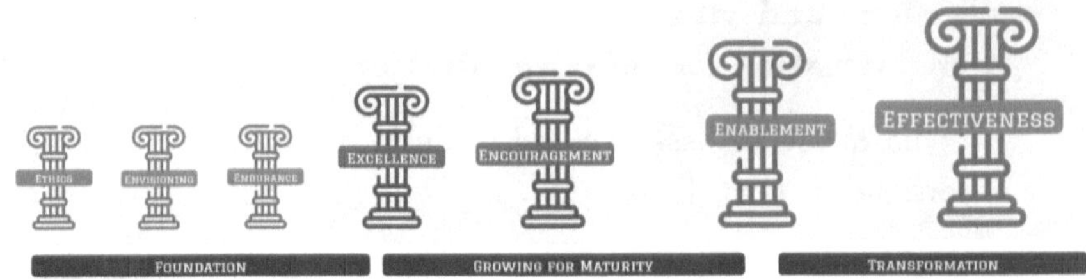

In the realm of leadership, a profound journey unfolds as one progresses from a solid internal **foundation** to a **transformative** external impact.

Following the **7E leadership framework** can logically improve **mental agility** for several interconnected reasons:

1. Holistic Development

The framework encompasses a broad range of attributes—ethics, vision, endurance, excellence, encouragement, enablement, and effectiveness. This holistic approach promotes comprehensive personal and professional growth, enhancing overall cognitive flexibility and adaptability, key components of mental agility.

2. Enhanced Decision-Making

By grounding leadership in **ethics**, leaders develop a clear set of values that guide decision-making. This clarity allows for quicker, more confident decisions, even in complex situations. When leaders are guided by a strong moral compass, they can navigate challenges without second-guessing their choices, fostering mental agility.

3. Visionary Thinking

The **envisioning** component encourages leaders to think strategically and anticipate future challenges. This forward-thinking approach sharpens critical thinking skills, enabling leaders to adapt their strategies in response to changing circumstances, a hallmark of mental agility.

4. Resilience in Adversity

Endurance teaches leaders to embrace setbacks as learning opportunities rather than obstacles. This mindset fosters resilience, which allows individuals to remain calm and adaptable under pressure, promoting a flexible thinking style that is crucial for mental agility.

5. Continuous Improvement

The pursuit of **excellence** encourages leaders to constantly seek ways to improve and innovate. This commitment to growth cultivates a mindset that is open to new ideas and approaches, enhancing cognitive flexibility and the ability to pivot when necessary.

6. Collaborative Problem-Solving

The **encouragement** and **enablement** aspects promote a culture of collaboration and empowerment. Engaging with diverse perspectives and ideas enhances creativity and flexibility in thinking, allowing leaders to adapt to challenges with agility and innovative solutions.

7. Long-Term Perspective

Focusing on **effectiveness** encourages leaders to look beyond immediate outcomes and consider the long-term impact of their actions. This broader perspective fosters strategic thinking, enabling leaders to adjust their approaches based on the evolving landscape of their organizations and markets.

By integrating the **7E leadership framework** into their leadership style, individuals can develop a more agile mindset that is adaptable, resilient, and innovative. Each element reinforces the others, creating a robust system that enhances mental agility, enabling leaders to navigate complexities and drive meaningful change effectively.

Imagine a leader at the beginning of their path, standing firmly on their values. They spend time reflecting on what truly matters, understanding that these core principles shape not just their actions but the environment around them. With a clear sense of self, they begin to form a vision that inspires not only themselves but also those they lead. This vision becomes a guiding light, a beacon that illuminates their journey and provides direction.

As this leader continues to grow, their focus broadens. They no longer operate in isolation; instead, they learn to influence and collaborate with their team. This expansion is like opening a window to fresh air—new ideas and perspectives flow in. The leader begins to empower others, trusting them to take ownership of the shared vision. Together, they navigate challenges and celebrate victories, building a culture of resilience and teamwork.

With time, the leader reaches a mature stage where their influence **transforms** not just individuals but entire organizations. They innovate boldly, introducing new ideas that reshape processes and drive success. Their leadership leaves an indelible mark, creating a lasting impact that resonates far beyond their immediate surroundings. This leader doesn't just aim for short-term results; they aspire to create a legacy, a positive change that endures.

The journey through these developmental stages illustrates how leadership evolves. From grounding in values to fostering collaboration and ultimately creating systemic change, each phase represents a step toward greater influence and responsibility. This journey is not just about personal achievement; it's about inspiring others and leaving the world better than they found it.

Through this framework, leaders discover that true power lies in their ability to connect deeply with their values, uplift their teams, and drive meaningful change in their communities and beyond.

By seeing leadership as a progression through these interconnected pillars, organizations can build leadership development programs that foster growth from values and vision, to resilience and discipline, ultimately ensuring leaders empower others and create lasting impact. The maturity in leadership evolves as the leader becomes more capable of leveraging each of these components cohesively.

Imagine a world where leaders stand firm on their principles, guiding others with unwavering integrity. Mahatma Gandhi walks through the streets, his calm demeanor inspiring millions. Each time he speaks, he stands as a beacon of truth and non-violence. In a time of great turmoil, he shows that ethical leadership means doing what is right, even when the world around him is chaotic. His actions resonate deeply, teaching others that true strength lies in moral courage.

Meanwhile, Alexander the Great gazes out over the vast territories he seeks to unite. He doesn't just see land; he envisions a future where diverse cultures come together. Each strategic move he makes is calculated and bold, illustrating how a visionary leader anticipates challenges and adapts seamlessly. His journey teaches us the importance of looking beyond immediate goals and daring to dream of a greater purpose.

As the Civil War rages on, Abraham Lincoln stands resolute in the face of despair. He embodies resilience, facing his own struggles yet never faltering in his mission to preserve the Union. Lincoln's determination shines through the darkest times, reminding us that endurance is crucial for leadership. His unwavering spirit encourages others to push forward, no matter the obstacles they encounter.

In the nascent stages of a new nation, George Washington's steady hands guide the ship of state. He faces challenges with discipline, demonstrating that effective leadership requires focus and self-control. His dedication shapes the future, showing how consistent effort lays the foundation for greatness.

As voices rise in the civil rights movement, Martin Luther King Jr. stands before a captivated crowd. His powerful words flow like music, each phrase igniting a fire of hope. Through his vision of unity, he encourages people to believe in a better tomorrow. King's ability to inspire not just through words, but through the warmth of his heart, illustrates the profound impact of encouragement in leadership.

John Adams, a mentor to many, walks alongside young leaders, nurturing their potential. His guidance is like sunlight breaking through the clouds, empowering them to rise and take charge. Adams shows us that true leadership is not only about personal achievement but about lifting others and fostering growth in those around us.

In a workshop filled with tools and ideas, Thomas Edison tirelessly experiments, a spark of creativity lighting his path. His mind buzzes with possibilities, and each failure becomes a stepping stone to success. Edison's relentless pursuit of innovation reveals how effective leaders embrace creativity, using it to make lasting change.

Through the stories of these remarkable figures, we see that the mind of a leader is a blend of vision, resilience, empathy, and integrity. Their lives become a source of inspiration, inviting us to lead with purpose and to create positive ripples in the world around us.

Once upon a time, in the ancient land of Egypt, during the reign of the Pharaohs, there was a story of an extraordinary leader named Pharaoh **Akhnaten**.

Unlike most Pharaohs, who followed in the footsteps of their predecessors and adhered strictly to traditional Egyptian customs, **Akhnaten** had a revolutionary vision that changed the course of Egyptian history.

At the time, Egypt was a land of immense wealth and power, worshiping a pantheon of gods with the sun god, **Amun**, being the most prominent. The temples of **Amun** were vast and wealthy, and the priests who managed them wielded great influence over Egyptian society. They had a powerful grip on both the state and its people.

However, **Akhnaten**, upon ascending to the throne, had a different vision. He believed in the worship of a single god, **Aten**, the sun disk, which represented the life-giving force of the universe. **Akhnaten's** leadership was about more than just a change in religious practice; it was about reshaping the values of his entire civilization. He was determined to break the stranglehold of the powerful Amun priests and lead Egypt towards unity under a single faith.

One of the most interesting aspects of **Akhnaten's** leadership was his courage to challenge the status quo. At a time when the gods of Egypt were deeply ingrained in every aspect of life — politics, economy, and social order — Akhnaten's decision to abandon the old gods was seen as radical. Yet, he believed that change was necessary for the future prosperity of Egypt.

Akhnaten's leadership style was highly innovative for his time. He didn't merely declare Aten the one true god; he built an entirely new city, **Akhetaten** (modern-day Amarna), where the people would worship Aten in peace and prosperity. The city became a symbol of his vision for a new Egypt, free from the old divisions and dominated by the harmony of a single belief system.

He also encouraged artistic and cultural expression in ways that were unprecedented. Under his rule, art flourished with a new naturalism, reflecting everyday life and the beauty of nature rather than the rigid and formalized styles of previous dynasties. This new artistic style was symbolic of his broader vision — a world where truth and natural order replaced the rigid hierarchies and traditions of the past.

However, **Akhnaten's** leadership was not without its challenges. The priests of **Amun** were not willing to give up their power without a fight. They conspired against him, and many nobles and common people, who had grown up worshiping the old gods, found it difficult to accept such a drastic change. Akhnaten faced opposition not just from the elites but also from the very people he sought to lead.

Despite these challenges, **Akhnaten's** leadership was marked by resilience. He stood by his beliefs and continued to promote Atenism, even in the face of opposition. He surrounded himself with loyal advisors and inspired his people with his vision for a united Egypt under a new faith.

Ultimately, **Akhnaten's** reign came to an end after 17 years, and after his death, Egypt returned to its old ways, reinstating the worship of the traditional gods. His city of **Akhetaten** was abandoned, and much of his legacy was erased by the following rulers, particularly his son, Tutankhamun, who restored the old religious order.

Though **Akhnaten's** religious revolution was short-lived, his leadership left a lasting impact on history. His boldness in pursuing his vision, even in the face of powerful opposition, showed the courage and conviction of a true leader. He challenged the deeply rooted traditions of Egypt, attempting to create a more unified and harmonious society.

Today, **Akhnaten** is remembered as one of the most fascinating and visionary leaders of ancient Egypt. His story serves as a testament to the power of leadership driven by conviction, the challenges of implementing radical change, and the lasting influence of innovative ideas, even in the face of opposition.

Let's reflect on the story of **Pharaoh Akhnaten** through the lens of the **7E Leadership Framework—Ethics, Envisioning, Endurance, Excellence, Encouragement, Enablement, and Effectiveness.**

1. Ethics

Akhnaten's decision to promote the worship of Aten over the established pantheon of gods can be seen as an ethical stance. He believed in the importance of integrity and aligning his leadership with a singular truth that he thought would benefit the society as a whole. By challenging the power of the Amun priests, he sought to dismantle corruption and redirect the focus towards a unified belief system.

Ethical leadership requires the courage to stand up for what is right, even when it goes against the grain. **Akhnaten's** actions were driven by a commitment to a higher principle, which is essential for leaders aiming to create meaningful change.

2. Envisioning

Akhnaten envisioned a new Egypt where people would worship one God, Aten. He didn't just challenge the existing order; he created a compelling vision for the future of his nation. His construction of Akhetaten symbolized this vision, providing a tangible space for people to embrace this new belief system.

Effective leaders must have a clear and inspiring vision that motivates others to follow. Akhnaten's innovative approach and his ability to create a new cultural and religious identity reflect strong envisioning skills.

3. Endurance

Akhnaten faced significant opposition from both the religious elite and the general populace. Despite the challenges, he endured through political resistance and social upheaval. His determination to promote Atenism showcases his resilience in maintaining his vision.

Endurance is critical for leaders who wish to implement transformative changes. Akhnaten's ability to withstand pressure exemplifies the importance of persistence in leadership.

4. Excellence

Under **Akhnaten's** rule, the arts flourished, and a new style emerged that was more naturalistic and reflective of real life. This dedication to excellence in artistic expression showed his commitment to improving culture and the societal experience.

Leaders should strive for excellence in all endeavors, inspiring others to pursue high standards in their work and contributions. Akhnaten's promotion of artistry reflects this principle.

5. Encouragement

Akhnaten encouraged new ideas and cultural expression. By promoting a new style of art and facilitating a shift in religious practice, he empowered his people to embrace creativity and innovation.

Encouraging others is vital for a leader to cultivate a supportive environment. Akhnaten's willingness to uplift and inspire his people demonstrates the importance of encouragement in leadership.

6. Enablement

Akhnaten established Akhetaten as a place where the worship of Aten could flourish. By creating a new city dedicated to his vision, he enabled his followers to practice their beliefs freely, providing them with the space and resources necessary to thrive under his new paradigm.

Effective leaders enable their followers by providing the tools, environment, and support needed for success. **Akhnaten's** actions illustrate the importance of enablement in fostering a community aligned with a leader's vision.

7. Effectiveness

While **Akhnaten's** reforms were ultimately short-lived, during his reign, he effectively shifted the religious landscape of Egypt and initiated significant cultural changes. His ability to mobilize resources to build a new capital and promote a new ideology showed his effectiveness as a leader in achieving his goals.

Leaders should measure their effectiveness by the impact they have on their communities. Despite the eventual rollback of his reforms, Akhnaten's ability to enact change during his time reflects a degree of effectiveness in his leadership.

Pharaoh **Akhnaten's** story exemplifies various aspects of the **7E Leadership Framework**. His ethical stance, visionary leadership, endurance in the face of adversity, commitment to excellence, encouragement of creativity, enablement of his followers, and effectiveness in implementing change all highlight the complexities and challenges of leadership.

Through this reflection, we see that successful leadership requires a multifaceted approach, with each of the 7E components playing a vital role in navigating the challenges of leading a community toward transformation.

Why Building the 7 E's of Leadership Mental Agility is So Challenging?

1. Ethics (Integrity, Trust, Moral Courage)

- **Moral Licensing**: Studies have shown that people who view themselves as highly ethical can sometimes rationalize minor unethical actions afterward, known as "moral licensing." Leaders with a history of integrity may feel they've "earned" some leniency, posing a risk to consistency.
- **Ethical Fatigue**: Research suggests that making constant ethical decisions can lead to decision fatigue, weakening resolve over time. Leaders repeatedly facing moral dilemmas may find it harder to uphold standards without support or rejuvenation.
- **Risk Aversion in Moral Courage**: Psychologists find that fear of judgment and career repercussions can deter leaders from taking morally courageous actións, especially in high-stakes environments where dissent is not well-tolerated.

2. **Envisioning (Visionary, Strategic, Boldness)**

    - **Planning Fallacy**: This cognitive bias, identified by psychologists, leads leaders to underestimate the time, costs, and risks of future actions, making bold visions difficult to realize as reality often diverges from initial plans.
    - **Confirmation Bias**: Leaders with a strong vision may focus on information that supports their ideas, ignoring counter-evidence. This bias can prevent leaders from adapting strategy when conditions change.
    - **Innovation Resistance**: Studies show that bold ideas often face organizational resistance, especially from those with a stake in the status quo, making it difficult for visionary leaders to gain widespread buy-in.

3. **Endurance (Resilience, Adaptability, Perseverance)**

    - **Burnout Syndrome**: Persistent high-stress situations, common in leadership, can lead to burnout, impacting resilience and adaptability. Neuroscience shows that chronic stress impairs cognitive flexibility, making adaptation to new challenges harder.
    - **Adaptability Paradox**: Research highlights that the more expertise leaders gain in one area, the less adaptable they become, due to "anchoring" in past successful approaches. Leaders must constantly work against this paradox to remain flexible.
    - **Adversity Response Cycle**: Studies show that repeated exposure to setbacks can erode resilience over time unless actively countered with positive reframing and stress management practices.

4. **Excellence (Discipline, Focus)**

    - **Attention Fatigue**: Cognitive science reveals that intense focus depletes attention reserves. Leaders often face this in high-demand environments, where multitasking and constant decisions hinder sustained focus on long-term goals.

- **Motivational Decline**: Research suggests that prolonged efforts to maintain high standards without immediate rewards can decrease motivation. Leaders may struggle to keep teams focused on excellence, especially during long projects.

- **Goal Dilution**: Having too many goals weakens commitment to each one. Studies show leaders who try to sustain excellence across numerous fronts may sacrifice quality, leading to diminishing returns.

5. **Encouragement (Influence, Collaboration)**

- **Empathy Fatigue**: Known as "compassion fatigue," this phenomenon occurs when leaders exhaust their capacity for empathy, making it harder to inspire and support team members over time.

- **Social Identity Theory**: Psychological research on in-group and out-group dynamics shows that team members may resist collaboration with those they perceive as different. Leaders must actively work against this to promote a truly collaborative culture.

- **Power Distance**: Studies show that perceived differences in authority can stifle team collaboration and open communication, especially in hierarchical cultures where subordinates feel less empowered to engage openly.

6. **Enablement (Empowerment, Transformation)**

- **Delegation Paradox**: Neuroscience research shows that people who are adept at tasks (often leaders) tend to believe they are the best suited to complete them, making delegation psychologically uncomfortable.

- **Imposter Syndrome**: Leaders who empower others may experience imposter syndrome, feeling inadequate as their influence shifts from direct action to enabling others. This can hold back true empowerment.

- **Resistance to Change**: Organizational research reveals that individuals often resist empowerment initiatives, especially if they've previously been in rigid structures. Leaders face the challenge of changing mindsets to embrace new, flexible roles.

7. **Effectiveness (Innovation, Impact)**

- **Status Quo Bias**: Leaders aiming for innovative solutions may find that both teams and stakeholders naturally resist change. Studies show that people prefer known risks over unknown opportunities, making innovation difficult.

- **Risk-Aversion Bias**: Psychological studies indicate that risk-averse leaders struggle with innovation, as fear of failure or loss prevents them from taking bold, impactful actions that could lead to breakthrough successes.

- **Difficulty Measuring Impact**: Research on decision-making shows that defining and measuring "impact" is inherently subjective, making it difficult for leaders to assess the success of their initiatives and make necessary adjustments.

Mastering these challenges requires leaders to balance short-term practical needs with long-term personal and organizational growth, often requiring dedicated reflection, feedback, and resilience-building techniques.

The principles of the **7E Leadership Framework** align deeply with the teachings of the **Upanishads**, which emphasize self-realization, ethical conduct, resilience, vision, and the interconnectedness of individuals with a higher purpose. Here's how each element of the 7E Framework resonates with Upanishadic wisdom:

1. **Ethics**

The **Upanishads** emphasize that leadership must be rooted in moral integrity and truth, where Dharma (moral duty) and Satya (truth) guide every action. In the **Taittiriya Upanishad**, the wisdom is clear: **"Satyam vada, dharmam chara"** – *"Speak the truth, follow righteousness."* This simple yet powerful teaching calls on leaders to act in alignment with universal principles of justice and truth, ensuring that every decision is based on what is right, not just what is convenient. In the context of leadership, these values urge leaders to lead by example, fostering an environment where integrity and righteousness are at the heart of every interaction. The **7E Leadership Framework** mirrors this Upanishadic wisdom by promoting ethical conduct and a commitment to justice, guiding leaders to create lasting, meaningful impact through their alignment with universal truths.

2. Envisioning

The **Upanishads** inspire leaders to develop a higher vision—one that transcends material pursuits and reaches toward a greater purpose. They stress the importance of having clear foresight, for it is vision that shapes reality. As the **Upanishads** say, **"Yatha drishti tatha srishti"** – *"As the vision, so the creation."* This means that a leader's vision is not just a mental image, but a powerful force that influences the outcome of their actions and the collective journey of their team. The Upanishads also use rich metaphors, like that of a charioteer guiding horses, to depict the mind's role in steering our senses. Just as the charioteer directs the horses with precision and wisdom, a leader must guide their thoughts and intentions to create clarity and purpose. When a leader has a strong, clear vision, it becomes the guiding light for themselves and their team, directing their efforts toward a unified and meaningful goal.

3. Endurance

The Upanishads place a strong emphasis on **resilience** and **perseverance**, seeing challenges not as obstacles, but as essential opportunities for growth. The **Shvetashvatara Upanishad** teaches, **"Amritasya putrah"** – *"You are the children of immortality,"* reminding us that the soul is limitless, and its strength can carry us through any hardship. This powerful teaching encourages us to rise above setbacks, drawing on inner strength and purpose to overcome adversity. For leaders, this message is particularly important: each challenge is an invitation to refine oneself, to grow stronger, and to develop the resilience that shapes lasting success. The path forward is not always smooth, but in every difficulty, there is a chance to purify the spirit and build the fortitude needed for greater accomplishments.

4. Excellence

In the Upanishads, the path to excellence is paved with **tapas** (discipline) and **sadhana** (dedicated practice). They teach that true mastery comes not from fleeting efforts, but from the consistent commitment to growth and improvement. The **Katha Upanishad** beautifully captures this spirit with the words, **"Uttisthata, Jagrata, Prapya Varannibodhata"** – *"Arise, awake, and stop not till the goal is reached."* This call to action urges us to pursue our goals with relentless determination, never giving up until we achieve excellence. It's a mindset that mirrors the 7E Leadership Framework, which emphasizes the importance of maintaining high standards and striving for continuous improvement, no matter the challenges we face.

5. Encouragement

The Upanishads deeply value encouragement and empowerment, teaching that true strength comes from unity and mutual support. They remind us that **"Anandam Brahma"** — "The ultimate reality is bliss" — and this bliss is found when leaders foster joy, support, and creativity within their teams. When leaders create an environment where team members feel valued and inspired, they unlock the highest potential in everyone. This aligns perfectly with the 7E Leadership Framework, which emphasizes nurturing teams and fostering collective growth, reminding us that success is not just an individual achievement, but a shared journey toward greatness.

6. Enablement

The Upanishads emphasize the transformative power of **Jnana Yoga** (the path of knowledge), and **Seva** (selfless service) as means to empower others. By sharing wisdom and creating opportunities, a leader helps others grow and reach their potential. The verse **"Tamaso ma jyotir gamaya"** — "Lead me from darkness to light" — beautifully captures the role of a leader, much like a guru, guiding their team from ignorance to knowledge, and from dependence to self-reliance. Through this guidance, leaders inspire growth, enlightenment, and independence in those they lead.

7. Effectiveness

The Upanishads emphasize the profound importance of aligning one's actions with **(Rta)**, the universal order, to create lasting impact and ensure sustainable success. This wisdom is beautifully encapsulated in the Bhagavad Gita, which is deeply rooted in Upanishadic philosophy. The verse **"Karmanye vadhikaraste, ma phaleshu kadachana"** teaches a timeless lesson: focus on performing your duties with dedication and integrity, without attachment to the outcomes. This approach reflects the essence of true effectiveness—channeling energy into meaningful contributions rather than being consumed by the pursuit of rewards.

Core Leadership Philosophy in the Upanishads

In the **Upanishads**, leadership is seen as more than just the pursuit of personal achievement. It's a spiritual journey that deeply connects individual growth with the well-being of the collective. Leaders are not simply those who accomplish goals; they are **guides**, lighting the way for others, helping them navigate their own paths to growth and fulfillment. The Upanishads teach that leadership is grounded in **self-awareness**, **moral integrity**, and a **higher purpose**, which collectively direct a leader's actions. As a leader, it is not just about what you achieve for yourself, but how you help others elevate, empowering them to realize their own potential and contribute to the greater good.

The **7E Leadership Framework** echoes the timeless wisdom of the Upanishads, blending ethical responsibility, visionary planning, resilience, excellence, encouragement, empowerment, and impactful action. By incorporating these teachings, leaders can foster transformation within themselves and inspire profound change in their teams and organizations, embodying the ideal of *"Vasudhaiva Kutumbakam"* (The world is one family).

| | Mental agility turns challenges into stepping stones | |

Let's dive into each pillar and uncover how they shape us into resilient and impactful leaders.

Part-1

Leadership Pillar-1 (Ethics)

Courageous Integrity: Leading with Trust and Moral Strength

- **Nelson Mandela: A Beacon of Trust**
- **Echoes of Resistance: The Legacy of the Sonderkommando and the White Rose**
- **The Flame of Courage: Leadership Lessons from Joan of Arc & Rani Lakshmibai**
- **From Chains to Triumph: The Indomitable Spirit of Harriet Tubman**
- **Leadership Gone Wrong: Stories of Corruption and Systemic Breakdown**

Imagine standing at the edge of a vast, dark forest. Ahead lies a winding path filled with obstacles and uncertainty. This is the journey of leadership, where courageous integrity shines like a bright beacon, guiding those who dare to lead with purpose. Leadership isn't just about making tough choices; it's about holding your ground when challenges arise, staying true to your values, and showing unyielding moral courage.

Throughout history, remarkable figures like Nelson Mandela, Joan of Arc, and Harriet Tubman have illuminated our understanding of true leadership. It's not merely about wielding power or seeking influence; it's about having the heart to fight for what's right, even when the going gets tough.

Take Nelson Mandela, for example. His journey was one of trust and unwavering strength. After spending 27 years in prison, he emerged not with bitterness but as a unifying force for a fractured nation. Imagine the grace it took to forgive those who wronged him! His dedication to rebuilding trust and leading South Africa to freedom speaks volumes. Mandela teaches us that authentic leadership transcends personal ambition; it's about uplifting others and nurturing entire communities.

Consider the brave resistance fighters during World War II, like the Sonderkommando and the White Rose. In the bleakest moments, they stood up against tyranny, fully aware that their courage might cost them their lives. Picture them quietly plotting and whispering their defiance, knowing that every small act of resistance could inspire others. Their legacy reminds us that moral courage, even in the smallest gestures, can spark significant change.

Then there's Joan of Arc, a fearless warrior, and Rani Lakshmibai, who led their people with an unshakable sense of justice. Visualize Joan rallying her troops, her spirit ablaze with determination as she stands firm against overwhelming odds. Their actions remind us that true leadership means fighting for something greater than oneself, weaving stories of moral conviction and relentless determination.

Harriet Tubman's life tells another powerful tale of leadership forged through personal struggle. After escaping slavery, she risked everything to lead others to freedom. Imagine her guiding weary travelers through the night, her heart pounding but driven by a profound sense of duty. Tubman's leadership wasn't about self-interest; it was a passionate call to help others, no matter the danger. Her courage and spirit embody the integrity that defines exceptional leaders.

But what happens when leaders lack this moral foundation? History shows us the downfall of those who fall into corruption. When integrity crumbles, trust vanishes, and systems unravel. Leaders driven by selfish ambition fail, leaving a trail of instability and division in their wake.

Courageous integrity teaches us that leadership isn't about sidestepping failure; it's about confronting it with strength and honesty. Leaders who inspire trust and act with moral conviction—like Mandela, Joan of Arc, and Tubman—are the ones who leave a lasting impact on history. This is the kind of leadership that builds not only successful organizations and nations but also a better world for everyone.

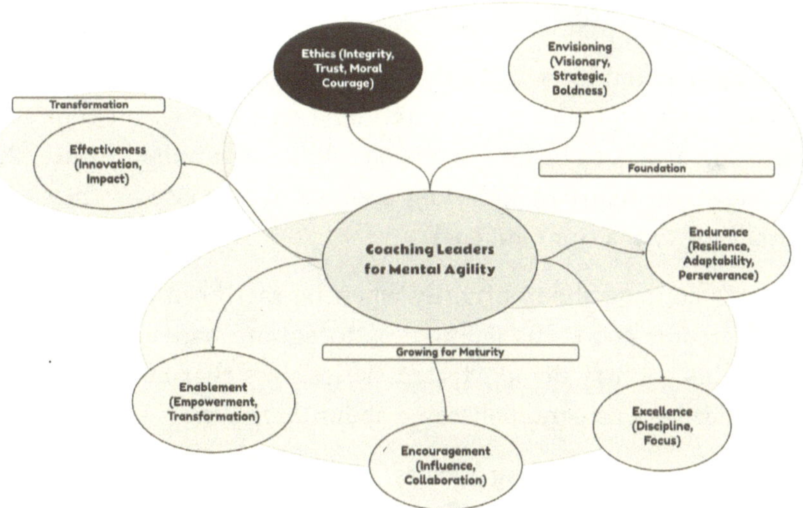

Coaching Leaders for Mental Agility: Story No 1

Nelson Mandela: A Beacon of Trust

> **"Trust is the glue of life. It's the most essential ingredient in effective communication. It's the foundational principle that holds all relationships."**
>
> \- **Stephen R. Covey**

Nelson Mandela, the revered South African leader, is a global symbol of trust and integrity.

His life and leadership exemplify how trust can transform societies and inspire individuals.

Nelson Mandela stood as a symbol of integrity and strength. Throughout his 27 years of imprisonment, he remained unwavering in his principles, steadfastly fighting for justice and equality. This dedication earned him the trust of millions who looked to him as a beacon of hope.

Mandela's empathy was striking. He had the remarkable ability to understand and share the feelings of others, even those who had oppressed him. After his release, he chose reconciliation over revenge, which helped heal a nation deeply scarred by division. This compassionate approach fostered trust among those who had once been adversaries.

With a clear vision for a democratic and inclusive South Africa, Mandela inspired those around him. He communicated this vision consistently, motivating others to believe in the possibility of a united future. People were drawn to his dream, feeling a sense of purpose as they worked together towards a common goal.

Mandela's courage shone brightly when he sacrificed his own freedom for the greater good. His willingness to endure hardship for the well-being of his country demonstrated selflessness that made people trust him as a leader who genuinely cared about their lives.

He was a master at building bridges, uniting communities that had been divided by race and politics. Through his efforts, he earned the respect and trust of diverse groups, showing that collaboration was possible even in the most challenging circumstances.

Leading by example, Mandela embodied the values he wished to see in others. His humility and respect for everyone set a standard for how leaders should act. He treated people with dignity, inspiring them to follow his path of service.

Mandela's transparent communication style further strengthened the bond between him and the people of South Africa. Even when the truth was difficult to hear, he spoke openly and honestly, which helped build a foundation of trust.

His advocacy for forgiveness and reconciliation was pivotal for the nation. By establishing the Truth and Reconciliation Commission, he encouraged South Africans to confront their painful pasts. This initiative paved the way for a future built on understanding and trust.

Mandela's inclusive approach ensured that all voices were heard and respected. He created an environment where everyone felt they belonged, fostering trust and unity among the people.

His resilience in the face of adversity was another source of inspiration. Mandela's unwavering commitment to his principles reassured the people that they could trust him to stand by his word, no matter the challenges he faced.

Through his life and actions, Nelson Mandela not only earned trust but also inspired a nation to rise together, demonstrating the power of integrity, empathy, and vision in the pursuit of justice and equality.

Here are some key aspects of how Mandela embodied and built trust:

Nelson Mandela is known for his legendary mental strength. He faced unimaginable challenges, yet he remained resilient throughout his life. To cultivate a similar level of resilience, one can adopt several key strategies inspired by his journey.

First, embracing forgiveness is essential. Mandela chose to forgive those who had imprisoned him. He understood that holding onto anger and resentment only harms oneself. By letting go of negativity, one can clear the mind and focus on positive growth.

Next, staying committed to personal goals is vital. Despite spending 27 years in prison, Mandela never wavered from his vision of a free and equal South Africa. He kept his eyes on the prize, reminding us all to remain focused on long-term aspirations, even when faced with daunting obstacles.

Maintaining a sense of optimism also plays a crucial role. Mandela believed in the power of hope and positivity. By cultivating a positive mindset, one can focus on the possibilities ahead instead of getting bogged down by difficulties.

Learning from adversity is another important strategy. Challenges and setbacks can serve as opportunities to learn and grow. Mandela used his time in prison to reflect on his experiences, developing his leadership skills and preparing for the future.

Practicing patience is equally essential. Change often takes time, and Mandela's life is a testament to the power of perseverance. It is important to be patient with oneself and to understand that resilience is built over time.

Finding strength in unity can also provide support. Mandela valued the power of collective action and teamwork. By building strong relationships and support networks, one can draw strength from others and offer help in return.

Cultivating discipline is another key aspect of resilience. During his imprisonment, Mandela maintained a disciplined routine, which helped him stay mentally and physically strong. Establishing daily habits that promote well-being can foster resilience in one's own life.

Finally, it is crucial to focus on the bigger picture. Keeping one's purpose and vision in mind, especially during tough times, can serve as motivation. Mandela's unwavering focus on the greater good kept him motivated through adversity. Identifying a broader purpose can help anyone stay resilient in the face of challenges.

By embodying these principles, one can nurture a mental fortitude that echoes Mandela's legacy, transforming challenges into opportunities for growth and unity.

By incorporating these strategies into your life, you can build mental stamina and resilience, drawing inspiration from Nelson Mandela's remarkable journey.

Let's go through these coaching questions with example answers to illustrate how they can help build mental stamina like Nelson Mandela.

Vision and Purpose

- **What is your ultimate goal or vision, and why is it important to you?** *Example*: "My ultimate goal is to start a nonprofit organization that supports education for underprivileged children. This is important to me because I believe education is the key to breaking the cycle of poverty and empowering individuals to improve their lives."

- **How does your current situation align with your long-term purpose?** *Example*: "Currently, I'm working as a teacher in a low-income area. This aligns with my long-term purpose because I am gaining firsthand experience and understanding of the challenges these children face, which will be invaluable when I start my nonprofit."
- **What values guide your decisions and actions?** *Example*: "The values that guide me are empathy, perseverance, and fairness. I strive to understand and support others, work hard despite obstacles, and ensure that everyone is treated with equal respect and opportunity."

Resilience and Overcoming Adversity

- **What challenges have you faced recently, and how did you overcome them?** *Example*: "Recently, I faced budget cuts at my school which limited resources for my students. I overcame this by organizing a community fundraiser and partnering with local businesses to donate supplies."
- **How can you reframe a current obstacle to see it as an opportunity for growth?** *Example*: "My current obstacle is the high stress level from balancing work and further education. I can reframe this as an opportunity to develop better time management skills and learn to prioritize my well-being."
- **What strategies have you used in the past to stay strong during tough times?** *Example*: "In the past, I stayed strong by maintaining a daily exercise routine, practicing mindfulness meditation, and seeking support from friends and mentors."

Patience and Persistence

- **What steps can you take today to move closer to your long-term goals, even if progress is slow?** *Example*: "Today, I can spend an hour researching potential grants for my future nonprofit and another hour networking with professionals in the field."

- **How do you maintain motivation when results are not immediate?** *Example*: "I maintain motivation by setting small, achievable milestones and celebrating each one. I also remind myself of the bigger picture and the impact my work will eventually have."
- **What past experiences have taught you the value of patience and persistence?** *Example*: "When I was learning to play the piano, it took me years to become proficient. This experience taught me that patience and consistent practice are essential for mastering any skill."

Forgiveness and Letting Go

- **Who do you need to forgive to free yourself from negative emotions?** *Example*: "I need to forgive a former colleague who wronged me. Holding onto this resentment only drains my energy and prevents me from moving forward."
- **How can letting go of past grievances help you move forward?** *Example*: "Letting go of past grievances will help me focus on the present and future, allowing me to channel my energy into positive actions and relationships."
- **What actions can you take to practice forgiveness and empathy daily?** *Example*: "Daily, I can practice forgiveness and empathy by putting myself in others' shoes, offering kindness even when it's difficult, and reflecting on the benefits of letting go of grudges."

Building Relationships and Support Networks

- **Who are the key people in your support network, and how can you strengthen those relationships?** *Example*: "The key people in my support network are my family, close friends, and professional mentors. I can strengthen these relationships by regularly checking in, offering my support, and expressing gratitude for their presence in my life."
- **How can you build trust and collaboration within your team or community?** *Example*: "I can build trust and

collaboration by being transparent about my goals and challenges, actively listening to others' ideas, and creating opportunities for teamwork and shared decision-making."

- **What role does empathy play in your interactions with others, and how can you enhance it?** *Example*: "Empathy allows me to connect deeply with others and understand their perspectives. I can enhance it by practicing active listening, asking open-ended questions, and reflecting on my interactions to ensure I'm responding with compassion."

Maintaining Optimism

- **What positive outcomes can you envision from your current challenges?** *Example*: "From my current challenges of tight deadlines and high workload, I envision becoming more efficient and developing better stress management techniques, which will benefit me in future projects."
- **How can you cultivate a mindset of hope and possibility?** *Example*: "I can cultivate a mindset of hope and possibility by regularly practicing gratitude, setting realistic yet ambitious goals, and surrounding myself with positive influences and inspirational stories."
- **What daily practices help you stay optimistic and focused on the future?** *Example*: "Daily practices that help me stay optimistic include journaling about my achievements, meditating to clear my mind, and reading motivational quotes or books."

Learning and Growth

- **What have you learned from your recent experiences, both successes and failures?** *Example*: "From my recent experiences, I've learned that resilience and adaptability are crucial. Successes have shown me the power of perseverance, while failures have taught me valuable lessons in humility and strategic planning."
- **How can you apply these lessons to improve your approach going forward?** *Example*: "I can apply these lessons by being more flexible in my planning, seeking feedback more actively,

and viewing setbacks as learning opportunities rather than roadblocks."

- **What new skills or knowledge do you need to develop to achieve your goals?** *Example*: "To achieve my goals, I need to develop better public speaking skills and gain more knowledge in nonprofit management. I can do this by taking relevant courses and seeking mentorship from experienced professionals."

Self-Discipline and Routine

- **What daily habits or routines help you stay mentally and physically strong?** *Example*: "Daily habits that keep me strong include morning exercise, a balanced diet, meditation, and setting aside time for personal development and relaxation."
- **How can you create a more disciplined approach to achieving your goals?** *Example*: "I can create a more disciplined approach by setting clear priorities, creating a structured daily schedule, and holding myself accountable through regular progress reviews."
- **What adjustments can you make to your routine to better support your mental stamina?** *Example*: "To better support my mental stamina, I can adjust my routine to include more breaks during work, dedicate time for hobbies, and ensure I get enough sleep each night."

Reflection and Self-Awareness

- **How do you take time to reflect on your experiences and emotions?** *Example*: "I take time to reflect by journaling every evening, meditating daily, and having regular check-ins with a trusted friend or mentor to discuss my thoughts and feelings."
- **What practices help you stay self-aware and in tune with your inner thoughts and feelings?** *Example*: "Practices like mindfulness meditation, regular journaling, and setting aside quiet time each day help me stay self-aware and connected to my inner thoughts and feelings."

- **How can you use reflection to enhance your resilience and decision-making?** *Example*: "Reflection enhances my resilience and decision-making by allowing me to learn from past experiences, understand my emotional responses, and make more informed, thoughtful choices moving forward."

By answering these questions with specific examples, you can gain a deeper understanding of how to build mental stamina, much like Nelson Mandela did. These answers provide practical steps and insights that can be applied to your own life and challenges.

Nelson Mandela's legacy as a beacon of trust is a testament to the power of integrity, empathy, visionary leadership, and resilience.

His life teaches us that trust is not built overnight but through consistent actions, sacrifice, and a genuine commitment to the well-being of others.

By embodying these values, Mandela not only led a nation through a transformative period but also left a lasting impact on the world, demonstrating that trust is the foundation of lasting change and unity.

Here are **five key takeaways** from Nelson Mandela's leadership and the way he embodied and built trust:

- **Integrity and Unwavering Principles**

  Throughout his 27 years of imprisonment, Mandela stayed true to his beliefs in justice and equality. His steadfast commitment to his principles, even in the face of adversity, earned him widespread respect and trust. People could rely on his integrity.

- **Empathy and Reconciliation**

  Mandela's ability to empathize, even with his oppressors, was remarkable. After his release, he chose reconciliation over revenge, which helped heal South Africa. His compassion and focus on unity fostered trust among people from all sides of conflict.

- **Visionary Leadership**

  Mandela communicated a clear vision for a democratic and inclusive South Africa. He inspired millions to work towards a common goal of unity and equality, and his consistency in pursuing this vision made him a trustworthy leader.

- **Selflessness and Sacrifice**

  Mandela's willingness to sacrifice his personal freedom for the greater good of his country showed immense selflessness. This act of putting others before himself demonstrated that he genuinely cared about the people, which helped build trust in him as a leader.

- **Bridge-Building and Inclusivity**

  Mandela worked to unite a deeply divided nation. He earned the respect and trust of diverse groups through his ability to bridge gaps and foster collaboration. His inclusive approach ensured that everyone's voice was heard, further strengthening trust.

These key takeaways highlight how Mandela's integrity, empathy, visionary leadership, sacrifice, and inclusiveness helped him build deep trust and bring about transformative change in South Africa.

Coaching Leaders for Mental Agility: Story No 2

Echoes of Resistance: The Legacy of the Sonderkommando and the White Rose

> **"When we are no longer able to change a situation, we are challenged to change ourselves."**
>
> **- Viktor E. Frankl**

Let me tell you a story about one of the darkest times in human history, a time when cruelty seemed to have no bounds, and yet, even in the depths of despair, there were glimmers of remarkable courage.

The story is about a group called the **Sonderkommando**, Jewish prisoners in Nazi concentration camps, particularly in Auschwitz.

Their role was among the most harrowing and tragic of the Holocaust.

The Sonderkommando faced unimaginable horrors as they were forced to work in the gas chambers and crematoria during one of history's darkest periods. Their grim responsibilities included the disposal of the bodies of countless victims murdered in the gas chambers. They meticulously removed the bodies, sorted through personal belongings, and operated the crematoria, all while grappling with the sheer weight of their tasks.

This group endured extreme dehumanization and brutality, living in a reality that stripped them of their identities and humanity. Isolated from other prisoners, they were treated as expendable tools by the Nazis, existing in a constant state of fear for their own lives. Their experiences highlight the depths of cruelty and the staggering impact of dehumanization during this horrific chapter in history.

Despite the horrific circumstances surrounding them, members of the Sonderkommando exhibited remarkable courage by engaging in acts of sabotage. They bravely attempted to disrupt the operations of the gas chambers and crematoria, striving to gather evidence of the unspeakable atrocities being committed. Some even risked their lives to smuggle information out of the camps, hoping to inform the outside world about the grim reality they faced.

Documentation became a vital act of resistance for the Sonderkommando. They worked tirelessly to record the atrocities they witnessed, ensuring that the truth would not be forgotten. A notable example is the writings and testimonies of survivors like Filip Müller, whose detailed accounts of the extermination process provide a chilling insight into the horrors of that time.

In addition to their documentation efforts, the Sonderkommando were also involved in planning and executing uprisings. One of the most significant revolts took place in October 1944 at Auschwitz, where the Sonderkommando succeeded in destroying one of the crematoria. This brave act incited a brief but intense revolt against the camp authorities, showcasing their indomitable spirit even in the face of overwhelming oppression.

The Sonderkommando endured a chilling reality marked by frequent executions. To eliminate any witnesses to their atrocities, the Nazis systematically executed members of the Sonderkommando, replacing them with new prisoners. This relentless cycle of loss deepened their sense of transience and despair, as they understood that their survival was precarious and temporary.

The moral and psychological toll on the Sonderkommando was staggering. Many grappled with the trauma of their harrowing duties, struggling to reconcile the ethical implications of their forced roles. Even as they sought to resist and bear witness to the horrors around them, the weight of their work hung heavily on their minds. The constant threat of execution loomed over them, compounding their anguish and despair. In the face of such overwhelming challenges, the strength of their spirit became a testament to human resilience in the darkest of times.

The accounts and testimonies of the Sonderkommando hold significant historical importance, shedding light on the scale of the Holocaust and the horrific mechanisms of the Nazi extermination process. Their narratives provide profound insights into the atrocities committed during this dark chapter in history and illustrate the extraordinary resilience of the human spirit amid unimaginable suffering.

Commemoration of the Sonderkommando's contributions to Holocaust documentation takes place through various memorials and historical records. Their experiences are honored as a testament to their suffering, resistance, and the remarkable capacity for endurance that individuals can exhibit even in the face of such brutality. These memorials serve not only as a reminder of the past but also as a call to remember the lessons learned from it, ensuring that the stories of those who endured and resisted are never forgotten.

The Sonderkommando story is one of profound tragedy and courage. Their forced participation in the extermination process and their acts of resistance illustrate the extreme conditions under which they lived.

Their efforts to document and resist highlight their resilience and moral courage, offering a poignant reminder of the Holocaust's atrocities and the enduring strength of the human spirit amidst overwhelming adversity.

The story of the Sonderkommando offers several profound key messages about human resilience, ethical integrity, and the capacity to endure under extreme conditions.

Here are the key messages we can learn:

Even in tough times, people can show great strength. The Sonderkommando, who faced terrible conditions, showed us how strong the human spirit can be. Their story reminds us that we can push through difficulties no matter how hard things get.

Having a clear purpose helps a lot during difficult times. The Sonderkommando resisted the Nazi regime because they wanted to fight against it. Having a goal can keep you motivated and help you take action when things seem hopeless.

Being creative and adaptable is also important. The Sonderkommando found new ways to resist, showing us that we should be flexible and think outside the box when facing challenges.

It's also crucial to take care of our emotional health. The Sonderkommando managed their stress and trauma, showing that mental strength is essential. We can build our emotional strength by taking care of ourselves, seeking support from others, and finding ways to cope with stress.

Standing up for what's right is vital, even when it's hard. The Sonderkommando acted on their morals, which reminds us to be brave and make decisions that align with our values, especially in tough situations.

Support from others can make us stronger. The Sonderkommando members helped each other, showing how teamwork and community can help us face challenges together. When we support each other, we can achieve more.

Finally, it's important to remember and share the truth. The Sonderkommando wrote down their experiences so history would not be forgotten. Sharing our stories helps future generations learn and remember important lessons.

This narrative not only honors those who faced incredible challenges but also inspires us to learn from their experiences. The key lessons teach us about strength, resilience, moral courage, and teamwork. By thinking about these lessons, we can better handle our own challenges and support others during tough times.

The Story of White Rose

During the time of Nazi Germany, a courageous group called the White Rose was formed by students and professors who wanted to stand up against the unfairness of the regime. Among them were two siblings, Hans and Sophie Scholl, along with their friend Christoph Probst, and other members like Alexander Schmorell, Willi Graf, and Professor Kurt Huber. Together, they shared a vision of justice and believed that people should know the truth about what was happening under Nazi rule.

The White Rose wanted to open the eyes of the German people to the harsh realities of the Nazi regime and encourage them to resist. They wrote and secretly spread powerful leaflets that spoke out against the government, urging people to stand up for their rights. At night, they also painted anti-Nazi slogans on walls in Munich, sending a bold message against the regime's lies.

In their leaflets, they exposed the cruel treatment of Jews and others, showing the injustices happening around them. While not everyone saw these leaflets, those who did were given hope and were encouraged to question what the government was doing.

Unfortunately, their bravery came at a cost. In early 1943, Hans, Sophie, and Christoph were caught while distributing leaflets at the University of Munich. Their arrest led to a swift and unfair trial. On February 22, 1943, Hans, Sophie, and Christoph were executed, along with some of their fellow members.

Even though their lives were tragically cut short, the legacy of the White Rose lives on. They are remembered as symbols of moral courage and resistance against tyranny. After the war, their story became a powerful reminder of standing up for what is right, and today, they are honored in Germany and around the world for their bravery.

The story of the White Rose teaches us the importance of moral courage. These brave individuals acted on their beliefs, even when it was dangerous. They showed that peaceful actions, like distributing leaflets, can challenge oppressive systems and make people question injustice.

At the same time, their sacrifice reminds us that speaking out against wrongdoings can have serious consequences. Their story encourages us to find the courage to fight for justice and freedom, even when it seems difficult. The legacy of the White Rose inspires us to stand up for truth and justice, no matter the risks.

The White Rose members' bravery and integrity remind us that resisting tyranny is important. They showed that exposing the truth and advocating for justice can make a difference, even when the risks are high.

Here are the major learnings and key messages from their resilience:

Instead of using violence, the White Rose fought against oppression through peaceful means. They wrote and handed out leaflets that spread hope and encouraged others to see the truth. These leaflets called for change and inspired people to resist the terrible things happening around them. Their example shows us that we can face challenges peacefully, using communication and education to create positive change.

The members of the White Rose were united by a shared vision of justice and humanity. This common goal gave them the strength to keep going, even when things were tough. We can learn from them to set clear goals in our own lives that match our values. By working together toward shared goals, we can achieve meaningful change.

The White Rose members showed what it means to be ethical leaders. They made difficult decisions that reflected their morals, even when it was dangerous. We can follow their example by leading with integrity and encouraging a culture of ethics and accountability in our communities.

Their story also highlights the importance of resilience. Despite constant threats and the possibility of being caught, they didn't give up. Their determination reminds us that setbacks are part of life. We can build our own resilience by staying focused on our goals and finding ways to handle challenges.

The White Rose's commitment to truth and justice teaches us how important it is to raise awareness about important issues. They believed that speaking out could inspire others, even in difficult times. This encourages us to educate our communities and stand up for what's right.

Collaboration and support among the White Rose members were key to their success. They understood that working together made them stronger. This spirit of teamwork can inspire us to build strong networks in our teams and communities, knowing that we can accomplish more together.

In every part of their struggle, the White Rose showed the way to **courage, resilience, and ethical leadership**. Their legacy inspires us to stay true to our principles and work for a better world where justice and truth are stronger than oppression.

The story of the White Rose teaches important lessons about leadership, courage, ethics, and resilience. By embracing these values, we can be inspired to act with integrity and pursue justice, especially in difficult times. Their example reminds us how powerful principled and courageous leadership can be.

Here are five key messages derived from the stories of the Sonderkommando and the White Rose:

- **Human Resilience in Adversity**: Both groups exemplify the incredible strength of the human spirit in the face of unimaginable suffering. They remind us that even in the darkest times, individuals can endure and resist oppression.
- **Moral Courage and Ethical Integrity**: The members of both the Sonderkommando and the White Rose acted on their principles, even when it put their lives at risk. Their stories emphasize the importance of standing up for what is right, highlighting the necessity of moral courage in our own lives.

- **The Power of Documentation and Truth**: Both groups utilized documentation and advocacy to raise awareness about the atrocities they witnessed. Their efforts to share the truth serve as a powerful reminder of the importance of preserving history and educating future generations.
- **Collaboration and Solidarity**: The strength found in mutual support and collaboration was vital for both groups. They showed how working together can amplify voices and strengthen resistance against oppressive systems, encouraging us to build strong networks in our own communities.
- **Finding Purpose in Difficult Times**: The Sonderkommando and the White Rose members found purpose through their acts of resistance. Their determination to combat oppression through non-violent means illustrates how a clear sense of purpose can inspire action and hope, even in bleak circumstances.

These messages highlight the extraordinary human capacity for courage, integrity, and resilience, urging us to reflect on our values and actions in our own lives.

Coaching Leaders for Mental Agility: Story No 3

The Flame of Courage: Leadership Lessons from Joan of Arc & Rani Lakshmibai

> **"Courage is found in unlikely places."**
>
> **– J.R.R. Tolkien**

Joan of Arc was a French military heroine and Roman Catholic saint who played a pivotal role in the Hundred Years' War. Born in a peasant family, she claimed to have received divine visions, inspiring her to lead the French army against the English invaders.

Joan of Arc, known as the "Maid of Orléans," is celebrated for her courage, faith, and extraordinary mental agility in the face of immense challenges.

Joan of Arc's story is a testament to the power of human potential and the importance of mental agility, leadership, and belief.

Her legacy continues to inspire people around the world, reminding us of the incredible things that can be achieved with courage, determination, and a clear sense of purpose.

Her ability to remain composed, adapt to rapidly changing situations, and navigate complex political and military environments makes her story particularly compelling.

The Siege of Orléans

At just 17 years old, Joan led French forces during the Siege of Orléans, a critical moment in the Hundred Years' War between France and England. The city had been under siege for months, and morale was low. Despite her lack of formal military training, Joan's mental agility and confidence helped rally the French soldiers.

Joan convinced the French leadership to let her lead an attack on the English forces. She demonstrated remarkable mental flexibility by working closely with experienced military commanders, adapting their strategies to the battlefield conditions. Her leadership revitalized the French army, leading to the lifting of the siege in 1429. Joan's ability to inspire and her keen sense of timing turned the tide of the war.

Her Trial and Quick Thinking

After being captured by the Burgundians and handed over to the English, Joan faced a politically charged trial for heresy. The trial was designed to trap her into making statements that would discredit her claims of divine guidance. Despite being a young peasant woman, Joan exhibited tremendous mental agility, skillfully answering her interrogators, and avoiding their traps.

When asked whether she believed she was in God's grace, a question designed to incriminate her, Joan famously replied:

"If I am not, may God put me there; and if I am, may God so keep me." - This response was brilliant in its simplicity and deflected the accusation, demonstrating her sharp intellect and ability to think on her feet in high-pressure situations.

Adapting to Political Complexities

Joan operated in a politically volatile environment. France was divided, and the loyalty of various factions was uncertain. She had to quickly learn how to navigate the complex dynamics of the French court, gaining the trust of key figures, including Charles VII. Despite being an outsider and a young woman, Joan's mental agility allowed her to understand political motivations and leverage her reputation as a divine messenger to influence the French king.

Her ability to adapt to the political landscape was evident when she persuaded Charles VII to allow her to accompany him to Reims for his coronation. This journey through enemy territory was a symbolic victory that solidified his claim to the throne and showed Joan's keen understanding of the power of symbolism and legitimacy in leadership.

Military Tactics and Quick Adaptation

During her military campaigns, Joan was known for her ability to quickly assess battlefield conditions and adapt strategies accordingly. In one instance, at the Battle of Patay in 1429, she was part of a surprise attack on English forces. When the opportunity presented itself, she urged the French commanders to act swiftly, capitalizing on the English army's disorganization. Her quick thinking led to a decisive victory, further boosting French morale, and cementing her status as a key military leader.

- **Quick Thinking Under Pressure**: In both combat and during her trial, Joan exhibited the ability to remain composed, think quickly, and respond strategically in high-stress situations.
- **Adapting to Unfamiliar Roles**: Despite lacking formal training, she seamlessly transitioned into roles of military leadership and political influence, demonstrating her mental flexibility.
- **Confidence in Decision Making**: Joan's self-belief, rooted in her spiritual convictions, allowed her to make bold decisions when others hesitated, displaying mental clarity and decisiveness.

- **Navigating Complex Power Structures**: Her understanding of political power and her ability to influence key figures showcased her agility in managing complex interpersonal dynamics.

Joan of Arc's mental agility, combined with her bravery and faith, allowed her to rise from an obscure peasant girl to a legendary figure who shaped the course of French history.

Her legacy endures as an example of leadership, adaptability, and resilience.

Rani Lakshmibai of Jhansi: A Tale of Courage

Rani Lakshmibai, born in 1828, was the queen of the princely state of Jhansi in northern India. She married the king of Jhansi, Raja Gangadhar Rao, and after his death in 1853, the British East India Company, which had been annexing Indian territories, sought to take control of Jhansi. They claimed that the state had no legitimate heir and demanded that the region be handed over to them.

In 1857, the Indian Rebellion against British rule began, and Rani Lakshmibai emerged as one of its most formidable leaders. Despite being a woman and facing overwhelming odds, she showed incredible courage and strategic acumen.

Rani Lakshmibai stood on the precipice of life and death, fully aware that opposing the British could very well cost her everything. Yet, despite the looming fear, she chose not to run but to face it head-on. She embraced the reality that her kingdom and her people needed her to fight, no matter the risks.

Rather than aiming for immediate, overwhelming success, Rani Lakshmibai began by setting smaller, more achievable goals. She first focused on strengthening Jhansi, fortifying its defenses, and rallying her troops. With each successful step forward, she gained momentum, building on these smaller victories to fuel the larger fight ahead.

Her mind was clear on one vision—a free Jhansi. Rani Lakshmibai held tightly to this image, seeing in her heart a sovereign land, free from foreign rule. This powerful vision of independence drove her, shaping her strategies and pushing her to act with unyielding commitment.

When setbacks came, as they often did, she didn't let doubt overtake her. Rani Lakshmibai practiced self-compassion. She didn't allow failure to define her; instead, she focused on her strengths—her courage, her leadership, and her determination. She remained her own greatest ally, even in the darkest moments.

Rani Lakshmibai knew she couldn't do it alone. She sought out support, forging alliances with local rulers and leaders who shared her desire to resist the British. These alliances gave her the resources and strength she needed, showing the power of unity in the face of oppression.

Each battle brought new lessons. After every encounter with the British forces, Rani Lakshmibai studied her experiences. She adapted, refining her strategies, becoming a more formidable leader each time. Every failure was not an end but an opportunity to grow stronger.

In battle, she took risks, but they were always calculated. Leading her troops into the fray, she often made daring maneuvers, knowing the stakes were high. Her courage wasn't reckless; it was guided by careful planning and a deep understanding of the risks involved.

Even when facing countless obstacles, Rani Lakshmibai never lost sight of the bigger picture. She didn't let temporary defeats cloud her vision. Her focus remained on the ultimate goal: defending her kingdom and ensuring the freedom of her people. This sense of purpose kept her steady through every challenge.

Amid the chaos of battle and political maneuvering, she maintained a clear, calm mind. Her ability to stay focused and mindful allowed her to make quick, effective decisions. In the heat of war, this mental clarity was often the difference between victory and defeat.

Rani Lakshmibai approached every challenge with a growth mindset. If something didn't go as planned, she learned from it, determined to grow, and improve. For her, each challenge was not a stumbling block but a stepping stone to greater wisdom and strength.

She celebrated every small victory. Each time her troops rallied, each time they defended Jhansi successfully, these moments were cherished.

They weren't just military wins; they were morale boosters that fueled her determination and kept her people fighting.

Curiosity was also her guide. Rani Lakshmibai remained open to new ideas, constantly adapting to the evolving nature of the rebellion. She wasn't afraid to try guerrilla tactics or explore innovative ways to outsmart the British forces.

Although Rani Lakshmibai didn't keep a literal journal, her courageous actions were etched into the pages of history. Her bravery, leadership, and unyielding spirit have been immortalized, inspiring generations to stand tall in the face of fear and fight for what is right.

Through every trial, Rani Lakshmibai showed what true courage looks like—steadfast, intelligent, and deeply rooted in purpose. Her life offers a powerful example of how, even in the most challenging times, one can rise, adapt, and lead with unwavering courage.

Rani Lakshmibai's resistance was ultimately unsuccessful, and she died in 1858, but her bravery and leadership left a lasting legacy. She is remembered as a symbol of resistance against colonial rule and a national heroine who fought valiantly for her people and her kingdom.

The story of Rani Lakshmibai of Jhansi exemplifies how courage, strategic thinking, and resilience can define a leader's legacy. Her willingness to face fear, set goals, and adapt to challenges provides a powerful example of leadership and bravery in the face of adversity.

Here are the top key messages derived from the texts about Joan of Arc and Rani Lakshmibai:

- **Unwavering Belief and Purpose**: Both Joan of Arc and Rani Lakshmibai exemplify the power of a strong belief in a cause. Their deep conviction motivated them to lead and inspire others, emphasizing the importance of having a clear vision and purpose in overcoming challenges.
- **Courage and Bravery**: Despite facing immense dangers, both figures demonstrated extraordinary courage. They were willing

to risk their lives for their beliefs, showcasing how bravery is essential in the fight against oppression.

- **Adaptability and Strategic Thinking**: Both leaders showed remarkable mental agility, adapting their strategies in response to rapidly changing circumstances. They were able to navigate complex political landscapes and military situations, highlighting the importance of flexibility in leadership.
- **Empowerment and Inspiration**: Joan of Arc and Rani Lakshmibai broke traditional gender roles, proving that women can be powerful leaders. Their stories continue to inspire others to challenge societal norms and fight for justice, encouraging empowerment among women and marginalized groups.
- **Resilience in the Face of Adversity**: Both figures encountered significant setbacks but remained determined. Their resilience and ability to learn from failures demonstrate that perseverance is crucial in the pursuit of goals, especially in challenging times.

These messages reflect the enduring legacies of both leaders and their powerful contributions to history and social change.

Coaching Leaders for Mental Agility: Story No 4

From Chains to Triumph: The Indomitable Spirit of Harriet Tubman

> **"Optimism is faith in action. It is the belief that tomorrow will be better than today because of what we do today."**
>
> **- Helen Keller**

Harriet Tubman is one of history's most revered leaders, celebrated for her extraordinary courage, resilience, and unwavering commitment to freedom and justice.

Her life and achievements offer profound lessons in leadership that continue to inspire individuals around the world today.

Harriet Tubman's Achievements as a Leader

1. Escaping Slavery and Pioneering the Underground Railroad

Born into the brutal world of slavery around **1822** in **Maryland**, **Harriet Tubman** was no stranger to suffering. From a young age, she faced the grim realities of being enslaved—long days of hard labor, frequent beatings, and the constant, heart-wrenching fear of being sold and permanently separated from her family. These early experiences shaped her into the resilient and fearless woman she would later become, fueled by a burning desire for freedom not just for herself, but for others.

In **1849**, Tubman made a courageous and daring escape to **Philadelphia**, leaving everything she had ever known behind. Navigating the treacherous path to freedom, she relied on the **Underground Railroad**, a secret network of safe houses and abolitionists willing to risk their lives for her liberty. Her escape was just the beginning of her journey; crossing into freedom was not enough—she knew she had a larger mission ahead.

Unlike many who escaped the chains of slavery, Tubman could not rest while others remained in bondage. Over the next **ten years**, she fearlessly returned to the South at least **13 times**, leading **70 enslaved individuals** to freedom. Each journey was fraught with danger—slave catchers, hostile environments, and betrayal loomed at every turn. Yet, Tubman's resolve never wavered. Her extraordinary bravery earned her the title of "**Moses**," symbolizing her role as a liberator guiding her people out of oppression.

2. Leadership During the Civil War

During the American Civil War, **Harriet Tubman** emerged not only as a symbol of courage and resilience but as an invaluable asset to the **Union Army**. She wasn't just a former enslaved woman turned freedom fighter; she became a **spy**, **nurse**, and **cook**, using her vast knowledge of the land and her strategic brilliance to aid the Union's efforts. Her unique understanding of Southern terrain and escape routes, gained from years as a conductor on the Underground Railroad, made her indispensable on the battlefield and behind enemy lines.

One of her most notable contributions came in **1863**, during the **Combahee River Raid**. Tubman led an operation in **South Carolina** that resulted in the liberation of over **700 enslaved people**. This mission, which required both military precision and bold leadership, was a testament to her tactical expertise. Guiding Union troops through Confederate territory, Tubman successfully coordinated the raid, showcasing not only her fearlessness but her ability to execute **complex, high-stakes operations** with remarkable skill. Her leadership in this daring mission cemented her role as one of the most remarkable strategists of her time.

3. Advocacy for Women's Suffrage

After the Civil War, Tubman continued her fight for equality by becoming an advocate for women's suffrage. She worked alongside prominent figures like Susan B. Anthony and Frederick Douglass, highlighting the intersectionality of racial and gender equality.

4. Legacy and Lasting Impact

Tubman's life story has become a powerful symbol of resistance against oppression. Her unwavering dedication to freedom and equality has inspired countless movements and individuals striving for social justice.

Tubman's legacy is honored through various means, including memorials, educational programs, and cultural representations. In 2016, she became the first woman to appear on a U.S. postage stamp in over a century, underscoring her national significance.

Why We Should Follow Harriet Tubman's Example

Harriet Tubman repeatedly ventured into slave-holding territories, risking her life with every step she took. The fear of capture, the constant threat of death—it was all very real. Yet she pressed forward, time and time again, showing an unwavering courage that defined her very existence. Her bravery teaches us the power of standing firm for what is right, even when the dangers are overwhelming. Tubman didn't just survive; she led others to freedom, fearlessly putting herself in harm's way to rescue those still in bondage.

At the heart of her actions was a deep sense of selflessness. Tubman wasn't motivated by personal gain; her focus was always on others. She risked everything, not just for her own freedom, but to ensure the safety and liberty of those who had none. Her selfless leadership showed what it means to put others first, to lead with compassion, and to make sacrifices for the greater good. Tubman's life was an embodiment of this spirit—time and time again, she placed the freedom of others above her own safety.

Her path wasn't easy. Born into slavery, Tubman endured unimaginable hardships—physical abuse, financial struggles, and the emotional scars of bondage. Yet, she remained resilient, never allowing these trials to break her spirit. Her determination to rise above the trauma of her past and keep pushing forward is a powerful example of overcoming adversity. Tubman's life shows us that resilience isn't just about surviving; it's about thriving in the face of hardship, using every obstacle as fuel to push forward.

What made Tubman an even more remarkable leader was her ability to plan and execute each mission with precision. She wasn't reckless in her bravery. Every move she made was calculated, grounded in strategic thinking. Her successful rescues were the result of meticulous planning, deep knowledge of the terrain, and an instinct for leadership that kept everyone safe. Tubman's leadership was not just about courage—it was about the ability to navigate complex situations with a clear head and a focused plan.

Tubman's commitment to justice and equality didn't end with her work on the Underground Railroad. Her entire life was a testament to the fight for freedom and equal rights. She stood tall as an activist, working tirelessly to dismantle systems of oppression and advocating for the rights of women and African Americans. Her dedication to justice serves as a powerful reminder that one person can indeed make a difference in the fight for equality. Tubman's legacy encourages each of us to engage in the struggle for a more just and equitable world.

Even long after her passing, Harriet Tubman continues to inspire. Her story is one of strength, moral conviction, and relentless determination, and it reaches across generations. Tubman's life reminds us that true leadership is born from integrity, and that each of us has the power to create meaningful change if we lead with courage and purpose. Through her example, we see that the fight for justice is never in vain, and that our actions today can inspire future generations to keep moving forward in the pursuit of freedom and equality.

Harriet Tubman's mental resilience and grit were key factors in her success as a leader and liberator.

Her extraordinary strength of character allowed her to overcome the immense challenges she faced throughout her life.

Here are some examples and actions that highlight her mental resilience and grit:

1. **Overcoming the Trauma of Slavery**

Harriet Tubman was born into slavery in **Maryland** around **1822**, where her childhood was filled with harsh abuse and cruelty. From a young age, she experienced severe physical punishment, but one moment in particular left a lasting mark on her life. When an overseer threw a heavy weight intending to hit another slave, it struck **Harriet** instead, causing a traumatic head injury. This injury led to lifelong struggles with **seizures**, **headaches**, and **narcolepsy**, making every day a battle for her health.

Despite these overwhelming challenges, Harriet Tubman never let her circumstances defeat her spirit. Even with the pain and difficulties caused by her injury, she found the strength to keep pushing forward. Her ability to endure both the physical suffering of her condition and the cruelty of slavery shows her incredible **mental resilience** and unwavering determination to overcome adversity.

2. **Escaping Slavery Alone**

In **1849**, Harriet Tubman made the bold decision to escape from slavery completely on her own. Fleeing from **Maryland**, she embarked on a dangerous journey, traveling nearly **90 miles on foot** to reach the safety of **Pennsylvania**, a free state. Along the way, Tubman faced countless threats, from the risk of being captured to the possibility of brutal punishment if caught. Despite the dangers that surrounded her, she pressed on with unshakable courage, determined to secure her freedom.

Tubman's solo escape demanded immense mental strength. Navigating unfamiliar and treacherous terrain, she had to trust her instincts and rely on the secretive **Underground Railroad**, a network of safe houses run by those who supported her cause. Her ability to keep going, despite the fear and uncertainty, showed the depth of her **mental fortitude**. Harriet's successful escape was not just a physical achievement—it was a powerful display of her sheer willpower and determination to break free.

3. Returning to Rescue Others

After gaining her own freedom, Tubman did not rest. She returned to the South multiple times over the next decade to lead approximately 70 enslaved people to freedom, including family members and strangers alike. Each trip was perilous, as slave catchers actively sought her, and the risks of betrayal and capture were high.

Tubman's repeated returns to slave-holding states, despite the personal risk, demonstrate her unyielding grit. She never wavered in her commitment to liberating others, even when her own life was on the line.

4. Facing Down Challenges on the Underground Railroad

Harriet Tubman faced constant dangers during her missions to free enslaved people. On one occasion, she overheard a group of men plotting to capture her and those she was guiding to freedom. Instead of panicking, Tubman calmly changed their route, avoiding the men and leading her group safely to freedom. Her ability to stay composed and strong in the face of such threats showed her incredible **courage** and determination.

Tubman's quick thinking and ability to remain calm under pressure were key to her success. She had a remarkable talent for solving problems on the spot, finding new paths when old ones became too dangerous. Her **leadership** and **resilience** meant that even in the most difficult situations, she never lost focus on her mission to bring people to freedom.

5. Decision to Carry a Revolver

On her dangerous missions to free enslaved people, Harriet Tubman carried a **revolver**. She used it not only to protect herself and those she guided but also to ensure no one in her group turned back. Tubman understood the power of fear and doubt, and she knew that if anyone tried to return, it could put the entire group at risk. Her weapon became a way to keep everyone moving forward, no matter how scared they were.

Tubman's decision to carry a weapon shows her incredible **mental toughness**. She was willing to make difficult choices to reach her goal of freedom for all. Tubman was prepared to do whatever it took to complete her missions, demonstrating her unshakeable determination and the strength to lead, even in the hardest moments.

6. Serving as a Union Spy During the Civil War

During the **Civil War**, Harriet Tubman took on multiple critical roles, serving as a **spy**, **nurse**, and **scout** for the **Union Army**. One of her most remarkable achievements was leading a raid along the **Combahee River** in **South Carolina**, which freed more than **700 enslaved people**. This mission required not only physical strength but also sharp **strategic thinking** and **mental resilience**, as Tubman carefully planned and executed the operation in the midst of war.

Tubman's ability to lead such complex and dangerous missions in the chaos of a war zone highlights her incredible **resilience**. Despite the stress, constant threats, and the demands of the battlefield, she remained laser-focused on her mission. Her endurance, both mentally and physically, was key to her success, proving her exceptional strength in the face of immense challenges.

7. Living with Lifelong Injuries and Pain

Tubman lived with the effects of her head injury for the rest of her life, experiencing seizures, headaches, and periods of unconsciousness. Despite these challenges, she continued to lead, serve, and inspire others well into her old age.

Her ability to persist in her efforts despite chronic pain and health issues is a powerful example of her mental and physical resilience.

Tubman's story is a testament to the power of perseverance, courage, and unwavering commitment to a cause greater than oneself.

Her life serves as a powerful inspiration for anyone facing adversity and striving to make a difference in the world.

> **"Our greatest glory is not in never falling, but in rising every time we fall."**
>
> **– Confucius**

Here are key takeaways:

- **Courage and Fearlessness in the Face of Danger**: Harriet Tubman demonstrated extraordinary courage by repeatedly risking her life to lead enslaved individuals to freedom through the Underground Railroad. Despite the ever-present threat of capture or death, her resolve never wavered, making her an iconic figure in the fight for freedom.
- **Strategic Leadership and Planning**: Tubman's success as a leader was not just due to bravery, but also her strategic mindset. Her role during the Civil War as a spy and her leadership in missions like the Combahee River Raid reflect her tactical expertise. Each mission was meticulously planned, showcasing her ability to navigate dangerous situations with precision.
- **Advocacy for Equal Rights**: Tubman extended her fight for justice beyond the abolition of slavery. After the Civil War, she became a vocal advocate for women's suffrage, aligning herself with other prominent activists like Susan B. Anthony. Her leadership encompassed both racial and gender equality.
- **Resilience in Overcoming Adversity**: Born into slavery and suffering from a traumatic head injury, Tubman displayed immense resilience throughout her life. Despite physical limitations and the emotional scars of her past, she continued to

fight for freedom and justice, proving that resilience involves not just surviving hardships, but thriving in spite of them.

- **Selfless Leadership**: Tubman's motivation was always driven by a deep sense of compassion for others. She returned to the South multiple times, putting others' freedom before her own safety. Her selflessness and commitment to the greater good defined her leadership and left a lasting legacy of service and sacrifice.

These takeaways highlight how Harriet Tubman's leadership, strategic brilliance, and resilience made her one of the most influential figures in the fight for justice and equality.

Coaching Leaders for Mental Agility: Story No 5

Leadership Gone Wrong: Stories of Corruption and Systemic Breakdown

> **"A people that values its privileges above its principles soon loses both."**
>
> **- Dwight D. Eisenhower**

Throughout history, corrupted leaders have left significant damage on the systems they governed, often leading to the downfall of entire civilizations, organizations, or nations.

By examining the actions of these leaders, we can understand what went wrong and what we should avoid in governance and leadership.

Nero (Roman Empire):

Nero, the Roman emperor, is widely remembered for his cruelty, tyranny, and self-indulgence. His reign was defined by political violence, including the murder of rivals, and his indifference to the well-being of the state.

Rather than focusing on the needs of his empire, Nero lived a life of luxury, draining resources for personal pleasure and entertainment. His obsession with gaining personal glory, such as through extravagant public performances, alienated the Roman Senate and led to widespread discontent among the populace.

Nero's selfish leadership destabilized the empire, both politically and financially. His neglect of state affairs and indulgent spending severely weakened Rome's foundations, playing a significant role in the eventual decline of the Roman Empire.

The lesson from Nero's rule is clear:

leaders must not prioritize their personal desires over the welfare of the people. Leadership requires a careful balance between personal interests and the responsibilities owed to the community. A leader's focus on self-gain can result in widespread instability and long-term damage to the system they are meant to protect.

Muammar Gaddafi (Libya):

Gaddafi's 42-year rule over Libya was characterized by dictatorship, eccentric behavior, and rampant corruption. He held onto power through practices like nepotism, bribery, and the use of violence. Even though Libya was rich in oil, these economic benefits did not extend to the broader population, as opportunities for growth were largely stifled. His personal control over the country's wealth and decisions meant that most citizens faced economic hardships despite the nation's resources.

When Gaddafi was overthrown, Libya was thrown into chaos, with civil war breaking out and various factions fighting for control. His centralized power left a vacuum that extremist groups took advantage of, resulting in long-term instability.

The lesson from Gaddafi's regime is that leaders should not create power structures that revolve solely around their own presence. For a nation to remain stable, power must be decentralized, and sustainable institutions need to be built to ensure long-term stability and prevent chaos after a leader's removal.

Hosni Mubarak (Egypt, 1981-2011)

During his 30-year reign, Hosni Mubarak's leadership in Egypt was characterized by widespread corruption, police violence, and nepotism. Mubarak and his family amassed immense wealth through embezzlement and questionable business deals, all while suppressing political opposition and restricting media freedom. The lack of transparency and accountability in his government led to growing economic stagnation. Poverty and unemployment surged under his rule, creating frustration among the Egyptian people. This deepening social unrest eventually culminated in the 2011 Arab Spring, when mass protests led to Mubarak's removal from power. His regime's legacy illustrates how long-standing corruption and political repression can erode public trust and destabilize a nation, showing that neglecting the welfare of citizens can lead to widespread revolts and systemic collapse.

The lesson to be drawn is that leaders must prioritize the people's interests and foster transparency to maintain stability and prevent uprisings.

Vladimir Putin (Russia, 1999-present)

Vladimir Putin's leadership in Russia since 1999 has been characterized by the centralization of power, the suppression of political opposition, and frequent accusations of corruption. Under his rule, many oligarchs and officials closely associated with Putin have accumulated vast wealth, while the general population has experienced limited economic gains. This concentration of power has severely weakened Russia's democratic institutions, eroding the rule of law and curbing political transparency. Putin's dominance over key sectors of both the economy and politics has made it difficult for opposition voices to challenge the system, further entrenching corruption and restricting accountability.

The lesson from Putin's rule is that excessive power concentration, combined with control over economic resources, weakens democracy, limits accountability, and fosters an environment where corruption can thrive. Sustainable leadership requires balanced governance, transparency, and empowering diverse political voices to ensure long-term stability.

True leadership doesn't hoard power—it empowers others, fostering teamwork and fresh ideas.

Learning from corrupt leadership is essential to avoid repeating the same mistakes and to foster better governance and accountability. Here are key lessons we can draw from these corrupt leaders and their failures:

1. The Importance of Transparency and Accountability

Corruption often thrives when leaders are not held accountable for their actions. For example, leaders like Muammar Gaddafi and Hosni Mubarak gained immense wealth through dishonest deals and embezzlement. During their rule, they manipulated resources for personal gain without anyone stopping them. Because there were no checks on their power, they put their own interests above the needs of the people, which led to frustration and unrest.

As their governments eventually collapsed, it became clear that strong systems of accountability are essential to prevent this kind of abuse of power. Leaders need to be monitored, with open decision-making processes that allow citizens and institutions to question and challenge their actions. By promoting honesty and transparency, societies can build trust and ensure that leaders focus on serving the public, not themselves.

One key takeaway to prevent corruption is by establishing checks and balances. When institutions are empowered to hold leaders accountable, corruption becomes less likely, and a fairer society can take shape. The downfalls of these leaders teach us that integrity in leadership isn't just a good idea—it's necessary for good governance.

2. Decentralization of Power

Leaders such as Vladimir Putin and Hosni Mubarak demonstrated a pattern of concentrating power within their own hands. By sidelining opposition and suppressing democratic institutions, they established a system where a single leader wielded substantial control over the government. This excessive centralization of power often leads to autocratic rule, where dissent is stifled, and innovation can be suppressed.

The key lesson here is that effective leadership is not about hoarding power but about decentralizing it. By fostering collaboration and ensuring that no single individual or group holds too much control, leaders can create a more dynamic and innovative environment. This approach not only supports democratic principles but also encourages diverse perspectives and creative solutions, which are crucial for effective governance and progress.

3. The Role of Ethical Governance

The story of Emperor Nero reveals a powerful lesson about leadership. Nero was more concerned with his own personal glory than with the well-being of Rome. His self-serving behavior and corruption eroded public trust and led to significant harm to the stability of the empire. When leaders focus solely on their own interests, they can cause widespread damage to the systems they are supposed to protect.

The takeaway from Nero's reign is that ethical leadership is essential for lasting success. True leaders prioritize the common good over personal gain, making decisions that are fair and driven by integrity. By focusing on what benefits everyone rather than just oneself, leaders build trust and ensure the long-term stability of their organizations or nations.

4. Building Strong Institutions

In Egypt, as the sun set over Cairo, a leader's control over the country began to fall apart. Hosni Mubarak, once a powerful leader, slowly weakened the institutions that were supposed to protect democracy. By using favoritism and harsh tactics, he broke the public's trust in the systems that should have protected their rights. Over time, the voices of the people were silenced under his rule, and the very systems meant to defend them crumbled.

When the Arab Spring protests swept through the region, these institutions collapsed, leaving chaos behind. The lesson from Mubarak's leadership is clear: *when leaders focus more on their personal power than on serving the people, they can destroy the systems that keep democracy strong.*

In times of crisis, a new way of thinking about leadership becomes important. Leaders must work to strengthen the democratic systems that will last even after they are gone. This means building institutions that are strong enough to survive tough times and adapt to changes. By focusing on transparency and accountability, leaders can make sure that these systems serve the people fairly.

History shows that real leadership is about creating institutions that protect the people, even after leaders leave. When leaders embrace this idea, they can help create a future where democracy thrives, and people's voices are heard.

5. Understanding the Long-Term Consequences of Corruption

In the world of leadership, corruption can have serious and long-lasting consequences. Throughout history, we've seen examples of corrupt leaders who cared more about their own short-term interests than the well-being of their people. One example is Muammar Gaddafi in Libya. His corrupt and oppressive rule eventually led to his downfall, which plunged the country into a civil war that caused suffering for many years. This shows us an important lesson: while corrupt leaders may benefit for a short time, the damage they cause can last for generations.

Sustainable leadership, on the other hand, is the opposite of corruption. It focuses on the well-being of the whole society instead of personal gain. Leaders who choose this path build trust and make sure that everyone is included. They focus on long-term benefits for their communities, helping create a peaceful and stable society. Unlike the short-lived benefits of corruption, sustainable leadership leads to lasting progress and peace.

This teaches us that true success in leadership comes from caring about the common good, not just individual ambition. It reminds us of the importance of integrity, trust, and the responsibility leaders have to their communities. When leaders nurture these values, they can inspire positive, lasting change and help create an environment where everyone can succeed.

6. Engaging with Diverse Voices

In countries where leaders are corrupt, they often silence people who disagree with them. Leaders like Vladimir Putin in Russia and Muammar Gaddafi in Libya show how oppressive governments stop different ideas from being shared. These leaders create fear, and people become afraid to speak up. Instead of encouraging new ideas, they push everyone to think the same way. This prevents societies from moving forward and makes it hard for change to happen.

In contrast, successful societies grow when there is open discussion and diverse opinions. Allowing people to share different ideas helps bring creativity and innovation. When people feel safe to express their thoughts without being punished, they contribute to a stronger and more dynamic environment. This openness helps prevent groupthink, where everyone just agrees without thinking critically, which can lead to bad decisions.

Leaders who welcome different viewpoints and honest conversations create a culture that is strong and flexible. They encourage others to think deeply and question the usual way of doing things, which leads to progress and positive change. By creating an inclusive environment, these leaders help their communities grow and adapt, making them ready to face challenges.

The lesson here is simple: to avoid the problems of corruption and stagnation, leaders must support the value of different opinions. This creates a strong, engaged, and empowered community.

7. The Importance of Upholding the Rule of Law

In a world where power can often take over justice, corrupt governments create situations where the rule of law breaks down. A clear example is Russia under Vladimir Putin, where his control over the legal system has weakened the independence of the courts. His actions have blurred the line between law and politics, making it harder for democratic processes to work and creating fear among those who speak out against him. Instead of being fair and independent, the courts become tools of the government, causing people to lose trust in the legal system. This creates an atmosphere of instability and distrust.

This example shows how important it is for leaders to uphold the rule of law. Leaders must respect the independence of legal institutions, making sure that justice is given fairly to everyone. When leaders focus on the rule of law, they help create a society where people can trust that their rights are protected, and that justice is available to all. By promoting fairness and honesty in legal matters, leaders can create a stable society where people feel safe and empowered.

The lessons from these examples teach us the importance of accountability and transparency in leadership. In a society where justice is fair and equal, citizens can thrive, knowing that laws protect everyone, including those in power.

By learning from corrupt leaders, future leaders can work to create fair, open, and inclusive systems that focus on the well-being of their citizens instead of personal gain.

> **"There is a sufficiency in the world for man's need but not for man's greed**."
>
> \- **Mahatma Gandhi**

Here are simple takeaways about leadership and corruption from the analysis:

- **Transparency and Accountability Matter**:

  Leaders who hide their actions and avoid being accountable, like Gaddafi and Mubarak, make corruption easy. Without checks on their power, they use resources for personal gain, which eventually leads to public anger and chaos.

- **Don't Hoard Power**:

  Leaders like Putin and Mubarak held onto too much power, stopping others from contributing or opposing them. Good leadership spreads power around, encouraging teamwork and fresh ideas.

- **Put Ethics First**:

  Nero, the Roman emperor, focused only on his own desires, which hurt his empire. A good leader makes decisions for the benefit of the people, not just for personal glory.

- **Build Strong Systems**:

  Mubarak's weakening of Egypt's institutions left the country vulnerable after he was removed. Leaders should build strong institutions that last and continue to serve people even after they leave.

- **Corruption's Long-Term Damage**:

  Leaders who focus on short-term personal gain, like Gaddafi, often cause long-lasting harm to their country. Good leadership focuses on what's best for the community over time.

In short, good leadership relies on being transparent, sharing power, staying ethical, building strong institutions, and avoiding corruption for the long-term good of society.

Part-1

Leadership Pillar-1 (Ethics)

Summary

Great leaders like Nelson Mandela, Harriet Tubman, and Joan of Arc all share something important: **they stayed true to their beliefs, no matter what challenges they faced.**

Even when the odds were against them, they never gave up. These leaders earned the trust of others because they always acted with integrity and stuck to their principles.

Imagine Nelson Mandela, who was imprisoned for 27 years but still held onto his dream of a free South Africa. Think of Harriet Tubman, who, despite the constant risk of being caught or killed, led many enslaved people to freedom. Or picture Joan of Arc, a young woman leading armies with nothing but her faith to guide her. These leaders didn't just talk about their values—they lived them, and that's why people believed in them.

But having strong beliefs wasn't enough on its own. These leaders also showed great moral **courage**. They took action, even when it was dangerous. The White Rose members, a group of German students, risked everything to speak out against the Nazis. The Sonderkommando, forced into terrible situations, still found ways to resist. Rani Lakshmibai, a queen who fought for her country's independence, knew she might not survive the battle but kept fighting anyway. These leaders remind us that sometimes, leadership means putting others before yourself and being willing to sacrifice for what's right.

They also had a clear vision. Mandela didn't just want an end to apartheid; he dreamed of a South Africa where everyone was equal. Tubman didn't just free slaves; she had a well-thought-out plan, knowing exactly how to get them to safety. These leaders didn't just react to events—they planned ahead and were ready for challenges. They didn't do it alone either; they worked with others, understanding, and helping people from different backgrounds.

One thing that defined them all was **resilience**. No matter how hard things got, they never gave up. Even when things seemed hopeless, they kept pushing forward. Mandela, Tubman, and Joan of Arc all faced moments where quitting might have seemed easier, but they stayed strong. They knew that leadership wasn't about short-term wins—it was about staying committed, even when the road was tough.

These stories aren't just about leading people; they're about doing so with strong ethics. Each of these leaders built their actions on a moral foundation. Their integrity, courage, empathy, and resilience inspired others to follow them. In the end, their ethical leadership helped create lasting change in the world, always aiming for justice and the greater good.

Skill	Definition	Key Actions to Develop
1. Trust and Integrity	Building trust through consistent honesty, transparency, and keeping commitments.	- Communicate openly. - Maintain confidentiality. - Model honesty in all interactions.
2. Moral Courage	The ability to make tough decisions based on ethics, even when they are unpopular or challenging.	- Practice addressing conflicts with fairness. - Take responsibility for mistakes. - Stand up for values.
3. Ethical Decision-Making	Making decisions aligned with moral principles and long-term benefits.	- Use ethical frameworks. - Consider the impact on stakeholders. - Reflect on past dilemmas for learning.
4. Fairness and Justice	Ensuring equitable treatment for all team members and stakeholders.	- Promote inclusion. - Resolve conflicts objectively. - Recognize and reduce unconscious biases.
5. Accountability	Owning decisions, actions, and outcomes while holding others to the same standard.	- Set clear expectations. - Acknowledge errors openly. - Implement regular accountability checks.
6. Empathy and Emotional Intelligence	Understanding and addressing the emotions and perspectives of others to build strong relationships.	- Practice active listening. - Show compassion in decision-making. - Adapt communication to individual needs.
7. Transparent Communication	Sharing both successes and challenges openly to align teams and stakeholders.	- Regularly share updates. - Be clear about goals and expectations. - Avoid withholding critical details.
9. Resilience and Adaptability	Thriving in the face of challenges and adapting to changes while maintaining ethical principles.	- Build mental agility through reflection. - Stay calm under pressure. - Learn from setbacks.

A 6-Month Plan to Enhance Ethical Leadership

Month 1: Building a Strong Ethical Foundation

Daily Actions:

- **Ethical Reflection:** Spend 5 minutes each morning reflecting on ethical principles and values.
- **Ethical News:** Read news articles or listen to podcasts about ethical issues in business and leadership.
- **Moral Courage Exercise:** Identify a challenging ethical dilemma and consider different courses of action.

Weekly Actions:

- **Ethical Dilemma Discussion:** Discuss ethical dilemmas with a mentor or colleague.
- **Ethical Self-Assessment:** Complete a self-assessment to identify areas for improvement.
- **Ethical Book Club:** Join a book club focused on ethics and leadership.

Month 2: Fostering Trust and Transparency

Daily:

- **Honest Communication:** Practice open and honest communication with colleagues and subordinates.
- **Active Listening:** Dedicate time to active listening during meetings and one-on-one conversations.
- **Empathy Exercises:** Put yourself in others' shoes and consider their perspectives.

Weekly:

- **Trust-Building Activities:** Organize team-building activities to foster trust and camaraderie.

- **Feedback Sessions:** Seek feedback from colleagues and subordinates to improve your leadership style.
- **Ethical Dilemma Case Studies:** Analyze real-world ethical dilemmas and discuss potential solutions.

Month 3: Cultivating Fairness and Justice

Daily:

- **Fairness Checklist:** Review your daily interactions to ensure fairness and equity.
- **Conflict Resolution:** Practice effective conflict resolution techniques.
- **Diversity and Inclusion:** Learn about diversity and inclusion and how to promote it in the workplace.

Weekly:

- **Diversity and Inclusion Training:** Attend a workshop or training session on diversity and inclusion.
- **Mentorship Program:** Mentor a junior employee to promote fairness and equality.
- **Bias Awareness Training:** Participate in bias awareness training to identify and address unconscious biases.

Month 4: Promoting Ethical Culture

Daily:

- **Ethical Decision-Making:** Practice ethical decision-making in daily situations.
- **Ethical Role Modeling:** Demonstrate ethical behavior in all interactions.
- **Ethical Communication:** Use clear and honest communication to avoid misunderstandings.

Weekly:

- **Ethical Code of Conduct Review:** Review your organization's code of conduct and discuss it with your team.
- **Ethical Dilemmas Workshop:** Participate in a workshop on ethical dilemmas and decision-making.
- **Ethical Leadership Training:** Attend a leadership training program that focuses on ethics and integrity.

Month 5: Building a Culture of Integrity

Daily:

- **Ethical Reflection Journal:** Write about ethical challenges and lessons learned.
- **Ethical Book Club:** Discuss ethical leadership books with colleagues.
- **Ethical Dilemmas Game:** Play ethical dilemma games to practice decision-making.

Weekly:

- **Ethical Audits:** Conduct regular audits of your team's ethical practices.
- **Ethical Leadership Coaching:** Seek coaching from an experienced ethical leader.
- **Ethical Retreat:** Organize a retreat to discuss ethical challenges and opportunities.

Month 6: Sustaining Ethical Leadership

Daily:

- **Ethical Self-Assessment:** Regularly assess your own ethical behavior.
- **Ethical Role Modeling:** Continue to demonstrate ethical leadership in all interactions.

- **Ethical Communication:** Practice clear and honest communication.

Weekly:

- **Ethical Leadership Training:** Attend a leadership training program focused on ethics and integrity.
- **Mentorship:** Mentor junior employees and share your knowledge and experience.
- **Ethical Reflection:** Dedicate time to reflect on your ethical journey and identify areas for continued improvement.

By consistently implementing this plan, individuals can develop a strong ethical foundation and become effective ethical leaders.

Coaching questions for reflection:

- **What core beliefs guide your actions in challenging situations?**
- **Can you share an experience where you had to stand firm in your beliefs despite significant challenges?**
- **What does moral courage mean to you, and how can you demonstrate it in your leadership?**
- **How do you cultivate trust with your team or followers?**
- **In what ways do you actively plan for the future while also responding to immediate challenges?**
- **How do you ensure that your actions align with your vision for your team or organization?**
- **What sacrifices have you made in your leadership journey for the sake of others?**
- **How do you respond when faced with setbacks or obstacles?**
- **Who do you collaborate with to achieve your goals, and how do you foster inclusivity in your leadership style?**

- **What lasting impact do you hope to have through your leadership, and how do you define success in this context?**

Concluding Reflection:

- **What one action can you take this week to embody the leadership qualities discussed in the chapter?**

These questions can help facilitate deeper reflection and dialogue, encouraging individuals to connect their personal experiences with the principles outlined in the text.

Part-2

Leadership Pillar-2(Envisioning)

Bold Minds, Bold Moves: Shaping the World Through Vision

- **Ratan Tata: Visionary Leadership and Resilience in Transforming Tata Group**
- **Revolutionary Vision: Mao Zedong and the Birth of Modern China**
- **The Remarkable Resilience of Lee Iacocca: A Story of Visionary Leadership and Strategic Boldness**
- **The Relentless Visionary Who Revolutionized Retail: Sam Walton**
- **How Microsoft Thrived Amidst Technological Evolution**
- **Trailblazing Leadership: Learning from Lee Iacocca's Journey**
- **From Humble Beginnings to Global Domination: The Dell Technologies Saga**
- **The iconic wartime leader of the United Kingdom during World War II**
- **Cultural Revolution: How Visionary Leaders Transformed Their Organizations**

In a world driven by bold visions and strategic thinking, there exist leaders who not only dare to imagine the future but also possess the unwavering courage to reshape it. These visionaries are not merely passive observers; they are active architects of change, skillfully navigating the complexities of uncertainty and transforming the landscapes of their industries and nations. Their journeys are marked by risks taken, conventions challenged, and movements inspired—each step paving the way for significant and lasting impact.

This chapter delves into the remarkable stories of leaders whose extraordinary vision and resilience have left indelible marks on the world. For instance, consider Ratan Tata, who took the helm of the Tata Group and transformed it from a traditional conglomerate into a global powerhouse, driving innovation and ethical business practices that resonate today. His leadership style emphasizes not just profit but also a commitment to social responsibility, demonstrating that a visionary leader can indeed harmonize business success with positive societal impact.

We also reflect on the revolutionary vision of Mao Zedong, whose ideological drive and strategies birthed modern China. Mao's leadership was characterized by an unwavering focus on transforming the socio-economic landscape of a nation, illustrating how bold, sometimes controversial decisions can reshape a country's future. His story serves as a powerful reminder of the far-reaching effects of visionary leadership on a national scale.

Similarly, Lee Iacocca's remarkable resilience and strategic boldness transformed Chrysler from the brink of bankruptcy into a thriving automotive giant. Iacocca's narrative is not just about saving a company; it's about redefining an industry through innovative thinking and courageous decision-making. His approach showcases the importance of adaptability and vision in overcoming seemingly insurmountable challenges.

Then there's Sam Walton, whose relentless pursuit of a visionary retail model changed the face of commerce forever. By founding Walmart, he created a shopping experience that prioritized customer satisfaction while driving efficiency and low prices. Walton's story embodies the essence of bold leadership—seeing a need and daring to fill it in a way that revolutionizes the market.

As we explore these visionary journeys—from the technological advancements that allowed Microsoft to thrive amidst evolving landscapes to the strategic brilliance of wartime leaders who navigated complex geopolitical landscapes—we uncover a common thread that unites these figures: their unwavering belief in the future they sought to create. Whether leading organizations through cultural revolutions or spearheading industrial transformations, these leaders exemplify what it means to possess a strategic vision and the boldness to realize it.

In this chapter, readers will discover how these leaders confronted uncertainty with clarity, embraced risk with purpose, and moved forward with resilience, ultimately crafting legacies that continue to inspire generations. Let their stories serve as powerful reminders that visionary leadership is not solely about predicting the future; it is about creating it through decisive action, innovative thinking, and an unyielding commitment to a better tomorrow.

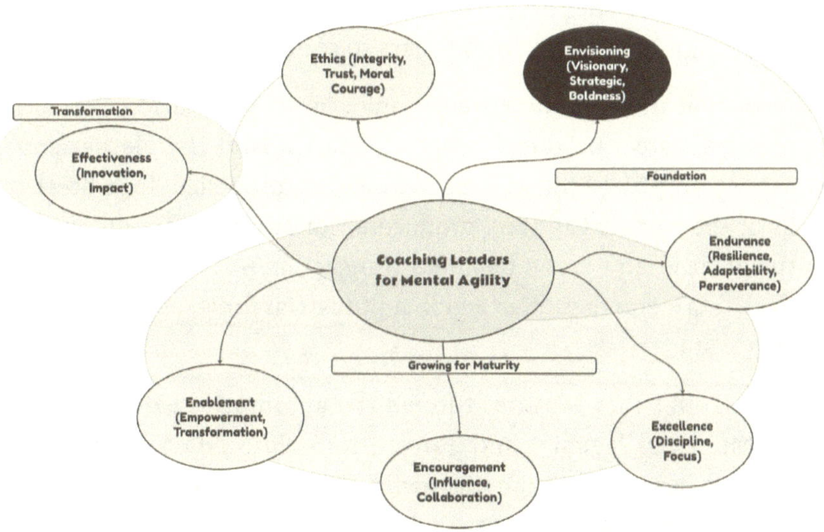

Coaching Leaders for Mental Agility: Story No 6

Ratan Tata: Visionary Leadership and Resilience in Transforming Tata Group

> **"You can't make a decision based on fear and the possibility of what might happen."**
>
> **- Ratan Tata**

Ratan Tata's tenure as Chairman of Tata Group is marked by numerous key achievements that reflect his leadership, vision, and strategic acumen.

Here are some of the most notable achievements:

1. Global Expansion and Strategic Acquisitions

In 2000, Tata Tea made a bold move that transformed its global presence by acquiring Tetley, one of the world's leading tea brands. This acquisition was not just about expanding the company's product line; it was a statement of Tata's ambition to become a global player in the consumer goods market. The Tetley deal opened doors to international markets and set the stage for Tata's global expansion, a vision that would only grow stronger in the years to come.

Just seven years later, Tata Steel made waves by acquiring Corus Group, a prominent steel producer based in the UK and the Netherlands, for an astounding $12 billion. This acquisition propelled Tata Steel to the ranks of the world's top steel producers, solidifying the company's global footprint. It wasn't just a business transaction—it was a milestone that marked Tata's emergence as a global industrial force, able to compete on the world stage.

Then, in 2008, Tata Motors stunned the automotive world by acquiring the prestigious Jaguar Land Rover from Ford for $2.3 billion. This acquisition wasn't just about owning luxury brands—it was about breathing new life into Jaguar Land Rover, investing in innovative models and cutting-edge technology. Under Tata's leadership, these iconic British brands were revitalized, regaining their stature in the global automotive market.

These acquisitions reflect Tata's bold vision for growth, an unwavering commitment to expanding on the world stage, and the ability to transform challenges into opportunities. The group's strategic moves serve as a powerful example of how thoughtful leadership and long-term vision can reshape industries and inspire lasting success.

2. Innovation in Product Development

In 2008, Tata Motors made a bold move by launching the Tata Nano, the world's most affordable car. Priced at around $2,000, it was designed to revolutionize transportation by making car ownership possible for millions of people who had never imagined it before. Though the Nano faced challenges along the way, its creation was a breakthrough in automotive innovation. Tata's vision wasn't just about selling cars—it was about democratizing mobility and providing affordable transportation to families across India. The Nano embodied the company's spirit of innovation, showing how bold ideas can drive change and open new possibilities for everyday people.

3. Strengthening Corporate Social Responsibility

Under Ratan Tata's leadership, Tata Trusts emerged as one of India's largest philanthropic organizations, making a profound impact across various social sectors. With a strong commitment to healthcare, education, and rural development, the Trusts advanced numerous initiatives that significantly contributed to societal welfare.

Ratan Tata and the Tata Group made substantial investments in social causes, establishing, and supporting vital institutions. One of their most notable achievements is the Tata Memorial Hospital, a leading cancer treatment center in India, which has transformed the lives of countless patients. Through these philanthropic efforts, Ratan Tata not only fostered a culture of giving back but also inspired a generation to prioritize social responsibility, demonstrating that business success can go hand in hand with meaningful contributions to society.

4. Resilience and Crisis Management

In November 2008, the horrific Mumbai terrorist attacks targeted multiple locations, including the iconic Taj Mahal Palace Hotel, part of the Tata Group. Amid this tragedy, Ratan Tata's leadership shone through with empathy and resilience. Instead of merely focusing on business recovery, Tata made the well-being of his employees and their families the top priority. Under his guidance, the company provided unwavering support to those affected, offering financial aid and emotional care. This compassionate response reflected Tata's deep commitment to his people, showing how true leadership emerges in moments of crisis.

Around the same time, the world was reeling from the global financial crisis. The Tata Group, under Ratan Tata's watch, faced immense pressure but remained steadfast. He led the company through this challenging period by introducing strategic cost-cutting measures and refocusing efforts on core businesses. Rather than retreating in fear, Tata made bold investments, positioning the company for long-term stability and growth. His calm yet decisive leadership allowed Tata Group to weather the storm, demonstrating that resilience, empathy, and forward-thinking are the cornerstones of lasting success.

Through these turbulent times, Ratan Tata's leadership proved to be both compassionate and strategic, showing how adversity can be met with unwavering resolve and deep humanity. His actions inspire others to rise in the face of crisis, to lead with empathy, and to always look ahead with courage.

5. Modernization and Growth

Ratan Tata spearheaded a transformative journey for the Tata Group, focusing on modernization and reorganization. He worked tirelessly to streamline operations and improve efficiency across the group's diverse range of businesses. His strategic approach involved making thoughtful divestments while simultaneously investing in key areas poised for growth.

Under his leadership, Tata Group became a global powerhouse, significantly enhancing its brand reputation. Through strategic acquisitions and a commitment to innovation, the company not only expanded its reach but also garnered international recognition. Ratan Tata's unwavering dedication to maintaining high standards of corporate governance and ethical practices set a benchmark in the business world, inspiring others to pursue excellence while prioritizing integrity. His vision not only shaped the Tata Group but also left an indelible mark on the global business landscape.

6. Advancing Infrastructure and Technology

The Tata Group, under Ratan Tata's leadership, made bold investments in infrastructure that transformed India. Projects like Tata Power and Tata Consultancy Services (TCS) were not just about building facilities; they were about paving the way for technological advancement and development across the country.

Ratan Tata's vision turned TCS into one of the largest IT services companies in the world. This wasn't just a business achievement; it reshaped the global technology landscape. By focusing on innovation and excellence, Tata inspired a generation of professionals to push boundaries and embrace change. His leadership showed that with the right investments and commitment, significant progress is possible, inspiring many to dream bigger and aim higher.

Ratan Tata's achievements reflect his strategic vision, commitment to innovation, and dedication to ethical business practices. His leadership not only transformed Tata Group into a global powerhouse but also set a standard for corporate social responsibility and resilience.

These accomplishments highlight his ability to drive growth, navigate challenges, and make a positive impact on society.

Ratan Tata's education and upbringing played a crucial role in shaping his leadership qualities and contributing to his achievements.

Ratan Tata was born into a family that carried a powerful legacy of leadership and philanthropy. His great-grandfather, Jamsetji Tata, had founded the Tata Group, laying the foundation for one of India's most respected business empires. His father, Naval Tata, was also a prominent figure in the business world. Growing up in such an influential family,

Ratan absorbed important lessons on business principles, leadership, and the importance of giving back to society.

From an early age, Ratan was immersed in the workings of the Tata Group, where he gained firsthand experience of the business world. He observed the complexities of running a large, diverse organization and the responsibility that came with leadership. *This early exposure instilled in him a deep understanding of the importance of maintaining high ethical standards, which would guide him throughout his career as he took on the immense responsibility of steering the Tata Group into new eras of growth and global success.*

Ratan Tata's educational journey began at Bishop Cotton School in Mumbai, where his formative years laid the groundwork for both his intellectual and social growth. The solid education he received here set the stage for the future responsibilities he would shoulder.

He then moved on to Cornell University in the United States, where he pursued a Bachelor of Science degree in Architecture with a focus on Structural Engineering. *This technical education sharpened his analytical abilities and problem-solving skills while giving him a deep understanding of design and planning.* It was during these years that Tata honed the mindset that would later help him navigate complex challenges in the business world.

To further strengthen his leadership capabilities, Tata attended the Advanced Management Program at Harvard Business School. *This experience broadened his perspective on global business practices and gave him a strategic edge that would prove essential in leading Tata Group to new heights.* His journey through these renowned institutions played a vital role in shaping the visionary leader he would become.

Ratan Tata began his journey with the Tata Group in 1962, immersing himself in the company by taking on various roles, from working on the shop floor to handling operations. This hands-on experience gave him a deep understanding of the business's inner workings, teaching him the critical importance of operational efficiency. Tata didn't just learn from the boardroom; he was in the trenches, seeing firsthand what it took to keep a company of that scale running smoothly.

His time in the United States, both in education and work, further shaped his vision. The global business practices and management techniques he encountered abroad gave him a broader perspective. This exposure was key in influencing his strategic thinking, particularly when it came to expanding Tata Group on an international level. Tata's blend of practical experience and global insight became the foundation of his innovative leadership style.

Ratan Tata was profoundly influenced by the mentorship of prominent figures within the Tata Group, especially his uncle, J.R.D. Tata. As a highly respected industrialist and the former Chairman of Tata Group, J.R.D. *Tata provided Ratan with invaluable guidance that shaped his approach to leadership and business. This mentorship instilled in him not only a deep respect for effective management but also a commitment to fostering innovation and integrity within the organization.*

From a young age, Ratan Tata absorbed the philanthropic values that defined the Tata family. This emphasis on giving back and upholding social responsibility became a fundamental part of his identity. *Throughout his career, he remained steadfast in his commitment to corporate social responsibility and ethical business practices, believing that true success lies in making a positive impact on society.* This blend of mentorship and ingrained values propelled Ratan Tata to lead with purpose and inspire those around him to do the same.

Ratan Tata's upbringing in a family with a strong business legacy, combined with his education in architecture, engineering, and management, provided him with a solid foundation for his leadership roles.

His exposure to global business practices and hands-on experience within Tata Group further shaped his approach to leadership and strategic decision-making.

Ratan Tata's Legacy: A Blueprint for Modern Leadership

Ratan Tata's tenure at the Tata Group offers a rich tapestry of leadership lessons. By examining his approach, we can identify key principles and apply them to contemporary leadership challenges.

Core Leadership Principles

Ratan Tata exemplified human-centric leadership, deeply understanding that people are the heart of any organization. His strong emphasis on social responsibility and employee welfare showed a commitment to nurturing talent and fostering a positive work environment, making every team member feel valued and essential.

With a keen strategic vision, Tata had an uncanny ability to anticipate industry trends. This foresight allowed him to position the Tata Group for future growth, ensuring that the company not only thrived but also stayed ahead of the curve in an ever-changing market.

Tata's approach to risk was both bold and prudent. He was unafraid to make significant decisions, yet he carefully calculated the potential outcomes, balancing ambition with caution. This thoughtful risk-taking contributed to the group's remarkable successes.

Ethical leadership was another cornerstone of Tata's philosophy. His unwavering commitment to ethical business practices fostered trust and credibility, not just within the organization but also among stakeholders and the public. This integrity set a standard that inspired others to follow.

Through his efforts, Tata transformed the Tata Group from a sprawling conglomerate into a more focused and competitive organization. This cultural transformation not only streamlined operations but also invigorated the company's spirit, paving the way for a bright future. Ratan Tata's journey is a testament to the power of leadership that values people, embraces strategic foresight, and maintains ethical integrity, inspiring generations to come.

Lessons for Modern Leaders

Purpose-driven leadership stands at the heart of effective management, guiding leaders to define a clear vision that resonates with the needs of society. This alignment not only motivates teams but also fosters a sense of belonging among employees, who feel valued and empowered to contribute their unique ideas and talents.

Creating a culture of empowerment is essential. When employees are encouraged to voice their opinions and take initiative, they become active participants in the organization's success. This collaboration leads to innovative solutions and a stronger sense of community within the workplace.

A long-term perspective is equally important in leadership. By making decisions that prioritize sustainable growth and meaningful impact, leaders lay the groundwork for a thriving future. This focus on longevity encourages thoughtful choices rather than quick fixes, ensuring the organization remains resilient in the face of challenges.

Ethical decision-making serves as the foundation for trust in business relationships. By prioritizing ethics in all dealings, leaders not only enhance their reputation but also inspire a culture of integrity within their teams.

Lastly, continuous learning keeps leaders agile and responsive to the ever-changing landscape of their industries. Staying updated on trends and adapting to new circumstances allows organizations to remain competitive and innovative, driving them toward lasting success. Through these principles, leaders can inspire those around them, creating an environment where everyone strives to achieve their best.

By studying Ratan Tata's leadership style, we can gain valuable insights into how to build successful and enduring organizations.

Here are some key messages about Tata's leadership vision:

- **Global Impact**: Tata's leadership vision emphasizes expanding the company's reach and influence globally. This includes strategic acquisitions and innovation to position Tata as a major player in various industries worldwide.
- **Innovation and Accessibility**: Tata aims to create innovative products that are not only cutting-edge but also accessible to a wider audience. This vision reflects a commitment to meeting the needs of diverse customers and improving their lives.

- **Social Responsibility**: A strong focus on corporate social responsibility is central to Tata's leadership vision. By prioritizing initiatives in healthcare, education, and community development, Tata demonstrates that businesses can play a crucial role in enhancing societal well-being.
- **Resilience and Empathy**: Tata's leadership vision includes a commitment to resilience in the face of challenges. Leaders are encouraged to prioritize the well-being of employees and stakeholders, showing empathy and support during tough times.
- **Ethical Governance**: Integrity and ethical practices are fundamental to Tata's leadership vision. By maintaining high standards of governance and corporate ethics, Tata sets an example for others, proving that success can be achieved while adhering to strong moral principles.
- **Empowerment and Growth**: Tata's vision promotes a culture of empowerment within the organization. By valuing employees and encouraging their growth, Tata fosters an environment where innovation and collaboration can thrive.

Overall, Tata's leadership vision combines a commitment to global growth, innovation, social responsibility, resilience, ethical governance, and employee empowerment, creating a comprehensive approach to sustainable and impactful leadership.

Coaching Leaders for Mental Agility: Story No 7

Revolutionary Vision: Mao Zedong and the Birth of Modern China

> **"To be a leader is to be a visionary and to be responsible for the future of the people."**
>
> **- Mao Zedong**

Mao Zedong (1893-1976) was a Chinese revolutionary and communist leader who played a key role in shaping modern China. He was born into a poor peasant family in Hunan province, and his early life was influenced by the hardships of rural living. As a young man, he got involved in radical politics, inspired by the May Fourth Movement, which called for changes in China. This led him to join the Chinese Communist Party (CCP) in the 1920s, starting his rise in politics.

With strong determination and vision, Mao quickly moved up in the CCP and became its chairman by 1943. His leadership stood out during the Long March from 1934 to 1935, a challenging journey that tested the strength of the Red Army and established Mao as a key leader in the party. This march was not just a military retreat; it symbolized endurance and commitment to their revolutionary goals.

Mao played a crucial role in the Chinese Revolution, which led to the creation of the People's Republic of China (PRC) in 1949. As the founding father of the PRC, he served as its chairman until he died, leaving a deep impact on the country. He developed a unique form of communist ideology known as Maoism, which focused on the power of peasants, the importance of mass mobilization, and ongoing class struggle.

In the late 1950s, Mao launched the Great Leap Forward, an ambitious campaign to quickly industrialize China and combine farms into larger collective farms. However, this plan led to widespread famine and economic failure, showing the dangers of his ideas.

The 1960s brought more upheaval when Mao started the Cultural Revolution, a movement aimed at removing capitalist and traditional elements from society. This time was marked by political purges, social chaos, and significant economic disruption. Mao's focus on ideological purity caused intense struggles in the country, affecting millions of people.

Even though his policies caused a lot of suffering, many people see Mao as the creator of modern China. They credit him with changing the economy and society, modernizing a nation that had faced many hardships. His charm and strong beliefs made him a powerful leader, but his authoritarian style concentrated power in the CCP and silenced dissent, creating a cult of personality around him.

Mao's legacy is a complicated mix of achievements and tragedies, showing the heavy burden of leadership and the deep impact of political ideas. His life story reminds us that one person's vision can shape the future of an entire nation, for better or for worse.

Mao Zedong faced numerous challenges throughout his leadership, and his approach to overcoming them often reflected specific traits and strategies:

Early in his career, Mao Zedong faced tough military challenges, especially against the Nationalist forces led by Chiang Kai-shek. These battles were difficult, but Mao didn't give up. Instead, he used guerrilla warfare tactics, which focused on being quick and surprising his enemies. With the help of support from rural communities, he was able to avoid larger Nationalist armies and gradually take control of more areas for the Communist Party.

Even as he grew in power, Mao's leadership in the Communist Party was not always safe. He faced strong opposition, especially in the early years and later during the Cultural Revolution. To keep his position, Mao took decisive action against his rivals and built a loyal following among party members and the public. His charm and strong ideas helped him unite people, creating a sense of loyalty and shared goals.

One of the most important moments in Mao's leadership was the Long March from 1934 to 1935. At that time, Communist forces were surrounded by Nationalist armies. In this challenging situation, Mao suggested a strategic retreat, leading his followers on a tough journey through difficult terrain. Although it was exhausting, this retreat allowed Mao to regroup and strengthen his leadership, making him a key figure in the Communist movement.

Mao aimed to change Chinese society with campaigns like the Great Leap Forward and the Cultural Revolution, but he faced many challenges. Still, he kept control by encouraging mass mobilization, getting rid of people he saw as enemies, and pushing for loyalty to his ideas among his followers. His charisma helped him inspire loyalty and gather support during these chaotic times.

Economically, Mao's policies were meant to quickly industrialize China and combine farms into larger collective farms, but they led to serious problems. The Great Leap Forward caused economic mistakes that resulted in widespread famine and unrest. Recognizing these failures, Mao adapted his approach and started to make changes. He introduced reforms like the "Household Responsibility System" in the late 1970s, which allowed individual farmers more freedom and improved agricultural productivity.

Mao's legacy is complex, filled with both great successes and major failures. His ability to deal with challenges came from being flexible, sticking to his beliefs, and being willing to change his strategies when needed. Through his journey, he not only changed the direction of China but also made a lasting impact on the world, showing the power of resilience and vision.

However, his leadership also led to significant human suffering and social upheaval, leaving a controversial and contested legacy in Chinese and world history.

From Mao Zedong's leadership, particularly in terms of stamina and endurance, several lessons can be drawn:

Mao Zedong showed great strength and determination as a leader, even when facing tough challenges. He didn't give up, despite losing battles and facing opposition within his own party. This shows how important it is for leaders to be strong and keep going during hard times.

Mao had a long-term plan to change Chinese society with communist ideas. He believed in making clear goals and having a strategy, even when things didn't go as planned. His focus on these goals kept him moving forward, no matter how hard it got.

Mao was deeply committed to his communist beliefs. His strong beliefs helped him get through difficult times and stay focused on his goals, even when others criticized him. This dedication gave him a purpose that motivated his actions.

While he stuck to his core beliefs, Mao also showed he could adapt. He changed his strategies when needed, which helped him handle various challenges. This flexibility allowed him to stay in power for a long time, proving that being able to adjust is important for solving problems.

Mao was good at getting support from the masses. He built strong loyalty among party members and the people, creating a network that helped him face challenges from inside and outside his party. This support made him stronger as a leader.

Mao's journey shows that learning from mistakes is important. His experiences, especially during the Great Leap Forward, taught him to think about what went wrong and change his policies. This ability to learn and improve was a key part of how he led.

Even with the controversial parts of his leadership, Mao's strength left a lasting impact on China and the global communist movement. His ability to lead through many years of change offers important lessons for leaders today. Whether seen as a positive force or a source of conflict, Mao's story reminds us of the complexities of leadership and how those who lead can make a lasting difference.

Mao Zedong's leadership stamina provides insights into the qualities of resilience, strategic planning, adaptability, and commitment to ideals that can inspire and inform leaders facing challenges in various contexts.

Mao Zedong, as a leader, was a complex and influential figure in 20th-century history, particularly in the context of China.

Here are some key aspects of his leadership:

Revolutionary Vision: Mao was driven by a revolutionary vision to transform China into a communist society. He saw himself as leading a movement to overthrow imperialism, feudalism, and capitalism, and to establish a socialist state that prioritized the peasantry and workers.

Charismatic and Authoritative: Mao possessed charismatic leadership qualities that enabled him to inspire and mobilize millions of people. His authoritative leadership style centralized power within the Communist Party and emphasized discipline and ideological purity.

Strategic Thinking: Mao demonstrated strategic thinking, adapting tactics to the changing political and military landscape. For example, during the Long March, he led his forces on a strategic retreat to evade encirclement by the Nationalist forces, which ultimately strengthened his leadership within the Communist Party.

Mass Mobilization: Mao's leadership relied heavily on mass mobilization. He leveraged propaganda, mass campaigns (such as the Great Leap Forward and the Cultural Revolution), and grassroots organizing to consolidate power and implement his vision for China.

Cultural and Social Engineering: Mao's policies, particularly during the Cultural Revolution, aimed to reshape Chinese society ideologically and culturally. This led to significant social upheaval, purges of perceived counter-revolutionaries, and the disruption of traditional institutions.

Legacy and Impact: Mao's leadership had a profound impact on China. He unified the country under communist rule, modernized certain sectors of the economy, and promoted gender equality and literacy. However, his policies also resulted in economic instability, human rights abuses, and political repression.

Controversy and Criticism: Mao's leadership is highly controversial. Critics argue that his policies, such as the Great Leap Forward and the Cultural Revolution, led to widespread famine, economic stagnation, and the loss of millions of lives. His authoritarian style of governance and suppression of dissent have also been subjects of criticism.

In conclusion, Mao Zedong's leadership was marked by revolutionary zeal, strategic acumen, and a commitment to transforming China.

However, his legacy is complex, with both achievements and significant challenges. Studying Mao's leadership provides insights into the complexities of governance, ideology, and the impact of leadership on society.

> **"The masses are the real heroes, while we ourselves are often childish."**
>
> **– Mao Zedong**

Mao Zedong's leadership offers several key insights:

1. **Revolutionary Vision**: Mao aimed to transform China into a communist society, with a focus on overthrowing imperialism, feudalism, and capitalism, prioritizing peasants, and workers.

2. **Resilience and Determination**: Mao's leadership was marked by his stamina, especially during difficult times like the Long March and internal challenges. He showed strength in adversity and the ability to persist.

3. **Adaptability and Strategic Thinking**: Mao's strategic flexibility, such as his use of guerrilla tactics and adapting his policies after failures, exemplifies the importance of adjusting plans when faced with challenges.

4. **Mass Mobilization**: Mao leveraged mass movements, grassroots campaigns, and propaganda to consolidate power, mobilize the population, and implement his policies.

5. **Complex Legacy**: Despite significant achievements in unifying China and promoting literacy and gender equality, his policies like the Great Leap Forward and Cultural Revolution caused widespread suffering, economic hardship, and loss of life. His leadership style also created a strong cult of personality, centralizing power, and stifling dissent.

Overall, Mao's leadership demonstrates both the power of vision and the risks of ideological extremism, showing the importance of resilience, adaptability, and the responsibility leaders bear in shaping their nations.

Coaching Leaders for Mental Agility: Story No 8

The Remarkable Resilience of Lee Iacocca: A Story of Visionary Leadership and Strategic Boldness Vision and Valor

> **"The very essence of leadership is that you have to have a vision. It's got to be a vision you articulate clearly and forcefully on every occasion. You can't blow an uncertain trumpet."**
>
> **— Reverend Theodore M. Hesburgh**

Imagine stepping into the shoes of Lee Iacocca, a leader who epitomized extraordinary mental resilience. His journey is a powerful example for all of us, starting from the moment he was fired as the president of Ford, a blow that could have defined his career. Instead of succumbing to defeat, Iacocca embraced the challenge ahead of him, transforming adversity into opportunity.

Lee Iacocca is a quintessential example of a leader who demonstrated extraordinary mental resilience.

His journey from being fired as the president of Ford to leading Chrysler's turnaround is a testament to his unwavering determination and ability to overcome adversity.

Lee Iacocca's mental resilience is exemplified through several key incidents and stories from his career that offer valuable lessons:

1. The Ford Mustang Launch

In the 1960s, Lee Iacocca spearheaded a project that would eventually become one of the most iconic cars in American history—the Ford Mustang. At the time, his bold idea for an affordable yet stylish sports car was met with skepticism by many of the higher-ups at Ford. Yet, Iacocca was undeterred.

He believed deeply in his vision and refused to back down, even when doubts surrounded him. Leading a team of equally dedicated and passionate individuals, Iacocca pushed forward. Together, they worked tirelessly, focusing on every detail—from the innovative design to the groundbreaking marketing strategies that would soon take the automotive world by storm.

When the Mustang finally hit the market, it was an instant sensation. In just two years, more than a million Mustangs were sold, securing Iacocca's reputation as a visionary leader. His story became one of perseverance, the power of believing in a bold idea, and the importance of rallying a team to bring that vision to life.

The lesson here is clear: Iacocca's unwavering belief in his vision, even in the face of resistance, shows how conviction and perseverance can turn a dream into a reality. His leadership inspired others to see what was possible and ultimately created a lasting legacy with the Mustang.

2. Firing from Ford

In 1978, after dedicating years of hard work to Ford and playing a major role in the company's success, Lee Iacocca was unexpectedly fired by Henry Ford II. The dismissal came as a significant blow, both personally and professionally. For someone who had poured so much into the company, it was a moment that could have easily left him defeated.

But Iacocca didn't let the setback define him. Instead, he saw it as an opportunity to take on an even greater challenge. Soon after, he joined Chrysler, a company teetering on the edge of bankruptcy. Determined to prove his resilience and capabilities, Iacocca threw himself into the task of turning Chrysler around.

What followed was nothing short of remarkable. Iacocca's leadership helped rescue Chrysler from financial collapse, restoring the company's fortunes and his reputation in the process. His ability to rise from such a difficult moment and tackle an even bigger challenge showed his incredible resilience.

The lesson in Iacocca's story is **powerful:** setbacks don't have to be the end. In fact, they can be the beginning of something greater. His determination to turn his firing into an opportunity proves the importance of resilience and shows how challenges can lead to even bigger successes when faced with courage and conviction.

3. Chrysler Turnaround

When Lee Iacocca took over as CEO of Chrysler in 1979, the company was on the brink of bankruptcy. Financial difficulties had brought Chrysler to its knees, and many doubted whether it could survive. But Iacocca wasn't one to back down from a challenge. He immediately set to work with a series of bold, strategic moves aimed at saving the struggling company.

One of his first steps was to negotiate government loans, a controversial yet necessary decision that bought Chrysler the time it needed to recover. He also implemented cost-cutting measures, streamlining operations to make the company leaner and more efficient. But it wasn't just about cutting back; Iacocca knew that innovation was key to Chrysler's revival. His team introduced the Chrysler minivan, a product that would go on to become a massive success and completely transform the company's fortunes.

By the mid-1980s, Iacocca's efforts had paid off. Chrysler had not only avoided bankruptcy, but it was also profitable again, standing stronger than ever. His bold decision-making and ability to act decisively under intense pressure were the driving forces behind this incredible turnaround.

Iacocca's leadership during this crisis teaches a valuable lesson: in times of adversity, strategic boldness and clear, decisive action can make all the difference. His vision and courage helped save a company that many had written off, showing how strong leadership can transform even the most dire situations.

4. Government Loan Guarantees

When Chrysler was on the verge of collapse, Lee Iacocca knew he had to take extraordinary action to save the company. In 1980, he made a bold and unprecedented move: securing a $1.5 billion loan guarantee from the U.S. government. At the time, it was a controversial decision that many doubted would succeed. But Iacocca was determined and personally took on the challenge.

He used his exceptional communication skills and credibility to lobby Congress and the administration. It wasn't just about asking for money; Iacocca presented a clear, realistic plan to turn Chrysler around. He promised that the government would be repaid in full, backing it up with a detailed strategy for making the company profitable again. His confidence and clarity won over skeptics, and his relentless advocacy ultimately paid off.

Thanks to Iacocca's efforts, Chrysler received the loan guarantees it desperately needed. The company used this financial lifeline to recover and eventually return to profitability. His success in securing the bailout was a defining moment, not only for Chrysler but for Iacocca's legacy as a leader.

Iacocca's story shows the power of effective advocacy. His ability to lead with vision, persistence, and strategic negotiation highlights the importance of not giving up, even when the odds seem stacked against you. His example inspires leaders to step up, communicate clearly, and fight for what they believe in.

5. Personal Challenges

Lee Iacocca's journey was not without personal challenges. Alongside the pressures of leading major companies, he faced deeply painful experiences, including health issues and the tragic loss of his first wife to diabetes. These personal hardships could have derailed anyone, but Iacocca remained steadfast in his commitment to both his professional and personal goals.

Rather than letting these challenges overwhelm him, Iacocca used them as motivation to do more. He channeled his grief into action, becoming a passionate advocate for diabetes research and education. His personal experiences fueled his philanthropic work, as he dedicated time and resources to finding a cure for the disease that had affected his family so profoundly.

This resilience didn't just make Iacocca a stronger person—it made him a more compassionate and determined leader. His ability to persevere through personal pain, while still excelling in his professional responsibilities, inspired those around him to rise above their own struggles.

Iacocca's story is a testament to the power of emotional resilience. It shows that even in the face of deep personal adversity, one can find the strength to move forward, grow, and make a difference. His life reminds us that true leadership is not just about success in business, but about how we respond to life's greatest challenges.

Lessons from Lee Iacocca's Mental Resilience with Examples and Actions

1. The Power of Visionary Leadership

When Lee Iacocca joined Chrysler in 1978, it didn't take him long to realize the company was teetering on the edge of bankruptcy. Instead of backing down from the overwhelming challenge, Iacocca boldly presented a vision that would breathe new life into the struggling automaker. His plan focused on creating fuel-efficient cars that would resonate with the changing needs of the market, as consumers began prioritizing vehicles that were not just stylish but also practical and economical.

To turn this vision into reality, Iacocca knew he had to clearly articulate it to everyone within the company. He made sure that his vision addressed Chrysler's immediate challenges and aligned with shifting market demands. But having a great idea wasn't enough—he also understood the power of effective communication. Iacocca consistently shared his plan across all levels of the organization, rallying employees around a common purpose and motivating them to work towards this shared goal.

As part of his strategy, he ensured that each department and team understood how their work played a crucial role in achieving the company's new direction. This alignment of goals across the organization fostered unity and purpose, making the turnaround not just a possibility but a reality.

Iacocca's story is a powerful example of how a clear, bold vision combined with effective communication and goal alignment can transform even the most dire situations. His leadership not only saved

Chrysler but set a blueprint for leaders facing their own challenges in today's ever-changing business landscape.

2. Turning Setbacks into Opportunities

In 1978, after a long and successful career at Ford, Lee Iacocca was unexpectedly fired. For many, this would have been a huge setback, but Iacocca didn't let it stop him. Instead, he took on a new challenge by joining Chrysler, a company that was struggling and close to bankruptcy. Under his leadership, Chrysler experienced one of the most amazing turnarounds in business history.

Rather than focusing on being fired, Iacocca saw it as a chance to grow. He came to Chrysler with fresh ideas and used his experience to guide the company through tough times. One of his major contributions was backing the development of the K-Car and the minivan—both of which became big successes and helped save the company.

Iacocca's story is a powerful example of resilience. He didn't just recover from his setback; he thrived. His journey shows us how important it is to embrace change and view challenges as new opportunities rather than the end of the road. His success also highlights the value of innovation, using creative ideas to solve problems during tough times. By building a resilient mindset in himself and his team, Iacocca proved that even in the hardest situations, the right attitude can lead to great success.

This story of determination and vision serves as an inspiring lesson for leaders, showing that with resilience and innovation, setbacks can lead to incredible achievements.

3. Strategic Boldness

Lee Iacocca faced a critical moment in Chrysler's history when he made the daring decision to request a $1.5 billion loan guarantee from the U.S. government. This unprecedented move was not just a gamble; it reflected his strategic boldness and unwavering confidence in his plan to revive the company.

Iacocca understood that taking calculated risks is essential in leadership. He believed in making bold decisions when necessary, ensuring that these choices were well-thought-out and supported by solid data.

Recognizing that survival sometimes depends on external support, he reached out for help, illustrating that asking for assistance can be a sign of strength, not weakness.

To rally everyone around his vision, Iacocca made sure to communicate the rationale behind his bold decision. By clearly explaining his reasoning, he gained the trust and buy-in of stakeholders, paving the way for Chrysler's turnaround. His journey serves as an inspiring reminder that great leaders are not afraid to take risks and that effective communication is key to rallying support for transformative changes.

4. Effective Advocacy

In 1979, Lee Iacocca spoke before Congress, making a case that would be vital for Chrysler's future. With confidence and clarity, he explained why loan guarantees were necessary, stressing that it wasn't just about saving Chrysler but also preventing harm to the broader economy if the company failed.

Iacocca's success wasn't by chance; it came from careful preparation. He gathered all the facts and built strong arguments that were hard to ignore. His skill in speaking made decision-makers understand the importance of helping Chrysler.

He also knew how important relationships were. Iacocca had built connections with key people, which helped strengthen his case. His story teaches us that to effectively advocate for any cause, we need to prepare well, communicate clearly, and build strong relationships. These efforts can turn challenges into opportunities and lead to significant outcomes.

5. Personal Resilience

Lee Iacocca faced many tough personal and professional challenges, like being unexpectedly fired from Ford and Chrysler's near bankruptcy. Despite this, he showed great resilience and determination, staying focused on his goals without letting setbacks stop him.

He understood the importance of keeping his eye on the bigger picture, even when things got difficult. Iacocca also made sure to take care of his own well-being, knowing that he needed to be strong to lead effectively during hard times. Instead of seeing challenges as failures, he viewed them as opportunities to learn and grow.

His journey teaches us that by staying focused, practicing self-care, and constantly learning, we can overcome challenges and come out stronger. Iacocca's story encourages us to face adversity with resilience and learn from every obstacle.

Learning from Lee Iacocca's life, we can develop a set of leadership coaching questions that focus on resilience, strategic thinking, and effective advocacy.

Here are some questions to inspire thoughtful reflection and growth in leaders:

- **What long-term vision do you have for your organization, and how do you plan to achieve it?** Reflecting on Iacocca's visionary leadership in transforming Chrysler.
- **How do you identify and leverage opportunities in times of crisis?** Inspired by Iacocca's ability to turn setbacks into opportunities.
- **How do you prepare for high-stakes negotiations or presentations?** Emphasizing the importance of thorough preparation like Iacocca's meticulous plan for securing the government loan.
- **What data and arguments do you gather before advocating for a significant change or initiative?** Reflecting on the importance of having comprehensive data and a strong case.
- **Can you describe a time when you faced a significant setback? How did you overcome it?** Drawing parallels to Iacocca's resilience during Chrysler's financial struggles.
- **How do you stay motivated and focused when facing challenges or setbacks?** Reflecting on Iacocca's determination and perseverance.
- **How do you tailor your message to connect with different stakeholders and decision-makers?** Inspired by Iacocca's compelling and persuasive testimony before Congress.

- **What strategies do you use to ensure your communication is both impactful and memorable?** Emphasizing the need for strong communication skills.
- **How do you cultivate relationships with key influencers and stakeholders in your industry?** Reflecting on Iacocca's ability to build and leverage important relationships.
- **What steps do you take to maintain and strengthen these relationships over time?** Emphasizing ongoing relationship management and trust-building.
- **How do you foster a culture of innovation and continuous improvement in your organization?** Reflecting on Iacocca's innovative approach to revamping Chrysler's product line.
- **What are some ways you handle resistance to change within your team or organization?** Drawing on Iacocca's experience in driving organizational change.
- **How do you continuously develop your own leadership skills and knowledge?** Inspired by Iacocca's lifelong learning and adaptability.
- **What legacy do you want to leave as a leader, and how are you working towards it?** Reflecting on Iacocca's impactful legacy in the automotive industry.

Lee Iacocca's story is not just a story but a rich source of timeless wisdom and practical advice that remains highly relevant.

It provides a comprehensive guide on leadership, resilience, and strategic thinking, making it a must-read for anyone looking to enhance their leadership skills and navigate the complexities of the modern business world.

> **"The greatest glory in living lies not in never falling, but in rising every time we fall."**
>
> **— Nelson Mandela**

A story to share with:

Amrutha *Thompson was the CEO of* ***InnovateX****, a tech startup with a revolutionary idea for a new AI product. Despite her innovative* ***vision****, she faced intense skepticism from investors and resistance within her own team. Many doubted whether her ambitious project could succeed.*

Determined to prove them wrong, ***Amrutha*** *remained steadfast in her* ***belief****. She passionately* ***communicated*** *her* ***vision*** *to her team, setting clear* ***goals*** *and* ***inspiring*** *them to push through the challenges. Her* ***commitment*** *to her* ***vision*** *was unwavering, even as doubts persisted around her.*

Just as ***InnovateX*** *began to show signs of progress,* ***Amrutha*** *faced a major setback: her top developer unexpectedly left the company. This departure threatened to derail the entire project. Rather than seeing it as a crushing blow,* ***Amrutha*** *viewed it as an opportunity to bring in fresh talent. She quickly hired a new developer whose innovative ideas actually improved the project's design.*

In addition to handling internal challenges, ***Amrutha*** *needed to secure substantial funding to complete the AI product. The funding market was highly competitive, and she knew she needed a bold approach.* ***Amrutha*** *developed a detailed plan and pitched it to several venture capitalists. She made a compelling case for the product's potential, showcasing how it could revolutionize the tech industry. Her* ***strategic*** *boldness and* ***confidence*** *won over the investors, securing the crucial funds* ***InnovateX*** *needed.*

Amrutha's *ability to advocate effectively was crucial in this process. She prepared meticulously, crafting powerful presentations, and leveraging her network to build support. Her persuasive* ***communication*** *convinced investors of the AI product's unique advantages and potential.*

On a personal front, ***Amrutha*** *faced significant challenges as well. Her mother fell seriously ill, adding to her stress and responsibilities. Despite these personal difficulties,* ***Amrutha*** *maintained a strong focus on her professional* ***goals****. She managed her time carefully, ensuring that her personal issues did not hinder her leadership. Her* ***resilience*** *in the face of personal adversity only strengthened her resolve.*

In the end, ***Amrutha's*** *dedication and strategic actions led* ***InnovateX*** *to success. The AI product was launched to great acclaim and quickly gained traction in the market. The funding she secured allowed the company to expand and grow, and her personal strength inspired her team.* ***Amrutha's*** *journey exemplified how vision,* ***resilience, strategic*** *boldness, and effective* ***communication*** *can drive a leader to overcome obstacles and achieve remarkable success.*

After reading Amrutha Thompson's story, here are the leadership steps I would take:

- I would make sure to explain my goals and vision clearly to my team, just like Amrutha did. By sharing my passion and setting clear objectives, I would help everyone understand what we're working towards and keep them motivated.
- When things go wrong, like losing a key team member, I would try to stay positive and see it as a chance to improve. Instead of getting discouraged, I would look for new talent or ideas that could make the project even better.
- I would take bold steps when needed, especially when trying to secure resources or convince others of my vision. Like Amrutha, I would carefully plan and confidently present my ideas to gain support from important stakeholders.
- If personal challenges arise, I would stay focused on my leadership duties, just as Amrutha did. Managing my time well and staying resilient would help me keep both my personal life and work on track.
- I would actively use my network to gather support for my projects, similar to how Amrutha secured funding. Preparing thoroughly for presentations and advocating for my ideas effectively would help me gain the backing I need.

By following these steps, I would aim to lead my team through challenges with confidence, adapt to changes, and achieve success, just like Amrutha did at **InnovateX**.

> **"If your actions inspire others to dream more, learn more, do more and become more, you are a leader."**
>
> **— John Quincy Adams**

Coaching Leaders for Mental Agility: Story No 9

The Relentless Visionary Who Revolutionized Retail: Sam Walton

> **"Walmart's success stems not only from its competitive pricing, but from the company's relentless pursuit of operational efficiency."**
>
> **— Harvard Business Review**

Sam Walton was the founder of Walmart and a highly influential figure in the retail industry.

His leadership and innovative approaches to business have made Walmart one of the largest and most successful companies in the world.

Sam Walton's ability to overcome challenges through innovative strategies, resilience, and a deep understanding of his business environment made him a legendary leader.

His actions provide valuable lessons in entrepreneurship, leadership, and strategic thinking that are applicable in various contexts and industries today.

Here are some key examples, along with the actions he took:

In 1962, Sam Walton opened the doors to the first Walmart store in Rogers, Arkansas, driven by a simple yet revolutionary idea: offering quality products at low prices. He believed that by keeping prices down, he could attract more customers, and in doing so, generate enough volume to make up for slim profit margins. This innovative approach transformed retail, laying the groundwork for Walmart's massive growth.

Walton's obsession with keeping costs low went beyond just pricing. He practiced what he preached, flying economy class, and staying in budget hotels. By leading with frugality, he infused Walmart with a cost-conscious culture that allowed the company to stick to its promise of low prices.

As Walmart expanded, Walton knew that innovation was essential to maintain the company's edge. In the 1970s, he invested in a state-of-the-art supply chain, building distribution centers and his own fleet of trucks. Walton wasn't just focused on cutting costs; he was changing the way inventory was managed. By embracing just-in-time inventory and cutting-edge satellite technology, he ensured that Walmart could restock stores quickly and offer more products at lower prices than the competition.

Sam Walton was ahead of his time when it came to technology. He introduced barcodes and computer systems to track inventory and sales, making Walmart one of the first retailers to use data for decision-making. With real-time information, Walmart could respond faster to customer needs, optimize inventory, and tailor its offerings to local preferences, all while keeping costs down.

One of Walton's key strategies was empowering his store managers. He gave them the freedom to make decisions that best served their local markets. Whether it was adjusting pricing or choosing products, managers had the autonomy to respond to their customers directly. This approach not only motivated store leaders but also ensured that Walmart was always connected to the needs of its customers.

At the heart of everything Walton did was the customer. His famous mantra, "There is only one boss. The customer," was more than just words. He would drop into stores unannounced, talking to shoppers and employees to get a firsthand sense of what was working and what wasn't. His open-door policy invited feedback, ensuring that Walmart's focus stayed on customer satisfaction.

The culture Walton built at Walmart was just as important as its business model. He introduced the Saturday Morning Meeting, a gathering where employees from all levels could discuss challenges, share ideas, and celebrate successes. Walton himself was always involved, fostering a sense of unity and purpose that made employees feel they were part of something bigger than just a retail company.

Walton's early adoption of technology put Walmart ahead of the competition. In the 1980s, he invested in satellite systems, allowing stores across the country to stay connected and communicate instantly. This technological leap enabled Walmart to streamline operations, cut costs, and provide better service to its customers.

Despite his relentless focus on building a business empire, Walton never forgot about the importance of giving back. He encouraged Walmart to support the communities where it operated, through donations, sponsorships, and volunteer work. His commitment to corporate social responsibility helped Walmart build a positive public image and fostered deeper connections with the people it served.

Walton's habit of visiting stores regularly set him apart from many CEOs. He didn't just rely on reports—he observed operations firsthand, talked to employees, and listened to their concerns. This hands-on approach allowed him to stay connected to the front lines, making decisions that were grounded in the day-to-day realities of the business.

Sam Walton's legacy is not just about creating a retail giant; it's about changing the way business is done. From innovation in supply chains to empowering employees, Walton's principles continue to shape Walmart's success today.

Sam Walton faced numerous challenges throughout his journey in building Walmart into the retail giant it is today. His responses to these challenges demonstrate his resilience, innovative thinking, and leadership.

Here are some key challenges Walton encountered, along with the actions he took to overcome them:

1. Starting with Limited Resources

Sam Walton's first store, a Ben Franklin franchise in Newport, Arkansas, was born from a dream but started with very limited financial resources. Unlike larger competitors, Walton didn't have the deep pockets or backing that could cushion his ventures. But instead of seeing this as a disadvantage, he turned it into an opportunity for innovation.

Determined to offer customers the best deals, Walton focused heavily on cost-cutting. He negotiated relentlessly with suppliers to get the best prices, kept a tight rein on inventory, and ran the store with a small, efficient team. Every penny saved meant he could offer lower prices, which drew more customers through the door. Walton also made smart decisions when it came to expanding his business. Rather than buying properties, he leased stores to avoid the heavy financial burden of ownership. This leasing strategy allowed him to grow quickly, opening new stores without getting weighed down by costly real estate purchases. His ability to stretch limited resources as far as possible laid the foundation for Walmart's remarkable growth.

2. Competition with Established Retailers

Sam Walton faced fierce competition from established retailers, especially in small towns where they already had a strong presence. It was a tough challenge, but Walton wasn't one to back down. He took a bold approach, introducing a discount retail model that focused on offering lower prices than his competitors. This was a risky move, but Walton understood the power of savings. Customers, eager to get more for their money, were willing to drive longer distances just to shop at his stores.

But Walton's strategy didn't stop at lower prices. He saw an opportunity where others didn't—in rural areas. While larger retailers concentrated on urban markets, Walton expanded Walmart into smaller towns, where big competitors were less likely to set up shop. By targeting these underserved areas, he created a space for Walmart to grow without having to go head-to-head with the retail giants in bigger cities. This combination of discount pricing and strategic expansion allowed Walmart to steadily carve out its place in the market, eventually outpacing the competition.

3. Overcoming Early Business Setbacks

When Sam Walton's first store in Newport thrived, he faced an unexpected blow. The landlord, seeing the store's success, refused to renew Walton's lease and took over the store for himself. It was a harsh lesson, one that could have easily ended Walton's ambitions. But instead of letting this setback define him, Walton chose to fight back with resilience and determination. He didn't give up.

With a clear resolve, he opened a new store in Bentonville, Arkansas. Armed with the lessons learned from Newport, Walton applied those insights to make his new venture even more successful. The experience shaped his thinking. He knew he had to be smarter about the future—particularly when it came to managing leases and choosing locations. Walton vowed that such a situation would never happen again. From then on, he made sure to own the properties where his stores stood, ensuring no one else could take away what he worked hard to build.

This experience not only showcased Walton's persistence but also sharpened his long-term vision. It was a turning point, where he learned that setbacks weren't the end—they were opportunities to grow stronger.

4. Managing Rapid Expansion

As Walmart grew bigger, it faced a new challenge. How could it keep all its stores running smoothly and consistently?

Empowering Store Managers

Sam Walton decided to give store managers more power. This meant that store managers could make decisions to suit their local customers and communities. This helped Walmart grow quickly while still keeping its core values.

Technology to the Rescue

Walton also invested in technology to help manage Walmart's growing network of stores. Satellite communication and data systems allowed Walmart to track inventory, sales, and operations in real-time. This helped the company expand smoothly and efficiently.

5. Building a Strong Supply Chain

Walmart, with its many stores spread across the country, had a big problem. Getting products to all those stores was a huge logistical challenge.

A Smart Solution: The Hub-and-Spoke System

To solve this problem, Sam Walton, Walmart's founder, came up with a clever idea. He created a hub-and-spoke system. This meant that products would be sent to central locations (the hubs) first. Then, these hubs would send the products to the individual stores (the spokes). This helped Walmart save money on shipping and get products to stores faster.

Technology to the Rescue

Walton also used technology to make Walmart's supply chain even better. He introduced barcodes and computer systems to track inventory and predict demand. This helped reduce waste and ensure that products were always available at a good price.

These changes made Walmart's supply chain more efficient and helped the company grow into a retail giant.

6. Maintaining Low Prices

Sam Walton faced a tough challenge as his company grew: keeping prices low for customers while still making a profit. This wasn't easy, especially as Walmart expanded. But Walton was determined to find a way to balance both.

He took direct action by negotiating with manufacturers to buy products in large quantities. By purchasing in bulk, he could secure lower prices and, in turn, pass those savings to his customers. This not only helped keep costs down but allowed Walmart to offer better deals than competitors.

In addition to this, Walton introduced Walmart's own private label products. These items, sold under Walmart's name, gave the company better control over pricing while still offering good quality. The private label strategy allowed Walmart to maintain its promise of low prices while also boosting profits.

Through these smart decisions, Walton managed to keep prices affordable for shoppers without sacrificing the company's bottom line, showing how innovation and thoughtful strategy could overcome challenges.

7. Public and Employee Perception

As Walmart expanded, the company faced growing criticism. People began to question its treatment of employees, pointing to low wages and tough working conditions. Others worried about the impact Walmart was having on small businesses, claiming the retail giant was driving them out of local markets. These issues threatened to tarnish Walmart's reputation.

Sam Walton didn't ignore these concerns. Instead, he took action to address them. Understanding that employees were the backbone of the business, Walton introduced profit-sharing programs. These plans gave workers a personal stake in the company's success, allowing them to share in Walmart's growth. This move not only boosted morale but also created a sense of loyalty and commitment among the workforce, transforming the way employees viewed their roles within the company.

But Walton didn't stop there. He believed that Walmart should be a positive force in the communities it served. He encouraged the company to get involved in local philanthropy, giving back to the people who supported the business. Walmart began investing in community service projects, improving public facilities, and helping those in need. This involvement showed that Walmart wasn't just focused on profits—it was also committed to making a difference in the lives of everyday people.

Through these initiatives, Walton showed that true leadership means listening to criticism, taking action, and working to create positive change, both for employees and for the communities that helped build the business.

8. Leadership Succession

As Sam Walton approached retirement, one of his biggest challenges was ensuring that Walmart would continue to thrive without him at the helm. He knew the future of the company depended on strong leadership and a commitment to the values that had made Walmart successful.

To prepare for this, Walton took a hands-on approach in grooming his successors. He spent years building a leadership team that shared his vision, one that understood the importance of cost efficiency, innovation, and a relentless focus on customer satisfaction. Walton worked closely with them, instilling the same principles and work ethic that had driven Walmart's rapid growth. He didn't just hand over the reins; he made sure the team was ready to lead with the same dedication he had brought to the company.

Walton also involved his family in the business, preparing them to take on leadership roles and carry his legacy forward. He wanted to ensure that the company's future was guided by people who understood not only the business side of Walmart but also the deeper values that made it a unique force in the retail world.

Even after his retirement, Walmart's continued dominance in the retail industry speaks to Walton's thoughtful planning and leadership. His focus on innovation, data-driven decisions, and customer service remains at the heart of the company's operations. Walton's careful planning and the strong foundation he built ensured that Walmart could continue to grow, even without him, demonstrating his true mastery as a leader who knew how to prepare for the future.

Several leaders have followed in Sam Walton's footsteps, adopting, and adapting his principles to build their own successful companies and make history. Here are a few notable examples:

1. Jeff Bezos (Founder of Amazon):

Jeff Bezos was inspired by Sam Walton's focus on customer satisfaction and keeping prices low. He took these core principles and applied them to Amazon, using technology to create a highly efficient operation that offered customers a huge range of products at competitive prices. Bezos's approach to making the customer the center of everything, much like Walton, helped Amazon grow rapidly.

Under Bezos's leadership, Amazon revolutionized the world of e-commerce and became one of the most valuable companies globally. He introduced groundbreaking innovations like one-click shopping, the

Prime membership program, and cloud computing services through Amazon Web Services (AWS). These innovations transformed the way people shop and interact with technology, leaving a lasting impact on the business world and consumer behavior.

2. **Howard Schultz (Former CEO of Starbucks):**

Howard Schultz was deeply inspired by Sam Walton's approach to building a strong company culture and prioritizing the customer experience. Walton's philosophy left a lasting impression on Schultz, who applied these principles at Starbucks. He didn't just want to sell coffee—he wanted to create an experience. Schultz believed in making Starbucks a place where customers could enjoy not only a cup of coffee but a welcoming atmosphere that felt like a second home.

Schultz's leadership had a profound impact on Starbucks. Under his guidance, the company grew from a small regional chain to a global coffee empire. His focus on providing employees with benefits, creating inviting store environments, and ensuring each customer's experience was memorable helped Starbucks become much more than just a coffee shop—it became a worldwide cultural icon.

3. Jim Sinegal (Co-Founder of Costco):

Jim Sinegal was greatly influenced by Sam Walton's focus on keeping prices low and running an efficient operation. Sinegal shared Walton's belief in providing customers with high-quality products at affordable prices, but he added his own twist by emphasizing bulk sales and introducing a membership model. This allowed Costco to offer even greater value to its customers.

Under Sinegal's leadership, Costco grew into one of the largest and most successful retail chains in the world. The company earned a reputation for its loyal customer base, fair treatment of employees, and its ability to consistently offer low prices without compromising on quality. Sinegal's approach transformed Costco into a trusted name in global retail.

4. Doug McMillon (Current CEO of Walmart):

Doug McMillon, who started his career at Walmart as an hourly associate, has been deeply shaped by Sam Walton's principles. He has carried forward Walton's legacy by focusing on innovation and e-commerce, while staying true to Walmart's core values of low prices and excellent customer service. McMillon's leadership is rooted in the belief that Walton's approach to serving customers can thrive even in a modern, digital world.

Under McMillon's leadership, Walmart has undergone significant transformations, particularly in expanding its e-commerce presence and integrating new technologies to improve customer service. His vision has helped Walmart adapt to the digital age, keeping it a dominant player in global retail while maintaining its foundational values.

5. Alice Walton, Jim Walton, and Rob Walton (Sam Walton's Children):

As the children of Sam Walton, Alice, Jim, and Rob Walton have played an important role in carrying on their father's legacy by staying actively involved in Walmart's operations and governance. They have remained committed to upholding the values Sam Walton established, ensuring that Walmart continues to thrive as one of the world's leading retailers.

The Walton family has not only preserved Walmart's global influence but also expanded its reach. Beyond their business roles, they have been deeply involved in philanthropy, supporting causes such as education and the arts through the Walton Family Foundation. Inspired by Sam Walton's leadership and innovative business practices, the family has made a lasting impact on both their industry and the world through their work and contributions.

> **"Walmart's ability to stay on top of innovation in retail has allowed it to continue dominating the market."**
>
> — **Jeff Bezos**, Founder of Amazon

The key messages from Sam Walton's leadership and the success of Walmart include:

- **Customer-Centric Philosophy**: Walton believed in serving the customer above all else. His mantra, "The customer is the only boss," guided Walmart's commitment to low prices and customer satisfaction.

- **Innovative Retail Strategy**: Walton's idea of offering quality products at low prices, coupled with his focus on cost-cutting and volume sales, revolutionized retail, allowing Walmart to grow rapidly.
- **Frugality and Leadership by Example**: Walton's personal frugality—flying economy class and staying in budget hotels—set the tone for Walmart's cost-conscious culture, essential for maintaining low prices.
- **Supply Chain Innovation**: Walton invested in technology and logistics, adopting the just-in-time inventory system and satellite communications to streamline Walmart's operations, and cut costs, giving the company a competitive edge.
- **Empowering Managers**: Walton empowered store managers with decision-making authority, fostering a sense of ownership and responsibility, which helped Walmart better respond to local market needs.
- **Resilience in the Face of Challenges**: Walton faced many challenges, from limited resources to losing his first store's lease. He used these setbacks to learn and improve, showing his resilience and adaptability.
- **Corporate Social Responsibility**: Walton emphasized giving back to communities through philanthropy and supporting local initiatives, which helped build a positive public image for Walmart.
- **Leadership Succession and Legacy**: Walton ensured a strong leadership succession plan, preparing both family members and executives to continue Walmart's growth, showing his long-term vision and strategic planning.
- **Influence on Other Leaders**: Walton's business principles inspired leaders like Jeff Bezos, Howard Schultz, and Jim Sinegal,

who adapted his customer-centric and cost-efficiency models to build their own successful companies.

Sam Walton's legacy continues to shape Walmart and the broader retail industry through his innovative approaches, leadership philosophy, and customer-first focus.

Coaching Leaders for Mental Agility: Story No 10
How Microsoft Thrived Amidst Technological Evolution

> **"Our mission is to empower every person and every organization on the planet to achieve more."**
>
> **- Satya Nadella**

Under Satya Nadella's leadership, Microsoft has undergone a remarkable transformation, redefining itself as a leading technology company focused on cloud computing, artificial intelligence, and digital innovation.

Here are some key highlights of Microsoft's journey under Nadella:

Satya Nadella, the CEO of Microsoft, has taken bold steps to transform the company into a powerhouse in the tech industry. He saw the immense potential of cloud computing early on and led Microsoft's shift towards a cloud-first, mobile-first approach. Under his guidance, Microsoft Azure has flourished, becoming one of the top cloud platforms. It competes fiercely with industry giants like Amazon Web Services and Google Cloud Platform. Businesses of all sizes have turned to Azure because of its strong infrastructure, wide range of services, and global accessibility. This growth in cloud computing has significantly boosted Microsoft's revenue.

Nadella also spearheaded the transition to subscription-based services, including Microsoft 365 and Microsoft Dynamics 365. By moving away from a traditional sales model to a subscription model, Microsoft has focused on creating lasting relationships with customers. This change has not only increased customer loyalty but has also provided the company with a steady and predictable income stream.

A spirit of collaboration and openness has thrived under Nadella's leadership. He has built bridges with competitors and industry peers, encouraging unprecedented partnerships. Embracing open-source technologies, he has supported initiatives involving projects like Linux and Kubernetes, making Microsoft a more inclusive and welcoming space for developers from all backgrounds.

Artificial intelligence has become a cornerstone of Nadella's strategy for Microsoft. He has heavily invested in AI research and development, placing it at the forefront of the company's initiatives. Microsoft's AI efforts encompass intelligent cloud services, conversational AI features like Cortana and Microsoft Teams, machine learning tools such as Azure Machine Learning, and AI-powered productivity solutions within the Microsoft Power Platform. These advancements have established Microsoft as a leader in AI innovation and adoption.

Nadella has also placed a strong emphasis on accessibility and inclusion within Microsoft's products and services. He believes that technology should be accessible to everyone, regardless of their abilities. Initiatives like AI for Accessibility aim to empower people with disabilities by harnessing AI solutions. The Xbox Adaptive Controller, designed for gamers with limited mobility, exemplifies this commitment. Through these efforts, Nadella has reinforced Microsoft's mission to use technology for positive social change.

In every aspect of his leadership, Nadella has not only focused on business growth but also on fostering a culture that values collaboration, innovation, and social responsibility. His vision inspires others to see the broader impact of technology in our lives and encourages them to work towards making it accessible to all.

Overall, Satya Nadella's leadership has transformed Microsoft into a more agile, innovative, and customer-focused organization, driving growth, and relevance in an increasingly digital world.

His vision, values, and strategic leadership have positioned Microsoft for continued success and impact in the years ahead.

"One inspiring story that exemplifies Satya Nadella's leadership style occurred during his early days as CEO of Microsoft. In response to a question about women's pay at the Grace Hopper Celebration of Women in Computing, Nadella initially suggested that women should trust the system to deliver fair compensation rather than asking for raises. However, he quickly recognized his mistake and ***publicly apologized, acknowledging the importance of advocating for equal pay and diversity in the workplace.***

This incident highlighted Nadella's ability to reflect on his actions, admit to shortcomings, and take proactive steps to rectify them. ***His willingness to listen, learn, and course-correct demonstrated humility, empathy, and a commitment to fostering an inclusive culture at Microsoft.*** *Nadella's response resonated with employees and observers alike, reinforcing his reputation as a leader who values diversity, equality, and continuous improvement."*

"Another example of Satya Nadella's leadership style is his emphasis on growth mindset and continuous learning. Under his leadership, Microsoft has embraced a ***culture of curiosity and experimentation, encouraging employees to take risks, learn from failures, and innovate relentlessly****. This approach was exemplified by the company's shift towards cloud computing and subscription-based services, which required a fundamental transformation in mindset and business strategy.*

Nadella's personal journey also serves as an inspiring example of leadership. He has spoken openly about his experiences overcoming adversity, including his son's struggle with cerebral palsy, which has shaped his perspective on ***empathy, resilience, and the importance of diversity and inclusion****. By sharing his own challenges and vulnerabilities, Nadella has connected with employees on a deeper level and fostered a sense of trust and authenticity within the organization.*

Furthermore, Nadella's focus on ***purpose-driven leadership*** *has been evident in Microsoft's initiatives to empower individuals and organizations worldwide through technology. Whether it's providing access to digital skills training, supporting sustainability efforts, or advancing accessibility and inclusivity in technology, Nadella has emphasized the role of technology as a force for positive change and societal impact. His visionary leadership and* *commitment to making a difference have inspired employees and stakeholders to rally behind Microsoft's mission of empowering every person and organization on the planet to achieve more."*

Satya Nadella's leadership had a profound impact on Microsoft's culture, strategy, and global influence.

Here's a deeper dive into how his values and approach have transformed the company:

Satya Nadella's leadership at Microsoft has been guided by strong values that have reshaped the company and driven its success. One of his key beliefs is in a "growth mindset." Nadella encourages employees to see challenges not as obstacles but as opportunities to learn and improve. This mindset has been essential in fostering a culture of innovation and continuous learning, which is crucial in the fast-changing tech industry.

Nadella also prioritizes empathy, urging leaders to focus on understanding customers and their needs. Under his guidance, Microsoft shifted from an inward-focused approach to one that places customers at the center of its strategy. This shift has fueled the success of products like Microsoft Azure and Microsoft 365, which are designed to solve real-world problems in ways that matter most to users.

In the workplace, Nadella has cultivated a collaborative and open environment. He encourages employees to work together, communicate freely, and take ownership of their ideas. This sense of empowerment has energized the company and allowed teams to contribute meaningfully to Microsoft's overall success.

One of Nadella's major cultural impacts has been moving Microsoft away from a "know-it-all" attitude to a "learn-it-all" approach. This change means the company now embraces continuous learning and adapting to new challenges, which aligns well with the fast pace of the tech world. As a result, Microsoft's products have become more customer-centric, focusing on user needs, and creating solutions that are easy to integrate into people's lives.

Nadella's leadership also extends beyond just products and company culture. He has championed making technology more accessible to all, including initiatives that help people with disabilities use Microsoft products. This includes adaptive controllers for gamers with disabilities and tools for users with visual impairments.

In addition, Nadella has led Microsoft in addressing the global digital skills gap. Through various training programs, the company is helping people around the world gain the skills they need in today's digital economy, creating a more digitally literate workforce.

Nadella has also placed a strong focus on sustainability. Under his leadership, Microsoft is striving to be carbon negative by 2030, setting an example for other tech companies to follow in terms of environmental responsibility.

Nadella's leadership has transformed Microsoft, both internally and externally, turning it into a company focused on values, innovation, and global responsibility. His approach to leadership has not only helped Microsoft grow but has also made it a leader in driving positive change in the world, inspiring leaders across various industries to lead with empathy, openness, and a growth mindset.

While his leadership style is widely admired, some critics point out potential challenges. For instance, the emphasis on collaboration can sometimes slow decision-making, and the focus on a growth mindset may overlook the value of deep expertise and experience. However, as the tech landscape continues to evolve, it will be fascinating to see how Nadella's leadership continues to shape Microsoft's future.

Here are some coaching questions about leadership we can ask and learn from the story of Satya Nadella and Microsoft's transformation:

Satya Nadella's leadership at Microsoft offers a powerful example of how visionary thinking, cultural transformation, and customer focus can reshape an organization. His journey was not just about making changes but also about recognizing opportunities and guiding the company towards a brighter future.

Nadella's ability to spot the rising potential of cloud computing early on set Microsoft on a new path. He steered the company towards a cloud-first strategy, understanding that this shift would unlock tremendous growth. But it wasn't just about jumping on the latest trend. Nadella had the foresight to balance this innovation with the company's legacy products. He ensured that while Microsoft invested heavily in cutting-edge technologies like AI, its cornerstone products like Office continued to evolve and meet customer needs.

Internally, Nadella worked to change the culture at Microsoft. He saw that the company's internal environment needed to be more open and collaborative, and he began fostering a mindset shift. Instead of operating in silos or competing against one another, employees were encouraged to work together, share ideas, and innovate collectively. This openness created a culture of trust, which was essential as Nadella introduced significant changes. He earned the buy-in of his employees by showing them the value of this new direction and empowering them to take ownership of their roles in the transformation.

Under Nadella's leadership, Microsoft also became more customer-focused. He and his team began to deeply understand what customers needed and found new ways to meet those demands. This focus led to the development of subscription-based services like Microsoft 365, which not only addressed customer needs for flexibility and accessibility but also built long-term relationships, improving loyalty and retention.

Nadella's leadership style played a critical role in these successes. He led by example, demonstrating through his own actions the behaviors and values he wanted to see across the company. He communicated openly and consistently, reinforcing the cultural shift he was driving. At the same time, he empowered employees to embrace new technologies and collaborate effectively, ensuring everyone felt a part of the company's future.

Through Nadella's leadership, Microsoft transformed itself into a more innovative, customer-driven, and collaborative organization, offering a blueprint for leaders everywhere. By reflecting on his decisions, culture-building strategies, and customer-centric mindset, leaders can find inspiration and practical guidance to implement in their own organizations, driving positive change and long-term success.

> **"We are not just building products. We are building a community of innovators who can solve problems together."**
>
> **– Satya Nadella**

Here are the central key messages about Satya Nadella's leadership and Microsoft's transformation summarized in five points:

- **Empowerment and Vision**: Nadella's mission is to empower every person and organization globally, using technology to help them achieve more and drive positive change.
- **Strategic Transformation**: Under his leadership, Microsoft has successfully shifted to a cloud-first and AI-focused strategy, with Azure becoming a top competitor in the cloud market, significantly boosting revenue.
- **Customer-Centric Approach**: Nadella has transitioned Microsoft to a subscription-based model, enhancing customer loyalty and ensuring long-term relationships by deeply understanding and addressing user needs.
- **Culture of Collaboration**: He has fostered a culture of openness and teamwork, encouraging a "learn-it-all" mindset that promotes continuous learning and innovation across the organization.
- **Commitment to Accessibility and Social Responsibility**: Nadella prioritizes making technology accessible to all, launching initiatives for individuals with disabilities and focusing on sustainability, including a goal to become carbon negative by 2030.

Coaching Leaders for Mental Agility: Story No 11

Trailblazing Leadership: Learning from Lee Iacocca's Journey

Lee Iacocca's accomplishments are most notable from his time as President of Ford (1970-1978) and later as CEO of Chrysler (1979-1992).

At Ford, Lee Iacocca made a significant impact by championing the development of the Ford Mustang. This iconic car shattered expectations and captured the attention of a younger generation, quickly becoming a symbol of freedom and power on the road. Its striking design and performance breathed new life into Ford, reviving the company's image and boosting sales in a time when they were desperately needed.

When Iacocca moved to Chrysler, he faced a formidable challenge. In 1979, the company stood on the brink of bankruptcy, but under his leadership, Chrysler successfully lobbied the U.S. government for loan guarantees. This bold and controversial move, while criticized by some, provided the lifeline needed to restructure and invest in new models. Thanks to Iacocca's vision, Chrysler not only survived but also thrived, producing successful vehicles like the Dodge Caravan minivan and the Jeep Cherokee. These innovative models resonated with changing consumer preferences, helping Chrysler regain market share and financial stability.

Iacocca's approach was not without its challenges. To ensure the company's survival, he made difficult decisions, implementing significant cost-cutting measures, including plant closures and workforce reductions. These decisions weighed heavily on him, knowing they would lead to job losses, but he believed they were essential for the company's recovery.

His reputation as a "turnaround artist" grew as he successfully revived both Ford and Chrysler during difficult times. Iacocca's charismatic leadership and exceptional communication skills allowed him to connect with the public and inspire confidence among employees. He became a figure of hope, rallying support and advocating for government assistance when it was needed most.

However, his strategies were not without criticism. Some argued that his focus on short-term success, exemplified by the Mustang and other iconic cars, overshadowed the importance of long-term investments in research and development. Additionally, while the government loan guarantees saved Chrysler, they sparked debates about the role of government intervention in the auto industry. Through all these challenges and achievements, Iacocca's story remains a testament to the power of leadership and vision in transforming the automotive landscape.

Lee Iacocca faced several significant challenges throughout his career, including:

During his time at Ford, Lee Iacocca faced significant financial struggles, especially in the late 1970s when the automotive industry was hit hard by an economic downturn and increased competition. These challenges forced Ford to reevaluate its operations and adopt cost-cutting measures to stay competitive.

Iacocca also had to navigate the complex world of corporate politics. Within Ford, he encountered resistance from internal stakeholders and competing interests, but he remained persistent, advocating for his vision, and pushing forward key strategic initiatives.

As a leader, Iacocca recognized the critical importance of product innovation and designing cars with the consumer in mind. However, bringing new models to market wasn't easy, as it required overcoming logistical and operational hurdles in an industry known for fierce competition and high consumer expectations.

Throughout his career, Iacocca faced economic uncertainty, including fluctuating market demands, regulatory changes, and geopolitical events that affected the auto industry. His ability to adapt to these unpredictable changes and anticipate market trends was key to his success.

In both his personal and professional life, Iacocca encountered setbacks. From disagreements with senior management to failed business ventures and public scrutiny, he faced numerous obstacles. Yet, his resilience and determination enabled him to overcome these challenges, eventually achieving lasting success and leaving a powerful legacy in the automotive world.

Lee Iacocca's leadership charisma wasn't just about showmanship; it translated into concrete actions that benefited the organizations he led.

Here's a deeper dive into how his charisma manifested and its impact:

Lee Iacocca stood out as a beacon of hope during tough times at Ford and Chrysler, his charisma radiating through the halls of both companies. With each gathering, he effortlessly rallied his employees, igniting a sense of unity and purpose among them. His powerful speeches resonated with a conviction that inspired confidence, urging everyone to work harder and persevere through challenges. Employees found renewed motivation in Iacocca's belief in their collective future, fostering a vibrant "can-do" attitude that lifted morale even in the darkest moments.

But Iacocca's influence extended beyond the workplace. He took to the public stage with the same fervor he displayed within the company, passionately advocating for the American auto industry during Chrysler's precarious journey toward bankruptcy. His heartfelt communications resonated with the public, investors, and government officials, garnering the support needed to secure critical loan guarantees. Iacocca's voice became a rallying cry for the industry, drawing people together in a shared vision for revival.

Innovation was at the heart of Iacocca's leadership style. He was not afraid to take calculated risks, championing bold ideas that others might have dismissed. The Ford Mustang emerged as a shining example of his visionary thinking. Iacocca's ability to connect with others helped him persuade key stakeholders to embrace groundbreaking concepts. This resulted in successful product launches that defied expectations and set new industry standards.

Under his leadership, a culture of openness blossomed within Ford and Chrysler. Iacocca encouraged a collaborative environment where ideas could flow freely, inviting employees to think creatively and challenge the status quo. This nurturing atmosphere sparked further innovation, allowing the companies to adapt and thrive in an ever-changing market.

Iacocca's mastery of communication played a vital role in his success. He had a remarkable ability to connect with a wide range of audiences, from blue-collar workers to government officials. By using clear language, relatable stories, and a dash of showmanship, he effectively delivered his message and improved communication both within the organizations and with external stakeholders.

The impact of Iacocca's leadership was profound. The Ford Mustang became not just a car but a symbol of youth, freedom, and innovation, revitalizing Ford's image and appealing to a broader audience. At Chrysler, his persuasive advocacy and ability to garner public support were instrumental in securing government loan guarantees that saved the company from the brink of collapse. With this financial lifeline, Chrysler could restructure and invest in new models, avoiding bankruptcy and setting the stage for a brighter future.

Yet, while Iacocca's charisma was a powerful tool, it is important to acknowledge its limitations. Overreliance on his personality could sometimes overshadow other essential leadership skills, such as strategic planning and long-term decision-making. In a complex world, effective leadership often requires a multifaceted approach, blending charisma with thoughtful strategy and vision. Nonetheless, Iacocca's story remains a powerful reminder of how inspiring confidence and championing innovation can transform organizations and bring about remarkable change.

Lee Iacocca's leadership style, while effective in his time, needs to be adapted for today's digital world.

Here's a breakdown of what we can learn from Iacocca and how to adapt it for the modern age:

In today's fast-paced digital world, leaders find themselves in a whirlwind of uncertainty, where the ability to inspire confidence and resilience within their teams is paramount. They know that clear communication is essential, so they work tirelessly to articulate a shared vision that unites their members. Celebrating each small success along the way keeps the team motivated and focused on the larger goals that lie ahead.

Leaders also recognize that innovation is crucial in this ever-changing landscape. They strive to create an environment where creativity flourishes, encouraging employees to think outside the box, experiment with new technologies, and embrace change as a constant companion in their work lives. It is in this culture of experimentation that great ideas are born and nurtured.

Effective communication is at the heart of successful leadership. Just as Lee Iacocca captivated diverse audiences with his charisma, today's leaders must master the art of connecting with people from all walks of life. They employ clear and concise communication strategies, especially through digital channels, ensuring that their messages resonate and guide their teams effectively.

Yet, in this dynamic age, charisma alone is not enough. Leaders must develop a wider skill set that encompasses data-driven decision-making and a deep understanding of digital technologies. They also need to foster collaboration across teams, ensuring that everyone feels included and empowered to share their ideas. While focusing on immediate wins is important, balancing short-term achievements with a long-term vision is equally vital. Leaders must invest in research and development to pave the way for sustainable growth.

The digital world is a sea of information, and modern leaders have access to vast amounts of data. They need to harness this wealth of analytics to make informed decisions, streamline processes, and gain a competitive edge. Agility and adaptability are essential traits, allowing them to pivot quickly as the landscape shifts beneath their feet.

Lee Iacocca's leadership style offers valuable insights for today's leaders. His journey was not without its challenges. He faced significant setbacks, including his firing from Ford and the daunting task of steering Chrysler away from near-bankruptcy. Overcoming these obstacles required immense mental resilience and a steadfast ability to persevere when the odds were stacked against him.

His success in turning around both Ford and Chrysler speaks to his strong capacity for navigating complex problems. Iacocca's knack for developing innovative solutions while keeping a laser focus on long-term goals is a testament to his mental agility. In a constantly evolving auto industry, he championed groundbreaking ideas like the Ford Mustang and adapted to changing consumer preferences with the Chrysler minivan.

Crisis management was another hallmark of Iacocca's leadership. Leading Chrysler through financial turmoil demanded quick thinking and the courage to make tough decisions under pressure. These moments showcased his mental stamina and ability to thrive in high-stress situations.

Iacocca's achievements reveal a relentless drive and an unwavering pursuit of success. This intrinsic motivation fueled his tireless efforts to revitalize Ford and Chrysler, inspiring those around him. His strong self-belief and confidence in his vision played a significant role in motivating employees and garnering external support.

In the end, Iacocca's story serves as a powerful reminder that in a world of constant change, resilience, adaptability, and a commitment to fostering a culture of innovation and inclusivity can lead to extraordinary transformations.

Overall, Lee Iacocca's leadership offers valuable lessons in inspiring confidence, championing innovation, and effective communication. However, modern leaders need to adapt his approach by incorporating data-driven decision making, agility, and fostering a culture of inclusion to thrive in the digital world.

Here are the central messages from Lee Iacocca's accomplishments and leadership style:

1. **Championing Innovation**: Iacocca's development of the Ford Mustang exemplified how visionary leadership and willingness to take risks can lead to iconic products that revitalize a company's image and appeal to new audiences.
2. **Crisis Management and Resilience**: During challenging times, particularly at Chrysler, Iacocca's ability to secure government loan guarantees was a testament to his resilience and strategic thinking, showcasing how effective leadership can guide a company away from the brink of bankruptcy.
3. **Effective Communication**: Iacocca's charismatic communication skills allowed him to connect with diverse audiences, inspire confidence among employees, and advocate passionately for the auto industry, emphasizing the importance of clear and relatable messaging in leadership.

4. **Balancing Short-Term and Long-Term Goals**: While achieving immediate successes, Iacocca faced criticism for not prioritizing long-term investments. His story highlights the need for modern leaders to balance quick wins with sustainable growth through research and development.

5. **Adapting Leadership Styles for the Digital Age**: Iacocca's experiences provide valuable lessons for contemporary leaders, underscoring the importance of incorporating data-driven decision-making, fostering inclusivity, and maintaining agility in a rapidly changing digital landscape.

Coaching Leaders for Mental Agility: Story No 12

From Humble Beginnings to Global Domination: The Dell Technologies Saga

> **"Recognize that there will be failures and acknowledge that there will be obstacles. But you will learn from your mistakes and the mistakes of others, for there is very little learning in success."**
>
> **– Michael Dell**

In 1984, Dell transformed the PC industry by changing how computers were sold. Instead of relying on traditional retailers, he sold directly to customers, offering lower prices and the ability to customize their machines. This innovation shifted the focus to customer needs and made technology more accessible.

Under his leadership, Dell expanded far beyond personal computers. By making strategic acquisitions and fostering organic growth, he turned Dell Technologies into a powerhouse, providing solutions in data storage, enterprise computing, and cloud services.

The company's financial success reflects Dell's sharp vision and leadership, growing it into a global tech giant with impressive revenue and profitability. His approach not only reshaped an industry but also positioned his company as a leader in the broader world of technology.

Dell reshaped the personal computer market by making PCs more accessible and affordable. His direct sales model allowed more people to own computers, accelerating the growth and widespread use of personal technology.

Understanding the growing need for customization, Dell gave customers the freedom to build PCs tailored to their specific needs. This shift toward personalization created a lasting trend that continues to shape the industry today.

By staying ahead of technological changes, from embracing cloud computing to expanding into enterprise solutions, Dell has ensured that his company remains competitive and relevant in the constantly evolving tech world.

Dell's leadership has always been defined by a focus on building a strong company culture rooted in innovation, efficiency, and customer commitment. This focus on culture became the backbone of Dell Technologies' success, driving the company forward.

His strategic acquisitions, like Alienware and EMC, showcased Dell's ability to identify opportunities for growth and expansion. These moves not only diversified the company's offerings but also expanded its reach into new markets.

Dell has never shied away from taking bold, calculated risks, such as taking the company private and later public again. While these decisions sparked debate, they ultimately played a key role in shaping the company's ongoing transformation and growth.

Michael Dell's journey to success wasn't without challenges. Some key hurdles he faced:

When Dell entered the PC market, it was up against established giants like IBM and Compaq. Competing against such powerful players required not only innovation but also the mental strength to stay focused and persevere. Dell had to carve out its space by offering better prices, innovative solutions, and superior customer service.

As the company grew rapidly, it faced the challenges of scaling up, managing a larger workforce, and maintaining its core values. Navigating this rapid expansion demanded tremendous mental resilience and a clear vision to keep everything on track.

The tech landscape is always shifting, and Dell had to constantly adapt to changes like the rise of cloud computing and new competitors. His ability to continuously learn, pivot, and embrace uncertainty showed remarkable mental agility.

Perhaps one of his boldest moves was taking the company private and then public again. These complex decisions involved navigating financial markets and managing investor relations, requiring a sharp, calculated approach to handle the risks and uncertainties that came with such strategic moves.

Dell's mental stamina was key to his success. Even when faced with immediate challenges, he never lost sight of his long-term vision for the company. His unwavering belief in his strategy helped him steer through tough times.

He had a strong ability to make tough decisions quickly, always ready to take action when needed. This decisiveness, paired with his openness to change, allowed him to overcome obstacles and seize new opportunities.

Resilience was a constant theme in Dell's journey. The tech world is full of setbacks, but Dell consistently bounced back, learning from his mistakes, and pressing forward. His ability to persevere through failures showed remarkable mental strength.

Dell's adaptability set him apart. He remained a lifelong learner, always open to new ideas and evolving his strategies to match the ever-changing technology landscape. His mental agility ensured he was never stuck in the past, always ready for the future.

Lessons for Today's World:

- **Focus on Long-Term Goals:** Don't get lost in the daily grind. Maintain a clear vision of your goals and don't be afraid to make short-term sacrifices for long-term gains.
- **Embrace Calculated Risks:** Calculated risks are an essential part of growth. Develop the ability to analyze situations, make informed decisions, and learn from both successes and failures.

- **Develop Mental Agility:** The world is constantly changing. Be open to new ideas, adapt your approach when necessary, and embrace lifelong learning.
- **Build Resilience:** Setbacks are inevitable. Learn to cope with challenges, bounce back from failures, and use them as opportunities to learn and grow.

Michael Dell's leadership style is known for its strengths that can be valuable in various aspects of life, beyond just business.

Here are some key personality traits and how they can be applied:

Dell saw the future of personal computers long before most did, recognizing the potential of a direct sales model to revolutionize the market. His forward-thinking mindset serves as a reminder to set ambitious goals and think far beyond the present. Just as Dell mapped out the future of his company, you can envision your path in life—whether it's career, education, or personal development.

When it came to decision-making, Dell acted swiftly, taking calculated risks without getting stuck in overthinking. In life, this translates to moving beyond hesitation and acting on your plans. By being decisive, you can face challenges head-on and seize opportunities that push you closer to your goals.

Dell's journey was fueled by relentless focus and determination. His constant drive to refine and improve his business model can inspire you to apply that same persistence in your personal endeavors. Whether learning a new skill, completing a tough project, or sticking to a fitness plan, it's about keeping your eyes on the goal and never giving up.

Customer satisfaction was at the core of Dell's business. He understood that success comes from meeting the needs of others. In everyday life, this principle of empathy can help you build better relationships and enhance communication, as you actively consider the perspectives and needs of those around you.

Finally, Dell believed in empowering those around him. He trusted his team to take ownership of their roles, encouraging collaboration and growth. You can bring this lesson into your life by trusting yourself and others. Delegate tasks, foster collaboration, and give people—including yourself—the space to learn, grow, and make decisions with confidence.

Dell's focus and determination stand out as key traits, but it's equally important to find balance in life. His relentless drive shows the value of commitment, but true success means not neglecting other areas of life in pursuit of a single goal. Like a tightrope walker, it's about keeping your eye on progress while making sure all aspects of life stay steady.

While Dell's leadership thrived in his unique context, it's a reminder that not every situation calls for the same approach. Adapting to the circumstances, whether at work or in personal relationships, shows real growth. The ability to shift gears and adjust strategies, just as Dell did when expanding his company, can lead to more effective outcomes.

Another essential aspect is self-awareness. Dell's confidence in making quick decisions played a huge role in his success, but not everyone may thrive with that style. Understanding your own strengths and limitations allows you to tailor your approach in ways that work best for you. Just as Dell knew his strengths and leaned into them, finding your personal rhythm is key to long-term success.

By exploring these below questions, you can gain deeper insights into how you can apply Michael Dell's leadership traits to your personal life and enhance your overall effectiveness and fulfillment.

Visionary Thinking:

- What long-term goals do you envision for yourself in your personal life?
- How can you apply forward-thinking strategies to achieve your personal aspirations?
- What steps can you take to align your actions with your future vision?

Decisive Action:

- What are some decisions you've been hesitant to make in your personal life, and what's holding you back?

- How can you overcome analysis paralysis and take decisive action towards your goals?
- What strategies can you implement to make quicker decisions while still considering the risks?

Focus and Tenacity:

- Describe a personal goal or project that requires long-term focus and perseverance. How do you plan to stay committed?
- What obstacles do you anticipate encountering, and how will you navigate through them?
- How can you break down your larger goals into smaller, manageable tasks to maintain momentum?

Customer Centricity:

- Reflect on a recent interaction where understanding someone else's perspective was important. How did you demonstrate empathy?
- In what ways can you incorporate customer-centric principles into your personal relationships or interactions?
- How do you currently gather feedback from others about their needs and preferences, and how can you improve this process?

Empowerment:

- Think about a situation where you delegated responsibility to someone else. How did it impact their growth and development?
- How can you empower yourself to take ownership of your personal goals and decisions?
- What opportunities exist for you to empower others within your personal or professional circles?

Additional Points:

- How do you currently maintain balance in your life between personal and professional commitments? What adjustments might you need to make?

- Can you think of a recent situation where you successfully adapted your approach based on the context? How did it impact the outcome?
- Reflect on a recent experience where self-awareness played a role in your decision-making process. How can you continue to develop this aspect of your leadership skills?

By understanding and applying these aspects of Michael Dell's leadership style, you can become more decisive, goal-oriented, and effective in various aspects of your life.

Successful leadership skills are transferable and can benefit you beyond the professional realm.

> **"We are all given the chance to succeed, but you have to seize the opportunity."**
>
> **– Michael Dell**

Coaching Leaders for Mental Agility: Story No 13

The iconic wartime leader of the United Kingdom during World War II

Winston Churchill, the iconic wartime leader of the United Kingdom during World War II, left a lasting legacy of leadership that continues to inspire leaders today.

His leadership style offers valuable insights and lessons that can be applied to contemporary leadership challenges.

Churchill wasn't born a strong leader; he was shaped by his experiences, both positive and negative.

His ambition, perseverance, intellectual curiosity, communication skills, and ability to adapt all played a role in his rise to prominence.

The crucible of World War II provided the ultimate test, where his strengths as a leader truly shone through, leaving a lasting legacy on the world stage.

In the early days of World War II, Winston Churchill faced a daunting challenge in the **Battle of the Atlantic**. Britain's survival depended on securing the vital shipping lanes that carried food, weapons, and supplies across the Atlantic Ocean. The German U-boats were merciless, sinking countless merchant ships, and threatening to choke off the lifeline to Britain. But Churchill refused to back down. He threw everything he had into the fight, pushing for advancements in anti-submarine technology, such as sonar, and directing naval resources with precision to counter the U-boat menace. Churchill didn't just lead behind closed doors; he understood the importance of keeping the public informed. He spoke openly about the sacrifices being made at sea and the critical role of the merchant sailors. Even as losses mounted, he never wavered in his determination, inspiring his nation to persevere, knowing that control of the Atlantic was essential for victory.

Around the same time, Churchill's mind was already turning toward the future invasion of Nazi-occupied Europe. The task of landing troops on the heavily defended beaches seemed almost impossible. But Churchill wasn't a man who accepted limitations easily. He envisioned the **Mulberry Harbors**, portable, pre-fabricated structures that could serve as temporary harbors, allowing Allied forces to land on the French coast during the D-Day invasion. It was a bold idea, one met with skepticism at first, but Churchill pushed forward, backing the engineers and soldiers tasked with bringing his vision to life. Though he kept the details of the project shrouded in secrecy, his unwavering belief in innovative solutions inspired those around him. When the Mulberry Harbors were finally deployed, they played a key role in the success of the invasion, proving Churchill's vision right.

Churchill also understood the value of alliances. With Britain's resources stretched thin, he knew that American support was critical. In 1941, Churchill traveled to the United States to meet with President Roosevelt. The **Lend-Lease Act** was his goal—convincing the U.S. to provide vital military aid to Britain without directly entering the war. Churchill's passionate appeals made it clear how dire the situation was. In person, he used not only his famous speeches but also his charm and eloquence to win over Roosevelt and others in Washington. It wasn't an easy task—many in Congress were reluctant to get involved in Europe's war—but Churchill's persistence paid off. His relentless diplomacy and clear communication about the global threat of Nazi Germany ultimately led to the passing of the Lend-Lease Act, providing Britain with much-needed support.

Churchill's leadership wasn't limited to strategy and diplomacy. During some of Britain's darkest hours, he was the voice that kept the nation united. In 1940, with British troops stranded on the beaches of Dunkirk, it seemed as though defeat was inevitable. But Churchill refused to give in. His powerful "We shall fight on the beaches" speech galvanized the country. It wasn't just words; it was a call to action. Ordinary civilians answered by sending a makeshift flotilla of boats to rescue over 330,000 soldiers, turning what could have been a devastating loss into a story of resilience and hope.

And when **The Blitz** rained destruction down on London, Churchill didn't hide in safety. He walked among the ruins, visiting bombed-out areas, and speaking with those who had lost everything. His calm and resolute demeanor gave strength to the people. Churchill was more than a leader in these moments—he became a symbol of endurance, standing tall amidst the rubble, showing that no matter the devastation, Britain would endure. His presence alone was a reminder that there was light at the end of the tunnel, even in the darkest of times.

These stories of Churchill's actions, his communication, and his steadfast perseverance reveal a man who led not just with his words but through his unbreakable spirit and visionary thinking, guiding Britain through one of the most challenging periods in its history.

These examples showcase how Churchill's leadership went beyond inspirational speeches.

He was a man who took decisive action, fostered innovation, and communicated effectively to achieve his goals.

His unwavering perseverance during a time of crisis served as a beacon of hope and a testament to his strong leadership.

Winston Churchill's leadership during World War II is a prime example of the psychological effects shaping leadership styles.

Lessons Learned:

Effective leadership hinges on several key elements that define how leaders inspire, communicate, and make decisions. To inspire others, leaders must harness the power of communication, motivating their teams through clear, passionate, and visionary messages. Belief plays a crucial role too, as a leader must hold a steadfast commitment to the vision, they are guiding their team toward.

In moments of crisis, decisive action is essential. Leaders must assess the situation, make tough decisions, and take calculated risks to steer their teams forward. Remaining composed under pressure is equally important, as emotional stability allows a leader to project confidence and reassure others in uncertain times.

Communication is a thread that runs through all aspects of leadership. It is not only about what is said but how it is delivered. A leader who communicates effectively can build trust, align teams, and ensure everyone is working toward the same goals, creating a cohesive and high-performing group.

Churchill's wartime leadership serves as a powerful reminder of the psychological aspects that shape effective leadership.

How these traits can be implemented in modern contexts and why they're still valuable?

Inspirational Leadership:

In today's work environment, leaders inspire their teams by creating a shared vision, fostering a culture that is positive and purpose-driven, and consistently recognizing and celebrating their employees' achievements.

This approach encourages motivation, strengthens engagement, and nurtures a sense of belonging within the team, making everyone feel valued and aligned with the bigger picture.

A leader's belief in a cause also holds great significance. By aligning a company's values with socially responsible initiatives, such as environmental sustainability or community efforts, modern leaders demonstrate their commitment to something larger than just profits. This passion resonates with people, drawing them toward leaders who are driven by a purpose beyond their personal goals.

Crisis Management:

In today's fast-paced world, decisive leadership is crucial. Leaders may need to quickly adapt to technological changes, steer through economic challenges, or manage public relations crises. Taking decisive action during these moments is essential for overcoming obstacles and providing clear direction during uncertain times.

Staying composed under pressure is equally important. Whether it's handling a product launch that went wrong or resolving a team conflict, leaders need to remain calm and collected. Composure enables them to think clearly, make well-informed decisions, and offer a sense of stability, which is vital for maintaining trust and confidence in challenging situations.

Communication Skills:

Leaders today have the opportunity to connect with their teams through a variety of communication platforms, from video calls to social media. Using these channels effectively allows leaders to keep their teams informed and engaged. Clear and transparent communication is key to building trust, encouraging collaboration, and ensuring that everyone is on the same page.

Honesty and transparency remain just as vital in today's information-driven world. Leaders should openly share challenges and setbacks while maintaining a focus on the future. This approach builds trust within the team, making it easier for everyone to work together toward solutions and common goals.

Example of a leadership of Elon Musk, CEO of SpaceX, and Tesla. Musk's approach to leadership echoes several of Churchill's key traits:

- **Inspirational Leadership:** Musk's ambitious vision for space exploration and sustainable energy has been a major source of inspiration. His ability to articulate a compelling vision for the future—such as colonizing Mars and accelerating the world's transition to electric vehicles—motivates both his teams and the broader public. Like Churchill, Musk's vision creates a shared sense of purpose that drives engagement and commitment.

- **Belief in a Cause:** Musk's belief in the transformative potential of technology and sustainable energy is central to his leadership. His commitment to addressing climate change through Tesla's electric vehicles and solar energy solutions, and his drive to make life multi-planetary through SpaceX, show his dedication to causes that he believes will fundamentally change the world. This unwavering belief attracts passionate supporters and fosters a strong organizational culture.
- **Crisis Management:** Musk has faced numerous challenges, from production delays at Tesla to technical hurdles at SpaceX. His decisive and often unconventional approach to crisis management—whether it's innovating solutions on the fly or making bold strategic moves—demonstrates his ability to handle crises effectively. For example, SpaceX's successful recovery and reuse of rockets after several failed attempts exemplify Musk's resilience and adaptive strategy.
- **Composure Under Pressure:** Musk is known for his intense work ethic and high-pressure environment, yet he remains focused on his long-term goals. Despite public scrutiny and the high stakes involved in his ventures, Musk's ability to remain calm and concentrated on his objectives helps steer his companies through periods of intense scrutiny and difficulty.

Musk's leadership showcases how Churchillian qualities can manifest in the high-stakes world of technology and innovation, demonstrating the timeless relevance of these traits in modern leadership.

Key message:

- **Decisive Action**: Churchill consistently made tough decisions during crises, from countering German U-boats in the Atlantic to spearheading innovative solutions like the Mulberry Harbors for D-Day, showcasing the importance of acting swiftly and effectively in challenging situations.

- **Effective Communication**: He connected deeply with the public through transparent, inspiring speeches, keeping people informed and motivated, especially during events like the Dunkirk evacuation and The Blitz.
- **Unyielding Perseverance**: Churchill's relentless determination in the face of adversity—refusing to back down even when losses mounted—served as a powerful example of resilience and leadership under pressure.
- **Strategic Vision**: His ability to anticipate future needs and champion innovative solutions, such as the Mulberry Harbors, reflected Churchill's forward-thinking mindset, ensuring success in key operations like D-Day.
- **Timeless Leadership Qualities**: Churchill's leadership—built on decisive action, communication, and perseverance—remains relevant today, influencing modern leaders like Elon Musk who inspire teams, tackle crises, and lead with a shared vision and purpose-driven goals.

Coaching Leaders for Mental Agility: Story No 14

Cultural Revolution: How Visionary Leaders Transformed Their Organizations

> **"Great things in business are never done by one person. They're done by a team of people."**
>
> **— Steve Jobs**

Changing an organization's culture is one of the most challenging tasks for a leader, but it can be crucial for turning around performance or adapting to new business environments.

Here are some key actions that leaders have taken to change organizational culture and improve their situations:

Lou Gerstner faced a challenge at IBM when the company was struggling to keep up with a rapidly changing tech industry. He knew that in order to transform the company, he needed to articulate a clear vision. Gerstner didn't just focus on selling hardware; he saw a future where IBM would become a provider of services and solutions. He communicated this vision tirelessly, ensuring that every employee understood the new direction. His leadership brought the company together under a common goal, and the shift in culture towards customer service became the cornerstone of IBM's turnaround.

Satya Nadella arrived at Microsoft at a time when the company was losing its innovative edge. Instead of just talking about change, Nadella led by example. He embraced a growth mindset, constantly learning, welcoming feedback, and encouraging new ideas. His leadership style was rooted in empathy and collaboration, which helped to transform the company's culture. Microsoft became more inclusive and innovative, and this cultural shift revitalized the company, restoring its position as a leader in the tech industry.

Herb Kelleher knew that for Southwest Airlines to thrive, employees needed to feel empowered. He believed that when employees are treated well, they, in turn, treat customers well. By giving them the freedom to make decisions that improved the customer experience, Kelleher created a culture where employees felt valued and engaged. This unique approach became a hallmark of Southwest's culture, making it one of the most admired airlines, known for its fun, efficient, and customer-centric service.

A.G. Lafley at Procter & Gamble recognized that innovation could only thrive in a collaborative environment. He broke down silos within the company by encouraging cross-functional teamwork and seeking ideas from outside sources. His "Connect + Develop" program fostered openness and collaboration, driving P&G to develop successful new products. This shift in culture helped the company regain its position as a leader in the market, with a renewed focus on creativity and innovation.

When Lee Iacocca took over Chrysler, the company was on the brink of collapse. Iacocca knew drastic measures were needed, so he made tough structural changes, cutting costs, and closing unproductive plants. At the same time, he focused on innovation, introducing new products like the minivan. These moves transformed the culture at Chrysler, making it more results-oriented and innovative, ultimately saving the company from bankruptcy and leading it to a successful recovery.

At Ford, Alan Mulally took a different approach to leadership. He introduced a business plan review process that held senior leaders accountable for their areas of responsibility. Mulally encouraged transparency, urging leaders to be honest about where they needed help. This culture of trust and accountability allowed Ford to navigate the 2008 financial crisis without needing a government bailout, reinforcing the importance of collaboration and transparency in leadership.

Jeff Bezos built Amazon with a relentless focus on the customer. Every decision he made was driven by a commitment to long-term customer satisfaction, not short-term profits. Bezos ingrained this culture of customer obsession across the company, pushing Amazon to innovate continuously and expand its services. This approach made Amazon a dominant force in e-commerce and beyond, as the company kept meeting and anticipating customer needs.

Tony Hsieh took a unique approach to leadership at Zappos by fostering open communication and transparency within the company. He encouraged employees to share their ideas and feedback, creating a sense of community and belonging. This open culture became a defining feature of Zappos' identity, leading to high employee engagement and customer satisfaction, and making the company a standout in the online retail space.

When Mary Barra took over as CEO of General Motors, she faced a culture that had been resistant to change, especially in light of safety scandals. Barra directly addressed these issues, holding the company accountable and focusing on safety, integrity, and transparency. By setting new standards and confronting resistance head-on, Barra helped rebuild trust in GM, leading to a more sustainable future for the company.

Bob Iger's leadership at Disney was marked by symbolic actions that signaled a shift in the company's direction. One of his first moves was to acquire Pixar, signaling a renewed focus on creativity and innovation. Iger also pushed for digital and global expansion, aligning the company with the future. These actions reinforced the importance of creativity and innovation at Disney, helping to rejuvenate the brand and driving its growth for years to come.

Each of these leaders shows how organizational culture can be transformed through clear vision, leading by example, empowering employees, and making strategic changes. Their actions provide powerful lessons on how to guide a company towards success by shifting its culture in the right direction.

By taking these actions, leaders can align the organization's culture with its strategic goals, driving improved performance and long-term success.

Organizational culture refers to the shared values, beliefs, norms, and practices that shape the behavior and interactions of people within an organization. It's the "personality" of the organization, influencing everything from decision-making and communication styles to employee engagement and innovation.

Changing organizational culture is a complex process that often requires strong, visionary leadership.

Here are examples from history that demonstrate how leaders have successfully changed organizational culture:

In the early 1990s, IBM was sinking under the weight of its own bureaucracy. It was a giant that had grown slow, deeply attached to its hardware roots while the world around it raced ahead, focusing on software and services. Lou Gerstner stepped in as CEO in 1993, ready to change everything. Rather than sticking with the old ways, Gerstner had a bold vision. He knew that for IBM to survive, it needed to shift its focus from just selling hardware to offering complete solutions that put the customer first. This was more than just a business decision—it was a cultural revolution. Departments that once worked in silos were encouraged to break down their walls and collaborate, pooling ideas and resources to serve customers better. Even the traditional dress code gave way to a more relaxed, approachable atmosphere, symbolizing the deeper shift toward agility and responsiveness. Under Gerstner's leadership, IBM rose from the ashes, transforming into a global leader in IT services and consulting, marking one of the most impressive corporate turnarounds in history.

When Satya Nadella took the reins at Microsoft in 2014, the company was caught in a rut. Internal conflict and competition stifled creativity, leaving Microsoft struggling to keep up in the fast-moving tech industry. Nadella, however, saw things differently. He wanted Microsoft to be a place where people worked together, where learning and collaboration fueled success. His first move was to champion a growth mindset—encouraging employees to be open to new ideas, to experiment, and to embrace failure as a part of innovation. Nadella also opened the doors to a more inclusive culture, where every voice was valued, leading to groundbreaking ideas and innovations. He even steered Microsoft toward embracing open-source technology, a major shift from the company's previous focus on proprietary software. Nadella's leadership breathed new life into Microsoft, pushing the company to become a leader in cloud computing and AI, solidifying its place as one of the most valuable companies in the world.

Herb Kelleher had a different idea when he founded Southwest Airlines. In an industry known for its strict rules and formality, Kelleher wanted to create something new—an airline where fun and friendliness ruled. He believed that happy employees would translate into happy customers. His leadership was as lighthearted as it was effective, encouraging employees to be themselves and have fun at work. Kelleher put his employees first, offering them job security and a sense of belonging, which empowered them to provide exceptional service. He also kept operations simple, cutting unnecessary costs and ensuring that flights were turned around quickly. Under his leadership, Southwest became a standout airline, thriving in an industry notorious for its ups and downs, all while consistently ranking high in customer satisfaction.

A.G. Lafley took over as CEO of Procter & Gamble (P&G) in 2000 when the company was stuck in a rut, hesitant to take risks and too focused on itself rather than its customers. Lafley knew that to grow, P&G needed to shift its mindset. His philosophy was simple but transformative:

the customer comes first. Everything P&G did had to revolve around understanding and meeting the needs of its consumers. Lafley also opened the door to new ideas, launching the "Connect + Develop" program, which encouraged collaboration with external partners. This influx of fresh thinking helped P&G break down internal barriers and foster a more agile, innovative culture. By empowering teams to make decisions close to the consumer, Lafley reduced bureaucracy and brought the company closer to the people it served. Under his leadership, P&G regained its momentum, launching successful new products and cementing its position as a leader in the consumer goods industry.

Lee Iacocca's arrival at Chrysler in 1979 marked the beginning of one of the most famous corporate turnarounds in history. The company was teetering on the edge of bankruptcy, bogged down by a bureaucratic, risk-averse culture. Iacocca stepped in with a clear vision: everyone, from the top down, needed to take responsibility. Personal accountability became the backbone of Chrysler's culture, driving the company to focus on results. Iacocca didn't just cut costs—he streamlined operations and focused on innovation, leading to the creation of the iconic minivan, which breathed new life into the company's product line. His clear and direct communication united the company around common goals, building trust and aligning everyone behind his vision. Thanks to Iacocca's leadership, Chrysler clawed its way back to profitability, becoming a symbol of American industrial resilience.

An exemplary Indian leader who has demonstrated these leadership principles is **Narayana Murthy**, the co-founder of Infosys.

Narayana Murthy's journey with Infosys is a living example of how visionary leadership and personal integrity can turn a small start-up into a global powerhouse. His story is not just one of business success, but of a leader who inspired by doing, not just telling.

From the very start, Murthy was not a man who demanded respect with grand gestures—he simply lived the values he believed in. His lifestyle remained simple, grounded in the very principles of transparency and ethics he expected of everyone at Infosys. When employees saw their leader walking the talk, upholding the highest standards of integrity, they followed suit. Trust wasn't just a policy at Infosys; it was the unspoken rule that Murthy demonstrated every day.

His vision for Infosys wasn't just whispered in boardrooms; it was shared passionately with every team member. Murthy had his eyes set on making Infosys a global IT leader, but his goals weren't wrapped in lofty words. Instead, he made sure everyone understood what excellence meant—delivering top-quality services with unwavering ethical standards. Murthy's vision wasn't just a directive, it was a call to action, something that sparked ambition and pride in everyone who worked with him. Under his leadership, the entire company moved toward this shared dream, united by a commitment to innovation and customer satisfaction.

Murthy wasn't the kind of leader who held the reins tightly; he believed in letting go, empowering his people to find their own paths to success. At Infosys, everyone, from fresh recruits to senior staff, knew their ideas mattered. It wasn't unusual to see new employees contributing to key decisions. Murthy's leadership style shattered hierarchies, fostering an environment where innovation thrived because people weren't afraid to take risks. He trusted his employees, and they responded by owning their work and driving the company's meteoric growth.

Infosys wasn't just a company—it was a community. Murthy made sure every employee felt like they belonged. He encouraged teamwork across departments and valued inclusivity, ensuring that different voices were heard and respected. This sense of belonging was amplified when Infosys introduced the Employee Stock Ownership Plan (ESOP), making employees not just workers but owners of the company's future. This built a culture of loyalty and commitment that became a bedrock of Infosys' success.

Above all, Murthy understood that staying still meant falling behind. His leadership was defined by a hunger to grow and adapt. He saw that technology was always evolving, and Infosys needed to evolve with it. Instead of resisting change, he embraced it, investing in upskilling his workforce and fostering a culture where innovation wasn't just encouraged—it was expected. Even when the global economy faltered,

Murthy's forward-thinking approach kept Infosys competitive, driving it to new heights.

Narayana Murthy's leadership didn't just guide Infosys through growth; it redefined what leadership means. He showed that leading by example, empowering others, and fostering a culture of collaboration and adaptability are the keys to building something truly extraordinary. His legacy at Infosys remains a testament to the power of vision, trust, and a relentless commitment to excellence.

Narayana Murthy's leadership at Infosys is a testament to the power of ethical leadership, clear vision, employee empowerment, collaboration, and adaptability. His commitment to these principles not only transformed Infosys into a global IT powerhouse but also set a benchmark for corporate governance and ethical business practices in India. Murthy's leadership legacy continues to inspire leaders across industries.

These examples illustrate that changing organizational culture is a complex and often challenging process that requires strong leadership, a clear vision, and a commitment to making deep, sometimes uncomfortable, changes.

Leaders who successfully change culture do so by aligning it with the organization's goals, empowering employees, fostering innovation, and maintaining clear and consistent communication. The long-term success of these leaders demonstrates the profound impact that cultural transformation can have on an organization's performance and legacy.

> **"Change the culture, change the game."**
>
> **— Connors and Smith**

The key messages from the above about changing organizational culture through leadership can be summarized as follows:

1. **Cultural Transformation is Critical for Organizational Success**: The leaders highlighted in these examples understood that culture shapes how a company operates, innovates, and responds to

challenges. Changing this culture was essential for turning around performance and adapting to new market conditions.

2. **Visionary Leadership is the Key to Cultural Change**: Leaders like Lou Gerstner, Satya Nadella, and Jeff Bezos had clear visions for their companies' futures. They communicated these visions tirelessly, ensuring everyone understood the new direction, which became the foundation for transformation.

3. **Leading by Example**: Satya Nadella and Narayana Murthy demonstrated the power of leading by example. They embodied the values they wanted their organizations to adopt, which fostered a culture of accountability, empathy, and growth.

4. **Empowering Employees**: Leaders like Herb Kelleher and A.G. Lafley believed in empowering their employees. By creating an environment where employees felt valued and were encouraged to take ownership of their roles, they fostered innovation and dedication, which contributed to their companies' success.

5. **Innovation Through Collaboration**: A.G. Lafley at P&G and Tony Hsieh at Zappos broke down internal silos and encouraged collaboration both within the company and with external partners. This openness led to more innovative ideas and stronger companies.

6. **Focusing on the Customer**: Lou Gerstner at IBM and Jeff Bezos at Amazon demonstrated how a customer-centric culture can drive long-term success. By prioritizing customer needs, their organizations adapted and innovated, resulting in sustained growth.

7. **Accountability and Transparency**: Leaders like Lee Iacocca and Alan Mulally emphasized the importance of personal responsibility and clear communication. This approach built trust, improved decision-making, and helped their organizations overcome significant challenges.

8. **Adaptability and Forward-Thinking**: Leaders like Narayana Murthy and Bob Iger understood the need to embrace change and

adapt to new trends. By fostering cultures that valued innovation and agility, they kept their companies competitive in evolving markets.

In essence, these leaders show that cultural transformation requires vision, communication, empowerment, collaboration, customer focus, accountability, and adaptability. Aligning the organization's culture with its strategic goals enables long-term success and leaves a lasting impact on performance and legacy.

Part-2

Leadership Pillar-2(Envisioning)

Summary

When we look at different leadership styles from people like Ratan Tata, Mao Zedong, Sam Walton, and Satya Nadella, one thing becomes clear: having a strong vision is crucial for effective leadership. Each of these leaders teaches us important lessons about how a clear vision can help organizations succeed in any industry.

Ratan Tata is a great example of someone who combines business growth with a sense of social responsibility. He doesn't just focus on making money; he also wants to make a positive difference in society. Tata shows that leaders can use their power to support social causes while growing their businesses. This way, he not only aims for financial success but also helps improve the lives of many people, proving that true leadership means caring about the well-being of society.

Mao Zedong and Sam Walton highlight how important it is for leaders to be resilient and adaptable. Mao's revolutionary ideas teach us that flexibility is essential when facing challenges. He demonstrates that a visionary leader needs to change their approach as needed. Walton's experience in retail shows how setbacks can turn into opportunities for growth. By adopting a mindset that embraces change, Walton turns challenges into chances for success.

Satya Nadella and Lee Iacocca show how empowering teams and communicating well are key parts of visionary leadership. Nadella creates a culture at Microsoft where learning is encouraged, and employees feel appreciated. His "learn-it-all" attitude inspires teamwork and creativity. Iacocca's strong communication skills help him connect with his team, building a shared vision that unites everyone towards common goals. Together, they illustrate that when leaders support their teams and communicate clearly, they create a solid foundation for success.

Sam Walton and Satya Nadella also emphasize the importance of focusing on customers. Walton believed that "the customer is the only boss," which transformed retail by making customer satisfaction a top priority. Nadella revamped Microsoft by shifting to a subscription-based model, showing that he understands what users want. This focus on customer needs highlights how visionary leaders can foster loyalty and drive growth by really listening to their audience.

Finally, ethics and integrity are essential to effective visionary leadership, as seen in the actions of Tata, Iacocca, and Alan Mulally. These leaders show that success should be based on strong moral values. Their dedication to ethical behavior builds trust and respect within their organizations, which is vital for long-term success. By sticking to these principles, they create a work environment where everyone feels empowered to work towards a common goal.

In conclusion, the leadership styles of Tata, Mao Zedong, Sam Walton, and Satya Nadella illustrate the many sides of visionary leadership. They all share common traits: a commitment to making a global impact, resilience when facing difficulties, empowering their teams, focusing on customers, and upholding strong ethics. These qualities help guide organizations through complex challenges and inspire collective success. By embracing these principles, today's and tomorrow's leaders can overcome obstacles and achieve their visionary goals, making a lasting difference in the world.

Key Skill	Action Steps	Follow-Up and Measurement
Visionary Communication	- Develop and articulate a clear, inspiring vision for the team or organization. - Share the vision regularly through meetings, emails, or presentations.	- Assess team understanding through feedback and surveys. - Track how well team members align their tasks with the vision.
Strategic Thinking and Adaptability	- Practice scenario planning and long-term goal setting. - Regularly review strategies and adjust based on emerging trends or obstacles.	- Hold quarterly reviews to assess strategic alignment and adjust where necessary. - Document and track changes in response to new insights.
Innovation and Problem-Solving	- Encourage creative brainstorming and solution-finding sessions. - Lead initiatives that challenge the status quo and promote experimentation.	- Measure the implementation of innovative ideas. - Track the number of successful innovations and their impact on outcomes.
Emotional Intelligence	- Practice active listening and empathy in all interactions. - Offer constructive feedback and celebrate achievements to build morale.	- Conduct regular team check-ins to gauge emotional well-being and engagement. - Measure improvements in team cohesion and trust.
Continuous Learning and Resilience	- Commit to ongoing professional development (e.g., attending workshops, reading books). - Reflect on challenges and setbacks to improve.	- Set a learning goal each month (e.g., read a book or attend a webinar). - Review progress in personal growth and resilience quarterly.

A 6-Month Plan to Enhance Visionary Skills

Month 1: Building a Strong Foundation

Daily:

- **Mindful Meditation:** 10 minutes daily to enhance focus and creativity.
- **Industry News:** Spend 30 minutes daily reading industry news and trends.
- **Vision Journaling:** Write down your thoughts and ideas related to your vision.

Weekly:

- **Vision Workshop:** Dedicate 1 hour to brainstorming and developing a clear vision statement.

- **Feedback Session:** Seek feedback from colleagues or mentors on your vision and communication skills.
- **Strategic Thinking Exercise:** Practice strategic thinking exercises, such as SWOT analysis or scenario planning.

Month 2: Developing Strategic Thinking

Daily:

- **Future Forecasting:** Spend 15 minutes daily imagining future possibilities and trends.
- **Problem-Solving Exercises:** Practice problem-solving techniques like root cause analysis and creative problem-solving.
- **Mind Mapping:** Use mind mapping to visualize ideas and connections between different concepts.

Weekly:

- **Strategic Planning Workshop:** Participate in a strategic planning workshop or session.
- **Industry Analysis:** Conduct a thorough analysis of industry trends and competitive landscapes.
- **Mentorship Session:** Meet with a mentor to discuss strategic challenges and opportunities.

Month 3: Enhancing Communication and Influence

Daily:

- **Public Speaking Practice:** Practice public speaking or presentation skills.
- **Active Listening:** Practice active listening during conversations and meetings.
- **Positive Affirmations:** Use positive affirmations to boost confidence and motivation.

Weekly:

- **Communication Workshop:** Attend a workshop on effective communication and persuasion.
- **Networking Events:** Attend industry events to connect with other leaders and expand your network.
- **Feedback Session:** Seek feedback from colleagues on your communication style.

Month 4: Fostering Innovation and Creativity

Daily:

- **Creative Thinking Exercises:** Practice creative thinking techniques, such as brainstorming or mind mapping.
- **Innovation Journal:** Document innovative ideas and solutions.
- **Experimentation:** Experiment with new ideas and approaches, even if they seem risky.

Weekly:

- **Innovation Challenge:** Participate in an innovation challenge or hackathon.
- **Visit Innovative Companies:** Visit innovative companies or organizations to learn from their practices.
- **Idea Generation Session:** Dedicate time to brainstorming new ideas and solutions.

Month 5: Leading with Empathy and Inspiration

Daily:

- **Empathy Exercises:** Practice empathy by putting yourself in others' shoes.
- **Inspirational Reading:** Read biographies or autobiographies of inspiring leaders.

- **Positive Reinforcement:** Recognize and appreciate the contributions of team members.

Weekly:

- **Team Building Activities:** Organize team-building activities to foster a positive team culture.
- **Coaching Sessions:** Provide coaching and mentoring to team members to help them develop their skills.
- **Self-Reflection:** Reflect on your leadership style and identify areas for improvement.

Month 6: Sustaining Visionary Leadership

- **Continuous Learning:** Attend conferences, webinars, and workshops to stay updated on industry trends.
- **Mentorship:** Seek mentorship from experienced leaders.
- **Feedback Mechanism:** Establish a regular feedback mechanism to gather input from colleagues and subordinates.
- **Strategic Planning:** Review and update your long-term strategy.
- **Celebrate Achievements:** Recognize and celebrate milestones and successes.

Remember: Consistent effort and practice are key to developing visionary leadership skills. By following this plan and seeking feedback, you can significantly enhance your ability to inspire, innovate, and lead effectively.

Coaching Questions to be asked:

1. **What is your vision for your organization, and how does it align with your personal values?**
2. **How do you ensure that your leadership approach supports both business growth and social responsibility?**

3. **Can you share a recent situation where you had to adapt your vision or approach to achieve a better outcome?**
4. **What strategies do you use to empower your team and ensure they feel valued in pursuing the shared vision?**
5. **How do you communicate your vision effectively to your team to foster a sense of connection and purpose?**
6. **In what ways do you prioritize understanding and addressing your customers' needs in your leadership strategy?**
7. **How do you gather and incorporate customer feedback into your decision-making process?**
8. **What steps do you take to build a culture of ethics and integrity within your organization?**
9. **Can you share an example where your commitment to ethics influenced a tough decision you had to make?**
10. **What legacy do you hope to create through your leadership, and how does that inform your vision?**

These questions aim to stimulate insightful discussions about leadership vision and its application in practice.

Concluding Reflection:

- **What one action can you take this week to embody the leadership qualities discussed in the chapter?**

This question can help facilitate deeper reflection and dialogue, encouraging individuals to connect their personal experiences with the principles outlined in the text.

Part-3

Leadership Pillar-3(Endurance)

Resilience in Action: Leading Through Life's Challenges

- **Relentless Leadership: Lessons from Sir Alex Ferguson's Triumph Over Adversity**
- **Leading with Resilience: Lessons from Ursula Burns' Transformative Leadership Journey**
- **The Iron Will: Patel's Mastery in Uniting a Nation**
- **Resilience in the Face of Darkness: Churchill's Mental Health Battle**
- **Navigating Setbacks: Leadership Insights from Churchill, Oprah, and Eleanor Roosevelt**
- **The Rise of the Wolf: A Tale of Leadership on the Steppe**
- **Leadership Lessons from UN Peacekeepers: Insights for Resilient and Effective Leadership**

As readers open this chapter, they embark on a journey through the dynamic world of leadership, where resilience drives every triumph. Each story unfolds like a vivid scene, filled with tension, growth, and the powerful force of perseverance. These aren't just tales of success—they invite readers to step into the leaders' shoes, to feel the weight of their decisions, and to witness firsthand how resilience guides them through the toughest challenges.

Sir Alex Ferguson stands on the sidelines, eyes sharp with determination, commanding his team not just through victory, but through moments of defeat. The roar of the crowd fades into the background as his focus sharpens. Readers see how years of resilience shaped not only his legendary career but the very fabric of leadership itself. He didn't just lead a football club—he transformed it, turning adversity into fuel for greatness.

Ursula Burns breaks into view, not just as a trailblazer, but as a force of quiet strength in a male-dominated corporate world. Readers watch her navigate towering boardrooms with grace and resolve, pushing through systemic barriers that would have stopped many. Her story pulses with the energy of someone who, despite the odds, redefined leadership through resilience, showing that courage and perseverance are the real keys to success.

Sardar Patel emerges as a unifier, standing resolute as a nation on the brink of chaos leans on his unwavering vision. He doesn't just piece together a fractured country—he embodies the iron will that leadership demands in the face of overwhelming adversity. His resilience pulls readers in, offering a close-up view of how true leaders hold firm, even as the world around them threatens to crumble.

Winston Churchill's presence fills the page, but it's the quiet moments of struggle that captivate. Readers find him alone, grappling with the weight of both war and personal battles. They witness the cracks in his public facade, where vulnerability slips through. But it's in these moments that Churchill's resilience shines the brightest. He doesn't shrink from his private demons; instead, he uses them to fuel his resolve, reminding readers that even the strongest leaders must confront their inner darkness to emerge stronger.

Oprah Winfrey and Eleanor Roosevelt step forward, each teaching readers that setbacks aren't failures—they're stepping stones. Oprah's story of overcoming early struggles plays out like a deeply personal confession, her resilience becoming the spark that ignites global change. Eleanor Roosevelt, moving through the public sphere with quiet strength, shows readers how to turn obstacles into opportunities. Their resilience, seen up close, is less about survival and more about growth—proof that real leaders transform challenges into fuel for their journey.

In the midst of this, the resilience of UN peacekeepers provides a glimpse into leadership on a global scale. Readers observe leaders negotiating across cultural divides, resolving conflicts, and navigating political turmoil. Their actions remind readers that true leadership is not about standing alone—it's about unity, compassion, and the strength that comes from embracing diversity.

By the time readers finish this chapter, resilience is no longer just an idea. It comes alive through these stories. Each leader's journey reveals the real essence of resilience—not simply as a trait, but as an active, lived experience. Readers come to see that resilience is the driving force behind leadership, shaping decisions, actions, and outcomes in the face of adversity. This chapter calls them not just to understand resilience, but to live it, to turn their own challenges into opportunities, and to lead with purpose and strength.

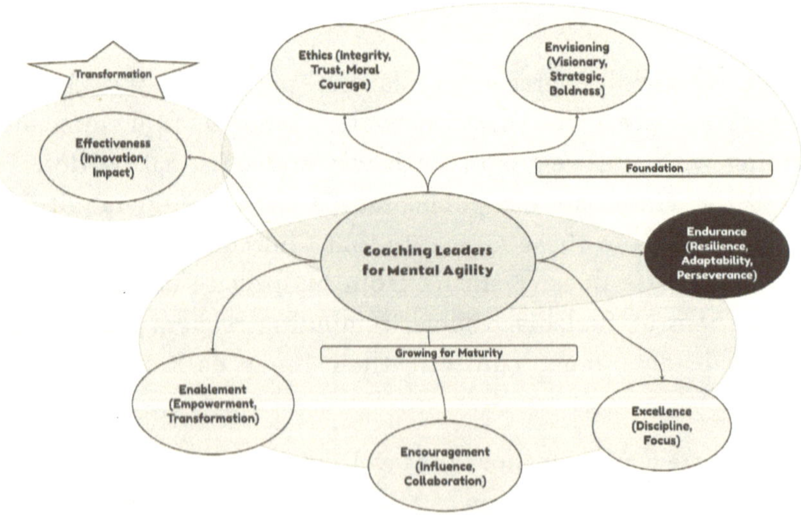

Coaching Leaders for Mental Agility: Story No 15

Relentless Leadership: Lessons from Sir Alex Ferguson's Triumph Over Adversity

Sir Alex Ferguson's tenure at Manchester United is a testament to exceptional leadership.

His ability to transform a team into a dominant force offers invaluable lessons for leaders across industries.

Sir Alex Ferguson, often regarded as one of the greatest football managers in history, demonstrated exceptional team building and performance management skills throughout his career.

Some real-time examples from his life that illustrate these qualities:

Sir Alex Ferguson's leadership at Manchester United offers an inspiring story of dedication, vision, and success. Starting in the early 1990s, Ferguson made a bold choice to promote young players like David Beckham, Ryan Giggs, and Paul Scholes to the first team, despite criticism from many people who doubted their readiness. But Ferguson believed in them, and this group of young players—later known as the "Class of '92"—proved him right. They went on to form the core of a team that dominated English football for over a decade, showing how great leaders believe in their team and invest in the future.

One of Ferguson's most amazing achievements came in 1999 when Manchester United won three major trophies in one season—the Premier League, the FA Cup, and the UEFA Champions League. This incredible accomplishment, called the "Treble," was possible because Ferguson knew how to balance the strengths of experienced players and young talents. In the Champions League final, Ferguson's decision to substitute two players—Teddy Sheringham and Ole Gunnar Solskjær—paid off when both of them scored late goals, turning a near-defeat into victory. Ferguson's leadership in these crucial moments showed his sharp tactical thinking and his ability to inspire his team to never give up.

Ferguson's leadership was also tested when his star player, Eric Cantona, was banned for eight months after an incident where he kicked a fan. Instead of abandoning Cantona, Ferguson supported him and made sure he was ready to play again when the ban was over. Cantona came back stronger than ever, leading Manchester United to win the Premier League in the 1995-1996 season. This moment shows how Ferguson was not only a tough leader but also loyal to his players, helping them grow even in difficult situations.

However, Ferguson wasn't afraid to make tough decisions. When high-profile players like David Beckham and Roy Keane became too focused on themselves rather than the team, Ferguson didn't hesitate to let them go, even though it was controversial. He understood that the team's success always came first, and he wanted to make sure no one was bigger than the club. This kind of leadership showed that Ferguson valued the long-term strength and harmony of the team over individual fame.

What really set Ferguson apart was his ability to manage change and keep the team competitive for over two decades. After the success of the Class of '92, Ferguson didn't stop there. He brought in new stars like Cristiano Ronaldo and Wayne Rooney, building another generation of champions. His ability to adapt and rebuild the team while still winning trophies proves that true leadership is about always thinking ahead and never becoming too comfortable with past success.

Ferguson was also known for his intense motivational style. His famous "hairdryer treatment," where he gave passionate halftime speeches, inspired his team to turn things around in tough matches. One such moment happened during a game against Sheffield Wednesday in 1994. Ferguson's fiery words during halftime fired up his team, leading to a thrilling comeback victory. This showed how Ferguson's demanding leadership style motivated his players to always give their best, even when the odds were against them.

In his 26 years at Manchester United, Ferguson won 13 Premier League titles, five FA Cups, and two UEFA Champions League trophies. His ability to maintain such high levels of success for such a long time demonstrates his incredible leadership, vision, and determination. His story is one of resilience and the belief that success isn't about winning once—it's about staying committed to excellence and pushing for more, no matter what challenges come your way.

These examples illustrate Sir Alex Ferguson's extraordinary ability to build, manage, and sustain successful teams, making him a master of team building and performance in the world of sports.

Sir Alex Ferguson faced numerous challenges throughout his career, but his ability to confront and overcome these obstacles is a testament to his leadership and management skills.

Here are some of the significant challenges he experienced, along with examples and the actions he took to address them:

1. Rebuilding Manchester United (1986-1990)

When Sir Alex Ferguson took the helm of Manchester United in 1986, he faced a daunting challenge. The club hadn't tasted victory in the league for nearly two decades, and a cloud of underachievement hung over the team. Off the pitch, a troubling drinking culture among players threatened to derail any hope of success.

But Ferguson wasn't one to shy away from tough decisions. With a fierce commitment to his vision, he introduced a strict disciplinary regime, swiftly moving out those who didn't share his ambition. He set about transforming the team, bringing in key players like Steve Bruce and Brian McClair, who would become essential to the club's future. But perhaps most importantly, he prioritized youth development, laying the groundwork for the legendary Class of '92—a group of young talents that would redefine the club's legacy.

The road was far from smooth. The early years were fraught with difficulties, and Ferguson even faced the looming threat of dismissal. Yet, he refused to back down. His unwavering determination and belief in his approach began to pay off. By 1990, Manchester United lifted the FA Cup, a victory that would ignite a remarkable journey and herald the dawn of a new era filled with triumphs and glory. Ferguson's story reminds us that resilience and vision can turn even the most challenging situations into extraordinary successes.

2. Overcoming the Alan Hansen Criticism ("You can't win anything with kids")

After several key players left the team, Sir Alex Ferguson faced a pivotal moment as he prepared for the 1995-96 season. He chose to embrace change by assembling a young squad, full of untapped potential. However, this bold decision did not come without criticism. Pundit Alan Hansen publicly scoffed, declaring that "you can't win anything with kids," casting doubt on Ferguson's strategy.

But instead of backing down, Ferguson stood firm. He saw the fire and talent in players like David Beckham, Paul Scholes, and the Neville brothers. He recognized their ability to rise to the occasion and took it upon himself to nurture their skills, giving them the stage to prove themselves.

As the season unfolded, Ferguson's unwavering belief began to pay off in ways that silenced the skeptics. The young squad fought fiercely, showcasing their talent and determination. By the end of the season, they had not only secured the Premier League title but also triumphantly lifted the FA Cup.

Ferguson's victory was more than just a win; it was a testament to his vision and faith in youth. His story inspires us all to trust in our convictions and embrace the potential of those around us, no matter how daunting the challenges may seem. It reminds us that sometimes the boldest choices lead to the greatest rewards.

3. Managing High-Profile Player Disputes (David Beckham)

In the early 2000s, a storm brewed in the dressing room of Manchester United as Sir Alex Ferguson's relationship with David Beckham began to sour. Beckham, once a vital part of the team, had become a global superstar, and Ferguson felt that the young player's rising celebrity status was becoming a distraction from the game. The tension reached a breaking point in 2003 after a match, when Ferguson accidentally kicked a football boot that struck Beckham above the eye. This incident sent shockwaves through the club, igniting a media frenzy, and raising questions about the future of both the player and the manager.

Amidst the chaos, Ferguson remained steadfast in his beliefs. He understood that the integrity and unity of the team had to come first, and he firmly believed that no player, no matter how talented, was bigger than the club itself. With a heavy heart but a clear vision, he made the tough decision to sell Beckham to Real Madrid. This move was met with controversy and disappointment among fans, yet Ferguson knew it was necessary to restore harmony and discipline within the squad.

In the wake of Beckham's departure, Manchester United continued to thrive, reaffirming Ferguson's authority as a leader who prioritized the team's success above individual accolades. This decision not only paved the way for a new chapter for the club but also demonstrated Ferguson's unwavering commitment to creating a united team ready to chase glory. The legacy of that choice echoed through the halls of Old Trafford, inspiring future generations to prioritize collaboration over fame.

4. The Battle with Arsenal and Arsène Wenger

In the late 1990s and early 2000s, a fierce rivalry ignited between Manchester United and Arsenal, with Arsène Wenger's team emerging as a formidable opponent. Known for their attractive and fluid style of play, Arsenal posed a significant challenge to United's dominance in English football, pushing Sir Alex Ferguson to adapt and evolve his strategies.

Recognizing the need for change, Ferguson rolled up his sleeves and set to work. He understood that to compete with Wenger's well-drilled squad, he needed to enhance his own team. With sharp insight, he brought in key players like Dwight Yorke and Jaap Stam, fortifying United's lineup with talent that could match Arsenal's physicality and skill on the pitch. But Ferguson didn't stop there; he was a master of mind games, often engaging in psychological tactics to rattle Wenger and his players, adding an extra layer of intrigue to their encounters.

This calculated approach bore fruit as Manchester United began to claim victory in several crucial matches against Arsenal. A standout moment came during the 1999 FA Cup semi-final replay, when Ryan Giggs unleashed a stunning solo goal that would go down in history. United's resilience in the face of Arsenal's challenge played a pivotal role in their treble-winning season, marking a triumphant era for Ferguson and his team. Through strategic adjustments and unwavering determination, Ferguson not only defended his legacy but also solidified Manchester United's position at the pinnacle of English football.

5. The Transition to a New Generation of Players (2003-2006)

After the departure of key players like Roy Keane and David Beckham, Sir Alex Ferguson found himself at a crossroads. The iconic Manchester United squad, once filled with star power and veteran leadership, needed a transformation to stay competitive both in the Premier League and on the European stage. The challenge loomed large, but Ferguson was determined to rise to it.

With a keen eye for talent, Ferguson set about rebuilding his team. He turned his attention to the future, recruiting young, dynamic players like Cristiano Ronaldo and Wayne Rooney, whose potential shone brightly. These fresh faces brought energy and ambition, while Ferguson also understood the importance of balance. To strengthen the squad further, he added seasoned professionals like Nemanja Vidić and Patrice Evra, whose experience would guide the younger players through the trials of top-level football. This blend of youth and experience became a cornerstone of Ferguson's strategy, allowing the team to evolve and adapt.

As the new-look Manchester United took shape, it quickly established itself as a powerhouse in European football. The team showcased its prowess on the pitch, clinching three consecutive Premier League titles from 2007 to 2009, a testament to Ferguson's vision and leadership. Their crowning achievement came in 2008 when they triumphed in the UEFA Champions League, solidifying their status as one of the continent's elite clubs. Through resilience and a clear focus on development, Ferguson's ability to rebuild his team not only preserved Manchester United's legacy but also paved the way for a new era of success.

6. Maintaining Success Amidst Personal Tragedy (2002)

In 2002, Sir Alex Ferguson faced an immense personal challenge that shook him to his core. His wife, Cathy, fell seriously ill, and the weight of her condition weighed heavily on him. Managing one of the world's biggest football clubs while grappling with this family crisis felt almost overwhelming. The prospect of stepping back from the high-pressure world of football to be with his family loomed large.

As he wrestled with the decision to retire, Ferguson ultimately chose to remain at the helm of Manchester United. His commitment to the club and its supporters was unwavering. Recognizing the need for support during this difficult time, he leaned on a strong coaching staff, ensuring that the team had the guidance it needed even as he faced his personal struggles.

Ferguson's decision to continue managing proved fruitful. Despite the turmoil in his personal life, he led Manchester United to success on the pitch. His remarkable resilience and dedication became a source of inspiration for both his players and the wider football community. Through the highs and lows, Ferguson demonstrated that true leadership is not just about managing a team but also about persevering through adversity, proving that strength can shine brightly even in the darkest of times.

7. Dealing with the Emergence of Chelsea Under José Mourinho (2004-2007)

When José Mourinho arrived at Chelsea, he brought with him not only a wealth of talent but also the backing of Roman Abramovich's significant financial resources. This shift created a new wave of competition in the Premier League, and Chelsea's dominance in the mid-2000s began to pose a real threat to Manchester United's long-standing position at the top of English football.

In response to this challenge, Sir Alex Ferguson knew he had to act decisively. He set about strengthening his squad, bringing in key players like Nemanja Vidić, Michael Carrick, and Edwin van der Sar, who would add depth and quality to the team. Understanding that Chelsea's style was characterized by physicality and tactical discipline, Ferguson also recognized the need to adapt United's own playing style. He instilled a mentality of resilience and determination in his players, urging them to rise to the challenge posed by their rivals.

Ferguson's strategic adjustments bore fruit when Manchester United regained the Premier League title in 2007. This victory not only marked a significant achievement for the club but also signaled the start of a new era of dominance. Through his vision and leadership, Ferguson not only responded to the challenges posed by Chelsea but also reaffirmed United's position as a powerhouse in English football.

8. Managing Cristiano Ronaldo's Departure (2009)

After winning both the Premier League and Champions League in 2008, Sir Alex Ferguson found himself at a pivotal moment in his career. Cristiano Ronaldo, the team's star player, left for Real Madrid in 2009, creating a gap that could have shaken the team's foundation. But Ferguson didn't panic. Instead of chasing another superstar to fill Ronaldo's shoes, he took a more thoughtful approach, one that would change the team's future.

Ferguson understood that relying on one star player wasn't the way forward. So, he focused on building a team that thrived on balance and teamwork rather than individual brilliance. He brought in new players like Antonio Valencia, Nani, and Javier Hernández—each one different, each bringing their own strengths to the table. With a clear vision, Ferguson molded a squad that could win as a unit, not just through the genius of one player.

This decision to prioritize the collective over the individual soon paid off. Under Ferguson's guidance, Manchester United continued to dominate, winning the Premier League again in 2011 and 2013. The team's success wasn't just about skill—it was about adaptability, teamwork, and Ferguson's ability to evolve the squad to meet new challenges. His genius wasn't in finding another Ronaldo but in creating a team that could perform without him, showing the world that true leadership lies in bringing out the best in everyone. Manchester United remained a force to be reckoned with, and Ferguson's legacy as a brilliant manager only grew stronger.

Through this story, Ferguson teaches us that true success comes not from clinging to one method but from adapting, evolving, and building something greater than the sum of its parts.

9. The 2011-2012 Premier League Title Loss

In the 2011-2012 season, Manchester United experienced one of the most painful moments in their history. The Premier League title was within their grasp, but in the final moments of the last game, Manchester City scored a stoppage-time goal to snatch the trophy away. The shock and disappointment were overwhelming, leaving the players and fans heartbroken. Yet, instead of letting this defeat break them, Sir Alex Ferguson turned the setback into an opportunity for growth.

Ferguson gathered his team and used the loss as motivation. He knew this wasn't the end of their story. With determination burning brighter than ever, he inspired his players to rise above the disappointment. The defeat became their fuel for the next season, pushing them to reclaim what had slipped away. Ferguson, always the strategist, made key moves in the transfer market, bringing in players who would strengthen the squad, including Robin van Persie, whose presence was crucial.

When the new season began, Manchester United was unstoppable. With van Persie leading the charge, scoring vital goals, and becoming a fan favorite, the team soared. They dominated the league, winning the Premier League with an impressive lead. This wasn't just a victory—it was a comeback, a demonstration of their resilience and Ferguson's leadership. As the team celebrated, this moment was even more special because it marked Ferguson's 13th and final Premier League title.

This victory symbolized more than just another trophy for United. It showed how setbacks can lead to greater triumphs when faced with the right mindset. Ferguson's unwavering belief in his team and his ability to turn a loss into fuel for success left a legacy that would inspire not only his players but also future generations of leaders.

10. Deciding When to Retire (2013)

Deciding when to retire after an immensely successful career is never an easy choice, and for Sir Alex Ferguson, this challenge weighed heavily on his mind. As he reflected on his time at Manchester United, he understood the importance of leaving the club in a strong position for whoever would take the reins after him. He wanted to ensure that his legacy would continue to thrive long after he stepped away.

In 2013, after clinching yet another Premier League title, Ferguson made the bold decision to retire. He wanted to exit on a high note, surrounded by the triumphs that had defined his career. With careful thought and consideration, he took steps to ensure a smooth transition. He recommended David Moyes as his successor, believing that continuity was vital for the club's future.

Although Moyes' time in charge was brief, Ferguson's legacy at Manchester United remained strong. His foresight in knowing when to step down showcased his leadership skills and allowed him to leave with dignity and success. This decision not only highlighted Ferguson's commitment to the club but also ensured that his impact would be felt for years to come, inspiring future leaders to consider not just their own journeys but also the paths they pave for others.

These examples highlight Sir Alex Ferguson's ability to navigate challenges with strategic thinking, resilience, and a relentless drive for success. His actions in the face of adversity are a masterclass in leadership and crisis management.

From Sir Alex Ferguson's leadership journey:

- **Resilience in Adversity**: Never give up, even when facing significant challenges. Keep pushing through tough times.
- **Team Building**: Focus on developing and empowering your team, understanding that a strong team is key to success.
- **Adaptability**: Be willing to adapt and change strategies when needed to stay ahead of the competition.
- **Long-Term Vision**: Have a clear vision for the future and make decisions that align with long-term goals, not just short-term gains.
- **Discipline and Consistency**: Maintain high standards of discipline and consistency in your approach to ensure sustained success.

Top Key Messages from Sir Alex Ferguson's Leadership Journey

- **Resilience in Adversity**: Effective leaders persist through challenges, demonstrating determination and grit even in tough times. Ferguson's ability to push through obstacles showcases the importance of resilience.

- **Team Building and Empowerment**: Fostering a strong, cohesive team is vital for success. Ferguson's emphasis on promoting young talent and nurturing team dynamics highlights the value of investing in people.
- **Adaptability and Strategic Change**: Leaders must be flexible and willing to adjust their strategies in response to changing circumstances. Ferguson's success in evolving his teams over the years exemplifies the need for adaptability.
- **Long-Term Vision**: Maintaining a clear vision and making decisions that align with long-term goals is crucial. Ferguson's approach to building future-oriented teams underscores the significance of a strategic outlook.
- **Discipline and Consistency**: High standards of discipline and consistent performance create a foundation for sustained success. Ferguson's relentless pursuit of excellence emphasizes the role of discipline in effective leadership.

Coaching Leaders for Mental Agility: Story No 16

Leading with Resilience: Lessons from Ursula Burns' Transformative Leadership Journey

> **"It does not matter how slowly you go as long as you do not stop."**
>
> **— Confucius**

I want to tell you a story that could completely change how you think about leadership.

It's the story of Ursula Burns, a woman who started as an intern at a company called Xerox and worked her way up to become the CEO—the first Black woman to ever lead a Fortune 500 company.

That's pretty remarkable, right?

But what's even more impressive is the leadership mindset she brought to the table, and the lessons we can learn from her journey.

Ursula Burns is a prominent business leader known for her trailblazing career and significant impact on the corporate world.

Ursula Burns' career offers valuable lessons in leadership, resilience, strategic thinking, and the importance of diversity and inclusion.

Her journey from an intern to a Fortune 500 CEO highlights the impact of perseverance, vision, and the willingness to embrace change.

Ursula Burns has had a distinguished career with several notable achievements:

In 2009, Ursula Burns made history when she became the first Black woman to lead a Fortune 500 company as CEO of Xerox. Her appointment was not just a personal achievement; it marked a significant milestone in the corporate world, highlighting the importance of diversity in leadership.

Under Burns's guidance, Xerox transformed its traditional business model. She shifted the company's focus from merely being a document technology provider to embracing a more diversified, services-oriented approach. This change included a strong emphasis on business process outsourcing and digital services, setting Xerox on a path for future growth.

A key moment in this transformation came with the strategic acquisition of Affiliated Computer Services (ACS) in 2009 for $6.4 billion. This move expanded Xerox's capabilities and played a crucial role in its transition toward a services-driven company.

In 2016, Burns successfully oversaw the spin-off of Xerox's business process outsourcing unit into a separate publicly traded company called Conduent. This strategic decision allowed Xerox to concentrate on its core document technology business while Conduent thrived in the services sector.

Throughout her career, Burns has been a passionate advocate for diversity and inclusion. She has dedicated herself to promoting equal opportunities for women and minorities in the corporate landscape, actively participating in initiatives aimed at enhancing workplace diversity.

Beyond her impressive corporate achievements, Burns has engaged in public service and philanthropy. She has served on various non-profit boards, working to improve education and economic opportunities for underserved communities.

Through her autobiography, "Where You Are Is Not Who You Are," and her appearances as a speaker at numerous conferences, Burns shares her experiences and insights. Her journey inspires many, embodying a leadership philosophy that encourages others to pursue their dreams while championing diversity and inclusion.

These achievements highlight Burns' impact on both her company and the broader business and social communities.

Ursula Burns' tenure as CEO of Xerox is marked by several achievements that highlight her impact on the company:

Under Ursula Burns's leadership, Xerox experienced a remarkable transformation in its business model, shifting its focus toward higher-margin services and outsourcing. Although the overall revenue faced challenges, this strategic pivot aimed to secure long-term growth for the company.

In 2009, Burns made a significant move by acquiring Affiliated Computer Services (ACS) for $6.4 billion. This acquisition expanded Xerox's capabilities in business process outsourcing and was a key step in its transition to a services-oriented model.

In 2016, she successfully oversaw the spin-off of Xerox's business process outsourcing unit, creating a separate publicly traded company named Conduent. This strategic decision allowed Xerox to concentrate on its core document technology business and represented a major milestone in the company's transformation.

During her tenure, Xerox's stock performance fluctuated, reflecting the broader challenges and achievements of its transformation journey. Despite these ups and downs, Burns focused on long-term value creation through her leadership and restructuring efforts.

Burns also played a crucial role in repositioning Xerox with a stronger emphasis on innovation and technology. She championed investments in research and development to drive growth in new areas, including digital services and data analytics.

Moreover, under her leadership, Xerox made significant strides in diversity and inclusion. The company increased representation and launched initiatives to foster a more inclusive workplace. Burns's role as the first Black female CEO of a Fortune 500 company was a landmark achievement, symbolizing progress in diversity within corporate leadership.

Through her efforts, burns not only transformed Xerox but also inspired countless individuals to pursue their goals, reinforcing the importance of innovation, resilience, and inclusivity in the corporate world.

Ursula Burns faced several significant challenges during her tenure as CEO of Xerox, and she took various actions to address them:

Xerox faced a significant challenge as it needed to transition from a traditional document technology company to a more services-oriented business in order to stay competitive in a rapidly changing market. Ursula Burns stepped in to lead this strategic transformation, focusing on business process outsourcing and digital services. She spearheaded the acquisition of Affiliated Computer Services (ACS), which was a pivotal move that expanded Xerox's capabilities in services and outsourcing. This shift was essential for diversifying the company's revenue streams and adapting to new market demands.

During the late 2000s and early 2010s, Xerox encountered another hurdle with the global economic downturn, which adversely affected its financial performance. In response, Burns implemented cost-cutting measures and streamlined operations to improve efficiency. She restructured the organization to align with the new strategic direction, which included divesting non-core assets and optimizing the company's overall structure.

Integrating ACS into Xerox presented its own set of challenges, particularly in aligning different business models and corporate cultures. Burns made the integration process a priority, working diligently to create a unified strategy that would bring both companies together effectively. Her efforts were aimed at achieving the desired synergies and enhancing Xerox's service capabilities.

Amid these changes, the impact on employee morale was a crucial concern. Leading such a major transformation during economic difficulties required strong leadership. Burns placed a strong emphasis on communication and transparency, engaging in regular dialogue with employees to keep them informed and motivated throughout the transition. Her resilient leadership style and commitment to employee development helped maintain high morale and fostered a positive corporate culture.

When it came time to spin off Xerox's business process outsourcing unit into a separate entity called Conduent, Burns managed the complex process with care. She ensured that both companies were well-positioned for success after the separation, focusing on defining strategic priorities for each entity and facilitating a smooth transition.

As the first Black female CEO of a Fortune 500 company, Burns faced scrutiny and high expectations. Embracing her role as a trailblazer, she became an advocate for diversity and inclusion within the corporate world. Burns actively promoted initiatives to enhance workplace diversity and used her platform to address critical issues related to representation and equal opportunities.

Through her remarkable leadership, Burns not only transformed Xerox but also inspired countless individuals by demonstrating the power of resilience, innovation, and a commitment to social responsibility.

Ursula Burns is a notable figure in the business world for several reasons:

Trailblazing Leadership: Burns is celebrated for being the first Black woman to lead a Fortune 500 company when she became CEO of Xerox in 2009. Her appointment was a significant milestone for diversity and inclusion in corporate leadership.

Transformational Change: During her tenure at Xerox, Burns led the company through a major transformation. She oversaw a strategic shift from a traditional document technology company to a services-oriented business, focusing on areas like business process outsourcing and digital services. This transformation was crucial in adapting to changing market conditions and technological advancements.

Resilience and Adaptability: Burns' leadership style is marked by resilience and adaptability. She effectively navigated Xerox through economic challenges, technological disruptions, and a competitive landscape, demonstrating her ability to steer a large corporation through complex changes.

Focus on Innovation and Growth: Under her leadership, Xerox invested in innovation and explored new business models. Burns emphasized the importance of technology and services in driving future growth, reflecting her forward-thinking approach.

Advocacy for Diversity and Inclusion: Burns has been a vocal advocate for diversity and inclusion in the workplace. Her career is a testament to breaking barriers and her efforts to promote equal opportunities for underrepresented groups in corporate settings.

Mentorship and Guidance: Burns has been a mentor and role model for many aspiring leaders. Her leadership style, characterized by a pragmatic approach, strategic thinking, and a commitment to employee development, offers valuable lessons for those interested in effective management and leadership.

Reading about Ursula Burns' leadership style provides insights into how she managed organizational change, fostered innovation, and championed diversity.

Her journey underscores the impact of visionary leadership and the importance of adapting to new business realities.

Here are a few key leadership lessons we can learn from Ursula Burns' inspiring story:

- **Perseverance and Resilience**: Ursula Burns' rise from intern to CEO shows that perseverance, even in the face of challenges, is essential for leadership success. She navigated the complexities of transforming Xerox while maintaining a focus on long-term goals.
- **Embracing Change**: Burns exemplifies how leaders must be adaptable and willing to embrace change. She led Xerox through a major transition from traditional document technology to a service-oriented model, showing that innovation and flexibility are key to staying competitive.
- **Visionary Leadership**: With her bold vision for the future of Xerox, Burns demonstrated that successful leaders think strategically and see opportunities beyond the present. Her ability to pivot the company towards digital services was a testament to forward-thinking leadership.
- **Commitment to Diversity and Inclusion**: Burns actively championed diversity, becoming a role model for underrepresented groups in corporate leadership. Her commitment to fostering a more inclusive workplace shows how leaders should advocate for equality and opportunity for all.
- **Leading with Integrity**: Throughout her career, Burns balanced business decisions with a deep sense of responsibility toward her employees and the communities she served. Her focus on transparency and communication helped maintain employee morale during challenging times.

Ursula Burns' journey is a powerful reminder that leadership is about resilience, vision, and creating positive change while lifting others along the way.

Coaching Leaders for Mental Agility: Story No 17

The Iron Will: Patel's Mastery in Uniting a Nation

> **"Faith is of no avail in the absence of strength. Faith and strength, both are essential to accomplish any great work."**
>
> **- Sardar Vallabhbhai Patel**

Sardar Vallabhbhai Patel, often referred to as the **"Iron Man of India,"** played a crucial role in unifying India after it gained independence from British rule in 1947.

At the time of independence, India was a patchwork of over 550 princely states, each with the option to join either India or Pakistan or remain independent.

The task of integrating these states into a united India was formidable, and Patel's leadership was instrumental in achieving this goal.

Sardar Patel's efforts were instrumental in creating a united India from a fragmented subcontinent.

His ability to combine diplomacy with firmness ensured that almost all the princely states acceded to India peacefully, with only a few exceptions where force was necessary.

His work not only strengthened India's territorial integrity but also laid the groundwork for the federal structure of governance that exists today.

Patel's legacy as the "Iron Man of India" is a testament to his determination, strategic vision, and leadership.

He is widely credited with preventing the Balkanization of India and ensuring that the country emerged as a unified and stable nation after independence.

Sardar Vallabhbhai Patel stood at the forefront of India's struggle for unity, wielding a blend of pragmatism and persuasion that would shape the nation's destiny. Known for his remarkable ability to connect with people, Patel, alongside V.P. Menon, the Secretary of the States

Department, embarked on a mission to bring the princely states into the fold of a newly independent India. With a calm yet compelling presence, he appealed to the princes' sense of patriotism, reminding them that joining a united India was not just a matter of policy, but a path toward stability, security, and prosperity for all.

To facilitate this integration, Patel and Menon introduced the Instrument of Accession, a groundbreaking legal document that offered princely states a way to join India while maintaining control over certain local affairs, such as land management and cultural practices. This instrument served as a vital framework, providing a sense of security and clarity as the states navigated their new roles in the Indian Union.

Yet Patel's approach was not solely diplomatic. He understood that sometimes firmness was necessary. When the Nizam of Hyderabad, Mir Osman Ali Khan, refused to accede to India, insisting on remaining independent or joining Pakistan, Patel faced a critical decision. With resolve, he authorized "Operation Polo," a military action that would bring Hyderabad into India's embrace. This decisive move underscored Patel's commitment to unity, even when faced with resistance. Similarly, he addressed the situation in Junagadh, where the Nawab sought to join Pakistan despite being surrounded by Indian territory and having a predominantly Hindu population. Patel's deft combination of diplomacy and calculated pressure ensured Junagadh's rightful place within India.

The challenge of integrating Jammu and Kashmir tested Patel's leadership further. The state, ruled by a Hindu Maharaja, Hari Singh, was caught in a precarious situation as tribal militias, supported by Pakistan, invaded. In a moment of crisis, the Maharaja signed the Instrument of Accession, allowing Indian forces to step in and defend Kashmir. This pivotal decision marked the beginning of the state's integration into India, although the complexities of the situation would echo through history.

Once the princely states began to join the Indian Union, Patel worked tirelessly to dismantle their separate administrative structures. He envisioned a unified administrative system that would reflect the diverse linguistic and cultural identities of the new states, laying the groundwork for modern India's governance.

Patel also recognized the importance of forging strategic alliances with the rulers of the princely states. He offered them privileges, titles, and pensions in return for their cooperation, easing the path to integration. This thoughtful negotiation not only smoothed the process but also helped prevent potential conflicts, fostering a spirit of collaboration in a time of transformation.

Through his unyielding determination and adept leadership, Patel became a pivotal figure in weaving the tapestry of India, ensuring that the nation emerged not just as a collection of states but as a united entity poised for a bright future. His story inspires, showing us the power of courage, diplomacy, and the unwavering commitment to a shared vision.

Sardar Vallabhbhai Patel faced significant challenges in unifying India after independence in 1947.

As India stood on the brink of independence, the nation faced a daunting challenge. The landscape was a patchwork of British-administered provinces and over 565 princely states, each governed by its own local monarch. Each of these rulers held the power to choose their future: they could join India, opt for Pakistan, or remain independent. This decision loomed over the nation like a dark cloud, threatening its very unity.

Among these rulers, many felt a deep reluctance to join India. They feared that aligning with the new nation would strip them of their sovereignty and the privileges that came with their royal titles. States like Hyderabad and Junagadh stood firm in their opposition, their leaders unwilling to relinquish the power they had wielded for generations.

The complexity of this situation was heightened by the rich tapestry of India's political and religious landscapes. Each princely state was unique, filled with diverse cultures and beliefs. Take Hyderabad, for instance; it was a Muslim-majority state that hesitated to join a nation predominantly Hindu. This apprehension added another layer of tension, as various groups grappled with their identities and aspirations within a newly forming India.

The risk of fragmentation loomed large, threatening to unravel the fabric of the nation. If a few influential states decided to carve their own path and declare independence, it could trigger a domino effect. The very idea of such disintegration sent shivers down the spines of leaders working tirelessly to forge a unified India.

As the nation teetered on the edge of possibility, the resolve to overcome these challenges grew stronger, driven by a shared vision of unity and belonging. It was a time when leaders emerged, ready to confront the daunting obstacles ahead and weave together the diverse strands of India's future.

Sardar Vallabhbhai Patel's leadership was marked by a remarkable blend of diplomacy, decisiveness, and vision. His ability to persuade the majority of princely states to join India peacefully reflected his exceptional diplomatic skills. However, when diplomacy failed in Hyderabad and Junagadh, his swift decision to use force demonstrated his decisiveness and strategic thinking, showing a leader unafraid to take bold action when necessary.

Patel's expertise extended beyond negotiation. His collaboration with V.P. Menon in crafting the Instrument of Accession revealed his profound understanding of legal and administrative matters, making him an invaluable architect of India's unification. Politically astute, Patel skillfully navigated a complex landscape, forging alliances that were essential in realizing his goals.

At the heart of his leadership was a clear vision of a unified India, a vision that he inspired others to pursue with equal determination. His courage and resilience shone through in his willingness to take daring actions, even in the face of immense challenges. Patel's legacy is one of unwavering leadership, strategic brilliance, and unshakeable commitment to his nation.

Sardar Patel's leadership in unifying India was marked by a combination of diplomatic skill, strategic decisiveness, and an unwavering commitment to national unity.

His ability to overcome the challenges posed by the princely states through a blend of persuasion, legal acumen, and, when necessary, force, serves as a powerful example of effective leadership in the face of complex and daunting obstacles.

The story of Sardar Vallabhbhai Patel's leadership in unifying India after independence offers several key lessons about leadership:

Sardar Vallabhbhai Patel exemplified visionary leadership. He didn't just dream of a united India; he relentlessly pursued it, day after day, his eyes always fixed on the goal of unifying a fractured nation. This clarity of vision made his leadership magnetic. People naturally followed, inspired by his unwavering focus and ability to see beyond the immediate challenges.

His diplomacy was another defining trait. Patel approached the princely states not with brute force but with negotiation, striking a delicate balance between firmness and tact. He understood that to unite India, he needed both strength and subtlety. He worked hard to understand the needs of the princely rulers and offered them concessions that didn't compromise his broader vision of unity. In leadership, negotiation and persuasion aren't optional—they are powerful tools to align diverse interests toward a common goal.

When the situation called for it, Patel was unflinching in his decisiveness. Faced with defiance in Hyderabad and Junagadh, he didn't hesitate to authorize military action. It was a tough call, but he knew that the unity of India was at stake. A leader must sometimes make bold, difficult decisions, even when others hesitate, to safeguard the integrity of their mission.

Patel also demonstrated remarkable adaptability. He didn't rigidly stick to one approach but used diplomacy, persuasion, or force depending on the circumstances. His focus remained on practical results, adjusting his methods to suit the moment. A great leader must have this flexibility, recognizing that success often comes from being pragmatic rather than dogmatically sticking to a single path.

His empathy for the princely states played a crucial role in their integration into India. Patel understood their concerns and addressed them by creating the Instrument of Accession, which gave them the autonomy they needed while still bringing them under the fold of India. This empathy made him a trusted leader. Understanding the perspectives of stakeholders and addressing their concerns is essential in building lasting trust and relationships.

In the face of numerous setbacks, Patel's persistence was unshakeable. He never wavered in his pursuit of a united India, even when obstacles seemed insurmountable. His resilience shines as a lesson for all leaders: the road to success is rarely smooth, but persistence through challenges is what creates lasting achievement.

Strategic alliances were a hallmark of Patel's leadership. He forged critical partnerships with princely states, using diplomacy and mutual agreements to bring them into the fold. This collaborative approach emphasizes that leaders don't succeed in isolation; they thrive by building strong networks and alliances that amplify their impact.

Patel was also a long-term thinker. His focus wasn't just on immediate political victories, but on securing a unified, stable India for future generations. A leader's decisions must always consider the long-term implications, ensuring that their choices today create a solid foundation for tomorrow.

Courage defined Patel's journey. In the face of seemingly insurmountable challenges, he held fast to his convictions, believing deeply in the importance of a united India. This courage wasn't reckless; it was rooted in a deep understanding of what was right and necessary. Leadership requires this kind of conviction, the ability to stand firm in the face of opposition.

Finally, *Patel's legacy is a testament to the lasting impact of true leadership. His efforts laid the groundwork for the united India we know today. Great leaders, like Patel, don't just think about their time in power—they think about the future, working tirelessly to build something that will endure and benefit generations to come.*

To develop the skills demonstrated by Sardar Vallabhbhai Patel, here are some powerful coaching questions that can guide reflection, growth, and action:

1. **Diplomacy and Negotiation**

   - How do you approach situations where you need to bring opposing parties to a common agreement? What strategies do you use to build trust and rapport with stakeholders?
   - Can you think of a recent negotiation where the outcome was not ideal? What could you have done differently to achieve a more favorable result?
   - How do you balance firmness and flexibility in negotiations? When do you know it's time to compromise, and when should you stand your ground?

2. **Decisiveness and Strategic Thinking**

   - How do you prioritize actions when faced with multiple challenges? What criteria do you use to decide when to take decisive action versus when to wait?
   - Can you recall a time when you had to make a tough decision quickly? What factors did you consider, and what was the outcome?
   - How do you ensure your decisions align with your long-term goals and vision? What methods do you use to evaluate the potential risks and benefits of your decisions?

3. **Legal and Administrative Expertise**

   - How do you stay informed about the legal and regulatory frameworks that impact your work? What resources or strategies do you use to deepen your legal knowledge?
   - When facing a complex legal or administrative challenge, how do you break it down into manageable steps? Who do you involve in the process?

- How do you approach problem-solving in legal or administrative contexts? What strategies do you use to ensure your solutions are both innovative and compliant?

4. **Political Acumen**

- How do you assess the political landscape within your organization or industry? What signs do you look for to understand power dynamics and alliances?
- Can you share an example of a time when you successfully navigated a politically sensitive situation? What was your strategy, and what was the outcome?
- How do you build and maintain relationships with key stakeholders? What steps do you take to ensure these relationships are beneficial for both parties?

5. **Leadership and Vision**

- How do you articulate your vision to others in a way that inspires and motivates them? What methods do you use to ensure your vision is understood and embraced by your team?
- What do you do to stay committed to your long-term goals, especially during challenging times? How do you keep your team aligned with these goals?
- How do you balance the need to lead with the need to listen? How do you create an environment where others feel empowered to contribute to your vision?

6. **Courage and Resilience**

- How do you handle fear and uncertainty when making difficult decisions? What practices help you maintain your courage in the face of adversity?
- Can you describe a situation where you faced significant challenges but persisted? What kept you going, and what did you learn from the experience?

- How do you build resilience in yourself and your team? What steps do you take to recover from setbacks and keep moving forward?

These coaching questions are designed to help individuals reflect deeply on their experiences, identify areas for growth, and develop the critical skills demonstrated by Sardar Vallabhbhai Patel. By regularly engaging with these questions, individuals can build the diplomatic, strategic, legal, political, leadership, and resilience skills necessary for effective leadership.

In summary, Sardar Patel's leadership in unifying India teaches us the importance of vision, diplomacy, decisiveness, adaptability, empathy, persistence, strategic alliances, long-term thinking, courage, and legacy-building in effective leadership.

> **"Work is undoubtedly worship but laughter is life. Anyone who takes life too seriously must prepare himself for a miserable existence."**
>
> **- Sardar Vallabhbhai Patel**

The leadership of Sardar Vallabhbhai Patel offers profound lessons in diplomacy, vision, courage, and resilience. His work in uniting a fragmented India after independence is a testament to the power of strategic leadership in the face of immense challenges. Here are some key messages that stand out from Patel's leadership journey:

- **Visionary Leadership**: Patel's unwavering commitment to a unified India exemplifies the power of having a clear and compelling vision. His ability to focus on the long-term goal of national unity inspired others to follow him with dedication.

- **Diplomacy and Negotiation**: Patel's use of tactful negotiation to persuade princely states to join India highlights the importance of diplomacy in leadership. By balancing firmness with empathy, he built trust and found common ground to achieve greater goals.

- **Decisiveness in the Face of Adversity**: Patel's willingness to make tough decisions, such as authorizing military action in Hyderabad and Junagadh, demonstrates that effective leaders know when to act decisively to protect the integrity of their mission, even under pressure.
- **Adaptability**: Patel's leadership showcased his ability to adapt to different situations, using a blend of diplomacy, persuasion, and force. This pragmatic approach underlines the importance of flexibility and adjusting strategies to meet the demands of the moment.
- **Persistence and Resilience**: Patel's relentless pursuit of Indian unity, despite numerous setbacks, reflects the importance of resilience. His perseverance in the face of adversity teaches that lasting success is often born out of unwavering commitment.
- **Strategic Partnerships**: Patel's alliances with princely states were instrumental in achieving his vision. He understood the value of building relationships and strategic partnerships to create a collective impact and drive lasting change.
- **Long-Term Thinking**: Patel's focus on creating a united India wasn't just for immediate gains but for the future stability of the nation. Leaders who think beyond the short term lay the foundation for sustainable success.
- **Courage and Conviction**: Patel's courage to stand by his convictions, even in the face of opposition, highlights the strength needed to lead boldly. His determination to create a unified India, regardless of the challenges, serves as an enduring example of courageous leadership.

These lessons from Sardar Patel's life remind us that true leadership requires vision, adaptability, courage, and the ability to inspire others to work toward a shared goal, even when the path is filled with obstacles. His legacy continues to inspire leaders to think strategically and act with conviction.

Coaching Leaders for Mental Agility: Story No 18

Resilience in the Face of Darkness: Churchill's Mental Health Battle

> **"The human spirit is stronger than anything that can happen to it."**
>
> **– C.C. Scott**

Winston Churchill, one of the most respected leaders in modern history, is admired not just for his strong leadership during World War II but also for his personal fight with depression, which he called his **"black dog."**

This term he used for his mental struggles has struck a chord with many, showing that even the greatest leaders can face serious mental challenges.

The Burden of Leadership During War

Churchill's most intense encounters with his "black dog" occurred during the early years of World War II.

As Prime Minister of Britain, he bore the colossal responsibility of steering the nation through the darkest days of the conflict.

The relentless pressure, coupled with the grim reality of facing a powerful enemy, pushed Churchill into deep periods of depression.

The onset of World War II marked a particularly strenuous time for Churchill. In 1940, following the fall of France and the evacuation of British forces from Dunkirk, Britain stood virtually alone against Nazi Germany.

The threat of invasion was real and imminent. Churchill's tireless efforts to rally the nation and sustain the war effort took a heavy toll on his mental health.

The weight of the nation's fate rested on his shoulders, amplifying his feelings of despair, hopelessness, and anxiety.

Manifestations of Churchill's Depression

Churchill's depression was more than just a passing sadness; it was a profound struggle that manifested in various ways. He experienced intense feelings of hopelessness and a pervasive sense of despair. There were times when the burden seemed almost too much to bear, leading to a loss of appetite and a diminished zest for life. These were not mere moments of melancholy but profound episodes that threatened to consume him.

At times, Churchill's depression led him to contemplate dark thoughts. He famously mentioned to his doctor that he avoided standing too close to the edge of train platforms or peering over the rails of a ship, fearing that a sudden impulse might drive him to jump. These admissions offer a stark glimpse into the depth of his struggles.

Churchill's Coping Strategies

Despite the severe challenges posed by his mental health, Churchill employed several coping mechanisms to manage his depression and continue his leadership duties. His ability to find solace in creative and physical outlets, lean on social support, and seek professional help serves as an enduring example of resilience.

1. Creative Outlets

Churchill found solace in creative pursuits, particularly painting and writing. He began painting later in life, and it became a vital therapeutic outlet. The process of capturing the world on canvas provided him with a form of escape, allowing him to channel his emotions into something tangible and beautiful. His paintings, often depicting serene landscapes and peaceful scenes, stand in stark contrast to the turmoil he felt within.

Writing was another crucial outlet for Churchill. A prolific author and historian, he penned numerous works during his lifetime, including his six-volume history of World War II.

Writing allowed him to express his thoughts, process the challenges he faced, and contribute to his enduring legacy. The act of writing also provided structure and purpose during moments of emotional turbulence.

2. Physical Activity

Churchill understood the importance of physical activity in managing his mental health. He was an avid walker and swimmer, finding that regular exercise helped to clear his mind and improve his mood.

His walks through the English countryside were not just a form of exercise but also a way to connect with nature and find peace amidst the chaos of war.

Swimming, another of Churchill's preferred activities, offered both physical exertion and a sense of liberation. The rhythmic motion of swimming, combined with the solitude it provided, allowed him to momentarily escape the pressures of his role.

3. Social Support

Churchill was fortunate to have a strong network of family and friends who provided emotional support during his darkest times. His wife, Clementine, was a steadfast partner who understood the complexities of his personality and the burdens he carried. Her unwavering support and companionship were crucial in helping him navigate his depression.

In addition to his family, Churchill maintained close friendships with several confidants who provided counsel and comfort. These relationships helped to alleviate his feelings of isolation and reminded him that he was not alone in his struggles.

4. Professional Help

Recognizing the severity of his depression, Churchill did not hesitate to seek professional help. He consulted with medical professionals, including psychiatrists, who provided guidance and treatment.

This willingness to seek help was a key factor in his ability to manage his depression while fulfilling his demanding role as Prime Minister.

Churchill's openness to medical intervention is noteworthy, especially in an era when mental health issues were often stigmatized. His proactive approach to managing his mental health, rather than succumbing to it, underscores his resilience and determination.

Overcoming the "Black Dog"

Despite the pervasive presence of his "black dog," Churchill's resilience and indomitable spirit allowed him to lead Britain through one of its most challenging periods. His ability to manage his depression while steering the nation to victory in World War II is a testament to his strength of character.

Churchill's story is a powerful reminder that even the most formidable leaders can struggle with mental health issues. His legacy teaches us that resilience is not the absence of struggle, but the ability to persevere in the face of it. His life serves as an inspiration to those who may feel overwhelmed by their challenges, showing that with the right support and coping strategies, it is possible to overcome even the darkest times.

Churchill's battle with depression, far from diminishing his legacy, adds depth to our understanding of him as a leader and a human being.

His willingness to confront his "black dog" head-on, seek help, and find ways to cope provides valuable lessons in leadership, resilience, and the importance of mental health awareness.

Point to note:

- Churchill's ability to lead a nation through its darkest hours while dealing with his own mental health challenges shows that resilience isn't about being unbreakable, but about continuing to move forward despite difficulties. Even in moments of personal struggle, he managed to fulfill his responsibilities, demonstrating the power of perseverance.
- Churchill didn't shy away from seeking professional help and using various coping mechanisms to manage his depression. This teaches us the value of acknowledging when we need help and

the importance of using available resources to take care of our mental health.

- Churchill's use of painting, writing, and physical activity as ways to manage his depression highlights how important it is to find healthy outlets for our emotions. Engaging in creative and physical activities can be powerful tools for coping with stress and improving overall well-being.
- Churchill's openness about his "black dog" shows that vulnerability does not diminish one's strength or capability. In fact, acknowledging our struggles can make us more relatable and can help break down the stigma surrounding mental health issues.
- The support Churchill received from his family and friends played a crucial role in helping him manage his depression. This emphasizes the importance of surrounding ourselves with supportive people who can provide comfort and encouragement during tough times.
- Churchill's story reminds us that no one is immune to mental health challenges, not even the most powerful and influential people. Understanding this can help us be more compassionate towards ourselves and others who may be going through similar struggles.

> **"When everything seems to be going against you, remember that the airplane takes off against the wind, not with it."**
>
> **– Henry Ford**

King Shivaji Maharaj: A Story of Leadership and Resilience

Shivaji Maharaj embarked on a formidable journey to establish his kingdom, facing immense challenges from powerful adversaries like the Mughal Empire and battling internal dissent. The landscape was fraught with difficulties, as betrayals from those he trusted, limited resources, and constant warfare tested his resolve at every turn.

Yet, amidst these adversities, Shivaji Maharaj's resilience shone through. He adapted to each setback, demonstrating remarkable strategic brilliance. His ability to pivot in the face of defeat and maintain his vision laid the groundwork for the creation of a strong and independent Maratha Empire. Each challenge he faced only reinforced his determination, proving that true strength lies in the ability to rise again and again, no matter how formidable the obstacles may seem.

Through his journey, Shivaji Maharaj not only built a kingdom but also inspired generations with his unwavering spirit and tenacity. His legacy reminds us that resilience can transform adversity into opportunity, paving the way for greatness.

In the early stages of his campaign, Shivaji Maharaj faced a mountain of military and administrative challenges. The complexities of warfare and statecraft weighed heavily on him, and he understood that he needed expert advice to navigate this daunting landscape. Recognizing the importance of collaboration, he reached out to seasoned generals and advisors, seeking their wisdom and insights. One of his most trusted allies, Tanaji Malusare, emerged as a key strategist who played a pivotal role in the successful capture of Kondana Fort. This willingness to seek help and counsel was crucial for Shivaji Maharaj as he overcame many initial hurdles.

Amidst the relentless pressures of warfare and governance, Shivaji Maharaj also understood the need to manage stress and maintain mental clarity. He engaged in various creative and physical activities to keep his mind sharp and spirits high. Known for his love of poetry, he actively patronized scholars and artists, immersing himself in their work for both creative expression and intellectual stimulation. Alongside this, he valued physical fitness, participating in rigorous training and horse riding, which kept him not only physically fit but also mentally agile.

Shivaji Maharaj faced numerous personal and public struggles, with the constant pressure of maintaining his kingdom against hostile forces and internal challenges. While historical records do not explicitly detail his admissions of struggle, his actions reflected a deep understanding of these challenges. He shared responsibilities with trusted advisors, showcasing a pragmatic approach to leadership. By communicating openly about the state's condition and strategic decisions, he demonstrated a form of openness that was vital for overcoming obstacles.

Moreover, Shivaji Maharaj's success was not solely his own; it hinged on the robust support network surrounding him. His family, allies, and loyal subjects played significant roles in his journey. His mother provided personal strength and guidance, while close confidants like Tanaji Malusare and Ramchandra Pant Amatya offered crucial strategic support. This network was instrumental in ensuring both his success and the stability of his kingdom.

Through these experiences, Shivaji Maharaj showcased the importance of seeking help, engaging in creative and physical outlets, being open about struggles, and cultivating a strong support network. His story inspires leaders to embrace collaboration, prioritize their well-being, and build meaningful relationships for a greater purpose.

King Shivaji Maharaj's story exemplifies how resilience, seeking help, engaging in creative and physical activities, being open about struggles, and valuing support networks can lead to significant achievements despite overwhelming challenges. His life serves as a testament to the power of leadership and personal strength in overcoming adversity and achieving greatness.

The top messages from these texts on leadership and setbacks are:

- **Resilience Through Adversity:** Both Churchill and Shivaji Maharaj demonstrated that true leadership is not defined by the absence of challenges but by the ability to persist through them. Their experiences underscore the importance of bouncing back from setbacks, which only strengthened their leadership.

- **Seeking Help and Collaboration:** Great leaders do not go it alone. Churchill sought professional help for his depression, while Shivaji Maharaj surrounded himself with trusted advisors like Tanaji Malusare to overcome challenges. Recognizing when to seek assistance is vital to overcoming adversity.

- **Creative and Physical Outlets for Mental Health:** Both leaders used creative and physical activities to manage their mental and emotional health. Churchill painted and wrote, while Shivaji Maharaj engaged in poetry and physical training. These outlets helped them maintain clarity and strength in the face of overwhelming pressure.
- **Vulnerability and Strength:** Churchill's openness about his struggles with depression ("black dog") shows that vulnerability doesn't diminish leadership; it humanizes it. Leaders who admit their struggles can break down stigmas, build trust, and inspire others.
- **The Power of Support Networks:** Both leaders leaned on strong support systems. Churchill relied on his family and friends for emotional support, and Shivaji Maharaj built a loyal network of allies. Strong relationships are essential for maintaining morale and achieving success in difficult times.

Coaching Leaders for Mental Agility: Story No 19

Navigating Setbacks: Leadership Insights from Churchill, Oprah, and Eleanor Roosevelt

> **"I have not failed. I've just found 10,000 ways that won't work."**
>
> **– Thomas Edison**

Winston Churchill's transformation from a political outcast to one of Britain's most revered wartime leaders is a fascinating tale of resilience, perseverance, and unwavering dedication to his country.

Early Setbacks and Exile:

Churchill's early political career was marked by ambition and controversy. In 1915, during World War I, he was First Lord of the Admiralty, overseeing the British Navy. He orchestrated the Gallipoli Campaign, a military strategy aimed at opening a new front against the Ottoman Empire to relieve pressure on Allied forces. The campaign turned into a disaster, resulting in heavy casualties and failure to achieve its objectives. Churchill bore much of the blame for the debacle, leading to his resignation from the Admiralty and a significant blow to his reputation.

After Gallipoli, Churchill entered a period of political exile. Despite his past successes and remarkable oratory skills, he struggled to regain political influence. He was viewed as reckless and unpredictable by his peers, which led to his isolation in British politics. During this time, he spent years on the political fringes, advocating for policies that often put him at odds with mainstream opinion, such as his early warnings about the rise of Nazi Germany in the 1930s.

Transformation and Leadership During World War II:

When World War II broke out, Britain needed strong and decisive leadership. By this time, Churchill's persistent warnings about the dangers of Nazi aggression had proved prophetic. In 1940, after the resignation of Prime Minister Neville Chamberlain following the failed policy of appeasement, Churchill was appointed Prime Minister. His return to power marked a pivotal moment not only in his career but in world history.

As Prime Minister, Churchill embodied resilience and defiance against the seemingly unstoppable German military. His speeches, filled with determination and optimism, rallied the British people during their darkest hour. Notably, during the Battle of Britain in 1940, Churchill's speeches such as "We shall fight on the beaches" and "This was their finest hour" inspired a nation under siege. Despite the odds, Churchill's leadership helped Britain withstand the Nazi onslaught, standing as one of the few European nations not to succumb to German occupation.

Key Transformation:

Churchill's story is one of remarkable transformation, from political missteps and exile to becoming the leader who would guide Britain to victory. His perseverance through years of political isolation allowed him to be prepared when Britain needed him most. The resilience he showed after the failure of Gallipoli gave him the strength to face adversity head-on during World War II. His unyielding belief in British survival, despite being surrounded by Nazi-controlled Europe, became a beacon of hope not only for Britain but for the Allied forces.

Churchill's return to leadership exemplified his ability to adapt, learn from past failures, and inspire those around him. His legacy remains tied to his leadership during World War II, but it was shaped just as much by the years he spent in political exile and his response to failure earlier in his career. Through his speeches, determination, and strategic vision, Churchill became a symbol of resistance and the personification of Britain's refusal to surrender.

In sum, Churchill's journey highlights that great leadership often arises from setbacks and challenges. His ability to learn from past mistakes, his resilience in the face of adversity, and his steadfastness in pursuit of his beliefs made him one of the most iconic leaders of the 20th century.

From Overcoming Shadows to Illuminating the World: The Oprah Winfrey Story

Imagine a young girl growing up in a rural town, her childhood marred by intense poverty and unimaginable abuse. This was Oprah Winfrey's reality. Born into a life of struggle, Oprah's early years were a tapestry of hardship. Raised in the harsh environment of rural Mississippi, she faced the cruel trials of poverty and the severe trauma of abuse from a young age. Her circumstances seemed insurmountable, and the future appeared bleak.

Yet, within the depths of her suffering, Oprah discovered a spark of resilience. She used her voice—a tool for expression and self-empowerment—as a beacon of hope. At the age of just 14, Oprah's story took a pivotal turn when she won a local oratory contest. This achievement was not just a personal victory; it was a glimpse into her potential.

Oprah's journey to success was not easy. Each step forward came with its own set of challenges. She moved to Nashville, Tennessee, to live with her father, who provided a stable environment and encouraged her education. Oprah seized this opportunity, excelling in school and eventually earning a scholarship to Tennessee State University. Her academic success, combined with her burgeoning talent in broadcasting, paved the way for her entry into the media world.

Her career began modestly with a job as a local news anchor. But Oprah's unique ability to connect with people and share their stories set her apart. Her empathy and authenticity resonated with audiences, leading to her breakthrough role as a talk show host. This was the beginning of an extraordinary transformation. The Oprah Winfrey Show became a cultural phenomenon, not just for its entertainment value but for its deep, heartfelt discussions on critical issues such as mental health, personal growth, and social justice.

Through her platform, Oprah didn't just entertain; she empowered. Her show became a space where people could confront their struggles and find hope. Oprah used her own experiences as a powerful tool for connection and healing. Her openness about her past inspired countless individuals to face their own challenges with courage and hope.

As Oprah's influence grew, so did her commitment to giving back. She founded the Oprah Winfrey Foundation and the Oprah Winfrey Operating Foundation, focusing on education, empowerment, and humanitarian work. Her philanthropic efforts have had a profound impact, including the establishment of the Oprah Winfrey Foundation Academy for Girls in South Africa, which provides educational opportunities for underprivileged girls.

Oprah Winfrey's story is not just one of overcoming adversity; it is a testament to the power of resilience and the ability to transform pain into purpose. From a victim of abuse to a global media mogul and philanthropist, Oprah's life is a shining example of how personal struggles can fuel a remarkable journey of empowerment and change. Her legacy is a reminder that no matter how difficult the beginning, one's story can evolve into something profoundly inspirational and impactful.

Eleanor Roosevelt: From Shyness to Advocacy

Picture a young Eleanor Roosevelt, emerging from a world of shadows and self-doubt. Her early years were far from the spotlight; they were filled with profound personal struggles that could have easily stifled her potential. Eleanor, born into a life of privilege, faced a turbulent internal landscape marked by crippling shyness and a marriage that strained her emotional resilience. Despite her privileged position, Eleanor's self-esteem was fragile, and her personal life was fraught with challenges that might have consigned her to obscurity.

The narrative of Eleanor Roosevelt's transformation is one of profound personal evolution. Her journey from a timid, insecure woman to an influential advocate for social justice and human rights was neither swift nor easy. It was a gradual, often painful process of self-discovery and empowerment. Eleanor grappled with her own fears and limitations, each step forward requiring immense courage.

As Eleanor navigated through her own struggles, she began to emerge from her self-imposed cocoon. Her evolution was catalyzed by a deep, unwavering commitment to making a difference. This transformation was not merely about overcoming shyness but about reimagining her place in the world. Her personal growth was mirrored by her increasing involvement in social and political causes, an arena where her voice would soon resonate powerfully.

When Eleanor assumed the role of First Lady of the United States, she was presented with a platform that was traditionally limited in scope. Rather than adhering to conventional expectations, Eleanor chose to redefine her role. She saw the position not as a passive one but as an opportunity to engage deeply with pressing social issues. Her approach was revolutionary; she became actively involved in policy discussions, using her influence on champion social justice, advocate for human rights, and address women's issues.

Eleanor Roosevelt's impact extended beyond her public duties. She actively reached out to marginalized communities and used her position to bring their concerns to the forefront of national discourse. Her work was groundbreaking for a First Lady, as she ventured into arenas previously reserved for men. Eleanor's initiatives were not only about addressing immediate needs but also about advocating for systemic change, creating a legacy of progress that would endure long after her tenure.

The essence of Eleanor Roosevelt's story is a powerful testament to the potential for personal transformation to drive public impact. Her journey from a reserved and self-doubting individual to a formidable advocate underscores a vital lesson: personal insecurities can be overcome, and personal growth can lead to extraordinary societal contributions. Eleanor's life serves as a compelling reminder that with resilience, determination, and a commitment to a larger purpose, even the quietest voices can effect significant, lasting change. Her legacy continues to inspire those who strive to make a difference, proving that profound change often begins with the courage to face and overcome one's own fears.

> **"Leadership is about navigating through adversity, not avoiding it."**
>
> **– Simon Sinek**

Key Takeaways from Leadership Legends

1. **Resilience Overcomes Challenges:** Churchill, Oprah, and Eleanor Roosevelt all faced significant setbacks but persevered. Their stories show that resilience is key to success.

2. **Personal Growth Drives Leadership:** These leaders transformed themselves personally. This growth helped them become better leaders and make a bigger impact.

3. **Seize Leadership Opportunities:** When the time is right, step up and lead. Churchill, Oprah, and Eleanor Roosevelt all took advantage of opportunities to make a difference.

4. **Mental Agility Is Essential:** Be flexible, adaptable, and open to new ideas. This mental agility is crucial for effective leadership.

Coaching Leaders for Mental Agility: Story No 20

The Rise of the Wolf: A Tale of Leadership on the Steppe

> **"If you are afraid, don't do it. If you are doing it, don't be afraid."**
>
> **- Genghis Khan**

In the harsh embrace of the Mongolian steppe, a young boy named Temujin shivered against the relentless wind.

Orphaned and ostracized by his tribe, his future seemed bleak. Yet, within this adversity, a fire burned – the flicker of ambition, the spark of a leader.

This boy, hardened by hardship, would rise to become **Genghis Khan,** the founder of the Mongol Empire, the largest contiguous land empire in history.

Vision Under the Open Sky:

Temujin didn't dream small. He envisioned a unified Mongolia, a nation of fierce horsemen galloping under a single banner. He rallied scattered tribes, not just through force, but by offering them a shared purpose, a chance to escape the cycle of petty warfare. He promised them strength, security, and a place at the heart of a mighty empire. This vision, like the endless steppe sky, ignited a fire in the hearts of his followers.

Resilience Forged in Steel:

Temujin's path wasn't paved with victories. Betrayal, defeat, and loss were constant companions. He was captured, enslaved, even escaped on horseback with a noose still around his neck. Yet, each setback tempered his spirit, honing his resilience like a blade against a whetstone. He learned from his mistakes, adapted his strategies, and emerged stronger from every challenge.

Adaptability: The Eagle's Eye:

The Mongols were masters of warfare, not because of brute force alone, but because of their ability to adapt. Genghis Khan studied his enemies, their strengths, and weaknesses. He adopted superior tactics from conquered peoples, integrating them seamlessly into his own military machine. Like an eagle surveying the battlefield, he saw opportunities others missed, exploiting them with ruthless efficiency.

Psychological Warfare: Whispers in the Wind:

Genghis Khan understood the power of fear. He sowed discord among his enemies, spreading rumors and exploiting existing rivalries. He used his fearsome reputation to precede him, demoralizing his foes before they even drew their swords. This psychological warfare, as subtle as the wind whispering through the tall grass, often proved as decisive as any battle.

Strategic Thinking: The Grand Chessboard:

Genghis Khan wasn't just a warrior; he was a brilliant strategist. He meticulously planned his campaigns, considering logistics, terrain, and weather. He anticipated his enemy's moves, playing a grand game of chess on a map stretching across the vast continent. His strategies, like intricate formations drawn in the sand, ensured his victories were swift and devastating.

Loyalty: The Wolf Pack's Bond:

Genghis Khan wasn't just a conqueror; he was a leader who inspired fierce loyalty. He recognized merit, promoting skilled warriors regardless of their background. He rewarded loyalty and punished betrayal with swift brutality. He created a sense of brotherhood among his soldiers, a feeling of belonging to a powerful and unstoppable pack. This unwavering loyalty became the bedrock of his empire.

Lessons from the Steppes:

Genghis Khan's leadership, born from the harsh realities of the steppe, offers valuable lessons for anyone seeking to lead. Vision, resilience, adaptability, the use of psychological tactics, strategic thinking, and the ability to inspire loyalty – these are the tools he wielded to forge an empire. Though his methods were often brutal, the lessons remain, echoing across the centuries like the thunder of Mongol hooves.

Genghis Khan's leadership and mental stamina were as formidable as the Mongol cavalry he led.

Let's delve deeper into the key aspects that made him such a successful, albeit brutal, leader:

Mental Toughness:

Genghis Khan's resilience was forged through the hardships of his early life. Orphaned, betrayed, and even enslaved, he faced immense adversity from a young age. These experiences shaped him into a leader of extraordinary resilience, teaching him to learn from setbacks and emerge stronger with each challenge he faced.

His unyielding willpower drove him to achieve his ambitions, no matter how insurmountable the obstacles appeared. Genghis Khan's iron will inspire his followers, motivating them to stand by him in even the most difficult of circumstances, while simultaneously instilling fear in his enemies.

Despite his reputation for calculated brutality, Genghis Khan had remarkable emotional control. In the heat of battle, he remained calm and focused, enabling him to make strategic, clear-headed decisions that often turned the tide in his favor. His ability to balance ruthlessness with measured composure made him a formidable and respected leader.

Leadership Strategies:

Genghis Khan was not only a conqueror but also a visionary leader who dreamed of unifying Mongolia into a powerful empire. He communicated this vision with great clarity and passion, successfully rallying disparate tribes under a single banner. His leadership was marked by his ability to inspire others to share in this grand ambition.

Beyond his leadership qualities, Genghis Khan was a master strategist. He meticulously planned his campaigns, carefully considering factors like logistics, terrain, and weather. He anticipated enemy moves and exploited their weaknesses with ruthless efficiency, turning battles in his favor through sheer strategic brilliance.

One of the key strengths of the Mongol army under Genghis Khan was its discipline and meritocracy. The army functioned like a well-oiled machine where discipline was paramount, and loyalty was rewarded. Genghis Khan promoted individuals based on their skills and abilities, regardless of their background. This approach fostered a culture of meritocracy and encouraged ambition among his fighters, further strengthening his forces.

Genghis Khan also understood the psychological aspects of warfare. He employed fear as a powerful weapon, using brutality to sow discord among his enemies. The fear he instilled often spread ahead of him like a storm, weakening his opponents' resolve before they even engaged in battle. This use of psychological warfare proved as effective as his military tactics in securing victories.

Additional positive aspects....

Genghis Khan's leadership was characterized by empowerment and inclusivity. His empire was known for promoting a meritocratic system where individuals were rewarded based on their skills and abilities, rather than their social status or background. This approach extended to his administration, where talented individuals from diverse ethnic backgrounds were appointed to key positions, fostering a sense of inclusivity and diversity within the empire.

His strategic leadership was evident in his military campaigns and conquests. Genghis Khan was a master tactician, carefully planning his military endeavors with a keen awareness of terrain, weather, and the strengths and weaknesses of his adversaries. A notable example of his strategic brilliance was the Battle of Khwarezmia, where he successfully used deception, speed, and surprise to defeat a much larger enemy force.

Genghis Khan also inspired immense loyalty and commitment among his followers. His charisma, leadership by example, and fair treatment of his soldiers earned him their unwavering devotion. He shared the spoils of conquest with his troops and provided for their families during times of need, creating a strong bond that motivated his soldiers to follow him into even the most perilous battles.

Adaptability and flexibility were key traits in Genghis Khan's leadership. He was known for changing tactics based on evolving circumstances, whether due to shifting alliances or battlefield conditions. For instance, when faced with enemies who had superior numbers or technology, he employed unconventional tactics like feigned retreats or ambushes to gain the upper hand.

Inclusivity was a hallmark of Genghis Khan's empire. He welcomed people of diverse ethnicities, religions, and cultures, recognizing the value of diversity. He actively integrated different traditions into his empire, fostering trade and cultural exchange, which led to economic prosperity and strengthened his vast, multicultural realm.

> **"Conquering the world on horseback is easy; it is dismounting and governing that is hard."**
>
> **- Genghis Khan**

The Dark Side:

It's important to acknowledge the dark side of Genghis Khan's leadership. His brutality towards those who opposed him was legendary. While his tactics were effective in their time, they wouldn't translate to modern leadership.

Lessons for Modern Leaders:

Genghis Khan's leadership strengths offer valuable lessons that can be applied today. One key strength is **resilience**. It's important to build the ability to recover from setbacks and learn from mistakes, turning challenges into opportunities for growth.

Having a clear and inspiring **vision** is another critical trait. A strong vision not only motivates you but also unites your team around a common goal, driving them toward success.

Strategic thinking is essential for effective leadership. By analyzing situations carefully and developing well-thought-out strategies, you can lead your team confidently toward achieving their objectives.

Adaptability is equally important. Continuously learning and adjusting your approach as needed will help you navigate changing circumstances and stay ahead.

Lastly, fostering a culture of meritocracy is vital. Recognizing and rewarding talent within your team builds loyalty, increases engagement, and drives overall performance.

Modern leadership demands ethical conduct, inspiring your team, and focusing on collaboration. The brutality of Genghis Khan's era is a historical footnote, but the core principles of resilience, vision, and strategic thinking remain valuable for leaders today.

> **"The strength of a wall is neither greater nor less than the courage of the men who defend it."**
>
> **- Genghis Khan**

Here are the top key leadership messages inspired by Genghis Khan's leadership style and experiences:

- **Vision with Purpose:** Genghis Khan had a clear, compelling vision to unite the Mongol tribes and create an empire. Modern leaders should aim to inspire their teams by providing a strong, unifying purpose, which creates a sense of belonging and motivates others to work toward shared goals.

- **Resilience in the Face of Adversity:** Genghis Khan faced betrayal, defeat, and even enslavement but always bounced back stronger. Leaders today must embrace resilience, learning from challenges and setbacks to continuously improve and lead with determination.

- **Adaptability and Innovation:** The Mongols succeeded not through sheer force but through strategic adaptability, adopting new tactics from other cultures. Leaders should be flexible, willing to adapt their strategies and embrace innovation in response to changing circumstances.

- **Psychological Insight and Influence:** Genghis Khan understood the power of psychological warfare, using fear and strategy to outmaneuver enemies. In modern leadership, understanding and influencing human behavior, fostering trust, and using emotional intelligence can be just as powerful in motivating and guiding teams.

- **Meritocracy and Loyalty:** Genghis Khan promoted individuals based on their skills and loyalty, regardless of their background. Today's leaders should recognize and reward merit, building a culture where talent is nurtured, and loyalty is fostered through fair and inclusive practices.

These timeless lessons focus on vision, resilience, adaptability, understanding human nature, and creating an environment where talent thrives, all essential for effective leadership.

Coaching Leaders for Mental Agility: Story No 21

Leadership Lessons from UN Peacekeepers: Insights for Resilient and Effective Leadership

> **"The UN is the world's conscience, and its leadership must reflect the highest ideals of humanity."**
>
> **– Kofi Annan, Former UN Secretary-General**

In Liberia, the United Nations Mission (UNMIL) was instrumental in bringing an end to the nation's devastating civil war in 2003. UN peacekeepers played a vital role in facilitating negotiations between the warring factions, building trust, and creating a pathway for a power-sharing government. Under the decisive leadership of Lieutenant General Daniel Opande, UNMIL ensured the safety of civilians and established a stable environment that paved the way for free and fair elections, marking a turning point in the country's history.

Similarly, in Namibia in 1989, the United Nations Transition Assistance Group (UNTAG) oversaw the nation's transition to independence. UNTAG peacekeepers carefully guided negotiations between South Africa and the Southwest Africa People's Organization (SWAPO), resulting in a ceasefire and the first free elections for the country. Martii Ahtisaari, as the UN Special Representative for Namibia, steered the complex political dynamics with strong leadership, ensuring a peaceful transfer of power that set Namibia on the course for independence.

In El Salvador, the United Nations Observer Mission (ONUSAL) was key to ending the 12-year civil war in 1991. UN peacekeepers fostered dialogue between the Salvadoran government and the Farabundo Martí National Liberation Front (FMLN) rebels, helping to rebuild trust. The leadership of Alain Dominique Touraine proved crucial as he encouraged compromise and guided both sides toward a peaceful resolution, allowing the country to begin its journey to recovery.

The United Nations Operation in Côte d'Ivoire (UNOCI) played a central role in resolving the violent post-election crisis of 2010-2011. Peacekeepers brokered talks between President Laurent Gbagbo and opposition leader Alassane Ouattara, defusing a potentially explosive situation. Y J Choi, the UN Special Representative, led efforts to foster international support and push both parties toward peaceful negotiation, preventing further bloodshed and stabilizing the country.

In the Philippines, after the Battle of Marawi in 2017, UN peacekeepers worked diligently to foster communication between the government and local communities. Leila Zerrougui's leadership was pivotal in advocating for the protection of civilians and focusing efforts on long-term recovery after the siege. By rebuilding trust and encouraging dialogue, the United Nations Mission in the Philippines (UNMPHIL) laid the foundation for sustained peace in the region.

The Good Friday Agreement of 1998, which ended decades of sectarian violence in Northern Ireland, was supported by UN peacekeepers, who helped facilitate crucial negotiations. They played a key role in bringing the British and Irish governments, political parties, and paramilitary groups to the table, ultimately leading to the establishment of a power-sharing government and a peaceful resolution to the conflict.

In Cambodia, UN peacekeepers were essential to the 1991 Paris Peace Agreements, which ended the country's civil war. They oversaw the ceasefire, monitored the repatriation of refugees, and assisted in disarming combatants, which laid the groundwork for democratic elections and a new transitional government.

The peace process in Indonesia's Aceh province in 2005 marked another significant achievement for UN peacekeepers, who supported negotiations between the Indonesian government and the Free Aceh Movement (GAM). The resulting peace agreement, known as the Helsinki Memorandum of Understanding, ended years of conflict, and enabled former rebels to reintegrate peacefully into civilian life.

In Mozambique, the 1992 Rome General Peace Accords ended 16 years of civil war between the ruling FRELIMO party and RENAMO rebels. UN peacekeepers were on the frontlines, facilitating negotiations, monitoring ceasefires, overseeing the demobilization of combatants, and assisting in clearing landmines to ensure a safer future for the nation.

Lastly, in Guatemala, the 1996 Peace Accords marked the end of a 36-year civil war. UN peacekeepers supported the negotiation process between the government and guerrilla groups, focusing on crucial issues like human rights, land reform, and indigenous rights. By monitoring the accords and strengthening democratic institutions, they played a key role in promoting reconciliation and rebuilding the country after decades of conflict.

Each of these examples highlights how UN peacekeepers, through negotiations and strong leadership, have consistently helped resolve conflicts, rebuild trust, and lay the groundwork for peace in some of the world's most turbulent regions.

These are just a few examples, and the work of UN peacekeepers continues in various conflict zones around the world.

Their dedication to negotiation, leadership, and building trust in challenging situations is a testament to the power of diplomacy and conflict resolution.

The stories of UN peacekeepers in conflict zones offer valuable insights into both leadership and human psychology.

Here's what we can learn:

Leadership:

Effective peacekeeping goes beyond mere presence; it requires a deep understanding of cultural nuances and communication styles. Imagine a peacekeeper stepping into a community, where every gesture and word holds significance. By showing genuine respect for these diverse cultural norms, they lay the foundation for trust. This trust becomes the bridge that connects them with various parties in a conflict, allowing for open dialogue and cooperation.

In the chaotic environment of conflict zones, adaptability is key. Picture a leader who navigates shifting circumstances, making swift decisions with only fragments of information at hand. Their ability to adjust strategies on the fly ensures that they can respond to new challenges, turning uncertainty into opportunity. Each choice made in these moments is not just about tactics; it's about guiding their team through the storm with confidence and clarity.

Collaboration is another essential element of successful peacekeeping. In this intricate dance, diverse groups come together, each bringing their unique perspectives and experiences. A leader fosters a collaborative atmosphere, encouraging dialogue and ensuring that every voice is heard. This environment allows for consensus-building, where conflicting parties can find common ground. As leaders guide these discussions, they create a space where cooperation flourishes, transforming tensions into partnerships.

However, peacekeeping is not without its emotional toll. The weight of responsibility can be heavy, and stress management becomes a vital skill. A leader who openly acknowledges their struggles while maintaining composure sets a powerful example for their team. They model resilience, showing that it's possible to remain steady in the face of adversity. This example not only uplifts the morale of their team but also inspires them to find strength within themselves.

Through cultural sensitivity, adaptability, collaboration, and effective stress management, peacekeepers become not just agents of stability but also beacons of hope. Their journey through challenging landscapes illustrates how understanding, flexibility, teamwork, and composure can pave the way for lasting peace.

Human Psychology:

In the complex world of conflict resolution, empathy and emotional intelligence become powerful tools for peacekeepers. Imagine a peacekeeper stepping into a heated negotiation, fully aware of the diverse emotions swirling around them. As they listen deeply to each party, they recognize the fears, hopes, and frustrations that drive their motivations. By showing genuine understanding, the peacekeeper fosters trust, creating an environment where dialogue can flourish, and solutions can be found.

Trust and legitimacy are the cornerstones of successful negotiations. Picture a peacekeeper who approaches all parties with unwavering neutrality. They engage each side with sincerity, demonstrating a true commitment to finding peaceful resolutions. This genuine desire for harmony resonates with those involved, allowing the peacekeeper to earn their trust. Only then can the path to resolution be illuminated, as both sides begin to see the peacekeeper as a fair mediator.

However, peacebuilding is not a sprint; it's a marathon that requires a long-term perspective. As challenges arise and tensions flare, the peacekeeper draws upon their understanding of psychology. They remain patient and persistent, knowing that real change takes time. Their steadfast commitment to sustained negotiation becomes a beacon of hope, inspiring others to stay the course, even when the journey feels daunting.

Despite their dedication, the environment in which peacekeepers operate can be incredibly taxing. Constant tension and exposure to atrocities weigh heavily on their spirits. Acknowledging the psychological impact of stress and trauma becomes essential in maintaining team morale. The peacekeeper creates a supportive atmosphere, where open conversations about mental well-being are encouraged. This recognition of emotional struggles not only uplifts their team but also strengthens the bonds between them, fostering resilience in the face of adversity.

Through the power of empathy, the importance of trust, a long-term perspective, and a commitment to mental well-being, peacekeepers navigate the intricate landscapes of conflict. Their journey highlights how understanding, patience, and compassion can transform despair into hope, paving the way for lasting peace.

Additionally:

- **Humanity's Capacity for Cooperation:** Despite deep-rooted conflict, these stories show how humans can overcome differences and work together towards peace.

- **The Importance of Active Listening and Communication:** Effective peacekeepers prioritize listening to all sides of a conflict and fostering open communication to find common ground.

By understanding the leadership skills and psychological considerations involved in UN peacekeeping missions, we gain valuable insights into navigating complex situations and promoting peaceful solutions in a world fraught with conflict.

To build mental resilience like UN peacekeepers, we can ask yourself the following psychology and leadership questions:

Self-Awareness:

- How well do I understand my own strengths, weaknesses, and emotional reactions?
- Am I aware of the biases and assumptions that influence my decision-making?
- Do I recognize when I need to seek support or take a step back to reevaluate a situation?

Emotional Regulation:

- How effectively do I manage my emotions, especially in high-pressure or conflict situations?
- Am I able to stay calm and composed under stress, or do I become easily overwhelmed?
- What strategies do I use to regulate my emotions and maintain focus during challenging times?

Resilience:

- How do I bounce back from setbacks, failures, or moments of adversity?
- Do I view challenges as opportunities for growth and learning, or do I see them as insurmountable obstacles?
- What practices or habits do I have in place to foster resilience and maintain a positive mindset?

Problem-Solving Skills:

- How do I approach complex problems or conflicts within my team or organization?
- Am I able to analyze situations objectively, consider multiple perspectives, and identify creative solutions?
- Do I seek input from others and collaborate effectively to address challenges?

Adaptability:

- How flexible am I in adjusting to changing circumstances or unexpected developments?
- Can I adapt my leadership style and strategies to meet the needs of different situations or environments?
- Do I embrace innovation and change, or do I resist new ideas or approaches?

Empathy and Communication:

- How well do I understand the perspectives and feelings of others, especially those from diverse backgrounds or cultures?
- Am I able to communicate effectively, listen actively, and foster open dialogue within my team or organization?
- Do I demonstrate empathy and compassion in my interactions, even during challenging or contentious discussions?

Motivation and Purpose:

- What drives me to lead and serve others, especially in demanding or high-risk environments?
- Am I able to maintain my motivation and sense of purpose over the long term, despite obstacles or setbacks?
- How do I inspire and empower others to stay committed to our shared goals and values?

By reflecting on these questions and actively working to develop your psychological and leadership skills, you can strengthen your mental resilience and leadership effectiveness, similar to UN peacekeepers facing complex and dynamic situations in their work.

> **"The United Nations stands as a symbol of collective leadership, where nations rise above their interests to serve humanity's greater good."**
>
> **– António Guterres, Current UN Secretary-General**

Here are the top key messages:

- **Leadership in Conflict Resolution**: Strong and adaptable leadership is essential for peacekeeping success. UN leaders like Lieutenant General Daniel Opande, Martii Ahtisaari, and others demonstrated resilience and decisive action, guiding nations through political turmoil and establishing peace.
- **Negotiation and Building Trust**: Peacekeepers play a vital role in fostering negotiations between conflicting parties, building trust, and encouraging dialogue. These actions create the foundation for peace agreements and long-term stability.
- **The Power of Diplomacy**: Diplomacy is central to peacekeeping efforts, as peacekeepers facilitate discussions, compromise, and peaceful resolutions. This diplomacy often results in transformative outcomes, such as ceasefires, free elections, and peaceful transitions to power.
- **Cultural Sensitivity and Empathy**: Successful peacekeeping requires deep cultural sensitivity and empathy, understanding the diverse emotions and motivations of the parties involved. This helps to create trust and makes it possible to resolve conflicts through dialogue.
- **Resilience and Mental Strength**: Peacekeepers face intense stress and adversity in conflict zones. Their resilience, emotional regulation, and ability to foster mental well-being within their teams are critical to maintaining morale and ensuring long-term success in peacekeeping operations.

Part 3

Leadership Pillar-3(Endurance)

Summary

The chapter dives deeply into the qualities that define strong leadership, bringing to life the stories of remarkable figures in history. At its core, it paints a vivid picture of resilience. Readers are drawn into moments where leaders like Sir Alex Ferguson, Ursula Burns, and Sardar Patel faced challenges head-on. In every setback, they didn't just persist—they adapted, using adversity as fuel to push forward with unwavering determination. Each of them showed that leadership is not about avoiding obstacles but learning to thrive in the face of them, constantly adjusting strategies to keep pace with a changing world.

Through Ferguson's bold decision to trust young, untested players and Burns' commitment to fostering a diverse and inclusive workplace, the chapter reveals how real leaders build their teams from within. Ferguson's young players evolved into legends, while Burns' focus on diversity created an empowered workforce. These moments highlight how leadership thrives on nurturing talent, unity, and a shared sense of purpose, driving long-term success.

Vision also leaps off the pages, as readers see how figures like Genghis Khan, Patel, and Burns imagined futures that others could not yet see. Their clear, bold goals weren't just ideas—they were calls to action that inspired those around them, leaving lasting legacies.

The chapter then shifts to moments of transformation, where Ferguson rebuilt his team over decades and Burns led Xerox through a complete overhaul. In these stories, adaptability isn't a choice—it's a survival skill. Their leadership wasn't static; it constantly evolved, responding to the demands of the moment, proving that staying competitive requires an open mind and a willingness to embrace change.

Finally, the chapter captures the relentless discipline and consistency that defined each leader's journey. They set high standards and held to them, ensuring that their teams delivered peak performance again and again. Through their actions, the chapter shows that true leadership isn't a one-time success but a lifelong commitment to excellence, driven by resilience, vision, adaptability, and an unshakeable belief in people.

Key Skill	Action to Develop the Skill	Follow-Up and Progress Check
1. Resilience and Adaptability	- Embrace challenges as opportunities for growth.	- Track instances where you faced challenges and how you adapted. Reflect weekly on how you handled adversity and what you learned.
	- Practice adjusting your strategy when facing setbacks.	- Seek feedback from peers and mentors about how you handle change and setbacks.
2. Emotional Intelligence	- Practice active listening to understand others' perspectives.	- Regularly assess how well you manage your emotions in high-stress situations and keep a journal of emotional responses.
	- Develop self-awareness and regulate emotions, especially under pressure.	- Set reminders to check in with your emotional state and reflect on your responses. Ask colleagues for feedback on your emotional management and interpersonal interactions.
3. Growth Mindset and Innovation	- Continuously seek learning opportunities and view failures as learning experiences.	- Set specific goals for skill development and reflect on progress every month. Share learning experiences with your team to inspire innovation.
	- Ask for constructive feedback regularly and act on it.	- Keep a "failure journal" where you document lessons learned and innovations tried.
4. Perseverance and Motivation	- Break large goals into smaller, manageable tasks and celebrate small wins.	- Review your progress weekly. Celebrate small achievements and track long-term goals. Evaluate your energy and motivation levels at regular intervals.
	- Develop strategies to stay motivated during monotonous tasks.	- Set up periodic check-ins with a coach or mentor to assess your focus and motivation levels.
5. Decision-Making and Stress Management	- Practice decision-making by weighing pros and cons of multiple options in both personal and professional settings.	- Reflect on your decisions regularly. Did they lead to positive outcomes? Adjust future decisions accordingly.
	- Use stress management techniques, such as mindfulness or time management, to keep clarity in high-pressure situations.	- Monitor how well you manage stress. Ask for feedback from colleagues on how calm and focused you appear during stressful situations.

A Daily, Weekly, and Monthly Plan to Improve Leadership Endurance

Daily Actions:

- **Mindfulness Practice:** Spend 10 minutes each morning practicing mindfulness techniques like meditation or deep breathing to reduce stress and increase focus.
- **Physical Activity:** Engage in physical activity for at least 30 minutes to boost energy levels and improve overall well-being.
- **Positive Affirmations:** Start your day with positive affirmations to cultivate a positive mindset.
- **Time Management:** Prioritize tasks and break them down into smaller, manageable steps.
- **Healthy Eating:** Fuel your body with nutritious food to maintain energy levels throughout the day.

Weekly Actions:

- **Self-Reflection:** Dedicate time to reflect on your week, identifying strengths, weaknesses, and areas for improvement.
- **Skill Development:** Commit to learning a new skill or improving an existing one, such as public speaking, negotiation, or time management.
- **Networking:** Connect with other leaders and professionals to exchange ideas and gain new perspectives.
- **Stress Management Techniques:** Practice stress-relief techniques like yoga, journaling, or spending time in nature.
- **Seek Feedback:** Ask for feedback from colleagues, subordinates, and superiors to identify areas for growth.

Monthly Actions:

- **Set Clear Goals:** Establish specific, measurable, achievable, relevant, and time-bound (SMART) goals for the month.

- **Review and Adjust:** Regularly review your progress and adjust your goals as needed.
- **Seek a Mentor:** Find a mentor who can provide guidance, support, and advice.
- **Continuous Learning:** Attend workshops, conferences, or online courses to stay updated on industry trends and leadership best practices.
- **Self-Care:** Prioritize self-care activities, such as hobbies, relaxation techniques, or spending time with loved ones.

By consistently implementing these strategies, individuals can enhance their endurance, resilience, and overall leadership effectiveness.

From this chapter on leadership, there are several coaching questions that can help leaders reflect on and improve their leadership approach. These questions are designed to encourage self-awareness, adaptability, and growth:

- **Resilience in Adversity:**
    - How do I respond when faced with significant challenges or setbacks in my leadership journey?
    - Can I think of a recent challenge where I showed resilience, and what did I learn from that experience?
    - In moments of adversity, how can I better maintain a long-term perspective while managing short-term pressures?
- **Team Building and Empowerment:**
    - How effectively am I fostering a culture of empowerment within my team?
    - What steps am I taking to nurture the potential of individuals and create a sense of unity and purpose in the team?

- Are there ways I could promote diversity and inclusion in my leadership, and how might this benefit the team's overall success?

- **Adaptability and Strategic Change:**
  - How open am I to changing my strategies when the circumstances around me evolve?
  - When was the last time I had to pivot or adapt my leadership approach? How successful was that change, and what did I learn?
  - How do I stay informed about new trends and challenges, and how do I adjust my leadership to stay competitive?
- **Visionary Leadership:**
  - Do I have a clear and compelling vision for the future of my team or organization? How effectively am I communicating this vision to others?
  - How do I inspire others to work toward long-term goals, even when faced with immediate challenges?
  - In what ways can I refine my vision to ensure that it remains relevant and motivates others?
- **Discipline and Consistency:**
  - What routines or habits do I have in place to ensure discipline and consistency in my leadership?
  - Am I maintaining high standards for myself and my team? If not, what areas require improvement?
  - How do I ensure that my team continues to perform at the highest level over time?
- **Developing Leadership Legacy:**
  - What kind of legacy do I want to leave behind as a leader?

  - How am I ensuring that my leadership contributes to long-term success, even beyond my tenure?
  - Am I nurturing future leaders, and how can I do better in mentoring and guiding others toward leadership roles?

- **Balancing Toughness and Empathy:**
  - How do I balance being tough and decisive with showing empathy and understanding in my leadership?
  - Are there times when my leadership style could benefit from being more adaptable or understanding, especially during difficult situations?

By reflecting on these questions, leaders can gain deeper insights into their leadership style, identify areas for growth, and take actionable steps to improve their effectiveness in guiding their teams and organizations.

Concluding Reflection:

- **What one action can you take this week to embody the leadership qualities discussed in the chapter?**

This question can help facilitate deeper reflection and dialogue, encouraging individuals to connect their personal experiences with the principles outlined in the text.

Part-4

Leadership Pillar-4(Excellence)

Mastering Excellence: Discipline as the Cornerstone of Leadership

- **The Power of Discipline: The Cornerstone of Effective Leadership**
- **The Alloy of Leadership: Forging Strength from Essential Qualities**
- **The Desert Fox's Strategies for Success**
- **Mastering Leadership: Discoveries from 'Neutron Jack!'**
- **The Cuban Missile Crisis: A Tale of Two Leadership Styles and Conflict Management**
- **The Heroic Stand at Thermopylae: Sparta's Last Stand**

In this chapter readers will step into a world where discipline reigns as the heart of effective leadership. Imagine a leader standing firm amid chaos, calmly charting a course through turbulent waters. This chapter unfolds stories of such leaders—individuals who didn't just dream of success but disciplined themselves to achieve it.

As we turn the pages, the narrative draws you in with the gripping tale of 'Neutron Jack' Welch, whose leadership at General Electric transformed a struggling company into a powerhouse. Picture him, unyielding and focused, making tough decisions that would shape the company's future. His story illustrates that discipline is not just about following rules but about making intentional choices that lead to remarkable outcomes.

Then, we journey back to the epic battlefield of Thermopylae. Imagine the brave Spartans, standing shoulder to shoulder, their resolve unwavering as they face insurmountable odds. Their heroic stand is a testament to disciplined focus and collective strength, proving that when leaders commit wholeheartedly, they can inspire their teams to achieve the seemingly impossible.

We also delve into the high-stakes drama of the Cuban Missile Crisis, where leaders like John F. Kennedy navigated intense pressure with clarity and purpose. Visualize the tension in the air as decisions were made that would impact millions. Here, discipline and strategic focus emerged as the guiding lights, demonstrating how effective leaders remain calm and resolute in the face of challenges.

Throughout the chapter, readers will find not just lessons but vivid illustrations of what it means to lead with discipline. Each story inspires, urging you to reflect on your own journey. What can you learn from these leaders? How can you cultivate a disciplined approach in your own life?

By the end of this chapter, you will not only grasp the concept of disciplined leadership but also feel a renewed sense of purpose. You will be ready to apply these insights, transforming your aspirations into reality through focused action. Let this chapter be a source of inspiration, guiding you to embrace the discipline that leads to excellence.

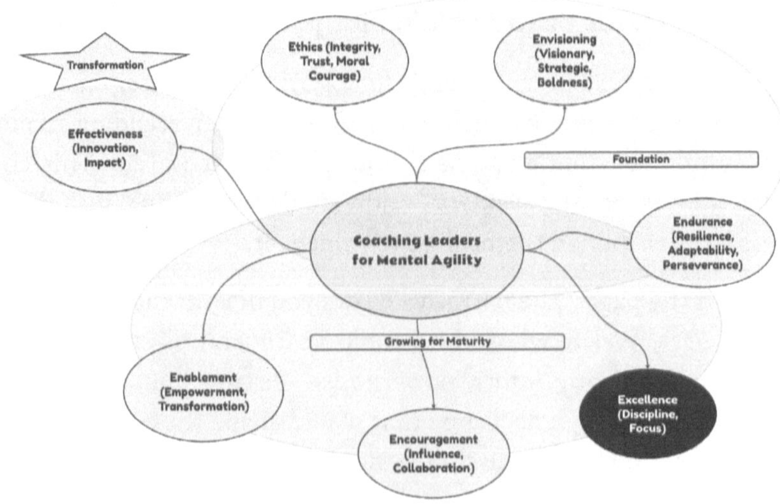

Coaching Leaders for Mental Agility: Story No 22

The Power of Discipline: The Cornerstone of Effective Leadership

> **"Discipline is choosing between what you want now and what you want most."**
>
> **– Abraham Lincoln**

Discipline is indeed the bedrock upon which leadership is built.

It's the unwavering commitment to a course of action, even in the face of challenges or distractions.

Building great discipline is challenging because it requires consistent effort, self-control, and the ability to prioritize long-term goals over immediate gratification.

Discipline often involves going against our natural tendencies for comfort, ease, and pleasure, making it a difficult but essential trait for effective leadership.

Why It's Difficult to Build Great Discipline

Humans naturally gravitate toward short-term pleasures, seeking immediate rewards over distant gains. Our brains are wired to prefer instant gratification, making it tough to resist urges that bring comfort in the moment. Discipline, however, asks us to go against this instinct. It requires us to step out of the routines where we feel safe and comfortable and into the unknown, even when it feels unsettling. True discipline is about challenging these deep-set tendencies and training ourselves to focus on long-term goals, even when the short-term rewards seem more tempting.

Consistency is the real test of discipline. It's not about one strong effort but about staying dedicated day after day, especially when the initial burst of motivation fades away. The toughest moments come when progress feels slow or when unexpected setbacks shake your resolve. It's easy to feel discouraged, but real discipline shines in those moments, pushing through failure and disappointment. It's about staying focused and committed, even when the journey becomes uncertain and the road ahead looks rough.

In a world filled with distractions, staying disciplined has never been harder. Social media, entertainment, and endless information constantly pull attention away from goals. But the distractions don't just come from outside—there are also the inner struggles. Doubts, fears, and the temptation to procrastinate can quietly sabotage the determination to stay on track. Acknowledging these distractions and inner conflicts is the first step toward overcoming them, recognizing that staying focused requires constant awareness and effort.

Sacrifice is at the heart of discipline. To build true discipline, we often have to give up immediate pleasures, trading short-term comforts for long-term achievements. This isn't easy, mentally, or emotionally. Leaders, in particular, face the challenge of balancing multiple responsibilities, which can make it difficult to maintain focus in one area without neglecting others. Discipline is about finding that balance, making the tough sacrifices while keeping your eye on the bigger picture.

Throughout history, many leaders have demonstrated discipline as a core component of their leadership, helping them to achieve remarkable success and become strong, effective leaders.

Here are some examples:

1. Mahatma Gandhi:

Gandhi's disciplined approach to non-violence and civil disobedience played a crucial role in India's struggle for independence from British rule. His strict adherence to principles like truth (Satya) and non-violence (Ahimsa) required immense self-discipline. Gandhi's personal life reflected this discipline as well; he maintained a simple lifestyle, followed a strict diet, and practiced regular fasting. His discipline inspired millions to join the independence movement, making him a powerful leader.

2. Winston Churchill:

During World War II, Winston Churchill's disciplined leadership was pivotal in guiding Britain through its darkest hours. Churchill was known for his rigorous daily routines, which included reading, writing, and strategic planning. His disciplined communication style, exemplified by his powerful speeches, helped to boost British morale, and maintain public confidence in the face of adversity. Churchill's ability to remain focused and resilient, even during setbacks like the Dunkirk evacuation, demonstrated his strong leadership.

3. Nelson Mandela:

Nelson Mandela's discipline was evident during his 27 years of imprisonment, where he remained steadfast in his fight against apartheid in South Africa. Despite harsh conditions, Mandela maintained a disciplined routine, educating himself and others, and never wavering in his commitment to justice and equality. His disciplined leadership ultimately paved the way for a peaceful transition to democracy in South Africa and earned him global admiration.

4. George Washington:

As the first President of the United States and the leader of the Continental Army during the American Revolution, George Washington exhibited remarkable discipline. Washington was known for his strict adherence to military discipline, which helped him maintain a cohesive and effective army despite numerous challenges. His disciplined leadership was also evident in his decision to step down after two terms as President, setting a precedent for the peaceful transfer of power and establishing the importance of democratic principles.

5. Margaret Thatcher:

Margaret Thatcher, the first female Prime Minister of the United Kingdom, was known for her disciplined approach to governance. Often referred to as the "Iron Lady," Thatcher maintained strict fiscal discipline, implementing policies that reduced government spending and curbed inflation. Her disciplined leadership style was characterized by a strong work ethic, meticulous preparation, and an unwavering commitment to her political beliefs, which enabled her to implement significant and lasting reforms in the UK.

6. Abraham Lincoln:

Abraham Lincoln's disciplined leadership during the American Civil War was crucial in preserving the Union and ending slavery. Lincoln was known for his thoughtful decision-making process, his ability to remain calm under pressure, and his disciplined approach to leadership. Despite facing immense criticism and personal tragedy, Lincoln remained focused on his goal of preserving the nation. His discipline in communication, especially through his speeches and letters, helped to articulate the moral purpose of the war and unite the country.

7. Julius Caesar:

Julius Caesar's disciplined military leadership was key to his success as one of Rome's greatest generals. His discipline extended to his strategic planning, rigorous training of his troops, and his ability to maintain strict control over his army. Caesar's disciplined approach allowed him to conquer vast territories and ultimately seize power in Rome. His leadership, though controversial, reshaped the Roman Republic and left a lasting legacy in history.

8. Queen Elizabeth I:

Queen Elizabeth, I demonstrated remarkable discipline in her leadership during a time of religious and political turmoil in England. Her disciplined approach to governance, diplomacy, and military strategy helped to stabilize the country and establish it as a major European power. Elizabeth's discipline in personal matters, including her decision to remain unmarried (the "Virgin Queen"), was part of her strategy to maintain control over her throne and avoid foreign influence. Her leadership style balanced firmness with political acumen, enabling her to navigate complex challenges and leave a strong legacy.

9. Alexander the Great:

Alexander the Great's disciplined leadership was evident in his military conquests, where he led his armies through difficult terrains and against formidable enemies. His rigorous training and preparation of his troops, along with his own personal discipline in studying various cultures and military tactics, allowed him to create one of the largest empires in history. Alexander's discipline in maintaining strong ties with his soldiers and managing logistics across vast distances was crucial to his success.

10. Martin Luther King Jr.:

Martin Luther King Jr. demonstrated extraordinary discipline in his leadership of the Civil Rights Movement in the United States. His commitment to non-violent protest, despite facing violence and hostility, required immense self-discipline. King's disciplined approach to organizing marches, delivering speeches, and negotiating with political leaders helped to advance the cause of racial equality. His disciplined communication, especially his famous "I Have a Dream" speech, inspired millions and remains a powerful symbol of the movement.

These historical leaders exemplify how discipline can be a key component of effective leadership, enabling leaders to achieve their goals, inspire others, and leave a lasting impact.

The leaders mentioned, built, and maintained strict discipline through a combination of personal values, experiences, and deliberate practices.

Here's how they did it:

1. Mahatma Gandhi

Mahatma Gandhi was a remarkable leader. He believed in truth and non-violence. These beliefs guided everything he did.

Gandhi had a strict daily routine. He would wake up very early, pray, fast, and think deeply about himself. He also ate simple food and lived a simple life. This helped him become mentally and physically strong.

Gandhi's experiences with injustice in South Africa and India made him even more determined to be disciplined. He knew that if he wanted to fight for civil rights and independence, he needed to be strong and focused.

2. Winston Churchill

Churchill was renowned for his strict daily routine, which involved reading, writing, and strategic planning. His disciplined approach to managing his time helped him remain productive and focused, especially during the war.

Even in the face of setbacks, like the evacuation at Dunkirk, Churchill's ability to stay disciplined was driven by his belief in the importance of perseverance and keeping public morale high.

Churchill's thorough study of history and military strategy gave him the knowledge and confidence needed to lead effectively during World War II. His preparation was key to his successful leadership.

3. Nelson Mandela

Nelson Mandela's 27 years in prison were a profound test of his discipline. During this time, he focused on studying, exercising, and maintaining a strong sense of purpose. His ability to stay disciplined under such harsh conditions was essential for his leadership later on.

Mandela's dedication to justice and equality was the driving force behind his discipline. He had a clear vision of a democratic South Africa, which kept him focused and motivated despite the numerous challenges he faced.

His discipline was also shown through his strategic patience. Mandela knew when to negotiate and when to stand firm, demonstrating exceptional self-control and strategic thinking in his decisions.

4. George Washington

George Washington's early military experiences instilled in him a strong sense of discipline, which he carried into his leadership of the Continental Army. He placed great importance on maintaining order, rigorous training, and high morale among his troops.

Washington's discipline was also driven by a profound sense of duty to the emerging nation. He believed in leading by example, upholding a strict code of conduct for both himself and his soldiers.

His disciplined commitment to democratic principles was further evident when he chose to step down after serving two terms as President. This decision set a lasting precedent and reflected his dedication to the ideals of democracy and leadership.

5. Margaret Thatcher

Margaret Thatcher's disciplined leadership was rooted in her strong work ethic. She was known for her meticulous preparation and deep understanding of the issues she addressed, reflecting her belief in the value of hard work.

Her discipline was also fueled by a clear vision for Britain's future. Thatcher's steadfast commitment to her economic and political beliefs helped her remain focused, even when facing significant opposition.

Thatcher's resilience was a crucial aspect of her leadership. Her ability to stay disciplined despite criticism and political challenges showcased her determination and what many described as her "iron will."

6. Abraham Lincoln

Abraham Lincoln was largely self-taught, and his disciplined study habits were crucial in shaping his leadership. He dedicated hours to reading, writing, and reflecting on law and governance, which provided him with a solid intellectual foundation.

Lincoln's discipline was deeply rooted in his strong moral convictions. His commitment to preserving the Union and ending slavery demonstrated his ability to maintain focus and composure under intense pressure, reflecting his disciplined character.

His approach to decision-making was also marked by discipline. Lincoln carefully considered diverse perspectives and weighed his options thoughtfully, which was essential for navigating the complex political landscape of the Civil War.

7. Julius Caesar

Julius Caesar's military training and experience instilled in him a strong sense of discipline, which he expected from his soldiers as well. This strict discipline played a significant role in his numerous military victories.

His disciplined approach to strategy and logistics was crucial for managing large-scale military campaigns across vast territories. Caesar's ability to think ahead and plan meticulously was a key factor in his effective leadership.

On a personal level, Caesar also maintained discipline in his conduct and decision-making. This self-discipline helped him navigate the political complexities of Rome and ultimately rise to power.

8. Queen Elizabeth I

Queen Elizabeth's disciplined approach to leadership was greatly influenced by her education. She was fluent in several languages and knowledgeable in literature and history, which prepared her to lead effectively.

Her ability to manage crises, such as the threat from the Spanish Armada, showed her calmness and focus under pressure. Elizabeth's disciplined response to such challenges highlighted her skill in navigating difficult situations.

In diplomacy and statecraft, Elizabeth's disciplined approach was crucial for building and maintaining alliances. These strategic partnerships were vital for England's security and prosperity during her reign.

9. Alexander the Great

Alexander the Great's disciplined military training began early in his life, preparing him to lead his armies through challenging campaigns. His personal dedication to studying different cultures and military tactics further strengthened his leadership.

He exemplified discipline by leading his troops through difficult conditions, sharing in their hardships. This approach earned him their loyalty and respect.

Alexander's relentless pursuit of his vision to build a vast empire drove him to push beyond conventional limits. His disciplined focus on this goal inspired his followers to strive for extraordinary achievements as well.

10. Martin Luther King Jr.

Martin Luther King Jr.'s disciplined commitment to non-violence was a cornerstone of his leadership in the Civil Rights Movement. Despite facing violent opposition, he remained steadfast in his dedication to peaceful methods, guided by his deep religious convictions and moral beliefs.

His disciplined approach to organizing protests, marches, and negotiations was crucial for the movement's success. King placed a strong emphasis on preparation, training, and coordination among participants, ensuring that each event was well-organized and impactful.

Even in the face of numerous setbacks, King's ability to remain focused on the long-term goals of the movement showcased his disciplined leadership. His resilience and unwavering commitment inspired others to persist in the struggle for civil rights.

These leaders built their discipline through a combination of personal values, experiences, education, and deliberate practices.

Their disciplined approaches to leadership not only helped them achieve their goals but also left lasting legacies.

Discipline is not just a personal trait; it's a cornerstone of effective leadership. It enables leaders to lead with consistency, uphold integrity, and achieve effectiveness in their roles.

By cultivating discipline in their own lives, leaders can inspire and empower others to do the same, creating a ripple effect that enhances the entire organization's performance and culture.

Discipline is a muscle that needs to be exercised regularly. Here are some activities to help you build it:

Setting clear goals and tracking your progress can make a big difference in reaching your dreams. It's important to define your goals specifically, breaking them into smaller, manageable steps that guide you forward. As you make progress, take the time to regularly check in on how you're doing. This not only keeps you motivated but also helps you stay focused on what needs to be done next. When you hit those small milestones, don't forget to celebrate. Rewarding yourself for these little wins reinforces the positive momentum and reminds you how far you've come.

Building mental resilience is equally crucial. By constantly pushing yourself beyond your comfort zone, you strengthen your ability to handle challenges. When you encounter setbacks, view them as opportunities to grow and learn rather than obstacles. Every failure offers a lesson. Along the way, positive self-talk can be a powerful tool. Encouraging yourself through affirmations helps boost your self-confidence and keeps you in a growth mindset.

Lastly, having the support of others plays a significant role in staying motivated. An accountability partner—someone who shares your vision and supports your journey—can help you stay on track. Joining groups with like-minded individuals can further fuel your drive, surrounding you with people who encourage your efforts and share in your successes.

> **"Discipline is the bridge between goals and accomplishment."**
>
> **– Jim Rohn**

Top Key Takeaways on Discipline in Leadership

- **Foundation of Leadership**: Discipline is crucial for effective leadership, requiring unwavering commitment to goals despite challenges and distractions.
- **Long-Term Focus Over Immediate Gratification**: True discipline involves resisting the urge for short-term rewards and prioritizing long-term goals, pushing through discomfort and self-doubt.
- **Continuous Effort and Consistency**: Building discipline demands ongoing dedication and resilience, particularly during setbacks or when motivation wanes; it's about maintaining focus over time.
- **Navigating Distractions**: Leaders must recognize and combat both external distractions (like social media) and internal conflicts (like procrastination) to remain disciplined in pursuing their goals.
- **Historical Examples of Discipline**: Prominent leaders like Mahatma Gandhi, Nelson Mandela, and Winston Churchill exemplified discipline in their pursuits, showcasing how this trait can lead to remarkable achievements and inspire others.

Coaching Leaders for Mental Agility: Story No 23

The Alloy of Leadership: Forging Strength from Essential Qualities

> **"A gem cannot be polished without friction, nor a man perfected without trials."**
>
> **– Seneca**

The human body is made up of elements that are found abundantly in the Earth.

About 99% of the human body is composed of six elements: oxygen, carbon, hydrogen, nitrogen, calcium, and phosphorus.

These elements are the building blocks of the molecules that make up our cells, tissues, and organs.

The elements in our bodies originated from the Earth and, ultimately, from the cosmos.

After the Big Bang, stars formed and eventually exploded in supernovae, creating heavier elements.

These elements were spread throughout the universe and eventually became part of planets, including Earth.

Material Leadership?

Material leadership is built from a combination of qualities, skills, and values that form the foundation of effective leadership.

These "materials" can be thought of as the core components or elements that define and shape a leader's ability to guide, inspire, and influence others.

Here's what leadership is "made of":

1. Vision and Purpose:

A leader needs to have a clear and inspiring vision for the future. This vision acts as a guide, showing the direction and giving the organization or group a sense of purpose.

Leaders are also motivated by a deep sense of purpose. This drives them to pursue meaningful and impactful goals, inspiring others to follow their lead and work towards a shared mission.

2. Integrity and Ethics:

Integrity is the foundation of strong leadership. Leaders must be honest, transparent, and consistent in everything they do, as this builds trust with their followers.

When faced with tough decisions, leaders need to rely on strong ethical principles. Making fair and just choices is essential for maintaining credibility and ensuring the well-being of their team or organization.

3. Empathy and Emotional Intelligence:

Empathy is key for leaders, as it helps them understand the needs, feelings, and viewpoints of others. This understanding builds strong relationships and creates a supportive environment.

Emotional intelligence is also essential. A leader's ability to control their own emotions and respond thoughtfully to the emotions of others is crucial for leading effectively and maintaining harmony within the team.

4. Courage and Resilience:

Leaders need to be willing to take calculated risks and make bold decisions, even when facing uncertainty or resistance. It's often these daring choices that lead to growth and success.

Resilience is equally important. The ability to bounce back from setbacks, adapt to new challenges, and keep pushing forward is crucial for achieving long-term success and overcoming obstacles along the way.

5. Communication and Influence:

Effective leaders know that clear communication is essential to success. Imagine a team gathered around a table, eager to start a project. The leader stands confidently at the front, sharing a vision that inspires everyone. As they speak, the team members nod in agreement, fully understanding the goals and expectations laid out before them. The clarity of the leader's words creates a sense of alignment, making each person feel included in the journey ahead. They leave the meeting feeling motivated, ready to contribute their best efforts toward a common purpose.

But clear communication is just the beginning. Leadership also requires the ability to influence and persuade others. Picture a situation where the leader must encourage the team to embrace a new idea. They don't just tell everyone what to do; instead, they share compelling stories and examples that resonate deeply. With enthusiasm and passion, the leader inspires the team to see the potential in the new approach. The team members begin to feel a sense of ownership over the idea, realizing that their contributions can make a real difference.

Through these actions, the leader demonstrates how effective communication, and the art of persuasion can bring a team together, igniting their passion and commitment. By clearly articulating their vision and influencing others with genuine inspiration, they create an environment where everyone is eager to take action and achieve great things together.

6. Accountability and Responsibility:

Leaders stand by the decisions they make, fully owning both the triumphs and the setbacks. They don't shy away from responsibility, showing maturity by embracing their role in every outcome. This accountability not only builds trust but also sets the tone for how a leader operates—reliable, grounded, and focused on growth.

But it's not just about personal accountability; great leaders ensure that their teams also take ownership of their responsibilities. By holding others accountable, they cultivate a culture where each member feels responsible for their role and is motivated to perform at their best. This creates an environment of trust, responsibility, and high performance, where everyone is committed to the collective success.

7. Adaptability and Innovation:

Leaders need to be flexible, able to adjust to changing situations, and open to new ideas and ways of doing things. This adaptability helps them navigate challenges and stay effective in a constantly evolving world.

They also encourage innovation by creating an environment where creativity can flourish. Great leaders inspire their teams to experiment, take risks, and continuously look for ways to improve and grow.

8. Collaboration and Team Building:

Leaders know the value of teamwork and focus on building strong, united teams that work well together to reach shared goals. They foster an environment where collaboration is key to success.

Effective leaders also empower their team members by giving them the freedom and support they need to succeed. They trust their team, allowing individuals to grow and perform at their best.

9. Visionary Thinking and Strategic Planning:

Leaders possess a strategic mindset, always planning for the long term and preparing for future challenges and opportunities. They think ahead and make decisions with the bigger picture in mind.

In addition, visionary leaders have the ability to inspire others by painting a clear and compelling vision of the future. They motivate people to work together towards achieving shared goals and aspirations.

10. Commitment and Dedication:

Leaders are deeply passionate about their mission or the organization they lead. Their strong commitment and dedication naturally inspire others to stay motivated and give their best efforts.

By leading through example, leaders set the standard for hard work and dedication. They serve as role models, showing others what it means to be truly committed to a cause or goal.

Drawing an analogy between the composition of leadership qualities and material science or metals helps to illustrate

how various elements combine to create strong, resilient, and effective leadership.

Here's how you can compare leadership qualities to different materials or metals:

1. **Vision and Purpose: Titanium**

Titanium is known for its strength and lightness, much like how a clear vision and strong purpose give direction and durability to leadership. Titanium's ability to withstand high stress without deforming is akin to how a strong vision provides stability and guides leaders through challenges.

2. **Integrity and Ethics: Gold**

Gold is a symbol of purity and value. It represents integrity and ethics in leadership. Just as gold does not tarnish and remains stable over time, a leader's integrity and ethical foundation should remain steadfast and unblemished, earning lasting trust and respect.

3. **Empathy and Emotional Intelligence: Copper**

Copper is highly conductive, symbolizing the way empathy and emotional intelligence allow a leader to connect and communicate effectively with others. Copper's flexibility and malleability represent the adaptability and understanding required to manage diverse emotions and perspectives in a team.

4. **Courage and Resilience: Steel**

Steel is a strong and resilient alloy, known for its toughness and ability to withstand pressure, similar to the courage and resilience leaders need to face challenges and bounce back from setbacks. Just as steel can be tempered to become even stronger, a leader's resilience can be strengthened through experience and challenges.

5. **Communication and Influence: Aluminum**

Aluminum is lightweight and versatile, representing the ease and adaptability of effective communication. Its widespread use in various industries highlights its importance, just as clear communication is essential in every aspect of leadership. Aluminum's reflective properties can also symbolize how effective leaders reflect and amplify the needs and voices of their followers.

6. Accountability and Responsibility: Iron

Iron is a fundamental building block in construction, much like how accountability and responsibility are foundational to leadership. Iron's strength and reliability represent how leaders must be strong and dependable, taking responsibility for their actions and decisions, much like iron's role in providing structural integrity.

7. Adaptability and Innovation: Nickel

Nickel is known for its ability to resist corrosion and its role in creating stainless steel, symbolizing adaptability, and innovation in leadership. Just as nickel prevents deterioration and enhances the durability of metals, a leader's adaptability and innovative mindset help them thrive in changing environments and protect their team from stagnation.

8. Collaboration and Team Building: Bronze

Bronze is an alloy made from copper and tin, symbolizing collaboration, and teamwork. Just as bronze combines different elements to create a stronger material, effective leadership is about blending different skills and perspectives to build a cohesive and resilient team.

9. Visionary Thinking and Strategic Planning: Platinum

Platinum is rare, valuable, and resistant to wear, much like visionary thinking and strategic planning in leadership. Just as platinum is used in high-precision applications, visionary leaders use strategic planning to navigate complex challenges and guide their organizations toward long-term success.

10. Commitment and Dedication: Tungsten

Tungsten is known for its incredible hardness and highest melting point among metals, symbolizing commitment, and dedication in leadership. Just as tungsten maintains its integrity under extreme conditions, a leader's dedication remains unwavering, inspiring others through their consistent effort and passion.

Here are historical leaders who exemplify the metal leadership analogy:

Throughout history, leaders have emerged, each leaving a unique mark on the world. Among them, George Washington stands out as a figure of unwavering strength and reliability. As the first President of the United States, he played a crucial role during the American Revolutionary War, demonstrating steadfast leadership. His commitment to establishing a new nation was as foundational as iron is in construction, symbolizing the solid groundwork upon which America was built.

Winston Churchill, the iconic British leader during World War II, displayed remarkable resilience and courage. In the face of adversity, he inspired the nation, guiding Britain through its darkest hours. His strength, much like steel, showcased the durability and toughness required to lead during times of crisis, reminding us that true leadership often shines brightest in the most challenging moments.

Nelson Mandela's journey towards ending apartheid in South Africa exemplifies visionary thinking and strategic planning. His leadership was characterized by a rare ability to see beyond division, guiding the nation toward unity and equality. Just as platinum is valued for its rarity, Mandela's vision for a reconciled South Africa highlighted the profound impact of visionary leadership.

Mahatma Gandhi's influence was rooted in empathy and emotional intelligence. He connected deeply with people, inspiring them through his philosophy of nonviolent resistance. His understanding of human emotions and ability to mobilize support reflect the adaptability of copper, showcasing the importance of empathy in effective leadership.

Margaret Thatcher, known as the "Iron Lady," exemplified commitment and dedication throughout her tenure as the UK's Prime Minister. Her leadership during significant economic reforms mirrored tungsten's hardness and high melting point. Her steadfastness in her policies set a strong example of what it means to be dedicated to one's vision, even in the face of opposition.

Abraham Lincoln, the 16th President of the United States, is celebrated for his integrity and commitment to justice. His leadership during the

Civil War and his efforts to abolish slavery resonate with the purity and value of gold. Lincoln's unwavering ethical stance showcased the importance of integrity in leadership, reminding us that true leaders uphold their values, even amidst turmoil.

Steve Jobs, the co-founder of Apple Inc., embodied adaptability, and innovation. He transformed technology and business models, much like nickel enhances alloys. His visionary approach revolutionized industries, illustrating how adaptability can lead to groundbreaking advancements.

Catherine the Great of Russia demonstrated effective collaboration and team-building skills. By integrating various influences and advisors, she strengthened her reign, much like bronze combines copper and tin to create a more robust material. Her leadership highlighted the power of collaboration in achieving greater outcomes.

Franklin D. Roosevelt skillfully used radio addresses to communicate directly with the American public. His "Fireside Chats" showcased his ability to connect and influence people, reflecting the versatility and reach of aluminum. Roosevelt's effective communication bridged the gap between leadership and the citizens, fostering a sense of unity during challenging times.

Indira Gandhi, the Prime Minister of India, exemplified vision, and purpose in her leadership. Her strong stance on national issues and her efforts to modernize India demonstrated resilience in the face of challenges. Gandhi's leadership was characterized by a profound sense of purpose, akin to titanium's strength, leaving a lasting impact on the nation she served.

These leaders not only faced their challenges but also inspired countless others through their actions. Their stories remind us that true leadership is marked by strength, resilience, empathy, and a commitment to a greater purpose, urging us to reflect on our own paths as we strive to make a difference in the world.

These leaders exemplify various qualities that align with the metals mentioned, showcasing how different traits contribute to effective and impactful leadership.

> **"Strength does not come from physical capacity. It comes from an indomitable will."**
>
> **– Mahatma Gandhi**

Top Key Takeaways on Leadership Qualities

- **Core Elements of Leadership**: Effective leadership is built on foundational qualities such as vision, integrity, empathy, courage, and communication, much like the essential elements that make up the human body.
- **Vision and Purpose**: A clear and inspiring vision serves as a guiding force for leaders, providing direction and motivating others to pursue meaningful goals.
- **Integrity and Accountability**: Integrity forms the bedrock of trust in leadership. Leaders must take responsibility for their actions and decisions, fostering a culture of accountability within their teams.
- **Empathy and Emotional Intelligence**: Understanding the needs and emotions of others is crucial for building strong relationships and creating a supportive environment, enabling leaders to respond effectively to their team's dynamics.
- **Adaptability and Innovation**: Leaders must be flexible and open to new ideas, encouraging innovation while navigating changing circumstances. This adaptability is essential for sustained success in a rapidly evolving world.

Coaching Leaders for Mental Agility: Story No 24

The Desert Fox's Strategies for Success

> **"Courage which goes against military expediency is stupidity, or, if it is insisted upon by a commander, irresponsibility."**
>
> **- Erwin Rommel**

Erwin Rommel, the "Desert Fox," was a fascinating and controversial figure in World War II.

His leadership style is often studied for its unique blend of strengths and weaknesses.

Erwin Rommel earned the nickname "Desert Fox" for several reasons, all related to his leadership and actions during the North African Campaign of World War II. **Here's is why?**

- **Cunning and Resourcefulness:** Like a fox, Rommel was known for his cunning and resourcefulness in the harsh desert environment. He excelled at exploiting weaknesses in enemy defenses and using his limited resources strategically, such as his "Ghost Division" bluff.
- **Surprise Attacks and Maneuvers:** Similar to a fox hunting its prey, Rommel was a master of surprise attacks and outmaneuvering his opponents. He often launched unexpected offensives, keeping the Allies off guard, and disrupting their plans.
- **Adaptability and Survival Instincts:** Foxes are known for their ability to adapt to their environment and survive in challenging conditions. Rommel displayed this same adaptability, adjusting his tactics to the desert terrain and changing circumstances on the battlefield.
- **Media Portrayal:** The Nazi propaganda machine heavily promoted Rommel's image as the "Desert Fox," portraying him as a brilliant and daring leader against all odds. This nickname stuck and became widely used by both Allied and Axis forces.

The "Desert Fox" moniker highlights Rommel's impressive skills in desert warfare, particularly his surprise tactics, resourcefulness, and adaptability.

In the heart of the North African desert during World War II, a remarkable leader named Erwin Rommel emerged, showcasing the essence of leadership under immense pressure. The Siege of Tobruk in 1941 became a defining moment, where Rommel faced relentless challenges. The scorching sun beat down on his troops, and the constant sound of combat filled the air. Yet, amidst this turmoil, Rommel stood firm at the frontlines, rallying his men with his unwavering spirit. He motivated his troops, reminding them of their strength, even when the odds seemed insurmountable. His determination to keep the fighting spirit alive, despite not capturing Tobruk, illustrated a profound mental resilience that inspired his soldiers.

The following year, in 1942, Rommel faced a daunting enemy force in North Africa. Instead of succumbing to despair, he crafted a brilliant deception known as the "Ghost Division" bluff. He skillfully maneuvered his limited panzer divisions to create the illusion of a much larger army, fooling the Allies into believing they were outnumbered. This bold move required not just strategic acumen but an incredible focus and composure under pressure. It was a testament to his ability to think creatively in the face of overwhelming odds, embodying the essence of tactical leadership.

As the tides of war shifted, Rommel found himself retreating from the Battle of El Alamein in 1942. His forces had initially tasted victory in North Africa, but now they faced a relentless push from the Allies. Even in the face of adversity, Rommel displayed remarkable grit and determination. He led a disciplined fighting retreat, prioritizing the safety of his men while inflicting damage on the advancing Allies. This strategic thinking, combined with his resilience, showcased his ability to turn defeat into a calculated retreat rather than a rout, demonstrating his skill as a leader who could adapt to changing circumstances.

The desert itself was a harsh and unforgiving environment, testing the mettle of every soldier. Rommel understood the importance of morale and shared the hardships with his troops. He often visited the frontlines, not as a distant commander but as a leader who endured the same struggles as his men. His presence inspired loyalty and camaraderie, helping to maintain their fighting spirit even amid brutal conditions.

Rommel's leadership was not set in stone; it evolved with the war. He began with aggressive tactics, pushing his forces forward with vigor, but as the landscape shifted, he recognized the need for a more defensive approach. This adaptability required a keen mind, capable of analyzing the changing battlefield and adjusting strategies accordingly. His willingness to pivot and adapt illustrated a profound understanding of the complexities of warfare, reinforcing his reputation as a formidable commander.

Through these moments of pressure, deception, grit, and adaptability, Rommel's legacy as a leader shines. His story serves as a powerful reminder of what it means to lead with courage and creativity, even in the darkest of times. In the face of adversity, Rommel's ability to inspire and navigate challenges left an indelible mark on history, offering lessons in leadership that continue to resonate today.

Here are some specific incidents that showcase both the strengths and weaknesses of Erwin Rommel's leadership:

In 1941, Rommel made a bold move during the Siege of Tobruk, defying direct orders to stay defensive. Instead, he launched a surprise attack on British forces in Libya, catching them off guard and nearly seizing the crucial port city. His audacity pushed the British back, though the advance eventually faltered due to logistical challenges and an inability to secure a decisive victory.

In the Battle of France in 1940, Rommel led the charge at the head of the 7th Panzer Division, commanding with relentless energy and presence. As the German blitzkrieg swept through France, Rommel's personal leadership on the front lines inspired his troops, raising their morale and significantly contributing to the swift victory.

Rommel's tactical brilliance shone in 1942 with the so-called "Ghost Division" in North Africa. Facing a larger Allied force, he strategically manipulated his limited resources, constantly shifting his panzer divisions to create the illusion of a much larger army. This clever deception stalled the Allied advance and bought him critical time.

Later that year, after his initial success in North Africa, Rommel found himself in retreat following the Battle of El Alamein. Forced to withdraw eastward due to overwhelming Allied forces, he displayed adaptability by leading a fighting retreat, reducing German losses while inflicting heavy casualties on the pursuing enemy.

However, Rommel's boldness sometimes crossed into overconfidence. In the Battle of Gazala in 1942, emboldened by his early victories, Rommel underestimated the strength of the British Eighth Army. Despite warnings from his own commanders, he launched an all-out offensive, which resulted in a costly defeat.

While Rommel's battlefield tactics were often brilliant, he lacked broader strategic vision. During the Nazi invasion of the Soviet Union in 1941, he initially opposed Hitler's decision but once involved, became solely focused on his own campaign without considering the larger war effort.

His strong-willed independence also led to friction with superiors. In 1943, after criticizing Hitler's unrealistic expectations and retreating from El Alamein, Rommel was removed from his command in North Africa. His outspoken nature clashed with Hitler's authoritarian control, showing the limits of his influence within the Nazi power structure.

While Rommel is often portrayed as a leader who treated Allied prisoners of war with compassion, his legacy is clouded by his association with the Nazi regime. Evidence suggests that he was aware of the killing of Jewish civilians in North Africa, yet he did nothing to oppose these atrocities, leaving his ethics open to question.

Learning from Rommel's Leadership:

- **Importance of Initiative and Inspiration:** Rommel demonstrates the critical role of bold leadership in motivating and inspiring troops.
- **The Dangers of Overconfidence:** His mistakes highlight the importance of strategic thinking and avoiding overestimating one's capabilities.
- **Balancing Tactics with Strategy:** Leaders need to excel at both battlefield tactics and understanding the bigger picture to achieve long-term success.
- **The Importance of Ethics:** Leadership must be coupled with ethical principles, especially in wartime situations.

Erwin Rommel's upbringing and circumstances likely played a significant role in shaping his leadership style. While these factors contributed to his strengths like tactical brilliance and the ability to motivate troops, they may also have contributed to his weaknesses like overconfidence and a lack of strategic vision.

Rommel grew up in a family with a deep military tradition, surrounded by a legacy of officers. This environment instilled in him a strong sense of discipline, duty, and respect for authority, fueling his ambition to excel in the military. His strict upbringing shaped his character, giving him a powerful work ethic and the resilience to endure hardship—traits that later became crucial in his leadership.

From a young age, Rommel was drawn to military history and strategy. His education placed heavy emphasis on battlefield tactics, sharpening his mind for strategic thinking and fostering his passion for military planning.

Rommel's experiences in World War I left a lasting impact. He witnessed the brutal realities of trench warfare, which may have driven his desire to develop innovative tactics that reduced casualties. However, these experiences also seem to have cultivated an aggressive approach, always seeking to break through stalemates and push forward with boldness.

His exceptional performance during the war earned him swift promotion, quickly rising through the ranks in the years that followed. This rapid ascent undoubtedly built his confidence, but it also laid the groundwork for the overconfidence that surfaced later in his career.

Rommel's rise to prominence was intertwined with the rise of the Nazi regime. Though not a fervent Nazi, he remained loyal and benefited from Hitler's favor, a connection that ultimately tarnished his legacy. His association with such a brutal dictatorship, despite his individual military brilliance, remains a shadow over his name.

How these factors might have contributed to his leadership:

- **Strengths:** His upbringing and experiences likely contributed to his strong work ethic, tactical brilliance, adaptability, and ability to motivate troops.

- **Weaknesses:** The strict hierarchy and focus on tactics might have instilled a lack of strategic vision and an underestimation of the broader picture. His rapid rise could have contributed to overconfidence and recklessness. His association with the Nazi regime remains a complex issue.

Here are five key messages from the text about Erwin Rommel and his leadership:

- **Cunning and Adaptability**: Rommel's ability to use resourcefulness and adaptability, particularly in the harsh desert environment, made him a formidable leader. His tactics, like surprise attacks and deceptive maneuvers, showcased his strategic brilliance.

- **Inspiring Leadership Under Pressure**: Rommel's personal presence on the frontlines and his motivational style helped boost the morale and loyalty of his troops, even under extreme conditions, demonstrating the importance of a leader's direct involvement.

- **Strategic Innovation**: Rommel's creativity and ability to think on his feet, such as the "Ghost Division" bluff, highlighted his tactical genius in facing overwhelming odds. This approach earned him respect and prolonged the fight despite limited resources.

- **Overconfidence and Missteps**: While Rommel's boldness often led to success, it also contributed to significant failures, such as underestimating the enemy at the Battle of Gazala. His overconfidence sometimes clouded his judgment, leading to costly defeats.

- **Ethics and Legacy**: Though Rommel was respected for his treatment of prisoners and battlefield conduct, his association with the Nazi regime and failure to oppose atrocities in North Africa cast a shadow over his legacy, emphasizing the importance of ethics in leadership.

Coaching Leaders for Mental Agility: Story No 25

Mastering Leadership: Discoveries from 'Neutron Jack!

Jack Welch's achievements as CEO of GE are significant.

He transformed the company into a global leader, increased profitability, and drove significant shareholder value.

However, his leadership style also had downsides, and some of his decisions may have had long-term consequences.

His most significant accomplishments:

Under Jack Welch's leadership, GE experienced extraordinary financial success. The company's stock price soared by more than 4,000%, an incredible growth that reflected the value he created for shareholders. Welch's strategies focused on increasing profitability by narrowing GE's focus to core businesses, streamlining operations, and selling off underperforming units. His ability to transform GE into a more efficient and profitable company was clear.

Welch also saw the importance of expanding globally. He pushed GE to become a truly international company, driving significant growth by tapping into new markets around the world. At the same time, he encouraged innovation, particularly in sectors like healthcare and aviation, helping GE maintain its competitive advantage.

One of Welch's most notable management practices was the "Work-Out" program. This initiative brought managers and employees together in a series of intense meetings where they openly discussed strategy, performance, and challenges. The program fostered transparency and improved problem-solving within the company.

However, it was the "Rank and Yank" system that caused the most controversy. By ranking employees on a bell curve and eliminating the bottom 10%, Welch aimed to create a high-performance culture, but this method also added pressure and tension among employees.

Welch was deeply committed to leadership development. He transformed GE's leadership program at Crotonville, focusing on finding and nurturing high-potential leaders to ensure a strong pipeline for the future.

Despite Welch's many successes, his leadership style faced criticism. The constant focus on performance, along with regular downsizing, may have created a stressful environment, hurt employee morale and increasing turnover. Some argued that his obsession with short-term results might have hindered long-term investments in research and development, potentially affecting GE's future after his departure.

Welch's personality was also a key factor in his leadership. His relentless drive for competition and excellence likely shaped GE's high-energy, competitive culture. His decisiveness allowed him to make quick, bold decisions that capitalized on opportunities and kept GE ahead of the competition.

Welch had a clear vision of GE's future as a global leader. His ability to see the bigger picture influenced his strategy, with a focus on core businesses and globalization that positioned GE for growth. Known for his direct communication style, Welch fostered a culture of openness and accountability, where employees knew what was expected and felt empowered to speak up.

But Welch's demanding nature also had downsides. The intense focus on performance created a high-pressure environment, with the "Rank and Yank" system possibly leading to fear and anxiety among employees. His short-term focus on results also raised concerns about whether GE neglected important long-term investments that could have been crucial for future innovation and success.

His leadership style, often referred to as "Neutron Jack" due to his focus on downsizing, emphasized several key areas:

Jack Welch's leadership at GE was marked by his bold approach to performance management. He introduced the "Rank and Yank" system, where employees were ranked on a curve, and the bottom 10% faced the risk of termination. This method pushed for high performance and fostered a culture of accountability, ensuring that only top performers remained. While this kept the bar high, it also created a sense of pressure among employees.

Welch's strategic focus was on simplifying GE's business. He streamlined the company by divesting underperforming units and honing in on core businesses where GE could dominate the market. This allowed the company to become more efficient and maintain its leadership in key sectors.

One of Welch's most defining contributions was his emphasis on speed and agility within the company. He believed in cutting through bureaucracy to encourage quick decision-making, which allowed GE to stay ahead in a rapidly changing business environment. His "Work-Out" program involved bringing managers and employees together to openly discuss strategies and challenges, fostering a culture of collaboration and ownership.

Welch also aimed to create a "boundaryless organization," where departments worked seamlessly across different units, breaking down silos and promoting teamwork.

Leadership development was a priority for Welch, and he revitalized GE's program at Crotonville to focus on grooming high-potential leaders. This emphasis on cultivating talent ensured a strong pipeline of future leadership.

Welch was quick to recognize the importance of global markets. He pushed GE to invest internationally, positioning the company for significant growth on the global stage.

However, Welch's leadership was not without its critics. The relentless focus on performance and downsizing created a high-pressure environment, potentially affecting employee morale and retention. Some argue that his pursuit of short-term results may have come at the expense of long-term innovation and investment, raising questions about the sustainability of his approach.

Overall, Jack Welch's leadership style left a lasting mark on management thinking. While his methods were not without criticism, his focus on performance, strategic clarity, cultural transformation, and leadership development continue to be relevant for businesses today.

Modern leaders often draw inspiration from Jack Welch's leadership style to navigate today's digital world. Some key concepts that are relevant include:

- **Visionary Leadership:** Like Welch, modern leaders focus on crafting a compelling vision for their organizations in the digital age. They articulate a clear direction for the future, leveraging technology to drive innovation and stay ahead of the competition.
- **Agile Decision-Making:** In the fast-paced digital environment, leaders must make decisions quickly and adapt to changing circumstances. Welch's decisive leadership style serves as a model for modern leaders who need to respond swiftly to market shifts and technological advancements.
- **Results Orientation:** Welch was known for his relentless focus on results, and modern leaders similarly prioritize outcomes in the digital era. They set clear goals and metrics for success, leveraging data analytics and performance management tools to track progress and drive performance.
- **Embrace of Change:** Welch was a proponent of change and encouraged a culture of continuous improvement at GE. Modern leaders recognize the importance of embracing change in the digital age, leveraging disruptive technologies and agile methodologies to drive innovation and transformation.
- **Empowerment and Collaboration:** Welch empowered employees to take ownership of their work and fostered a collaborative culture at GE. Modern leaders promote empowerment and collaboration in digital workplaces, leveraging technology to facilitate communication, collaboration, and knowledge sharing across teams and departments.
- **Customer-Centricity:** Welch emphasized the importance of understanding and meeting customer needs at GE. Modern leaders prioritize customer-centricity in the digital age, leveraging data and technology to gain insights into customer preferences and deliver personalized experiences that drive loyalty and satisfaction.

Coaching Leaders for Mental Agility: Story No 26

The Cuban Missile Crisis: A Tale of Two Leadership Styles and Conflict Management

> **"When written in Chinese, the word 'crisis' is composed of two characters—one represents danger and the other represents opportunity."**
>
> **-John F. Kennedy**

The Cuban Missile Crisis of 1962 stands as a pivotal moment in history, a tense standoff between the United States and the Soviet Union over Soviet missile deployments in Cuba.

The Cuban Missile Crisis offers a comprehensive look into various aspects of human psychology, from decision-making and communication to emotional intelligence and conflict resolution.

While the crisis ultimately ended peacefully, it showcased the contrasting leadership styles of **John F. Kennedy and Nikita Khrushchev**, and the delicate dance of conflict management during a nuclear standoff.

John F. Kennedy: Deliberative and Collaborative

As a young president facing one of the most dangerous international crises of his time, John F. Kennedy demonstrated a leadership style marked by deliberation and collaboration. When the Cuban Missile Crisis emerged in 1962, Kennedy gathered a diverse group of advisors known as the Executive Committee of the National Security Council (ExComm), composed of military officials, diplomats, and political experts. This team provided Kennedy with a range of perspectives, ensuring that no single view dominated the decision-making process.

In managing this high-stakes conflict, Kennedy promoted open dialogue within ExComm, welcoming differing opinions. Rather than rushing to action, he carefully considered all possible responses, including military invasion and diplomatic options. Ultimately, Kennedy decided on a strategic naval "quarantine" of Cuba to prevent further Soviet missiles from reaching the island. This decision reflected a balanced approach, seeking to avoid war while still addressing the threat.

Kennedy also prioritized communication, both with the American public and Soviet leader Nikita Khrushchev. Through televised addresses, he kept the nation informed of the situation, emphasizing the seriousness of the threat. At the same time, he maintained a direct line of communication with Khrushchev, using diplomatic channels to make his intentions clear and work toward de-escalation.

Nikita Khrushchev: Impulsive and Secretive

Khrushchev, the experienced Soviet leader, displayed a more impulsive and secretive style of leadership during the Cuban Missile Crisis. Unlike Kennedy, who encouraged open discussion and deliberation, Khrushchev made decisions without much consultation and kept his plans somewhat vague. This ambiguity added to the tension between the U.S. and the Soviet Union.

In terms of conflict management, Khrushchev handled the situation in a less collaborative manner. He initially downplayed the severity of the crisis and sent mixed signals, which only intensified the standoff with the U.S. His impulsive actions were in sharp contrast to Kennedy's more measured approach.

When it came to communication, Khrushchev's early messages to Kennedy were marked by threats and warnings, reflecting the escalating hostility. However, as the crisis reached its peak, he shifted his stance and ultimately agreed to withdraw the missiles from Cuba in exchange for a U.S. promise not to invade the island. Additionally, there was a secret deal to remove U.S. missiles from Turkey, signaling a more diplomatic resolution after days of intense standoff.

The Outcome: A Delicate Balance

The Cuban Missile Crisis highlights the importance of effective conflict management in leadership. While both Kennedy and Khrushchev made mistakes, Kennedy's willingness to listen to diverse perspectives, manage internal conflict within his team, and communicate clearly with the Soviets ultimately helped avert nuclear war.

Lessons Learned:

- **Collaboration and Open Communication:** The crisis underscored the value of collaboration and open communication in leadership, especially during times of crisis.
- **Considering Multiple Perspectives:** Leaders benefit from hearing dissenting voices and considering a range of options before taking action.
- **The Peril of Miscommunication:** Clear communication between leaders is crucial to avoid misunderstandings and escalation during a conflict.

The Cuban Missile Crisis remains a stark reminder of the consequences of poorly managed leadership conflict, particularly on the world stage. It showcases how leadership styles, communication strategies, and the ability to find common ground can have a profound impact on global security.

The Cuban Missile Crisis of 1962 presented a multitude of challenges for leaders on both sides, forcing them to make critical decisions under immense pressure.

Here's a breakdown of some key challenges faced by the leaders involved:

Challenges for John F. Kennedy (US):

The presence of Soviet nuclear missiles in Cuba created a serious military threat to the United States during the Cuban Missile Crisis. President Kennedy had to carefully weigh his options to prevent a potential nuclear attack, while at the same time avoiding any aggressive action that might lead to a broader war with the Soviet Union.

Domestically, Kennedy faced significant pressure from within the U.S. government and among the public to take a tougher approach. Many believed that a stronger stance was necessary to counter the Soviet threat, but Kennedy understood the risk of escalating tensions, so he had to find a more measured response.

In addition to external pressures, Kennedy also had to manage internal conflict within his administration. His advisors were divided on the best course of action, with some favoring military intervention and others advocating for diplomacy. Kennedy's challenge was to unite his team and select a strategy that had broad enough support to be successfully carried out.

Throughout the crisis, Kennedy also had to maintain public confidence. While the situation was incredibly tense and dangerous, he couldn't reveal all the sensitive details of the negotiations to the public. His ability to project calm and resolve helped reassure the American people, even as secret negotiations continued behind the scenes.

Challenges for Nikita Khrushchev (Soviet Union):

When the Soviet Union agreed to remove its missiles from Cuba during the Cuban Missile Crisis, it risked a loss of prestige on the world stage. Nikita Khrushchev, the Soviet leader, had to strike a balance between demonstrating Soviet strength and avoiding a direct military conflict with the United States. The withdrawal of the missiles could be viewed as a retreat, which could damage the image of Soviet power.

Within the Soviet Union, Khrushchev likely faced significant domestic pressure, especially from military leaders and political factions who may have disagreed with his handling of the situation. Some may have favored a more aggressive approach or believed the missiles in Cuba were a strategic advantage that shouldn't have been abandoned so easily.

In addition to managing external relations, Khrushchev also had to contend with internal dissent. The decision to remove the missiles would not have been universally popular among Soviet leadership, particularly given the military benefits the missiles offered in terms of their proximity to the U.S.

Finally, Khrushchev had to think about how the removal of the missiles would affect the Soviet Union's broader military strategy. He likely needed to explore alternative ways to maintain a military advantage over the United States while navigating the political fallout of the crisis.

Communication Challenges:

During the Cuban Missile Crisis, the risk of misunderstandings between the United States and the Soviet Union was extremely high. Cold War tensions created a volatile atmosphere where even small miscommunications could lead to disastrous consequences. Communication between the two superpowers was often indirect, relying on back-channel messages and intermediaries, which made it easier for intentions to be misinterpreted.

Secrecy also played a major role in the crisis. Both sides had to keep their internal discussions and military preparations hidden from the other, which added another layer of complexity. This secrecy, while necessary for protecting national security, increased the risk of miscalculations. With limited information about each other's true intentions, the U.S. and the Soviet Union had to navigate the crisis carefully, trying to avoid actions that could unintentionally escalate into war.

Overall, the Cuban Missile Crisis presented a complex set of challenges for leaders on both sides. They had to weigh military threats, manage domestic pressures, navigate internal conflicts, maintain public confidence, and overcome communication hurdles - all while facing the ever-present possibility of nuclear war.

Key Personality Traits and Leadership Styles

In the midst of the Cuban Missile Crisis, John F. Kennedy faced an unprecedented moment that tested his leadership and composure. Instead of yielding to the immediate pressures to launch a military strike, he opted for a blockade. This decision was not just strategic; it reflected a deep calmness that allowed him to think clearly in the face of chaos. As Kennedy stood resolute, he demonstrated to his team and the nation that staying composed in crises is vital. Leaders today can draw inspiration from his example, recognizing that maintaining a calm demeanor fosters rational decision-making and reassures their teams during challenging times.

Kennedy also understood the power of collaboration. He formed the Executive Committee of the National Security Council, or ExComm, bringing together a diverse group of advisors to weigh different perspectives. This inclusive approach didn't just lead to better decisions; it created a sense of unity among his advisors. Leaders today should take this lesson to heart, embracing collaborative decision-making by actively seeking input from their teams and valuing the insights of various stakeholders. When leaders create a culture of collaboration, they unlock the potential for innovative solutions and stronger team dynamics.

Communication is another pillar of effective leadership, and Kennedy excelled in this area. His clear and direct messages to the public, along with his diplomatic back-channel conversations with the Soviet Union, showed how crucial effective communication is during a crisis. In today's world, leaders must prioritize clarity and transparency in their messaging. By ensuring their words are easily understood, they can build trust and eliminate ambiguity. This commitment to clear communication fosters stronger relationships with their stakeholders and enhances overall team morale.

Strategic patience was a hallmark of Kennedy's leadership. He and Khrushchev both recognized the importance of allowing diplomacy the time it needed to work, rather than rushing into decisions that could have dire consequences. For today's leaders, this means practicing the art of patience and waiting for the right moment to act. Flexibility is equally important; being able to adapt strategies based on new information or changing circumstances can make all the difference in navigating complex situations.

Empathy and emotional intelligence played a crucial role in Robert F. Kennedy's negotiations. He demonstrated a profound understanding of the human element in diplomacy, considering the perspectives and motivations of the Soviet negotiators. This ability to empathize is essential for today's leaders, who must not only address the needs and concerns of their teams but also foster meaningful connections with their partners and even adversaries. Cultivating empathy creates a more supportive and engaged team environment, where everyone feels valued and heard.

Courage and moral fortitude were defining traits of the Kennedy leadership. Despite intense pressure from military advisors and public opinion, the Kennedys stood firm in their commitment to seek a peaceful resolution. Their moral courage serves as a powerful reminder for leaders today. Often, making the right decision requires taking a stand that may not be popular. True leadership means adhering to one's principles, even when faced with opposition.

Finally, the Kennedys exemplified proactive crisis management. By implementing a naval blockade and engaging in secret negotiations, they demonstrated the importance of anticipating potential crises and preparing for them in advance. Today, leaders should embrace a proactive mindset, developing plans to address challenges before they escalate. By being proactive rather than reactive, they can effectively mitigate risks and navigate obstacles with confidence.

In summary, the lessons drawn from Kennedy's leadership during a turbulent time resonate powerfully today. By embodying calmness, fostering collaboration, communicating effectively, exercising strategic patience, demonstrating empathy, showing moral courage, and embracing proactive management, leaders can inspire and guide their teams through any crisis they face.

Applying These Lessons in Today's Leadership

- **Cultivate Calmness**: Develop stress management techniques and train your team to stay calm under pressure.
- **Foster Collaboration**: Build diverse teams and create mechanisms for inclusive decision-making processes.
- **Communicate Clearly**: Prioritize clear, consistent, and transparent communication both internally and externally.
- **Practice Strategic Patience**: Be willing to take the time necessary to make informed decisions. Stay flexible and adapt as situations evolve.
- **Enhance Emotional Intelligence**: Invest in emotional intelligence training for yourself and your team to better understand and respond to the emotional dynamics within your organization.
- **Demonstrate Courage**: Stand by your values and make decisions based on what is right, even in the face of opposition.

- **Prepare for Crises**: Develop comprehensive crisis management plans and conduct regular drills to ensure readiness.

By incorporating these traits and styles into their leadership approach, contemporary leaders can navigate complex challenges more effectively, inspire their teams, and achieve sustainable success.

Here are several ways the crisis helps us understand human psychology:

During the Cuban Missile Crisis, the world hung in the balance as leaders grappled with the terrifying prospect of nuclear war. President John F. Kennedy and Soviet Premier Nikita Khrushchev faced intense pressure, and their decision-making processes revealed a delicate dance between instinct and reason. Under such high-stress conditions, they had to navigate their natural fight-or-flight responses while weighing the consequences of their choices. This dynamic offers valuable insights into how individuals and leaders make decisions in crises, informing strategies for better crisis management in the future.

The formation of Kennedy's Executive Committee of the National Security Council, known as ExComm, brought together a diverse group of advisors, but it also posed the risk of groupthink. In moments where harmony seems preferable, decision-making can veer off course, leading to irrational outcomes. Kennedy recognized this danger and actively encouraged open debate and dissent within ExComm. This approach not only fostered a richer discussion but also served as a crucial lesson for leaders today: promoting an environment where differing viewpoints are welcomed can lead to better decision-making.

As the crisis unfolded, the significance of communication became clear. The leaders learned that clear and direct communication was essential to prevent misunderstandings that could escalate tensions. Kennedy's use of diplomatic channels showed how effective communication could defuse potentially explosive situations. Today, this lesson resonates beyond international diplomacy; in personal and professional settings alike, clear communication can resolve conflicts and foster understanding.

Kennedy and Khrushchev also demonstrated remarkable emotional intelligence. They made a conscious effort to understand each other's perspectives and motivations, which played a vital role in finding a peaceful resolution. Their ability to empathize with their adversaries illustrates that emotional intelligence can enhance interpersonal relationships and negotiations, leading to more collaborative outcomes. Leaders today can benefit greatly from developing empathy, as it helps bridge divides and builds stronger connections.

Throughout the crisis, leaders assessed various risks associated with their decisions, from military action to implementing a blockade. This ongoing evaluation highlighted how individuals and groups manage risk under uncertainty. Understanding risk perception and management is crucial; training in these areas can better equip individuals and organizations to navigate high-stakes situations confidently.

The resolution of the Cuban Missile Crisis without resorting to war was a remarkable achievement in conflict resolution. Kennedy utilized back-channel communications, practiced patience, and made strategic concessions to de-escalate the situation. These strategies serve as important lessons in conflict resolution that can be applied in everyday life, encouraging practices like active listening and negotiation to resolve personal and professional disputes effectively.

However, the crisis also revealed human fallibility. Mistakes, miscalculations, and sheer luck played significant roles in the unfolding events. Recognizing this fallibility encourages leaders to develop systems that mitigate the impact of errors. Implementing checks and balances, peer reviews, and contingency plans can help organizations navigate critical situations more effectively.

As Kennedy and Khrushchev faced immense stress and uncertainty, their psychological resilience came to the forefront. They demonstrated coping mechanisms that allowed them to manage extreme pressure. Developing resilience through techniques like mindfulness and building strong support systems can enhance an individual's ability to handle stress in high-pressure environments.

The moral and ethical dilemmas faced by these leaders were profound. They had to balance national security with the potential for catastrophic loss of life, reflecting the complexity of ethical decision-making in leadership. Studying these dilemmas provides valuable lessons for ethical training, helping individuals and leaders make informed and principled choices.

The Cuban Missile Crisis serves as a rich source of lessons on decision-making, leadership, communication, and ethics. By immersing themselves in the experiences of Kennedy and Khrushchev, today's leaders can draw inspiration and guidance to navigate their own challenges with wisdom and resolve.

> ***"You must never confuse faith that you will prevail in the end—which you can never afford to lose—with the discipline to confront the most brutal facts of your current reality, whatever they might be."***
>
> **- James Stockdale**

Here are the top 5 central messages from the provided text about the Cuban Missile Crisis:

- **Leadership and Decision-Making in Crisis**: John F. Kennedy and Nikita Khrushchev displayed contrasting leadership styles during the Cuban Missile Crisis, with Kennedy favoring collaboration and open discussion, while Khrushchev was more impulsive and secretive. Effective crisis leadership involves careful decision-making, collaboration, and clear communication to prevent escalation.
- **The Role of Communication in Conflict Resolution**: Clear and direct communication between the U.S. and the Soviet Union was critical in de-escalating tensions. Kennedy's televised addresses and diplomatic back-channel conversations helped defuse the situation, emphasizing the importance of open, transparent communication in resolving conflicts.
- **The Peril of Miscommunication and Secrecy**: The crisis highlighted the dangers of miscommunication and secrecy.

Misunderstandings, exacerbated by vague and indirect messaging from Khrushchev, increased tensions. The importance of maintaining open lines of communication during conflicts was made evident to avoid potentially disastrous outcomes.

- **Collaboration and Diverse Perspectives in Leadership**: Kennedy's approach to assembling the Executive Committee (ExComm), which included a diverse group of advisors, showcased the value of collaboration. Encouraging dissenting voices and considering multiple perspectives leads to more informed decisions, a valuable lesson for leadership today.
- **Emotional Intelligence and Patience in Conflict Resolution**: Both leaders demonstrated emotional intelligence by considering each other's perspectives, which allowed for strategic patience and negotiation. Kennedy's calm demeanor and ability to listen, as well as Khrushchev's eventual concession, underscored the significance of empathy, patience, and flexibility in resolving high-stakes conflicts.

Coaching Leaders for Mental Agility: Story No 27

The Heroic Stand at Thermopylae: Sparta's Last Stand

> **"Come back with your shield – or on it."**
>
> **– Sparta**

The Battle of Thermopylae (480 BC)

The Battle of Thermopylae was an important fight during the Greco-Persian Wars. A small Greek army, led by King Leonidas of Sparta, made a heroic stand against a much larger Persian army led by King Xerxes.

Leadership and Mental Strength:

King Leonidas and his 300 Spartan warriors, along with a few thousand other Greeks, defended a narrow pass called Thermopylae against the huge Persian army. Even though they were greatly outnumbered and knew they were likely going to die, Leonidas and his men chose to fight.

Their goal was to slow down the Persians so the other Greek city-states could get ready for future battles.

Spartan Discipline and Bravery:

The Spartans were trained from a young age to be disciplined, brave, and honor-bound. At Thermopylae, their strength and commitment were evident. Despite facing certain death, they fought with great skill and courage, holding the pass for three days. Their sacrifice showed their dedication to their homeland and became a symbol of ultimate bravery.

Strategic Impact:

Although the Greeks were eventually defeated when a traitor showed the Persians a secret path, their stand at Thermopylae delayed the Persian advance. This gave the Greek city-states time to unite and prepare for future battles, like the important naval battle at Salamis. Leonidas and his men inspired all of Greece to keep fighting against Persian control.

Outcome:

The battle ended with the death of Leonidas and his men, but their sacrifice became a symbol of courage and leadership.

The Battle of Thermopylae is remembered as one of history's greatest last stands, showing how true leadership sometimes means making the ultimate sacrifice for a greater cause.

The Battle of Thermopylae offers several profound lessons in leadership and mental stamina, particularly in the face of overwhelming odds.

> **"A king does not need to be safe. He needs to be fearless."**
>
> **– Spartan**

Here are the key takeaways:

1. Courage in the Face of Adversity:

True leadership demands immense courage, especially when facing seemingly insurmountable challenges. King Leonidas and his 300

Spartans exemplified this by standing their ground despite knowing they faced almost certain death. Their bravery became a powerful symbol that inspired others to keep fighting. In leadership, tough decisions often need to be made, even when the odds are against success. Courage in such moments can inspire and motivate others to take action, even in the face of overwhelming adversity.

2. Sacrifice for the Greater Good:

Leonidas and his men made the ultimate sacrifice by giving their lives to delay the Persian advance, allowing the rest of Greece time to prepare for battle. Their selflessness prioritized the larger goal of preserving Greek freedom over their own survival. Effective leaders recognize that personal sacrifice might be required for the greater good. This often means placing the needs of the team or organization above one's own interests, demonstrating a commitment to the collective success rather than individual gain.

3. Strategic Thinking and Resourcefulness:

Choosing Thermopylae as the battleground was a strategic move that played to the strengths of the Greek forces while neutralizing the advantages of the much larger Persian army. By effectively leveraging the terrain, the Greeks were able to hold off the Persians far longer than anyone anticipated. This example highlights the importance for leaders to think strategically and use their resources wisely. Understanding both the strengths and weaknesses of their own team and their opponents allows leaders to make decisions that maximize their advantages and achieve their goals.

4. Resilience and Mental Stamina:

The Greeks' ability to hold their ground against a vastly superior force for three days exemplified extraordinary resilience and mental toughness. Despite knowing that their chances of survival were slim, they remained focused and fought with unwavering determination. This lesson underscores the importance of mental stamina for leaders, particularly when navigating prolonged and challenging situations. Resilience enables leaders to maintain their resolve, guiding their teams through difficult times while keeping morale and focus intact.

5. Leading by Example:

Leonidas led his men from the front, fighting alongside them and sharing in their hardships. This approach not only inspired deep loyalty but also demonstrated that he was willing to endure the same risks and dangers as his soldiers. By leading through example, he built trust and commitment within his ranks. This lesson highlights the importance of leaders actively participating in the challenges faced by their team. When leaders are seen working as hard as their followers and confronting the same obstacles, they foster greater trust, inspire increased effort, and strengthen loyalty.

6. Inspiring Through Vision and Purpose:

The stand at Thermopylae was far more than a strategic military defense; it was a profound act of defending Greek freedom and resisting tyranny. Leonidas and his men were driven by a deep sense of purpose, which transformed their sacrifice into a meaningful and enduring story. This illustrates that leaders who clearly articulate a compelling vision and purpose are capable of inspiring others to fully commit to a cause. When a leader instills a strong sense of purpose, it becomes a powerful motivator, helping individuals persevere through challenging times and stay dedicated to their goals.

7. Accepting and Managing Risk:

Leonidas fully grasped the risks of holding Thermopylae but chose to accept them for the strategic advantage it offered. By sending away the bulk of the Greek army and remaining behind with a small contingent, he demonstrated a keen ability to manage risk effectively. This decision highlights a crucial lesson for leaders: they must assess and manage risks carefully, making tough choices that weigh immediate dangers against long-term objectives. Often, this involves accepting certain losses to secure a larger victory in the end.

8. Legacy and Influence:

The tale of Thermopylae has persisted through the ages, serving as a powerful symbol of resistance and the strength of the human spirit. Leonidas and his men crafted a legacy that has inspired countless generations, demonstrating how their courage and sacrifice left an indelible mark on history. For leaders, this story highlights the importance of striving to leave a positive legacy through their actions. The influence of leadership extends beyond immediate challenges, shaping the future and impacting generations to come.

In summary, the Battle of Thermopylae teaches that great leadership is about more than just winning battles; it's about demonstrating courage, resilience, strategic acumen, and the willingness to make sacrifices for a higher cause. These qualities not only help in overcoming immediate challenges but also in creating a lasting legacy that can inspire others for generations to come.

> **"The secret to happiness is freedom... And the secret to freedom is courage."**
>
> **- Spartan**

The Battle of Thermopylae holds profound lessons in leadership, demonstrating values such as courage, sacrifice, and resilience. Here are the key takeaways from this historic event:

- **Courage in Adversity:**

  King Leonidas and his 300 Spartans faced overwhelming odds but stood firm, knowing death was inevitable. Their bravery inspired Greece to continue resisting Persian control. In leadership, showing courage in the face of adversity motivates others to persevere, even when success seems unlikely.

- **Sacrifice for the Greater Good:**

  Leonidas and his men willingly sacrificed their lives to delay the Persian advance, giving Greece time to prepare. True leadership often requires putting the team's or organization's needs above personal interests, demonstrating commitment to a larger cause.

- **Strategic Thinking:**

  By choosing the narrow pass of Thermopylae, the Greeks neutralized the Persian army's size advantage. This highlights the importance of strategic thinking—leaders must assess their strengths and weaknesses to turn challenges into opportunities.

- **Resilience and Mental Stamina:**

  The Greeks held their position for three days despite overwhelming pressure. This teaches that resilience and mental toughness are vital for leaders, especially when facing prolonged challenges, allowing them to guide their teams with focus and determination.

- **Leading by Example:**

  Leonidas fought alongside his men, sharing their risks and hardships. Leaders who lead from the front inspire trust, loyalty, and greater effort from their followers, demonstrating that they are willing to face the same challenges as their team.

- **Vision and Purpose:**

  The stand at Thermopylae was not just about military strategy but about defending freedom. Leaders who articulate a compelling vision and purpose inspire deep commitment from their teams, even in the face of great difficulty.

- **Managing Risk:**

  Leonidas accepted the high risks of holding Thermopylae, balancing the immediate threat against long-term goals. Leaders must learn to assess risks carefully, sometimes accepting losses in the short term to secure future success.

- **Legacy and Influence:**

  The story of Thermopylae endures as a symbol of resistance and strength, illustrating that leadership creates a lasting legacy. Great leaders aim to leave a positive impact that inspires generations to come.

In summary, Thermopylae teaches that great leadership is about courage, sacrifice, strategy, and resilience. These values not only overcome immediate challenges but also create an enduring legacy of inspiration and strength.

Part 4

Leadership Pillar-4(Excellence)

Summary

As this chapter has demonstrated, effective leadership is rooted in key principles that have remained consistent across history and industries. Discipline, as seen in leaders like Gandhi and Churchill, is fundamental to long-term success, requiring unwavering focus, resilience, and the ability to overcome distractions. These qualities are mirrored in business leaders like Jack Welch, whose leadership at General Electric drove remarkable financial growth and innovation, even as his methods stirred controversy.

Core leadership elements—such as vision, integrity, empathy, and adaptability—are vital for guiding teams through both challenges and opportunities. In times of crisis, like the Cuban Missile Crisis or the Battle of Thermopylae, leaders such as John F. Kennedy and King Leonidas demonstrated the importance of strategic thinking, emotional intelligence, and courage. Their decisions, grounded in empathy and collaboration, highlight the impact of clear communication and the ability to inspire others in the face of adversity.

Ultimately, leadership is about leaving a lasting legacy—whether by fostering growth, navigating crises, or defending a higher purpose. The lessons drawn from these examples serve as timeless reminders that great leaders not only achieve success but also inspire those around them to strive for greatness.

A 6-Month Plan to Enhance Excellence Skills

Daily Actions:

- **Mindful Practice:** Spend 10-15 minutes daily practicing mindfulness or meditation to improve focus and reduce stress.

- **Continuous Learning:** Dedicate 30 minutes daily to reading books, articles, or taking online courses related to leadership, management, or industry trends.
- **Self-Reflection:** Spend 5-10 minutes each day reflecting on your actions and identifying areas for improvement.

Weekly Actions:

- **Set Clear Goals:** Set specific, measurable, achievable, relevant, and time-bound (SMART) goals for the week.
- **Seek Feedback:** Request feedback from colleagues, subordinates, or a mentor to gain insights into your performance.
- **Skill Development:** Dedicate time to develop a specific skill, such as public speaking, negotiation, or strategic thinking.
- **Team Building:** Organize team-building activities to foster collaboration and improve team morale.

Monthly Actions:

- **Performance Review:** Conduct a self-assessment of your performance and identify areas for improvement.
- **Professional Development:** Attend workshops, conferences, or webinars to expand your knowledge and skills.
- **Mentorship:** Seek a mentor to provide guidance and support.
- **Goal Setting and Review:** Set monthly goals and review your progress at the end of each month.

Additional Tips:

- **Embrace Challenges:** View challenges as opportunities for growth and learning.
- **Practice Positive Thinking:** Cultivate a positive mindset and focus on solutions rather than problems.

- **Prioritize Tasks:** Use time management techniques to prioritize tasks and avoid procrastination.
- **Seek Feedback:** Actively seek feedback from colleagues and superiors to identify areas for improvement.
- **Continuous Learning:** Commit to lifelong learning and stay updated on industry trends.
- **Celebrate Successes:** Recognize and celebrate your achievements, no matter how small.

By consistently implementing these strategies, individuals can significantly improve their excellence skills and achieve greater success in their careers.

Skill	Key Actions to Take	Follow-Up/Reflection
1. Commitment to Quality	- Set and communicate clear quality standards. - Conduct regular quality reviews. - Address gaps immediately.	- Are quality standards consistently met? - What improvements have been implemented?
2. Continuous Improvement and Innovation	- Seek feedback from peers and teams. - Implement a "lessons learned" practice after projects. - Encourage creative solutions.	- What innovations were introduced? - How is feedback incorporated into processes?
3. Achievement Orientation	- Define SMART (Specific, Measurable, Achievable, Relevant, Time-bound) goals. - Track progress regularly. - Reward and celebrate successes.	- Were goals met on time? - How are milestones communicated and celebrated?
4. Leadership Through Example	- Model disciplined work habits. - Demonstrate resilience during challenges. - Actively mentor team members.	- How does the team perceive your leadership? - Are team members motivated and engaged?
5. Growth Mindset and Adaptability	- Commit to regular skill-building activities. - Attend workshops and read industry updates. - Embrace challenges positively.	- What new skills have been developed? - How have challenges strengthened adaptability?

Here are some thought-provoking leadership coaching questions derived from the text, designed to stimulate reflection and discussion on key leadership principles:

Questions on Discipline and Commitment

1. **How do you maintain discipline in your leadership role, especially when faced with challenges?**
   - Reflect on the strategies you employ to stay committed to your goals.
2. **Can you share an instance where you had to resist the temptation of immediate gratification to achieve a long-term goal?**
   - Discuss the impact of that decision on your leadership journey.
3. **What specific actions do you take to cultivate consistency and resilience in yourself and your team?**
   - Consider methods to encourage ongoing dedication among your team members.
4. **How do you identify and address distractions—both internal and external—that impede your focus?**
   - Explore techniques for managing distractions effectively.

Questions on Core Leadership Qualities

5. **Which foundational qualities of leadership—vision, integrity, empathy, courage, or communication—do you believe are most crucial in your current role, and why?**
   - Prioritize these qualities based on your experiences.
6. **In what ways do you ensure that your vision is clearly communicated and understood by your team?**
   - Consider tools or methods you use to inspire and motivate others.

7. **How do you model integrity and accountability in your leadership style?**
    - Share examples of how you take responsibility for your actions and decisions.
8. **What strategies do you use to develop emotional intelligence and empathy in your interactions with team members?**
    - Reflect on the importance of understanding others' emotions in leadership.

Questions on Leadership Development and Innovation

9. **How do you foster an environment of innovation and adaptability within your team?**
    - Discuss practices that encourage creativity and flexibility.
10. **What lessons have you learned from leaders like Jack Welch regarding leadership development and performance management?**
    - Reflect on both positive and negative aspects of Welch's approach.

Questions on Crisis Leadership

11. **During times of crisis, how do you balance decisive action with collaboration and communication?**
    - Share your approach to crisis management.
12. **Can you think of a moment when clear communication helped de-escalate a tense situation? What role did you play?**
    - Reflect on the power of communication in conflict resolution.

Questions on Historical Examples and Lessons

13. **What lessons can modern leaders learn from the contrasting leadership styles of Kennedy and Khrushchev during the Cuban Missile Crisis?**
    - Analyze the impact of their approaches on the outcome of the crisis.
14. **How can the bravery and sacrifice demonstrated by King Leonidas and his men at Thermopylae inspire your leadership practices?**
    - Consider how courage and sacrifice are relevant in your context.
15. **In what ways do you assess risks and make decisions that may involve short-term losses for long-term success?**
    - Reflect on your risk management strategies.

Questions on Legacy and Influence

16. **What kind of legacy do you aspire to leave as a leader?**
    - Discuss your vision for your impact on others and the organization.
17. **How can you ensure that your leadership style positively influences future generations?**
    - Consider mentorship, role modeling, and other forms of influence.
18. **What stories from your own leadership journey exemplify the qualities of courage, resilience, and sacrifice?**
    - Share personal experiences that reflect your leadership values.

Conclusion

These questions can serve as powerful tools for self-reflection and group discussions among leaders seeking to enhance their effectiveness. They encourage deeper consideration of the core elements of leadership while drawing on historical examples and personal experiences to foster growth and understanding.

Concluding Reflection:

- **What one action can you take this week to embody the leadership qualities discussed in the chapter?**

This question can help facilitate deeper reflection and dialogue, encouraging individuals to connect their personal experiences with the principles outlined in the text.

Part-5

Leadership Pillar-5(Encouragement)

Leading Through Connection: The Importance of Influence and Collaboration

- **Impression Management: Crafting How Others Perceive You**
- **The Expectation Effect: Why Leaders Need the Self-Fulfilling Prophecy**
- **The Mastery of Social Influence in Leadership**
- **The Psychology of Extreme Followers and the Leaders They Crave**
- **Shaping Behavior Through Reinforcement**
- **Mary Barra: A Trailblazing Leader**

In the realm of leadership, the ability to influence and encourage stands as a pillar of effective guidance. It is not merely about issuing commands or making decisions; it's about crafting an environment where individuals feel valued and motivated to contribute their best. This journey begins with the delicate art of impression management, where leaders consciously shape how they are perceived. By understanding their own strengths and weaknesses, leaders can project authenticity, which fosters trust and sets a collaborative tone within their teams.

As readers delve into the principles of the expectation effect, they will discover the powerful dynamic at play: a leader's belief in their team's potential can ignite a transformative self-fulfilling prophecy. When leaders express high expectations, their team members often rise to meet them, resulting in elevated performance levels and morale. This insight emphasizes that the words spoken by a leader carry weight, influencing not only outcomes but also the culture within an organization.

The chapter further explores the psychology behind social influence, revealing how leaders can master the nuances of human behavior to inspire loyalty and commitment. It highlights that true leadership transcends authority; it involves understanding the emotional and psychological needs of followers. Figures like Mary Barra serve as compelling examples of this principle, demonstrating how visionary leadership and authentic connection can drive substantial organizational change.

By examining the ways in which behavior can be shaped and reinforced, readers will grasp the profound impact they have on their teams. Strategies for fostering collaboration and creativity emerge as essential tools in a leader's toolkit. This chapter not only illustrates how to influence effectively but also invites readers to reflect on their own leadership styles.

Ultimately, this exploration reveals that leadership is less about exerting control and more about cultivating an atmosphere of encouragement and growth. As leaders embrace these insights, they will be empowered to inspire those around them, creating a culture that thrives on collaboration and shared success. In this environment, individuals are not just employees; they become passionate contributors to a collective vision, working together to overcome challenges and achieve remarkable results.

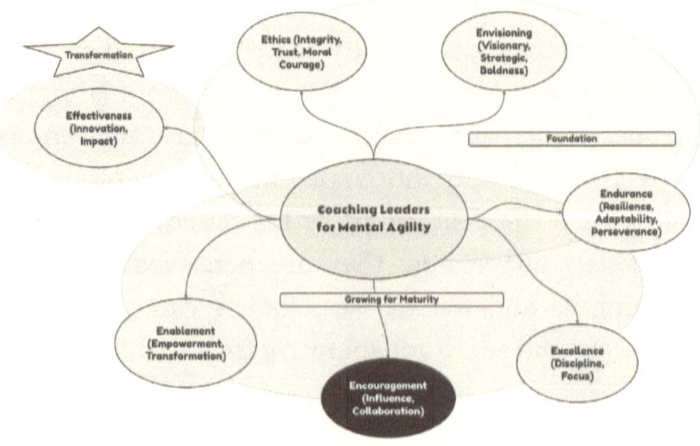

Coaching Leaders for Mental Agility: Story No 28

Impression Management: Crafting How Others Perceive You

> **"You never get a second chance to make a first impression."**
>
> **— Will Rogers**

Impression management is a critical skill for leaders.

It involves consciously shaping how others perceive you, your team, and your organization. Here are some actionable steps:

Self-Awareness

Imagine a leader who takes a moment each week to reflect on their strengths and weaknesses. They think about what they believe in and how it shapes their decisions at work. This leader knows exactly what they stand for, and you can see it in the way they act.

Now, picture this leader regularly chatting with their team, asking for thoughts on how they're doing. They welcome feedback like it's a gift. When a team member shares their view, the leader listens carefully, nodding and taking notes. This openness creates a warm atmosphere where everyone feels comfortable sharing their ideas.

This leader also pays attention to their feelings. They notice when frustration bubbles up during a tough meeting and take a deep breath to stay calm. By understanding their emotions, they can handle tough situations with poise, making decisions that keep the team moving forward.

Focusing on these simple but powerful actions, this leader builds a genuine presence. Their team feels inspired and supported, turning the workplace into a positive and productive space for everyone.

Strategic Communication

Imagine a leader standing in front of their team, speaking with confidence. Every word they say matches the values they believe in. When they talk about their goals, the team can feel the passion behind the words. You can see heads nodding and smiles appearing as everyone feels the trust grow.

Now, picture this leader sharing a story about a tough project that turned into a big success. As they recount how the team worked late nights, faced challenges, and celebrated together, you can almost see the excitement in the room. The team feels a part of that story, connected to a shared mission, ready to tackle whatever comes next.

Next, think about a meeting where the leader listens intently. They lean forward, nodding as team members share their ideas. You can see the respect in their eyes; they make everyone feel important. By really listening, the leader builds a space where everyone wants to contribute, knowing their voices matter.

By focusing on clear communication, sharing inspiring stories, and listening with care, this leader lights a spark in their team. Together, they create a positive atmosphere where everyone is excited to work toward meaningful goals.

Building Relationships

To build a strong leadership presence, it's important for leaders to form real connections with key people around them. Networking becomes essential as they meet others who share similar goals and values. These relationships not only help open new opportunities but also create a supportive community that works together for success.

Mentorship is another vital piece. When leaders take the time to guide and encourage their team members, they help them grow their skills and build their own reputations. This supportive approach boosts confidence, allowing individuals to shine and make valuable contributions to the organization.

Collaboration is equally important for creating a positive workplace. When leaders promote teamwork and cooperation, they create an atmosphere where everyone feels valued and motivated to reach shared goals. This spirit of working together strengthens connections and enhances the impact of their collective efforts.

By focusing on networking, mentorship, and collaboration, leaders can inspire their teams and create a vibrant organizational culture that reflects everyone's dreams and ambitions.

Crisis Management

To handle challenges well, leaders need to be ready for anything that might go wrong. They think ahead, imagining possible problems and making plans to tackle them. This way, when something unexpected happens, they can jump into action without hesitation.

When a crisis hits, clear communication is key. A good leader gathers the team and speaks openly, sharing what's happening and what the plan is. This honesty builds trust and keeps everyone on the same page, even when things are chaotic.

Strong leadership also shines through in tough times. Imagine a leader who stays calm, even when pressure mounts. They make decisions confidently and guide their team with a steady hand. This not only helps get through the immediate trouble but also inspires the team to stay strong and focused.

By being prepared, communicating openly, and leading with confidence, leaders can turn challenges into chances for growth, inspiring their teams to rise above difficulties together.

Ethical Considerations

Authenticity in leadership shines through like a beacon. Imagine a leader who walks into a room and speaks from the heart, sharing real thoughts and feelings without trying to impress anyone. This genuine approach allows team members to connect on a deeper level, building trust and making them feel valued.

When a leader is transparent, they invite their team into the process. Picture a leader explaining the goals and reasons behind decisions openly, creating a space where everyone feels informed and included. This honesty not only clarifies the path forward but also strengthens the bond between the leader and their team, making everyone feel like they are part of something bigger.

Respect is also key. Imagine a leader who greets everyone—whether they are a senior manager or a new intern—with kindness and appreciation. This simple act cultivates an atmosphere where everyone feels valued and motivated to contribute. When team members know they are treated with dignity, they are more likely to give their best efforts.

By being authentic, transparent, and respectful, leaders create a positive environment where people feel inspired to strive for excellence. It's in this supportive space that collaboration thrives, and everyone works together toward shared goals.

As a leader, your actions and behaviors significantly influence how others perceive you and your organization. Effective impression management is crucial for building trust, inspiring teams, and achieving organizational goals.

Steve Jobs: The Master of Image Crafting

Steve Jobs was a quintessential example of a leader who carefully cultivated his public image.

Steve Jobs stood on the stage, not just as a CEO, but as a visionary who seemed to see the future before anyone else. He moved with purpose, his black turtleneck and jeans becoming a symbol of his unique style. There was something about the way he spoke, as if he knew things that others hadn't even imagined yet. His confidence and passion for innovation made Apple more than just a company—it became a symbol of creativity and cutting-edge technology.

When Jobs stepped in front of the cameras, every word felt calculated, yet natural. He knew the power of communication and made sure that his message always came across clearly. Whether in interviews or keynotes, he delivered his ideas with a sharpness that left no room for misunderstanding. His ability to shape conversations about technology and innovation was unmatched.

Then came the product launches—events that felt less like corporate presentations and more like magic shows. The lights dimmed, and the audience leaned in, waiting for Jobs to reveal the next groundbreaking device. Every detail of these demonstrations was choreographed to perfection. As he swiped across screens and introduced sleek new gadgets, the crowd erupted in applause, fully captivated by his storytelling and the sense of revolution that filled the air.

Steve Jobs wasn't just selling products—he was offering a glimpse into the future. With each carefully planned appearance, he invited millions of people to share his vision, transforming Apple into more than a brand. It became a movement, fueled by his unwavering belief in the power of innovation.

Indira Gandhi: A Symbol of Strength and Resilience

Indira Gandhi, India's first female Prime Minister, employed impression management to solidify her leadership.

Indira Gandhi stood at the helm of a nation in turmoil, her calm yet firm presence a beacon of strength. When the Bangladesh Liberation War erupted, she didn't hesitate. Her decisions were swift, her focus sharp. In the face of overwhelming pressure, she led with unwavering resolve, earning the respect of allies and opponents alike. Every move she made during that period cemented her image as a leader who would not back down in times of crisis.

On the streets of India, her voice rang with the fervor of a patriot. She spoke directly to the people, her words laced with pride for the country's past and hope for its future. Through her speeches, she painted herself not just as a leader, but as someone who deeply cared for the nation's heart and soul. Her ability to tap into that shared love for the homeland drew crowds to her side and made her a towering figure in Indian politics.

Though born into a political dynasty, Indira Gandhi didn't simply follow tradition. She embraced modern ideas, showing the nation that progress didn't mean letting go of the past. She balanced tradition with innovation, pushing the country forward while honoring its roots. Her leadership was a testament to resilience and vision, leaving behind a legacy that encourages others to step forward boldly, with confidence in their own unique paths.

Nelson Mandela: The Icon of Reconciliation

Nelson Mandela's impression management was centered around forgiveness, unity, and reconciliation.

Nelson Mandela walked out of prison after 27 years, not with bitterness, but with a quiet strength that captured the world's attention. Every step he took was a reminder of the struggle he had endured, and yet, his spirit had not been broken. Instead, his time in prison had deepened his resolve. People everywhere saw in him the power of a man who had faced great suffering and still held on to hope. His story became a beacon for millions, showing just how strong the human spirit can be when faced with challenges.

As president, Mandela did something many found impossible—he reached out to those who had once oppressed him. Rather than seeking revenge, he chose forgiveness. His actions spoke louder than words. He worked to bring together a country that had been torn apart by racial divisions. In choosing unity over division, Mandela showed the world that true leadership is about compassion, understanding, and the ability to forgive.

On the global stage, Mandela's calm presence and ability to connect with others earned him respect from leaders across the world. His charm and diplomacy transformed how South Africa was seen. He stood not just for his nation, but for the values of freedom and justice. Mandela's legacy continues to inspire people everywhere, showing us that forgiveness and resilience have the power to heal and bring hope.

These great figures knew that how others saw them mattered. By aligning their actions with their beliefs, they shaped their public image, built trust, and achieved their goals. Their legacies remind us that leadership is not just about what you say, but how you live your values every day.

These questions encourage self-reflection and strategic planning.

Self-Presentation:

Think about how you present yourself. What do you wear or how do you act that shows the image you want others to see? For instance, if you wear smart clothes to work, how do you think that makes your coworkers view your professionalism? It might make them take you more seriously.

Adjust the way you talk to fit the image you want. How can you change the way you communicate to sound more confident? For example, instead of saying, "I think this might work," you could say, "I believe this will work well." Using stronger words can help people see you as more capable in meetings.

Flattery and Agreeableness:

Think about how you can support others. How can you give sincere compliments or show you care to connect better with people? For example, think about a time when a teammate shared a good idea. Instead of just saying, "Great job," you could say, "I really liked how you handled that presentation. It made the information clear and easy to follow!" This way, you're building a stronger bond.

Stay true to yourself while getting along with others. How can you agree with people without losing your own voice? Imagine you're in a meeting and someone shares an idea you like, but you also have a different thought. You could say, "I see what you mean, and I think adding this might help too." This shows you respect their idea while still sharing your own.

Highlighting Achievements:

Think about your achievements. What are some successes you can share that show who you are at work? For example, can you recall a project where you solved a big problem? When it's time for your performance review, you could say, "I helped the team finish a project two weeks early by organizing our tasks better." This helps your manager see your value.

Share your wins in a friendly way. How can you talk about what you've done without sounding like you're bragging? Imagine you're chatting with a colleague, and you say, "I really enjoyed working on that last project; we all put in a lot of effort, and it paid off!" This way, you're sharing your success, but you're also giving credit to the team.

Managing Appearances:

Imagine you're giving a presentation, standing in front of an audience. How are you standing? Are your arms crossed, or are they open and relaxed? The way you carry yourself in that moment speaks louder than your words. Take a moment to picture it. Are you sending the right message? Does your body language show confidence, or does it suggest uncertainty? Every gesture, every movement, paints a picture for your audience, shaping how they see you.

Now, think about the power of non-verbal cues. A simple smile, a steady posture, or even making eye contact can completely change how people perceive you. Instead of telling them you're confident, you're showing them without saying a word. What if you could practice these small adjustments, standing a little taller, looking more engaged, or using your hands to emphasize key points? How would that shift the way others see you, and how you see yourself?

By paying attention to these details, you're not just presenting information—you're projecting the person you want to become.

Selective Disclosure:

Imagine you're in a job interview, and the conversation shifts to your experience. What do you say first? Do you talk about your years in a completely different field, or do you focus on the roles that directly connect to the position you're applying for? Picture how the interviewer's expression changes as you highlight the most relevant parts of your background. You're steering the conversation, carefully choosing which parts of your story will resonate most.

Now, think about a networking event. You're meeting new people—what details do you share? Do you mention a personal hobby or stick to your professional achievements? It's not just about what you say but how it fits the moment. Picture yourself weighing each story, deciding if it will help others see you as competent and relatable, or if it might steer the conversation in the wrong direction.

In each situation, you're not telling everything about yourself—you're crafting a narrative that fits. You're showing people what matters most in that moment, based on what will leave the strongest impression.

Social Media Curation:

Imagine someone visiting your LinkedIn profile—what do you want them to see? You can curate it by sharing content that aligns with your career goals, like posting articles about industry trends, celebrating team achievements, or highlighting your skills through thoughtful comments. Each post or update adds to the story of who you are professionally, so it's important to be intentional about what you share.

Now, think about how you present yourself offline, in meetings or at events. Does it match your online presence? The key is making sure there's no disconnect. If your social media showcases professionalism, positivity, and expertise, your in-person interactions should reflect the same qualities. Whether you're at a conference or posting online, your actions and words should consistently represent your values and career aspirations.

By curating your online profiles and ensuring they match who you are in real life, you create a strong, authentic professional image that people can trust.

Role Enactment:

Imagine the role you want to have in your organization. Is it a leadership position? Picture yourself already acting like a leader, even in your current role. You take initiative, offer solutions, and support your team. Every day, you show qualities like responsibility, clear communication, and decision-making, laying the groundwork for the role you're aiming for.

Now think about the different roles you play at work—sometimes you're a team member, other times you may need to step up as a leader. When you're part of a team, you listen, collaborate, and contribute, but when you're leading, you guide the group, set direction, and make decisions. You adapt your behavior based on the situation, knowing when to step back and when to take charge.

By consistently embodying the qualities of the role you want and adjusting your behavior to fit different situations, you're not just waiting for a promotion—you're showing you're ready for it.

Emotional Display:

Imagine you're in a tough meeting, but instead of showing frustration, you choose to smile and stay positive. Even when things are challenging, your enthusiasm shines through. You nod, engage, and keep your tone upbeat, signaling to others that you're handling the situation with confidence and optimism. By doing this, you're not just reacting—you're reinforcing an image of someone who stays positive under pressure.

Now, picture a stressful situation where emotions are running high. Instead of letting the stress take over, you take a deep breath and focus on staying calm. You speak clearly, avoid raising your voice, and keep your body language relaxed. This approach shows that no matter how tough things get, you're in control. By managing your emotions, you project a steady, professional image that others can trust.

Through simple techniques like showing positivity and staying composed, you're able to shape how others see you—even in difficult moments.

Networking and Relationship Building:

Think about the people you already know—friends, colleagues, mentors. Who among them can vouch for your skills or help you make valuable connections? Imagine reaching out to a trusted colleague to ask for a recommendation, or to a mentor for advice on your next career move. Their endorsement could boost your credibility and open doors that might otherwise be closed.

Now, picture yourself at an industry event, meeting new people who are leaders in your field. You're striking up conversations, exchanging ideas, and building relationships that could help you reach your career goals. These connections don't happen by accident—you're actively seeking out opportunities to meet the right people, whether it's at conferences, networking events, or even online groups.

By nurturing your existing relationships and building new ones, you're not just expanding your network—you're positioning yourself for success.

Strategic Timing and Setting:

Imagine you're in a meeting, waiting for the right time to share your idea. The conversation is moving quickly, but you're paying attention.

When there's a pause and everyone seems ready for the next thought, that's your moment. By speaking up at just the right time, you make sure your idea stands out and gets the attention it needs.

Now think about having a casual chat with coworkers. It's not a formal meeting, but you can still bring up your achievements in a relaxed way. Maybe you mention a project you're proud of, but you do it naturally, like part of the conversation, rather than giving a formal presentation.

In any setting, whether it's a meeting or a casual talk, you're choosing how and when to share your strengths. By reading the room and adjusting to the situation, you can show your best side at the perfect moment.

By asking these coaching questions, individuals can gain a deeper understanding of how to effectively manage impressions, enhance their image, and achieve their personal and professional goals.

> **"People will forget what you said, people will forget what you did, but people will never forget how you made them feel."**
>
> **— Maya Angelou**

Here are the top key messages derived from the text about impression management for leaders:

- **Self-Awareness and Emotional Intelligence:**

  Effective leaders are self-aware, regularly reflecting on their strengths, weaknesses, and values. They actively seek feedback from their team, create an open atmosphere for communication, and manage their emotions to maintain composure during challenging situations. This self-awareness fosters a genuine presence that inspires and supports the team.

- **Strategic Communication and Relationship Building:**

  Leaders must communicate clearly and confidently, aligning their words with their values. By sharing inspiring stories and listening actively, they build trust and a positive atmosphere. Additionally, forming authentic connections through networking, mentorship, and collaboration enhances the leader's impact and strengthens the team's cohesion.

- **Crisis Management and Preparedness:**

  Leaders should anticipate potential challenges and develop strategic plans to address them. During a crisis, clear communication and decisive action are crucial. By staying calm under pressure and guiding their team effectively, leaders can turn challenges into growth opportunities, reinforcing team resilience.

- **Authenticity and Ethical Leadership:**

  Authenticity in leadership is vital for building trust and respect. Leaders should be transparent in their decision-making processes, showing genuine care for their team. By embodying respect, kindness, and honesty, they create a supportive environment where collaboration and shared goals can flourish, ultimately leading to organizational success.

These key messages emphasize the importance of self-awareness, communication, relationship-building, and authenticity in effective leadership and impression management.

Coaching Leaders for Mental Agility: Story No 29

The Expectation Effect: Why Leaders Need the Self-Fulfilling Prophecy

> **"The greatest discovery of all time is that a person can change his future by merely changing his attitude."**
>
> **— Oprah Winfrey**

A self-fulfilling prophecy is a belief or expectation that comes true simply because one acts as if it is already true. This psychological phenomenon can significantly impact our lives, relationships, and even societies.

How It Works?

Imagine you have a big presentation coming up, and as the date approaches, a familiar thought creeps into your mind: "I'll probably mess this up." This thought isn't just a passing concern; it begins to settle in, taking root as a belief about how things will go.

As the day draws closer, this belief starts to shape your actions. You feel the anxiety building up, and instead of preparing, you find yourself skipping practice sessions and avoiding the materials you need to study. You might even tell yourself that there's no point in trying since you expect to fail. Each choice to hold back reinforces your belief, pushing you further into a cycle of doubt.

Finally, the day of the presentation arrives. You walk into the room feeling unprepared and anxious. When it's time to speak, your mind goes blank, and the words you had hoped would flow easily seem to escape you. The performance is shaky, and as you finish, you hear that nagging inner voice whisper, "See? I knew I would mess it up."

This experience illustrates a powerful cycle: your beliefs shape your actions, and those actions ultimately lead to the outcomes you expect. The moment you start doubting yourself, you may unknowingly set yourself up for failure. Recognizing this cycle can empower you to break free from limiting beliefs and inspire confidence in your abilities.

Examples of Self-Fulfilling Prophecies

Education: Imagine a classroom filled with excited students. The teacher walks in and sees her gifted students as special. She encourages them with high expectations, and they start to believe in themselves. Because of her support, they work harder and do better than their classmates.

Workplace: Picture a team meeting where a manager praises one of the employees for their great work. This praise makes the employee feel valued and motivated, so they continue to do well. But if another employee is often criticized, they start to feel less confident and may not perform as well. Positive words can really help people shine, while negative ones can hold them back.

Relationships: Think about a couple sitting together, but one person is feeling insecure and worried that their partner might cheat. Because of this fear, they start asking lots of questions and acting suspicious. This behavior creates tension and mistrust between them. Ironically, the more they worry about being betrayed, the more likely they are to push their partner away, leading to the very situation they fear.

Mitigating the Effects

Challenge Negative Beliefs: When a negative thought pops into your head, like "I can't do this," take a moment to question it. Instead of believing that thought, try replacing it with something positive, like "I'm capable and can learn." This shift can make a big difference in how you feel and what you can achieve.

Focus on Evidence: Think about what you believe. Is it based on facts or just assumptions? Take some time to gather information and see if your beliefs hold up. For example, if you think you're not good at something, look for evidence of times when you've succeeded. This can help you see things more clearly.

Mindful Awareness: Start paying attention to your thoughts and actions. Notice if you have patterns where you expect negative outcomes, like thinking "I always mess things up." Recognizing these patterns can help you change your mindset and break the cycle.

Open Communication: If you have worries or expectations, talk about them with others. Sharing your thoughts can prevent misunderstandings and help you feel more connected. Whether it's with friends, family, or coworkers, open communication can lead to better relationships and clearer expectations.

By understanding the concept of self-fulfilling prophecies, we can become more aware of their impact on our lives and take steps to create positive outcomes.

Steve Jobs: The Reality Distortion Field

Steve Jobs, the visionary founder of Apple, is a prime example of how a strong belief, or "reality distortion field," can shape an organization's trajectory. Jobs possessed an unwavering confidence in Apple's ability to create groundbreaking products. This belief was so infectious that it inspired employees to push beyond perceived limitations, ultimately leading to the creation of iconic products like the iPod, iPhone, and iPad.

Jobs' conviction in Apple's destiny was a self-fulfilling prophecy. His belief in the company's potential influenced his decisions, the company culture, and ultimately the products that changed the world.

The "Bank Run" Phenomenon

A classic example of a negative self-fulfilling prophecy occurs during bank runs. If rumors circulate about a bank's financial instability, depositors may fear losing their money. This fear can lead to a mass withdrawal of funds, causing the bank to collapse, thus confirming the initial rumor.

The "Peter Principle"

While not strictly a self-fulfilling prophecy, the Peter Principle is closely related. It suggests that people are promoted based on their success in previous roles, but eventually reach a level of incompetence. This can create a self-fulfilling cycle where individuals are promoted beyond their capabilities, leading to decreased performance.

These examples illustrate the powerful impact of beliefs and expectations on outcomes. Understanding the concept of self-fulfilling prophecies can help leaders cultivate positive mindsets, set ambitious goals, and create high-performing organizations.

Elon Musk and Tesla

Elon Musk had a dream—a world where electric vehicles weren't just an alternative, but the new normal. He wanted to create cars that weren't just environmentally friendly but also fast, sleek, and exciting to drive. His goal for Tesla was clear: to build electric vehicles that could stand toe-to-toe with traditional gasoline cars, and even surpass them.

But it wasn't just talk. Musk was relentless in sharing his vision with the world. Through social media, product launches, and bold public statements, he made sure people knew what Tesla was aiming for. He didn't shy away from setting the bar high, pushing his team to design cars that were not only cutting-edge but also beautiful. The message was simple: electric cars could be desirable, powerful, and the future of driving.

And slowly, the world began to believe it too. As Tesla rolled out new models, each more innovative than the last, consumers and investors took notice. People started to see electric vehicles not just as a trend but as the next big leap in automotive technology. Tesla's market value skyrocketed, and the company became a symbol of progress and sustainability, proving that Musk's vision wasn't just a dream—it was the future.

Jeff Bezos and Amazon

In the early days of Amazon, Jeff Bezos had a vision that seemed almost too ambitious. He wanted to make Amazon the most customer-focused company in the world, a place where anyone could find anything they needed at low prices and get it delivered quickly. It wasn't just about selling books or products—it was about creating an experience that customers would trust and return to, again and again.

Bezos didn't just talk about this vision; he lived it. Every decision, every new feature, every innovation was driven by his relentless focus on customer satisfaction. He communicated this goal clearly to his team, setting high expectations and pushing them to think bigger. One of his key strategies was Amazon Prime, a service that offered fast, free shipping. It wasn't just about convenience; it was about showing customers that Amazon valued their time and loyalty.

As Amazon expanded its offerings, so did the trust of its customers. They knew they could rely on Amazon for whatever they needed, whenever they needed it. Bezos' unwavering commitment to his vision paid off. Amazon grew rapidly, becoming the go-to place for online shopping. Through his leadership and focus on innovation, Bezos turned his vision into a reality, creating a company that dominates the e-commerce world and revolutionized how people shop.

Mark Zuckerberg and Facebook

Mark Zuckerberg had a visionary dream: he wanted Facebook to be more than just a social network; he envisioned it as a powerful platform that could connect people across the globe. His goal was to simplify communication and make social interactions easier and more accessible for everyone.

To bring this dream to life, Zuckerberg set ambitious goals for the growth and impact of Facebook. He didn't just keep these aspirations to himself; he actively communicated his vision through public statements and strategic decisions. Each announcement was a reminder of his commitment to building something extraordinary. Moreover, Facebook continuously rolled out new features designed to boost user engagement, ensuring that more and more people could connect and share their lives.

Zuckerberg's unwavering confidence and focus on fostering connectivity and enhancing user experience turned into a remarkable reality. This dedication transformed Facebook into the leading social media platform, a place that profoundly influenced the way billions of individuals connect, communicate, and share information with one another. Through his vision and determination, Zuckerberg didn't just create a platform; he sparked a global movement that reshaped social interaction for people everywhere.

Reed Hastings and Netflix

Reed Hastings had a bold vision for Netflix. He imagined transforming the company from a simple DVD rental service into a leading digital streaming platform that would revolutionize how people consumed media. This was not just a dream; it was a mission to reshape the entertainment landscape.

To turn this vision into reality, Hastings set high expectations for Netflix's growth and innovation. He poured significant investments into original content and cutting-edge technology, all aimed at enhancing the streaming experience for viewers. Hastings didn't keep his ambitions to himself; he shared this vision openly with investors, employees, and customers, making sure everyone understood the direction in which Netflix was heading.

His unwavering commitment to innovation and excellence soon became a self-fulfilling prophecy. Under Hastings' leadership, Netflix revolutionized the entertainment industry, emerging as the go-to platform for streaming movies and TV shows. The impact was profound, setting a new standard that other streaming services aspired to reach. Through his vision and determination, Hastings didn't just create a successful business; he changed the way people around the world enjoy entertainment, inspiring countless others to think big and pursue their dreams.

Leaders need to understand and harness the self-fulfilling prophecy because it has the power to transform individual and organizational performance.

By setting high expectations, communicating belief in their teams, and reinforcing positive behaviors, leaders can create a cycle of success and continuous improvement.

This approach not only drives immediate results but also builds a resilient, motivated, and high-performing organization poised for long-term success.

> **"People tend to become what they expect of themselves."**
>
> **— John Steinbeck**

Here are the top four messages from the provided text on self-fulfilling prophecies:

- **Beliefs Shape Actions**: A self-fulfilling prophecy occurs when an individual's beliefs or expectations influence their actions, leading to outcomes that confirm those beliefs. For example, if someone believes they will fail a presentation, their lack of preparation may result in a poor performance, reinforcing their initial doubt.

- **Positive Expectations Can Inspire Success**: High expectations and positive reinforcement can lead to improved performance. In educational settings, a teacher who believes in her students can motivate them to achieve more. Similarly, a manager's praise can boost an employee's confidence, leading to better results.

- **Open Communication and Mindfulness Are Key**: To mitigate negative self-fulfilling prophecies, it's essential to challenge negative thoughts, focus on evidence, and practice mindful awareness. Open communication with others can also help clarify expectations and reduce misunderstandings.
- **Leaders Can Foster Positive Prophecies**: Leaders like Steve Jobs, Elon Musk, and Jeff Bezos exemplify how strong beliefs can drive organizations to achieve remarkable success. By setting high expectations and instilling confidence in their teams, leaders create a culture that encourages innovation and fosters a self-fulfilling cycle of success.

Coaching Leaders for Mental Agility: Story No 30

The Mastery of Social Influence in Leadership

> **"In the long history of humankind, those who learned to collaborate and improvise most effectively have prevailed."**
>
> **— Charles Darwin**

Social influence is the process of changing someone's thoughts, feelings, or behaviors. It's a powerful tool that leaders can use to motivate teams, enact change, and achieve goals. Here's a breakdown of the key attributes and parts of social influence:

Attributes of a Socially Influential Leader:

Leaders are more likely to influence others when they are perceived as honest, competent, and ethical, building credibility and trust. Clear and effective communication is essential for leadership, as those who can articulate their vision, listen actively, and use storytelling can connect with others on a deeper level.

Empowering others by delegating tasks, providing growth opportunities, and recognizing achievements fosters a sense of ownership and inspires action. Positive relationships are built through empathy, emotional intelligence, and collaboration, which helps leaders create a strong bond with their team. Additionally, adaptability is crucial; leaders who can learn, embrace change, and stay connected to the needs of others are able to adjust their approach for the best possible outcomes.

Parts of the Social Influence Process:

The source of influence is the leader or individual communicating the message, whose credibility and personal attributes greatly affect how receptive people are. The message itself is the content being communicated, and it can be most effective when it offers a clear vision, compelling arguments, or inspiring stories. The channel refers to the method of communication, whether through speeches, presentations, or even nonverbal cues, all of which influence how the message is received. The receiver is the target audience, and understanding their needs, perspectives, and motivations helps ensure that the message resonates with them. Ultimately, the outcome is the desired change in behavior, attitude, or belief, with social influence aiming to move people toward a specific goal.

Additional Considerations:

People are more likely to follow behaviors they see others adopting, a concept known as social proof. Leaders can use this by showcasing successful examples or testimonials to encourage similar actions. Additionally, we tend to be more influenced by those we like and respect, meaning a leader's ability to build positive relationships is crucial in gaining influence. Scarcity, or the perception that resources or opportunities are limited, can make them more desirable, and leaders can ethically use this to prompt action. Authority also plays a key role, as people often defer to those in positions of power. However, it is essential for leaders to exercise this authority responsibly to avoid misuse of their influence.

By understanding these attributes and parts of social influence, leaders can develop effective strategies to inspire and motivate others. Remember, true social influence is built on trust, respect, and a genuine desire to create positive change.

1. Nelson Mandela: Forgiveness and Reconciliation:

Nelson Mandela's leadership in South Africa is a powerful example of social influence through forgiveness and reconciliation. After 27 years imprisoned by the white apartheid regime, Mandela emerged advocating for racial unity and healing. His message of forgiveness resonated deeply, inspiring both Black South Africans yearning for justice and white South Africans apprehensive about the future. He understood the importance of social cohesion for a truly free South Africa, and his influence transcended past grievances to build a new nation.

2. Martin Luther King Jr.: The Power of Non-violent Protest:

Martin Luther King Jr.'s leadership in the American Civil Rights Movement is another prime example of social influence. He advocated for racial equality through non-violent protests, powerful speeches, and civil disobedience. His "I Have a Dream" speech remains iconic, captivating millions with its vision of a just America where race wouldn't dictate one's opportunities. King's influence transcended race lines, inspiring people of all backgrounds to join the fight for equality.

3. Rigoberta Menchú Tum: The Voice of the Indigenous:

Rigoberta Menchú Tum, a Mayan Guatemalan activist, used her platform to raise awareness about the Guatemalan Civil War's atrocities against indigenous peoples. She gave voice to the voiceless, sharing her experiences of persecution and loss. Her courage and unwavering commitment to human rights garnered international attention, pressuring the Guatemalan government, and influencing global discourse on indigenous rights.

4. Malala Yousafzai: Education for All:

Malala Yousafzai, a Pakistani activist, became a global symbol of female education rights after being shot by the Taliban for advocating for girls' education. Her bravery and determination to continue her fight despite the attack inspired a global movement advocating for education equality. Malala's influence used social media and public appearances to raise awareness and pressure governments to prioritize girls' education.

5. Lech Wałęsa: Solidarity and the Fall of Communism:

Lech Wałęsa, a Polish shipyard electrician, became the leader of the Solidarity trade union movement in Poland. Solidarity used strikes and peaceful protests to challenge communist rule. Wałęsa's charisma and unwavering commitment to workers' rights inspired millions of Poles and galvanized international support. His influence ultimately played a key role in the collapse of communism in Poland and Eastern Europe.

Here are some strategies you can implement to improve your social influence as a leader:

Develop Trust and Credibility:

To be an effective leader, it's crucial to lead by example. By living out your values and demonstrating the behaviors you expect from others, you build trust and respect within your team. Being authentic and transparent further enhances your leadership; people respond more positively to leaders who are genuine, open, and honest. Additionally, keeping your promises is essential for maintaining credibility and inspiring trust. Following through on your commitments ensures that others see you as reliable and principled.

Communication is Key:

To be an effective leader, you need to become a skilled communicator. This means articulating your vision and ideas clearly and concisely, while tailoring your communication style to suit your audience. Practicing active listening is also essential; you should pay genuine attention to the concerns and perspectives of others. Additionally, emphasizing empathy is crucial. Showing understanding and compassion for the challenges faced by those you lead fosters a supportive and respectful environment.

Empower and Inspire Others:

Effective delegation involves trusting your team members and entrusting them with responsibilities. It's essential to provide opportunities for growth by offering mentorship and support to help individuals develop their skills. Recognizing and rewarding achievements is also important; celebrating successes and acknowledging contributions fosters motivation and morale. Moreover, inspiring your team with a shared vision helps by painting a clear picture of the future you're working towards and illustrating how each person's efforts contribute to that vision.

Build Positive Relationships:

To be an effective leader, it is crucial to show genuine interest in people by taking the time to get to know your team members on a personal level. Building strong relationships fosters a sense of trust and connection. Additionally, fostering collaboration and teamwork creates an environment where individuals feel comfortable working together toward a common goal. Equally important is practicing conflict resolution; addressing disagreements constructively and finding solutions that benefit everyone helps maintain a positive and productive work environment.

Stay Relevant and Adaptable:

To thrive in today's world, it's important to be a lifelong learner. Always look for new opportunities to gain knowledge and improve your skills so that you can stay relevant and adaptable in an ever-changing environment.

Being open to change and innovation is equally essential. Embrace new ideas and different ways of doing things, and encourage your team to do the same. This mindset fosters creativity and keeps you ahead in a competitive landscape.

Additionally, staying connected to the people you are trying to influence is crucial. Understanding their needs, concerns, and motivations helps you build stronger relationships and communicate more effectively.

Additional Tips:

Developing strong storytelling skills is key to connecting with your audience on a deeper, emotional level. By sharing compelling stories, you can engage people in a way that resonates with them and leaves a lasting impact.

Social media is a powerful tool to reach and communicate with a wider audience. It allows you to share your message, build connections, and engage with people across different platforms, expanding your influence.

Maintaining a positive attitude is also important. Optimism and enthusiasm can be contagious, and your positive energy can inspire and motivate those around you, creating a more uplifting and productive environment.

By incorporating these strategies, you can develop your social influence as a leader and inspire others to follow your vision. Remember, true social influence is built on trust, respect, and a genuine desire to empower those around you.

Mahatma Gandhi's style of social influence was unique and highly effective. Here's a deeper look at the key aspects of his approach:

Non-Violence (Satyagraha):

The core of Gandhi's philosophy was "Satyagraha," which means "truth force" or "soul force." It focused on non-violent resistance as a means to bring about social change. This approach involved acts such as civil disobedience, boycotts, and hunger strikes. Gandhi believed in the power of moral authority, and by refusing to use violence, he exposed the injustices of British rule. His actions drew international attention and appealed to the moral conscience of both his oppressors and the global community. Gandhi's willingness to endure personal hardship and imprisonment for his beliefs inspired millions of Indians to join the independence movement. This collective sacrifice helped foster a sense of unity and shared purpose among his followers.

Leadership by Example:

Gandhi embraced a life of simplicity, rejecting the opulence of the British elite. He chose to wear homespun khadi cloth and lived modestly, aligning himself with the masses who were suffering from poverty. Gandhi didn't just advocate for non-violence—he lived it. By leading protests from the front, he put himself at risk, showing his unwavering commitment to the cause. His deep sense of empathy and understanding extended to both the Indian people and the British, as he sought common ground and worked towards peaceful coexistence.

Effective Communication and Mobilization:

Gandhi was a powerful speaker, known for captivating audiences with his messages of truth, justice, and non-violence. He communicated in simple terms, making his words resonate with people from all walks of life. Understanding the importance of involving the masses, Gandhi organized peaceful marches, demonstrations, and boycotts that played a key role in bringing the struggle for independence to the forefront. India, with its diverse religions and ethnicities, was united under Gandhi's leadership. He emphasized the importance of national unity while respecting cultural and religious differences, which was vital to the success of the independence movement.

Impact and Legacy:

Gandhi's leadership style not only achieved Indian independence but also inspired countless social movements around the world that embraced non-violent resistance. Leaders like Martin Luther King Jr. and Nelson Mandela drew inspiration from his principles.

Limitations:

It's important to acknowledge that Gandhi's approach wasn't without limitations. His focus on non-violence was sometimes criticized for being idealistic, and his vision for a united India faced challenges after independence.

Mahatma Gandhi's style of social influence, rooted in non-violence, leadership by example, and effective communication, remains a powerful model for peaceful social change. His legacy continues to inspire movements fighting for justice and equality around the globe.

> **"People will forget what you said, people will forget what you did, but people will never forget how you made them feel."**
>
> **- Maya Angelou**

Here are the top key messages about social influence and leadership:

- **The Power of Trust**: Leaders must be perceived as honest, competent, and ethical to build credibility and effectively influence others. Trust is the foundation of strong leadership.

- **Effective Communication**: Clear, compelling communication is essential for leaders. It involves articulating a vision, actively listening, and engaging with team members to foster connection and understanding.
- **Empowerment and Collaboration**: Empowering team members by delegating tasks and recognizing their achievements inspires a sense of ownership and motivates them to contribute more actively to the team's goals.
- **Adaptability to Change**: Successful leaders are adaptable and open to change. They embrace new ideas and remain connected to the needs of their team, allowing them to respond effectively to evolving challenges.
- **Historical Examples of Influence**: The leadership styles of figures like Nelson Mandela, Martin Luther King Jr., and Mahatma Gandhi illustrate how powerful social influence can drive significant societal change through trust, non-violence, and effective communication. Their legacies serve as enduring models for inspiring others.

Coaching Leaders for Mental Agility: Story No 31

The Psychology of Extreme Followers and the Leaders They Crave

> **"If your actions inspire others to dream more, learn more, do more, and become more, you are a leader."**
>
> \- **John Quincy Adams**

Leader-follower relations are a two-way street that significantly impacts a follower's development as a leader themselves.

Key aspects:

Leader Behaviors that Foster Follower Development:

Effective leaders help their teams grow by providing opportunities for skill development and leadership. They assign challenging tasks, offer constructive feedback, and delegate responsibilities in ways that allow individuals to stretch their capabilities. Through coaching and mentoring, leaders guide their team members in recognizing their strengths, addressing weaknesses, and refining their leadership styles.

Leaders also empower their followers by trusting their judgment and giving them the autonomy to take initiative. This creates an environment where people feel confident in making decisions. Moreover, leaders set a strong example by demonstrating essential qualities like integrity, communication, and sound decision-making. By involving team members in key leadership opportunities, such as meetings or presentations, leaders provide valuable experience and help their teams build a leadership presence for future success.

Follower Behaviors that Enhance Leader Development:

Followers who take initiative and actively participate in decision-making demonstrate clear leadership potential. By proposing new ideas and getting involved, they not only show their readiness to lead but also benefit from valuable learning experiences. Those who are open to feedback and actively seek constructive criticism further demonstrate a commitment to growth and improvement.

When followers take responsibility for their mistakes, they show accountability, a critical trait for any leader. Building strong relationships with colleagues and leaders helps them create a supportive network that fosters personal and professional development.

Lastly, those who pursue continuous learning, by seeking new skills and expanding their knowledge, strengthen their leadership capabilities and prepare themselves for future challenges.

The Context also Matters:

- **Organizational Culture:** A supportive and positive organizational culture that values learning, and development fosters an environment where both leaders and followers can thrive.
- **Challenges and Setbacks:** Challenges and setbacks can be valuable learning experiences if handled constructively. Leaders can help followers learn from their mistakes and emerge stronger leaders.

Historical Examples:

- **Nelson Mandela and the ANC (African National Congress):** Mandela's leadership provided a vision and empowered followers within the ANC to fight for racial equality in South Africa. Many followers, like Oliver Tambo and Walter Sisulu, developed their own leadership skills through their experiences in the movement.
- **Indra Nooyi at PepsiCo:** Nooyi was known for mentoring and promoting talented women within the company. Her leadership helped create a pipeline of female leaders who could follow in her footsteps.

Here are some historical examples that illustrate the impact of personality, values, culture, and context:

Throughout history, various leaders have demonstrated distinct personality traits, values, and cultural influences that shaped their leadership styles. These characteristics often inspired or challenged those around them, revealing how the context of their time influenced their approach to leadership.

Winston Churchill, the British Prime Minister during World War II, stood as a beacon of hope for his nation. With a charismatic and determined spirit, he inspired the British people to persevere through the darkest days of the conflict. His speeches rang out with conviction, instilling a sense of unwavering belief in victory. Each word he delivered motivated the nation, rallying them to stand firm in the face of immense challenges. The weight of his leadership shone through as he led by example, showing that resilience was possible, even in the bleakest times.

In stark contrast, Joseph Stalin ruled the Soviet Union with an iron fist. His ruthless personality dominated his leadership style, creating a top-down approach that left little room for dissent. Under his regime, rapid industrialization took place, transforming the country into a formidable power. However, this came at an enormous cost. The suffering endured by countless individuals echoed the values of Stalin's leadership, which prioritized the state's goals over the rights of its people. His legacy serves as a reminder of how the pursuit of power can overshadow compassion.

On the other side of the world, Martin Luther King Jr. emerged as a guiding light for the American civil rights movement. His leadership was anchored in shared values of non-violence and racial equality. King's unwavering commitment fostered trust among his followers, who faced immense opposition yet found motivation in their collective resolve. They marched together, driven by the belief that a better future was possible. King's ability to connect deeply with people showcased the strength of shared values in mobilizing change.

The American Revolution epitomized a clash of values that shaped a nation. Colonists yearned for self-governance, fueled by their desire for freedom and autonomy. This aspiration stood in direct conflict with the British crown's desire for control. The tension between these opposing values ignited a revolution, a battle for independence that would ultimately reshape the course of history.

Cultural contexts also play a vital role in shaping leadership. Genghis Khan, the founder of the Mongol Empire, exemplified a leadership style that thrived within his nomadic culture. His effectiveness as a leader was apparent among his people, as he skillfully united tribes and expanded his empire. However, his expansionist tactics often led to brutal conquests outside of his cultural realm, leaving a legacy marked by both innovation and destruction.

Leadership styles can vary significantly across cultures. In many Western societies, democratic leadership is common, valuing collaboration and input from others. In contrast, Eastern cultures might lean toward more hierarchical structures, where authority is respected, and decisions flow from the top down. Despite these generalizations, effective leaders recognize the importance of adapting their approach to fit the unique cultural context in which they operate.

Amid times of crisis, leadership can evolve significantly. Abraham Lincoln faced one of the greatest challenges in American history during the Civil War. His leadership style adapted as the war progressed, showcasing his ability to make tough decisions that would ultimately preserve the Union. Lincoln's values of unity and perseverance guided him through the tumult, demonstrating the importance of adaptability in leadership.

Steve Jobs, the co-founder of Apple, was a visionary leader who revolutionized technology. His passion for innovation fueled Apple's success, pushing boundaries in design and functionality. However, Jobs' demanding leadership style created a challenging environment for some employees. His relentless pursuit of excellence illustrated the complex relationship between personality and context in leadership, revealing that greatness often comes with its own set of challenges.

These leaders, with their varied personalities, values, and cultural influences, shaped their eras in profound ways. Their stories remind us that leadership is not a one-size-fits-all approach. Instead, it is a dynamic interplay of individual traits and the contexts in which they operate, revealing the profound impact leaders can have on their followers and society.

Here are a few examples that showcase how followers can become great leaders themselves:

Throughout history, many great leaders have inspired those around them, imparting lessons that shaped future generations. Among these leaders, Alexander the Great stands out. His trusted generals, Ptolemy and Seleucus, fought bravely by his side during his legendary conquests. As they marched into battle with him, they watched closely, absorbing Alexander's military tactics and the vision he had for building an empire.

When Alexander passed away, his generals didn't just mourn the loss of their leader; they took the skills they had learned and set out to create their own legacies. Ptolemy ventured to Egypt, where he established the Ptolemaic dynasty, while Seleucus founded the Seleucid Empire in the east. Their achievements were a testament to the profound influence Alexander had on their journeys, as both dynasties emerged as major powers in the Hellenistic world.

In a different era, another remarkable partnership unfolded between Moses and his devoted aide, Joshua. For years, Joshua stood alongside

Moses, learning how to lead the Israelites out of Egypt and into a new life. He observed Moses' strength as he faced numerous challenges, his unwavering faith as he sought divine guidance, and his ability to foster a strong sense of community among the people.

When Moses died, Joshua felt the weight of responsibility settle upon his shoulders. He knew it was his turn to lead. With determination and a clear vision, he guided the Israelites into the Promised Land, fulfilling the dream they had long awaited.

Mary McLeod Bethune, a formidable civil rights leader, and the founder of the National Council of Negro Women, also left a lasting impact through her mentorship. Dorothy Height began her journey working closely with Bethune, soaking up her wisdom on social activism, community organizing, and advocating for racial equality. Under Bethune's guidance, Height grew and evolved, ultimately becoming the president of the NCNW herself. She didn't just carry on Bethune's legacy; she became a powerful voice for civil rights and women's empowerment, making a significant mark on the movement.

In the tech world, the relationship between Steve Jobs and Tim Cook exemplified a different kind of leadership legacy. Tim Cook served as Jobs' right-hand man and Chief Operating Officer at Apple. During this time, he absorbed Jobs' extraordinary vision for innovation, design, and branding. Cook learned not just from Jobs' successes, but also from his challenges.

After Jobs' untimely passing, Cook took the helm as CEO of Apple. Faced with the challenge of leading the company into a new era, he embraced the opportunity. With a steady hand, Cook guided Apple through significant growth and diversification, ensuring that the spirit of innovation Jobs had instilled continued to thrive. He respected the legacy of his predecessor while also forging a new path forward, proving that leadership is about both honoring the past and shaping the future.

These stories of mentorship and legacy highlight how the influence of great leaders transcends their lifetimes. Whether in the battlefield, on a spiritual journey, in the fight for civil rights, or in the world of technology, the lessons learned from these leaders inspire and empower those who follow them.

Here's how leaders can cultivate a loyal and engaged following, along with the mindset traits that support this endeavor:

Building a Great Follower Base:

A leader begins by crafting a clear and inspiring vision that aligns with the values and aspirations of their followers. This vision instills a sense of purpose and encourages everyone to contribute toward a common goal, reminiscent of Martin Luther King Jr.'s iconic "I Have a Dream" speech.

Being genuine and transparent is essential for building trust. Followers are more inclined to respect a leader who stays true to themselves and their values. Open and honest communication plays a vital role as well. By keeping followers informed about decisions and being open to feedback, a leader fosters a sense of shared responsibility and trust.

Leaders also empower their followers by giving them ownership of tasks and projects. By effectively delegating and providing the necessary resources and support, they help followers build confidence and develop their own leadership skills.

Recognizing and appreciating the contributions of followers, both large and small, is crucial. Celebrating successes and acknowledging hard work not only motivates individuals but also reinforces positive behaviors.

Finally, investing in the growth and development of followers is vital. By offering opportunities for learning, a leader demonstrates that they value their team, leading to a more skilled and engaged workforce.

Mindset Traits for Building a Strong Follower Base:

Imagine a leader who sees their role not as a position of power but as a commitment to serve. This leader dedicates themselves to creating a nurturing environment where each follower can flourish and share their unique talents. In this space, everyone feels valued, encouraged to contribute their best ideas and efforts.

Now picture this leader as someone deeply attuned to the emotions and experiences of their team. They listen actively, striving to understand each individual's feelings and perspectives. This empathy forms the bedrock of trust, weaving strong connections that make the team feel like a family, united by a common purpose.

Humility shines through in this leader's approach. They are aware of their strengths and openly acknowledge their weaknesses, inviting feedback and learning from those around them. This openness fosters a culture where everyone feels comfortable sharing their thoughts, knowing their voices matter.

Instead of chasing quick wins, this leader focuses on the long game. They build relationships that stand the test of time, prioritizing sustainable success over immediate results. Followers know they can rely on this leader not just for guidance but for a commitment to their collective growth.

Collaboration thrives under this leader's watchful eye. They cultivate an atmosphere of teamwork, encouraging individuals to come together and share ideas. This sense of community transforms the team into a powerful force, united in their mission and driven by a shared vision.

In this vivid landscape of leadership, each interaction nurtures growth, trust, and connection, turning the team into a dynamic collective that thrives on collaboration and mutual respect.

Throughout history, there have been numerous examples of **extreme followers** who took their devotion to a leader or cause to dangerous and destructive extremes. Here are a few cautionary tales:

- **Nazi Germany and the SS (Schutzstaffel):** The SS was a paramilitary organization within the Nazi Party known for its brutality and fanatical loyalty to Adolf Hitler. Fueled by Nazi ideology and propaganda, SS members committed horrific acts of genocide and violence during the Holocaust. Their blind obedience to Hitler and the Nazi regime illustrates the dangers of extreme follower behavior.
- **The Peoples Temple and Jim Jones:** In 1978, cult leader Jim Jones orchestrated the mass murder-suicide of over 900 people at the Peoples Temple in Jonestown, Guyana. Jones' followers,

isolated from the outside world and indoctrinated with his ideology, willingly participated in this tragedy. This example highlights the power of manipulation and control that extreme leaders can exert over their followers.

- **The Assassination of Abraham Lincoln:** John Wilkes Booth, a fervent Confederate sympathizer, assassinated President Abraham Lincoln in 1865. Booth's extreme devotion to the Confederacy and hatred for Lincoln led him to commit this act of violence, demonstrating the destructive potential of follower extremism in the context of political conflict.
- **The Crusades:** The Crusades were a series of religious wars fought between Christians and Muslims for control of the Holy Land. While many factors contributed to the Crusades, the religious fervor and unquestioning obedience of Christian followers to the Pope and the idea of reclaiming Jerusalem played a significant role in the violence and devastation these wars caused.
- **The Khmer Rouge and Pol Pot:** The Khmer Rouge, led by Pol Pot, was a brutal communist regime that ruled Cambodia from 1975 to 1979. Pol Pot's radical ideology and ruthless methods resulted in the deaths of millions of Cambodians. The extreme devotion of his followers, often indoctrinated from a young age, facilitated the regime's horrific crimes.

These are just a few examples, and the motivations and contexts surrounding extreme follower behavior can vary widely. However, they all underscore the importance of critical thinking, questioning authority, and maintaining a sense of individual morality.

Here are some additional points to consider:

- **Social and Psychological Factors:** Extreme follower behavior can be influenced by social isolation, charismatic leadership, and the promise of belonging to a larger cause.
- **Deindividuation:** In large groups, individuals may feel less accountable for their actions, making them more susceptible to following orders without question.

- **The Importance of Education and Critical Thinking:** Encouraging critical thinking skills and promoting media literacy can help individuals resist manipulation and extremist ideologies.

Traits of Leaders that Attract Extreme Followers:

Imagine a leader standing before a crowd, radiating charisma and confidence. This figure embodies hope and solutions, captivating those who seek direction in a chaotic world. They promise to be the savior, much like a cult leader or a charismatic politician, offering a sense of belonging to those who feel lost.

Now, picture another leader, unwavering in their vision, rallying followers with a powerful ideology. Even if that vision is built on shaky ground, it becomes a beacon for those yearning for purpose. History remembers such figures—those who ignited revolutions and led nations into battle, driven by distorted beliefs that captivated the masses.

Consider the chilling effectiveness of a leader who fosters an "us versus them" mentality. By creating a clear division, they draw followers into a tight-knit community, unified against a perceived enemy. This tactic has echoed throughout history, as dictators and extremist groups have thrived on the power of exclusion, giving people someone to blame for their struggles.

Then, there are the leaders who project an image of strength and control, appealing to those wracked with insecurity. In their presence, followers may find themselves submitting to harsh rules and commands, prioritizing obedience over ethics, all in search of stability in uncertain times.

Lastly, envision leaders who exploit the vulnerabilities of society. They prey on fears and anxieties, offering simplistic answers to complex problems. In moments of desperation, those feeling marginalized may find themselves lured by the promises of demagogues and populist figures, clinging to hope where none seems to exist.

Through these dynamics, we see the intricate dance between leadership and followership, a powerful interplay that shapes societies and influences the course of history. Each interaction reveals not just the qualities of leaders but the deep-seated desires and fears of those who choose to follow them.

The Challenge of Assigning Credit:

The question of who deserves credit, the leader, or the followers, is complex. While leaders exploit these vulnerabilities and manipulate situations, followers also have a responsibility to think critically and resist blindly following harmful ideologies.

Here are some additional points to consider:

- **Shared Responsibility:** In some cases, there might be a shared responsibility. The leader creates the environment, but the followers have a choice to participate or not.
- **Social and Psychological Factors:** It's important to consider the social and psychological factors that might make individuals susceptible to extreme leadership, such as poverty, lack of education, or social isolation.
- **The Importance of Individual Agency:** Even within extreme follower groups, individuals can make choices to resist or break free. Highlighting stories of those who defy the leader can be a powerful message.

Here are the top key messages from the text:

- **Mutual Growth in Leadership**: The relationship between leaders and followers is dynamic, with effective leaders nurturing their followers' development through skill-building, mentorship, and empowering them to take initiative. This reciprocal relationship fosters a new generation of leaders.
- **The Impact of Organizational Culture**: A supportive and positive organizational culture plays a critical role in nurturing leadership qualities in both leaders and followers. Challenges can serve as valuable learning experiences when approached constructively, highlighting the importance of a conducive environment.
- **Historical Examples of Mentorship**: The journeys of historical figures like Alexander the Great, Moses, and Mary McLeod

Bethune demonstrate how mentorship shapes future leaders. These leaders not only inspire but also equip their followers with the skills needed to pursue their own paths to leadership.

- **Building Trust and Engagement**: Leaders who communicate openly, remain genuine, and empower their followers create a strong foundation of trust. Recognizing and appreciating followers' contributions further enhances engagement, fostering a loyal and motivated team.
- **Critical Thinking and Individual Agency**: While leaders can influence followers profoundly, it is essential for individuals to think critically and resist harmful ideologies. Followers share the responsibility for their choices, emphasizing the importance of personal agency within leadership dynamics.

Coaching Leaders for Mental Agility: Story No 32

Shaping Behavior Through Reinforcement

> **"The consequences of an act affect the probability of its occurring again."**
>
> **- B.F. Skinner**

Effective leaders often use reinforcement techniques to shape and change behaviors within their organizations. These techniques help establish desired behaviors, motivate employees, and foster a positive and productive work environment.

In a company called **Innovate Inc.,** the CEO, Sarah, was renowned for her ability to inspire and motivate her employees through various reinforcement techniques.

She believed in recognizing and rewarding good behavior while addressing issues constructively.

Positive Reinforcement

1. **Praise and Recognition** One day, Alex, a project manager, completed a challenging project ahead of schedule. During the

weekly team meeting, Sarah publicly praised Alex's efforts, highlighting his dedication and creativity. She also sent him a personal note of appreciation. This public recognition boosted Alex's morale and motivated other team members to strive for similar achievements.

2. **Rewards and Incentives** In the sales department, manager Linda decided to introduce a new incentive program. Employees who exceeded their sales targets would receive bonuses or extra vacation days. This initiative not only motivated the sales team to perform exceptionally but also set a benchmark for others to aim for, fostering a culture of excellence.

Negative Reinforcement

1. **Removing Negative Conditions** Emma, a software developer, consistently met her deadlines and produced high-quality work. Noticing this, Sarah decided to reward her by reducing her workload pressure. She assigned Emma a preferred project and offered more flexible working hours. This action reinforced the importance of meeting deadlines without the need for punitive measures, encouraging others to follow suit.

Punishment

1. **Constructive Feedback** However, not all behaviors were positive. When Jake, another project manager, frequently missed deadlines, Sarah scheduled a one-on-one meeting with him. She explained how his delays were impacting the team and offered suggestions for improvement, such as better time management strategies. This constructive feedback helped Jake understand his shortcomings and work towards improving them.

2. **Disciplinary Actions** In another instance, Mark, a team member, was habitually late to work. After a few verbal warnings, Sarah implemented a progressive discipline process. She issued a written warning and eventually had to suspend Mark when the behavior didn't change. This approach emphasized the importance of punctuality and accountability within the team.

Extinction

1. **Ignoring Undesirable Behavior** In meetings, Emily, a junior analyst, often disrupted discussions seeking attention. Sarah decided to ignore these interruptions and instead only responded to Emily's constructive contributions. Over time, Emily's disruptive behavior decreased as it no longer received the attention she sought, and she started contributing more productively.

Continuous and Intermittent Reinforcement

1. **Continuous Reinforcement** During the rollout of a new project management system, Sarah knew it was crucial to establish the new behavior quickly. She consistently recognized and rewarded employees who used the system correctly, ensuring it became a part of the company's routine.

2. **Intermittent Reinforcement** Once the system was well-established, Sarah switched to intermittent reinforcement. Occasionally, she would publicly acknowledge or surprise reward employees who continued to use the system effectively. This kept the behavior consistent without over-reliance on constant rewards.

Through these various reinforcement techniques, Sarah fostered a positive and productive work environment at Innovate Inc., demonstrating the power of thoughtful leadership in shaping organizational behavior.

Real-World Example: Google

Application: Google is known for its innovative use of reinforcement techniques to foster creativity and productivity.

Techniques Used:

- **Positive Reinforcement:** Google offers extensive praise, recognition, and rewards. Employees are given perks like bonuses, vacation days, and even time to work on personal projects (20% time) when they meet or exceed expectations.

- **Constructive Feedback:** Google uses regular performance reviews and feedback sessions to guide employees. Constructive feedback helps employees understand areas for improvement and encourages continuous development.

- **Supportive Environment:** Google removes negative conditions by creating a supportive and flexible work environment. For instance, employees have access to wellness programs and flexible working arrangements, which reduce stress and promote well-being.

1. Franklin D. Roosevelt (FDR) and the New Deal

During the darkest days of the Great Depression, the United States faced overwhelming economic challenges. Millions were out of work, and poverty swept across the nation. It was a time of uncertainty, but President Franklin D. Roosevelt believed the country could rise again. His bold plan, known as the New Deal, aimed to restore hope and rebuild the economy.

Roosevelt introduced programs like the Civilian Conservation Corps (CCC) and the Works Progress Administration (WPA), which gave millions of people jobs. Men and women who had lost everything suddenly had work again, building roads, parks, and public buildings. Through these programs, Roosevelt reinforced a powerful idea: the government could step in and provide meaningful change, offering people the dignity of work and a way to rebuild their lives.

The introduction of Social Security was another monumental step. It offered financial security to the elderly and unemployed, ensuring that in times of need, no one would be left behind. This act reshaped the public's understanding of government, showing that it could protect its citizens and provide a safety net when life became difficult.

Through the New Deal, Roosevelt didn't just alleviate immediate hardships. He transformed how Americans viewed their government, instilling a belief that, in moments of crisis, the government could lead the way to recovery and renewal. His leadership gave the nation hope during its most trying times, showing that together, they could build a better, more secure future.

2. Mahatma Gandhi and Nonviolent Resistance

Mahatma Gandhi was the leader of India's fight for independence from British rule, but he took a unique approach. Instead of using violence, Gandhi believed in nonviolent resistance, a method he practiced with unwavering commitment.

One of the most powerful examples of this was his Satyagraha campaigns. Gandhi organized peaceful protests and acts of civil disobedience, encouraging people to stand up against injustice without raising a hand in anger. Those who followed his principles of nonviolence were praised and often became symbols of courage in their communities. Their actions proved that strength didn't always come from force but from moral conviction.

The Salt March was another defining moment in this struggle. In defiance of British laws, Gandhi led a 240-mile march to the Arabian Sea to make salt, a basic necessity that the British controlled. This act of peaceful rebellion was covered by the media and became a global symbol of resistance. It showed the world the power of nonviolent protest, inspiring millions and reinforcing Gandhi's belief that change could be achieved without violence.

However, Gandhi was firm in his principles. Whenever a movement took a violent turn, he would withdraw his support. By doing this, he sent a clear message: true progress could only come from peace, and he would not stand behind actions that betrayed his ideals.

Through his leadership, Gandhi showed that nonviolence was not just a strategy but a powerful tool that could change the hearts of millions. His unwavering commitment to peace reshaped how people viewed resistance and proved that even the mightiest oppressors could be challenged through peaceful means.

3. Martin Luther King Jr. and the Civil Rights Movement

Martin Luther King Jr. became the heart of the American Civil Rights Movement, leading the fight against racial segregation and discrimination through nonviolent means. He believed deeply in the power of peace to drive change and inspire a better future.

King often publicly recognized those who followed his path of nonviolence. One of the most notable examples was the Montgomery Bus Boycott, where participants bravely stood against injustice by refusing to ride segregated buses. King praised their courage, showing the world that nonviolent protest was not only effective but carried a moral strength that violence could never match.

His speeches, especially the iconic "I Have a Dream" speech, ignited hope and determination in his supporters. With his powerful words, King painted a picture of a future where everyone, regardless of race, would live in equality and justice. These speeches weren't just words; they were calls to action that inspired millions to join the movement.

At the same time, King was firm in his stance against violence. Whenever violence erupted, whether from authorities or protesters, King condemned it, reminding everyone that the movement's strength came from peace, not aggression. This reinforced his belief that lasting change could only come through nonviolent resistance.

King's leadership reshaped the way Americans viewed justice and equality. His relentless dedication to nonviolence led to monumental changes, including the Civil Rights Act of 1964 and the Voting Rights Act of 1965. Through his example, he showed that courage, peace, and perseverance could tear down even the strongest barriers of injustice.

4. Nelson Mandela and the End of Apartheid

Nelson Mandela led South Africa through its most challenging chapter, fighting against the injustice of apartheid and eventually becoming the nation's first black president. His leadership was grounded in the ideals of peace, forgiveness, and reconciliation, which guided the country through a difficult transition.

Instead of seeking revenge against those who had enforced apartheid, Mandela chose a path of unity. He encouraged former adversaries to come together, praising those who supported the vision of a new, democratic South Africa. By emphasizing the power of reconciliation, he showed the country that healing was possible only through collaboration and mutual respect.

Mandela also established the Truth and Reconciliation Commission, a bold step that allowed individuals to come forward and confess their wrongdoings under apartheid in exchange for amnesty. This move reinforced the importance of truth and forgiveness, helping the nation confront its painful past while moving forward without hatred.

Throughout this process, Mandela stood firm against retribution. He openly criticized any attempts at revenge, reminding his country that violence would only lead to more suffering. His commitment to peace shaped the mindset of millions, helping South Africa move from oppression to a hopeful future.

Mandela's leadership inspired a sense of national unity, showing the world that even the most divided nations could heal when led by courage and compassion. His vision for a peaceful South Africa continues to inspire generations worldwide.

Here are some more stories to look into.

1. Winston Churchill and World War II

During World War II, Winston Churchill stood as a pillar of strength for the United Kingdom, leading the nation through one of its darkest times. As Prime Minister, he faced the daunting task of keeping the country united and motivated in the face of relentless attacks and hardship.

Churchill's speeches became a lifeline for the British people. His powerful words, like those in his famous "We shall fight on the beaches" address, inspired courage, and resilience. He spoke directly to the hearts of the people, reminding them of their strength and determination, and fostering a deep sense of pride in their shared struggle.

Beyond his speeches, Churchill made sure to honor those who played vital roles in the war effort. He recognized the bravery of soldiers on the front lines, the pilots who defended the skies, and even the civilians who faced bombings with unshakable resolve. By celebrating these everyday heroes, Churchill reinforced the idea that everyone's contribution was crucial to the nation's survival.

At the same time, Churchill demanded accountability from his leaders and military officials. He made it clear that dedication and competence were essential for victory, holding those in power responsible for their actions. This reinforced the importance of discipline and commitment to the war effort.

Through his leadership, Churchill helped lift the spirits of a weary nation. His words and actions united the British people, strengthening their resolve to endure—and ultimately, triumph. His unwavering belief in their resilience became a beacon of hope that led them through the storm of war.

2. John F. Kennedy and the Space Race

During the Cold War, President John F. Kennedy sought to inspire the American people and establish the United States as a leader in space exploration. His vision for the future was bold and clear, and he believed that reaching for the stars would unite the nation in a common goal.

Kennedy famously declared, "We choose to go to the Moon," setting an ambitious target that captured the imagination of the country. His words were more than just a statement—they were a call to action. He praised the hard work of NASA scientists and engineers, recognizing their creativity and determination, and reinforcing the idea that with persistence, anything was possible.

As the space program achieved milestones like the Mercury missions, Kennedy made sure to publicly celebrate each success. His recognition of these accomplishments built national pride and confidence in American innovation, making people believe that the dream of landing on the Moon was within reach.

Kennedy also understood the global stakes. By framing the space race as a competition with the Soviet Union, he created a sense of urgency. The pressure to succeed wasn't just about science—it was about proving America's strength and leadership in the world.

Through his inspiring vision and reinforcement of progress, Kennedy sparked a wave of excitement and determination across the nation. His leadership laid the groundwork for the historic Apollo 11 Moon landing in 1969, showing that a clear goal, combined with unwavering belief, can lead to extraordinary achievements.

3. Abraham Lincoln and the Emancipation Proclamation

President Abraham Lincoln faced one of the most difficult challenges in American history: preserving the Union during the Civil War while confronting the issue of slavery. As the nation fractured, Lincoln understood that his leadership would shape not only the future of the country but also the fate of millions enslaved.

In 1863, Lincoln issued the Emancipation Proclamation, a bold and historic step. By declaring the freedom of enslaved people in the Confederate states, Lincoln sent a clear message—this war was not just about preserving the Union, but also about fighting for freedom and human dignity. His decision turned the war into a moral cause, reinforcing the idea that the Union's struggle was aligned with justice and equality.

Lincoln didn't stop there. He regularly praised the courage and sacrifice of Union soldiers, acknowledging how African American soldiers played a crucial role in the fight. By doing this, Lincoln reinforced the importance of every soldier's contribution, and showed that the fight for freedom was a shared mission, regardless of race.

Despite immense pressure and countless setbacks, Lincoln never wavered in his commitment to keep the country united. His firm stance, even when faced with opposition from all sides, reinforced the importance of national unity and the need to see the war through to its end.

Lincoln's leadership didn't just preserve the Union. By redefining the war as a fight for human rights, he strengthened the resolve of the people, leading to the ultimate abolition of slavery. His actions showed that, with courage and moral clarity, even the most impossible battles can lead to profound change.

4. Susan B. Anthony and the Women's Suffrage Movement

Susan B. Anthony stood at the forefront of the movement for women's right to vote in the United States. With unwavering determination, she dedicated her life to a cause that many viewed as impossible. She recognized that the fight for suffrage was not just her own but a collective effort that required the support of many.

To uplift her fellow suffragists, Anthony often praised their hard work and commitment. She celebrated the small victories and recognized the sacrifices that each activist made. This recognition created a strong sense of community among the women fighting for the same goal, encouraging them to keep pushing forward.

Anthony understood the power of education in motivating others. She organized lectures, petitions, and rallies, using these platforms to inform and inspire supporters. Her words ignited a fire in those who listened, making them realize the importance of their voices in the struggle for equality. Through her efforts, she showed that every action, no matter how small, contributed to the larger fight for voting rights.

When faced with unjust laws, Anthony did not back down. She boldly challenged the system, even risking arrest to stand up for what she believed in. Her bravery became a symbol of the determination needed to achieve change. By facing these challenges head-on, she reinforced the message that resilience was essential in the fight for justice.

Through her tireless work and inspirational leadership, Susan B. Anthony played a crucial role in galvanizing the women's suffrage movement. Her efforts contributed significantly to the passage of the 19th Amendment in 1920, which finally granted women the right to vote. Anthony's legacy serves as a powerful reminder that perseverance, courage, and collective action can lead to monumental change.

These examples illustrate how historical leaders used reinforcement techniques to influence and change people's thoughts and behaviors.

Through a combination of positive reinforcement, public recognition, and strategic denouncements, these leaders were able to guide their followers toward new ways of thinking and acting, ultimately leading to significant social, political, and scientific advancements.

Understanding reinforcement techniques is essential for leaders aiming to inspire, motivate, and guide their teams effectively. By strategically applying these principles, leaders can cultivate a positive work environment, enhance performance, and foster long-term commitment.

1. **Ignite Motivation:** Positive reinforcement fuels employee engagement by acknowledging and rewarding achievements. Public recognition, tangible rewards, and opportunities for growth can significantly boost morale and productivity. For instance, publicly praising an employee for a successful project not only acknowledges their contribution but also inspires others to strive for excellence.

2. **Shape Desired Behaviors:** Negative reinforcement, when used judiciously, can redirect behavior towards desired outcomes. By removing negative consequences when employees exhibit positive actions, leaders can encourage consistent performance and adherence to standards. For example, offering flexible work arrangements to employees who consistently meet deadlines can foster a sense of autonomy and responsibility.

3. **Correct Course:** Constructive feedback and, when necessary, disciplinary action are crucial for addressing undesirable behaviors. By providing clear expectations and consequences, leaders can guide employees towards improved performance while maintaining a respectful and supportive environment.

4. **Eliminate Distractions:** Extinction, or the purposeful ignoring of negative behaviors, can be an effective strategy to reduce disruptive actions. By focusing attention on positive contributions, leaders can create a more productive and harmonious workplace.

5. **Sustain Positive Change:** Consistent and strategic reinforcement is vital for long-term behavior change. A balanced approach, combining continuous and intermittent reinforcement, can help solidify new habits and prevent complacency. For instance, recognizing employees' achievements consistently during a new project implementation can establish desired behaviors, while intermittent rewards can maintain motivation over time.

6. **Cultivate a Thriving Culture:** By skillfully employing reinforcement techniques, leaders create a positive work culture that fosters employee

well-being, loyalty, and innovation. A culture of recognition, growth, and support drives higher job satisfaction, reduced turnover, and enhanced team cohesion.

7. **Elevate Leadership Impact:** Mastering reinforcement techniques empowers leaders to make informed decisions, address challenges proactively, and optimize team performance. By aligning rewards with desired outcomes, leaders can demonstrate their commitment to employee success and organizational goals.

In essence, reinforcement techniques are invaluable tools in a leader's arsenal. By understanding and applying these principles effectively, leaders can inspire, motivate, and guide their teams towards exceptional performance and lasting success.

> **"You cannot change your destination overnight, but you can change your direction overnight."**
>
> **- Jim Rohn**

Here are the top key messages distilled from the text on reinforcement techniques used by effective leaders:

- **Motivation Through Recognition**: Effective leaders, like Sarah at Innovate Inc., utilize positive reinforcement strategies such as praise and rewards to boost employee morale and motivate team members. Public recognition and incentive programs foster a culture of excellence and inspire others to achieve similar successes.
- **Constructive Feedback and Accountability**: Leaders must address undesirable behaviors through constructive feedback and, when necessary, disciplinary actions. Providing clear expectations and supportive guidance helps employees understand their shortcomings and encourages improvement while maintaining a respectful work environment.
- **Creating a Supportive Environment**: By removing negative conditions, such as excessive workload pressures, leaders can

reinforce desired behaviors without punitive measures. A supportive and flexible work environment enhances employee well-being and promotes productivity.

- **Balanced Reinforcement Approaches**: The use of continuous and intermittent reinforcement is essential for sustaining positive behavior changes. Consistently recognizing achievements helps establish new habits, while occasional rewards maintain motivation over time, preventing complacency.
- **Cultivating a Thriving Work Culture**: Mastery of reinforcement techniques allows leaders to cultivate a positive organizational culture characterized by employee recognition, growth, and support. This culture drives higher job satisfaction, reduces turnover, and enhances overall team cohesion and performance.

These messages emphasize the importance of reinforcement techniques in effective leadership and their role in shaping organizational behavior.

Coaching Leaders for Mental Agility: Story No 33

Mary Barra: A Trailblazing Leader

> **"I think one of the most important things that I can do as a leader is to create an environment where people can thrive, where they can take risks, where they can fail, and where they can learn from their failures."**
>
> **- Mary Barra**

Mary Barra is a quintessential example of a modern-day leader who has transformed a behemoth corporation while breaking glass ceilings. Her journey from a co-op student inspecting car parts to the CEO of General Motors is a testament to her grit, determination, and strategic acumen.

Mary Barra began her remarkable journey at General Motors in 1980, stepping into the world of engineering as a co-op student. Eager to learn, she gained hands-on experience in various engineering roles while diligently working toward her degree. This early exposure to the inner workings of the automotive industry ignited her passion for innovation and teamwork.

Upon graduating, Barra dove into a range of engineering and management positions within GM. She contributed to vehicle development and manufacturing, showcasing her commitment to excellence. With each role, she honed her skills and built a reputation as a capable leader who understood the complexities of the automotive landscape.

As she rose through the ranks, Barra held several significant positions that showcased her leadership prowess. In her role as Vice President of Global Manufacturing Engineering, she took charge of overseeing manufacturing processes, striving to improve efficiency across the board. Her ability to foster collaboration and streamline operations marked her as a visionary in her field. Later, as Vice President of Global Human Resources, she focused on enhancing GM's organizational culture, prioritizing the well-being and growth of employees.

Barra's journey reached a pivotal moment when she became the Executive Vice President of Global Product Development. In this role, she led the charge in developing new vehicles, managing product planning, design, and engineering. Her strategic vision and commitment to innovation played a crucial role in shaping GM's future.

On January 15, 2014, Mary Barra made history by being appointed as the Chairperson and CEO of General Motors, becoming the first woman to lead a major global automaker. This groundbreaking achievement symbolized not just a personal victory but a significant step for women in leadership roles across industries.

However, her initial days as CEO were far from easy. She faced the daunting task of addressing the aftermath of a major ignition switch recall crisis that had shaken the company to its core. Barra stepped up to the challenge with resilience and clarity, implementing extensive reforms and fostering open communication within the organization. Her leadership during this turbulent time demonstrated her ability to navigate complex issues while maintaining a focus on the company's long-term vision.

Mary Barra's journey from a co-op student to the CEO of General Motors serves as a powerful inspiration. It showcases the impact of hard work, adaptability, and a commitment to continuous improvement. Her story reminds us that leadership is not just about holding a position but about inspiring others, driving change, and navigating challenges with courage and integrity.

Mary Barra's tenure as CEO of General Motors (GM) has involved navigating a range of complex challenges.

Here are some notable challenges she faced and the actions she took to overcome them:

In her early days as CEO of General Motors, Mary Barra faced an enormous challenge when she inherited a crisis rooted in a massive ignition switch recall. This issue, which had begun before her leadership, had resulted in tragic accidents and lost lives, severely tarnishing GM's reputation. Determined to restore trust, Barra took decisive action. She implemented sweeping reforms to enhance safety practices, introducing a rigorous review process that prioritized transparency with regulators and the public. Understanding the importance of culture, she fostered an environment of accountability, encouraging open dialogue about safety concerns so that issues could be addressed proactively.

As the automotive landscape shifted dramatically due to the rise of electric vehicles and autonomous technologies, Barra recognized the urgency for GM to adapt swiftly. She led the charge toward a new era of innovation, making substantial investments in research and development for electric and self-driving vehicles. The launch of the Chevrolet Bolt EV marked a significant milestone in this transition, showcasing GM's commitment to an electric future. Barra also established strategic partnerships with tech companies like Cruise Automation, reinforcing GM's position in the evolving market.

Financial performance presented another hurdle as GM grappled with declining market share and economic pressures from both new competitors and traditional rivals. To combat this, Barra implemented a restructuring plan designed to streamline operations and reduce costs. This included closing unprofitable plants and focusing on core markets.

Under her guidance, GM revamped its product lineup, prioritizing high-demand models like SUVs and trucks to boost profitability.

With growing concerns about environmental sustainability and stricter emissions regulations, Barra embraced the need for change. She set ambitious goals for GM to become a leader in sustainability, pledging to achieve carbon neutrality by 2040. Under her leadership, GM adopted sustainable manufacturing practices and increased its investment in zero-emission vehicle production, aiming to position the company as an industry pioneer in environmental responsibility.

Barra also navigated the complexities of global trade and supply chain disruptions. Recognizing the challenges posed by trade tensions and tariffs, she worked diligently to diversify GM's supply sources and enhance the flexibility of its operations. By emphasizing local sourcing strategies, Barra aimed to reduce the company's reliance on international suppliers, fostering resilience in GM's supply chain.

Throughout these transformations, employee morale became a critical focus for Barra. The organizational changes and restructuring efforts had understandably affected the workforce's spirit. To address this, she prioritized employee engagement, implementing new leadership practices that emphasized communication and transparency. Barra championed diversity and inclusion initiatives, creating a more inclusive workplace that ultimately enhanced employee satisfaction and cohesion.

Mary Barra's journey at GM is a powerful illustration of how effective leadership can turn challenges into opportunities. Through her unwavering commitment to safety, innovation, sustainability, and employee well-being, she has not only guided GM through turbulent times but has also inspired a new generation of leaders to embrace change and strive for excellence.

Mary Barra's approach to these challenges highlights her leadership skills in managing crises, driving innovation, and steering GM through periods of significant change.

Her actions reflect a commitment to transforming GM into a more agile, customer-focused, and sustainable company.

Mary Barra, the Chairperson and CEO of General Motors (GM), offers several valuable lessons in leadership and accomplishment:

Mary Barra stands as a transformative force at General Motors, driving the company through a remarkable period of change. With a clear vision for the future, she has championed the shift toward electric vehicles and autonomous driving technologies. Her forward-thinking mindset not only highlights the importance of innovation but also underscores the necessity of adapting to the rapidly changing automotive industry.

Under her leadership, GM has committed to investing significantly in new technologies, exemplified by the development of the Chevrolet Bolt EV and advancements in self-driving cars. This dedication to innovation reflects the need for continuous progress to remain competitive and meet the evolving needs of customers.

Barra has also prioritized environmental responsibility, pushing GM toward a sustainable future. She set ambitious goals to reduce carbon emissions and transition to renewable energy sources, acknowledging the critical role of environmental stewardship in modern business leadership.

In the face of challenges, including the impact of the COVID-19 pandemic, Barra has demonstrated remarkable resilience. She has successfully navigated GM through turbulent times, making strategic decisions that showcase her ability to lead through adversity. Her approach provides a powerful lesson in resilience and strategic thinking.

Emphasizing diversity and inclusion, Barra has worked diligently to create a more inclusive workplace at GM. By prioritizing diverse perspectives, she highlights the value of varied experiences in driving innovation and fostering a strong organizational culture.

Barra's leadership style centers on empowering her teams, encouraging collaboration and engagement among employees. She believes that strong leadership is about cultivating an environment where individuals feel valued and motivated to contribute to the company's success.

With a customer-centric approach, Barra has prioritized understanding and responding to market needs. This focus on aligning GM's strategies with customer demands is crucial for effective product development and marketing.

Her bold decision-making has positioned GM for future growth. By making significant investments in electric and autonomous vehicles and undertaking restructuring initiatives, she demonstrates the importance of aligning actions with long-term goals.

Known for her transparent communication style, Barra builds trust and credibility with employees and stakeholders. Effective communication is essential for navigating organizational change and fostering a positive workplace culture.

Finally, Barra has emphasized ethical leadership and corporate responsibility. She has worked to improve safety standards and address past issues, reinforcing the importance of integrity in leadership.

Through her visionary leadership, Mary Barra inspires others to embrace change, foster innovation, and prioritize sustainability, showcasing the profound impact that one leader can have on an entire industry.

Mary Barra's leadership at GM offers valuable insights into driving transformation, embracing innovation, and fostering a positive organizational culture, all while navigating complex challenges and prioritizing sustainability.

Key Takeaway:

- **Visionary Leadership:** Emphasizes the importance of having a forward-looking vision and adapting to industry changes to drive transformation.
- **Innovation Focus:** Highlights the need for continuous investment in new technologies and innovation to stay competitive and meet evolving customer needs.
- **Commitment to Sustainability:** Demonstrates the value of setting ambitious environmental goals and transitioning to sustainable practices to address growing environmental concerns.
- **Resilience in Crisis:** Shows the significance of navigating challenges and making strategic decisions during uncertain times to maintain organizational stability and growth.

- **Inclusive Leadership:** Underlines the importance of fostering diversity and inclusion to create a more collaborative and representative workplace.
- **Employee Engagement:** Reflects the need to empower employees and build a positive organizational culture to drive success and enhance morale.
- **Customer-Centric Approach:** Illustrates the value of understanding and responding to market needs to align business strategies with customer demands.
- **Strategic Decision-Making:** Demonstrates the importance of making bold, strategic decisions aligned with long-term goals for future growth and success.
- **Transparent Communication:** Emphasizes the role of clear and transparent communication in building trust and managing organizational change effectively.
- **Ethical Leadership:** Reinforces the significance of ethical practices and corporate responsibility in maintaining integrity and improving organizational standards.

Part 5

Leadership Pillar-5(Encouragement)

Summary

In this chapter, readers embark on a journey through the leadership lessons learned from Mary Barra, the inspiring CEO of General Motors. Barra's career offers a treasure trove of insights into effective leadership practices, urging readers to think deeply about what it means to lead with purpose.

Imagine a leader who navigates change with a clear vision, guiding their organization through turbulent waters. Barra embodies this visionary leadership, showing how essential it is to adapt and evolve in a fast-paced world. She encourages others to look ahead, embracing innovation as the driving force behind success. By consistently investing in new technologies and ideas, leaders can meet the ever-changing needs of their customers, staying one step ahead of the competition.

Sustainability is another core theme in Barra's leadership approach. She exemplifies how ambitious environmental goals can transform a company's practices, making them more responsible and responsive to global ecological challenges. Through her actions, readers can see that true leadership includes a commitment to the planet, inspiring others to follow suit.

Barra's resilience shines brightly during times of crisis. She navigates challenges with strategic decision-making, proving that stability and growth are possible even when the path is unclear. Her calm and focused demeanor encourages others to face difficulties head-on, reminding them that every challenge is an opportunity for growth.

Fostering an inclusive workplace is another hallmark of Barra's leadership style. She understands that diverse teams not only enhance collaboration but also reflect the society we live in. By creating an environment where everyone feels valued, she builds a culture of respect and understanding, encouraging people to bring their whole selves to work.

As the chapter unfolds, readers learn that engaging employees is crucial for driving success. Barra champions a positive organizational culture where empowerment leads to heightened morale and performance. She advocates for truly understanding customer needs, aligning business strategies to meet those demands effectively.

Strategic decision-making is portrayed as an art form in this chapter. Bold decisions, rooted in a long-term vision, pave the way for future growth and success. Barra's commitment to transparent communication fosters trust within her team, creating an open environment where ideas can flourish, and change can be managed effectively.

Moreover, the chapter emphasizes the importance of ethical leadership. Barra stands as a beacon of integrity, demonstrating that ethical practices and corporate responsibility are foundational to maintaining trust and respect in any organization.

Readers discover that effective leaders harness the power of recognition to motivate their teams. Barra's acknowledgment of achievements boosts morale, fostering a culture of excellence. Constructive feedback becomes a vital tool for improvement, allowing individuals to learn and grow while maintaining a respectful atmosphere.

Creating a supportive environment emerges as a key factor in promoting productivity. By alleviating negative conditions, leaders can enhance employee well-being, which translates into higher performance. The chapter also reveals the importance of balanced reinforcement techniques—both consistent and occasional recognition—to sustain positive behaviors over time.

The relationship between leaders and followers is portrayed as dynamic and reciprocal. Leaders nurture their followers' growth through mentorship and skill-building, highlighting how this mutual development fosters a new generation of leaders. A supportive organizational culture plays a critical role in nurturing leadership qualities, making learning a shared journey.

Open communication is celebrated as a cornerstone of trust and engagement. When leaders genuinely appreciate their followers' contributions, they strengthen team loyalty and motivation. Historical examples of mentorship illustrate the profound impact of leaders on their followers, showcasing how guidance shapes future generations.

The chapter delves into the influence of social dynamics, underscoring the importance of trust, effective communication, and adaptability. Readers are reminded that true leaders embrace change and remain connected to the needs of their teams, drawing inspiration from figures like Nelson Mandela and Martin Luther King Jr.

Finally, the concept of self-fulfilling prophecies emerges, revealing how beliefs can shape actions. Positive expectations can inspire success, and leaders play a crucial role in creating an environment where high expectations are the norm. By cultivating a culture that encourages innovation and growth, leaders can drive remarkable achievements.

In conclusion, this chapter serves as a guide for aspiring leaders, emphasizing the importance of self-awareness, emotional intelligence, and authenticity. It inspires readers to cultivate a supportive and thriving organizational environment where every individual can flourish. Through Mary Barra's example, they are reminded that effective leadership is not just about directing others; it's about empowering them to rise and shine.

Leadership Skill	Action Steps	Follow-Up / Measurement
1. Recognition and Appreciation	- Acknowledge individual and team contributions regularly.	- Review team feedback: Have team members share how they feel about the recognition provided.
	- Provide timely, specific, and sincere praise, both publicly and privately.	- Track frequency of recognition (e.g., how often you celebrate wins, big or small).
	- Create a routine (e.g., weekly shout-outs during meetings).	- Observe improvements in team morale and engagement over time.
2. Empathy and Active Listening	- Schedule one-on-one check-ins with team members.	- Ask for feedback on whether team members feel heard during meetings or check-ins.
	- Practice active listening during conversations, focusing on understanding team concerns and ideas.	- Measure effectiveness by asking team members how well they think you understand their challenges and needs.
	- Demonstrate empathy by acknowledging their emotions and providing solutions or support.	- Reflect on the emotional atmosphere within the team (Is there a sense of being valued?).
3. Empowerment and Autonomy	- Delegate tasks with clear expectations, providing team members autonomy in how they approach tasks.	- Evaluate if team members feel empowered by seeking their input on decision-making and task delegation.
	- Involve team members in decision-making processes whenever possible.	- Review the results of projects where autonomy was given, checking for innovation or ownership demonstrated.
	- Encourage independent thinking and problem-solving.	- Track improvements in innovation or problem-solving when autonomy is granted.
4. Positive Communication and Constructive Feedback	- Use positive reinforcement consistently (acknowledge efforts, reinforce desired behaviors).	- Assess how well team members respond to feedback by tracking changes in their performance or engagement.
	- Provide constructive feedback in a manner that is supportive and solution-oriented.	- Use feedback surveys to gauge how team members view the feedback process.
	- Foster an open and transparent communication environment where feedback is a two-way street.	- Evaluate the openness of the team (Are team members comfortable giving feedback to you?).
5. Creating a Supportive and Collaborative Environment	- Encourage collaboration by creating spaces for team members to share ideas and solutions.	- Observe if team collaboration improves by measuring how frequently team members collaborate on tasks.
	- Organize team-building activities or informal check-ins to strengthen team bonds.	- Track team cohesion through regular pulse checks or informal discussions on team dynamics.
	- Address conflicts constructively and ensure that resolutions align with team goals.	- Follow up on conflict resolution effectiveness by seeing if the team is more cohesive after resolving conflicts.

Daily, Weekly, and Monthly Program to Improve Encouragement Leadership Skills

Daily Actions:

1. **Acknowledge Efforts:**
    - **Action:** Every day, identify at least one team member's contribution and publicly acknowledge it. This could be in meetings, emails, or quick messages.
    - **Example:** "Great work on the presentation, your creativity really made a difference!"
2. **Active Listening:**
    - **Action:** Make time to actively listen to team members' ideas and concerns during meetings or one-on-one check-ins.
    - **Example:** Ask, "What do you think could improve in this project?" and genuinely consider their response.
3. **Check-In:**
    - **Action:** Have brief check-ins with team members, asking about their work and any support they need.
    - **Example:** "How are you feeling about the current project? Is there anything I can do to support you?"

Weekly Actions:

1. **Team Acknowledgement:**
    - **Action:** Set aside time each week to recognize the collective team's achievements, not just individual ones.
    - **Example:** "This week, we made great progress as a team—let's celebrate our teamwork!"
2. **Encourage Peer Support:**
    - **Action:** Encourage peer-to-peer recognition. Ask team members to acknowledge each other's work in meetings.

- **Example:** "Who would like to share a positive experience about a teammate this week?"

3. **Provide Constructive Feedback:**

- **Action:** Offer feedback not only when things go wrong but also when things go right.
- **Example:** "I noticed you handled that challenge well—what strategies did you use? How can I help you do more of that?"

Monthly Actions:

1. **Team Building Activities:**

- **Action:** Organize one team-building activity each month to foster collaboration and trust.
- **Example:** A team lunch, brainstorming session, or collaborative project that promotes teamwork.

2. **Celebrate Successes:**

- **Action:** End each month by celebrating achievements and setting the tone for continued success.
- **Example:** "We hit our monthly goals and surpassed expectations. Let's recognize those who went above and beyond."

3. **Reflection and Feedback:**

- **Action:** Conduct a feedback session where team members can share their experiences about how they've been encouraged and supported.
- **Example:** "What do you need more of from me as a leader to help you succeed in the upcoming month?"

Measurement & Results Tracking:

1. **Daily:**
   - **Metric:** Number of acknowledgments and positive feedback given.
   - **Self-Review:** Did I recognize at least one person's effort today?
2. **Weekly:**
   - **Metric:** Number of peer-to-peer recognitions encouraged and team morale.
   - **Self-Review:** Did I create an open environment where team members felt valued and heard?
3. **Monthly:**
   - **Metric:** Team engagement and satisfaction levels (survey or feedback).
   - **Self-Review:** Did I organize a successful team-building activity or recognition event?

By consistently applying this plan, the leader can significantly improve their encouragement skills, fostering a motivated and collaborative team environment.

Here are some key coaching questions about leadership based on the insights from the text:

Visionary Leadership

1. **What is your vision for your organization, and how do you communicate it to your team?**
2. **How do you adapt your vision in response to industry changes?**

Innovation Focus

3. **What steps are you taking to foster a culture of innovation within your team?**
4. **How do you identify and invest in new technologies that align with customer needs?**

Commitment to Sustainability

5. **What ambitious environmental goals have you set for your organization?**
6. **How do you promote sustainable practices among your team members?**

Resilience in Crisis

7. **Can you share a recent challenge you faced and the strategic decisions you made to navigate it?**
8. **How do you maintain organizational stability during uncertain times?**

Inclusive Leadership

9. **What initiatives are you implementing to foster diversity and inclusion in your workplace?**
10. **How do you ensure that all voices are heard and valued in your organization?**

Employee Engagement

11. **What strategies do you use to empower your employees and boost morale?**
12. **How do you cultivate a positive organizational culture?**

Customer-Centric Approach

13. **How do you gather and respond to feedback from your customers?**

14. **In what ways do you align your business strategies with customer expectations?**

Strategic Decision-Making

15. **What bold, long-term decisions have you made for your organization, and what guided those choices?**

16. **How do you ensure that your decisions align with the overall vision of your organization?**

Transparent Communication

17. **What practices do you have in place to promote open and transparent communication within your team?**

18. **How do you build trust through your communication style?**

Ethical Leadership

19. **How do you uphold ethical practices within your organization?**

20. **What role does corporate responsibility play in your leadership approach?**

Reinforcement Techniques

21. **How do you recognize and celebrate achievements within your team?**

22. **What feedback mechanisms do you have in place to promote improvement while maintaining respect?**

Organizational Culture

23. **What steps do you take to cultivate a supportive and positive organizational culture?**

24. **How do you leverage challenges as opportunities for learning and growth within your team?**

Building Trust and Engagement

25. **How do you build trust with your team members?**
26. **What methods do you use to appreciate and acknowledge your team's contributions?**

Personal Growth and Development

27. **In what ways do you mentor and develop the leadership skills of your followers?**
28. **How do you balance your personal growth as a leader with the development of your team?**

Reflection and Future Growth

29. **How do you measure your effectiveness as a leader, and what areas do you believe you need to improve?**
30. **What legacy do you want to leave as a leader, and how do you plan to achieve it?**

These questions can serve as a foundation for coaching discussions, helping individuals reflect on their leadership style and effectiveness while encouraging them to consider their own practices and goals.

Concluding Reflection:

- **What one action can you take this week to embody the leadership qualities discussed in the chapter?**

This question can help facilitate deeper reflection and dialogue, encouraging individuals to connect their personal experiences with the principles outlined in the text.

Part-6

Leadership Pillar-6(Enablement)

Catalysts of Change: The Role of Leaders in Empowering Others

- **Learning Leadership from Maria Montessori**
- **Empathetic Leaders Mindset**
- **How Alan Mulally's Leadership Drove a Historic Turnaround**
- **From Rubble to Riches: The Rise of a Post-War Powerhouse**

In a world filled with challenges and opportunities, great leaders emerge as catalysts of change, illuminating paths that empower others to grow and thrive. Imagine a classroom where every child's curiosity is not just acknowledged but celebrated. Maria Montessori, a pioneer in education, transformed how we view learning and leadership. She envisioned an environment where children explore freely, guided by their interests. In her classrooms, children become active participants in their education, discovering their strengths and passions. Montessori's methods remind us that when leaders create nurturing spaces, they unlock the potential within each individual.

Transitioning from education to the corporate world, we meet empathetic leaders who understand that connection drives success. These leaders do not merely manage tasks; they build relationships. Envision a workplace where leaders listen deeply, recognizing the unique challenges their team members face. They foster an environment of trust and collaboration. This is evident in companies that prioritize employee well-being, leading to higher morale and productivity. By practicing empathy, leaders empower their teams to voice their ideas and contribute to a shared vision, knowing that their contributions are valued and respected.

Consider the inspiring journey of Alan Mulally, who stepped into the troubled Ford Motor Company during a time of crisis. Faced with immense challenges, he turned the company around with a vision grounded in empowerment. Imagine walking through Ford's headquarters, where employees feel a renewed sense of purpose and ownership over their work. Mulally engaged his team, inviting them to share their thoughts and strategies. His approach was simple yet profound: by empowering his employees to take ownership of their work, he sparked innovation and resilience. His story illustrates how leaders can transform organizations by creating environments where everyone feels they can contribute. Mulally's leadership style reflects a deeper understanding of what it means to empower others, showing that effective leadership is about more than just making decisions; it's about building a culture where every voice matters.

Lastly, let's reflect on the remarkable journeys of leaders who have risen from adversity. Picture a community rebuilt from the ground up, where a leader stands firm amid challenges, inspiring hope, and determination. These leaders, such as those who rebuilt their communities after wars or natural disasters, remind us that true empowerment often emerges from struggle. Their resilience and commitment to their people inspire those around them to find strength in difficult times. They exemplify how overcoming challenges not only builds character but also strengthens a community's spirit and resolve.

As you explore the stories of these leaders, remember that empowerment is not just a strategy; it's a philosophy that can transform organizations and communities. Each example reveals how the power of encouragement and understanding can lead to profound transformations. These narratives invite you to reflect on your leadership journey and consider how you, too, can be a catalyst for change in your own sphere of influence.

Leadership is not merely about position or authority; it's about how you influence and uplift those around you. By embracing the principles of empowerment, empathy, and resilience, you can create an environment that inspires others to rise and thrive. So, as you delve into these powerful stories, consider how you might embody the same spirit of empowerment in your own life and leadership journey.

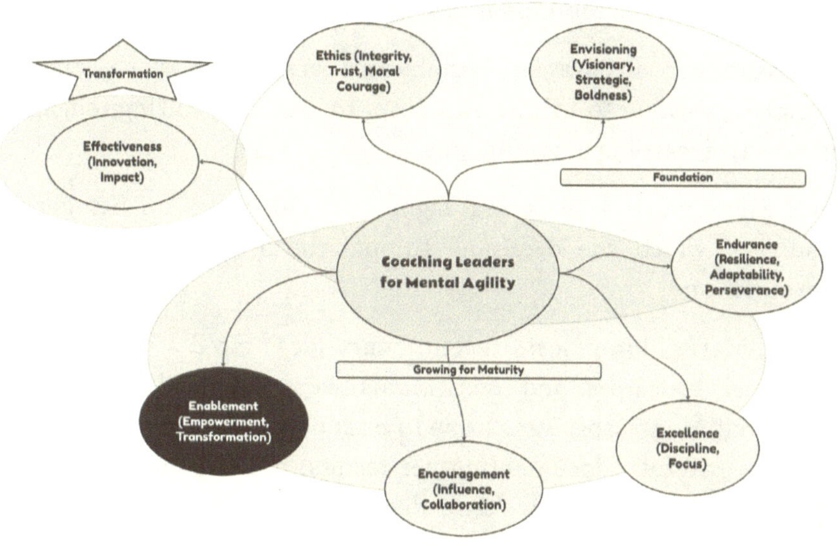

Coaching Leaders for Mental Agility: Story No 34

Learning Leadership from Maria Montessori

> **"To aid life, leaving it free, however, is the most important duty of the educator."**
>
> **- Maria Montessori**

Dr. Maria Montessori was an Italian physician and educational pioneer.

She became one of the first female doctors in Italy, initially focusing on psychiatry and working with children with disabilities.

Her observations of these children sparked her lifelong interest in education.

In 1907, she opened her first school, the "Casa dei Bambini" (Children's House), where she implemented her educational approach.

Maria Montessori's leadership style has had a profound and lasting impact on education worldwide.

Her emphasis on child-centered learning, independence, and respect for the individual has influenced many educational philosophies and practices beyond the Montessori method itself.

Montessori schools are now established across the globe, and her principles continue to inspire educators to create nurturing, engaging, and effective learning environments.

Maria Montessori faced several significant challenges on her journey to success, which she overcame through resilience, innovation, and determination.

At first, Maria Montessori's revolutionary ideas faced a wall of doubt. Traditional educators and institutions were skeptical, resistant to change. But Montessori wasn't one to back down easily. She set up pilot programs, carefully documenting her results, proving the effectiveness of her approach. Her first "Casa dei Bambini" (Children's House) in Rome became a shining example of her methods, turning skeptics into believers as her ideas gained recognition and spread.

As one of Italy's first female physicians, Montessori also faced gender discrimination. The barriers were undeniable, but her perseverance was stronger. She excelled academically, broke into professional spaces dominated by men, and earned respect through her groundbreaking work with children and her contributions to medical science. Her success spoke louder than the prejudice she faced.

When World War II disrupted her work, forcing her to leave Europe, Montessori didn't stop. In India, she adapted her methods to new cultures, training teachers and continuing to spread her educational philosophy far beyond Europe. Her passion for learning knew no borders.

Montessori's journey was also marked by financial struggles. Early on, resources were scarce, and funding was hard to come by. But she didn't let that stop her. She found supporters—powerful figures and organizations—who believed in her vision and helped finance her schools and training centers. Through writing books and delivering lectures, she raised both funds and awareness for her cause.

Her methods weren't always understood. Critics, especially in traditional educational circles, misinterpreted or misapplied her ideas, leading to pushback. Yet Montessori remained unwavering. She emphasized thorough teacher training to ensure her philosophy was correctly implemented. Establishing the Association Montessori International (AMI), she safeguarded the integrity of her approach, ensuring her vision would continue to flourish as she had intended.

Maria Montessori's journey was not an easy one, but her determination and belief in her methods paved the way for a global movement that continues to inspire education today.

Her journey offers several leadership lessons that can inspire and guide us today:

Maria Montessori's journey was one marked by resilience and determination, with obstacles ranging from gender discrimination to the upheavals of war. At every turn, she encountered resistance to her ideas and personal setbacks, yet she never wavered from her mission. Her persistence is a testament to the power of staying focused and committed even when the odds seem overwhelming. She showed that true leaders find growth in adversity and remain steadfast in pursuit of their goals, regardless of the challenges ahead.

Montessori wasn't afraid to break away from tradition. She introduced bold, innovative ideas that transformed education, placing the needs and independence of the child at the center of learning. This forward-thinking approach challenged the norms of the time, proving that real progress comes from daring to think differently. Through her work, Montessori exemplified how great leaders push boundaries and embrace creativity, seeing opportunities where others see limits.

What fueled Montessori through every challenge was her deep passion for education. Her work wasn't just a profession; it was her purpose.

She believed wholeheartedly in the potential of every child and was relentless in her efforts to spread her educational philosophy. Her unwavering commitment demonstrates how passion and purpose can drive leaders to inspire others and achieve meaningful change. It is this sense of purpose that gives leaders their energy and guides them through even the toughest moments.

Montessori also understood the importance of adaptability. When World War II forced her to leave Europe, she brought her methods to India, proving her ability to adjust and embrace new cultural contexts. Her willingness to adapt, to learn from different environments, showed that effective leaders must be flexible, able to shift their approaches as circumstances evolve.

At the heart of Montessori's educational philosophy was empowerment. She believed in giving children the freedom to learn, grow, and take ownership of their education. Her methods empowered students to become self-motivated and independent learners. This principle of empowerment extends to leadership as well, where true leaders support and trust their teams, providing the tools and autonomy needed to thrive.

Montessori was committed to lifelong learning. She constantly researched, refined, and expanded her methods, demonstrating a thirst for knowledge that never faded. Her dedication to personal and professional growth serves as a reminder that leaders must never stop learning. Staying curious and open to new knowledge keeps leaders effective and innovative.

Despite the many difficulties she faced, Montessori never worked alone. She built a supportive network of influential figures and organizations that believed in her vision. This collaboration helped her overcome financial hurdles and expand her reach. Her story highlights the importance of building strong networks—leaders need allies and supporters to achieve their full potential.

Throughout her life, Montessori remained true to her principles. Even when her methods were criticized or misunderstood, she stayed consistent in her values and never compromised her beliefs. This integrity earned her trust and credibility, qualities essential for any leader who seeks to inspire and guide others.

Montessori didn't just talk about her ideas; she lived them. She led by example, embodying the principles she taught through her own actions and results. Her ability to show, rather than tell, set a powerful example for those around her. This kind of leadership—leading by example—creates a culture of accountability and inspiration.

Her clear vision of transforming education and improving child development was always at the forefront of her work. Montessori communicated this vision effectively, drawing others to her mission. Her leadership showed how vital it is for leaders to have a compelling vision that can motivate and unite people around a shared purpose.

Maria Montessori's life is a masterclass in resilience, innovation, and visionary leadership. Her legacy continues to inspire leaders across many fields, demonstrating that with passion, adaptability, and a clear vision, anything is possible.

To improve our leadership style and mindset based on the Montessori principles, we can ask ourselves the following questions:

1. **Child-Centered Approach**
    - How well do I understand and support the unique potential of each individual in my team?
    - Do I create opportunities for my team members to pursue their interests and develop at their own pace?
2. **Empowerment and Independence**
    - How can I provide the tools and environment needed for my team to work independently and confidently?
    - In what ways can I foster a sense of autonomy and self-responsibility within my team?
3. **Respect and Observation**
    - Am I taking enough time to observe my team's needs and interests before making decisions?
    - Do I respect the individual choices and learning processes of my team members?

4. Prepared Environment

- Is the working environment structured to facilitate independent and effective work?
- How can I better organize resources and tools to promote self-discipline and freedom within limits?

5. Holistic Development

- Am I addressing the social, emotional, and practical skills development of my team, in addition to their professional growth?
- How can I incorporate activities that promote overall well-being and community sense in my team?

6. Innovation and Adaptability

- Am I open to new ideas and willing to adapt my methods based on feedback and observations?
- How can I encourage innovation and adaptability within my team to meet our specific needs?

7. Training and Mentorship

- How can I improve the training and development opportunities I provide to my team?
- In what ways can I act as a mentor to support the growth and success of my team members?

Examples of Applying These Questions

Child-Centered Approach:

How well do I understand and support the unique potential of each individual in my team?

Action: Conduct one-on-one meetings to discuss individual goals and tailor tasks to align with each team member's strengths.

Empowerment and Independence:

How can I provide the tools and environment needed for my team to work independently and confidently?

Action: Create a resource hub with all necessary tools and information easily accessible and encourage team members to take ownership of projects.

Respect and Observation:

Am I taking enough time to observe my team's needs and interests before making decisions?

Action: Implement regular feedback sessions where team members can voice their needs and preferences and use this information to guide decision-making.

Prepared Environment:

Is the working environment structured to facilitate independent and effective work?

Action: Design the workspace to be functional and organized, ensuring that team members have easy access to what they need to perform their tasks efficiently.

Holistic Development:

Am I addressing the social, emotional, and practical skills development of my team, in addition to their professional growth?

Action: Integrate team-building activities and wellness programs that promote overall personal development and a sense of community.

Innovation and Adaptability:

Am I open to new ideas and willing to adapt my methods based on feedback and observations?

Action: Foster a culture of experimentation where new ideas are encouraged and tested, and adapt strategies based on what works best.

Training and Mentorship:

How can I improve the training and development opportunities I provide to my team?

Action: Establish a mentorship program and offer regular training sessions to enhance skills and knowledge.

By reflecting on these questions and taking corresponding actions, leaders can create a supportive and empowering environment that fosters creativity, independence, and growth, much like Maria Montessori did in her educational philosophy.

> **"A person's character is determined by the way they respond to their environment."**
>
> **– Maria Montessori**

Here are four key messages from the text about Dr. Maria Montessori that are suitable for a 10th-grade student:

- **Resilience and Determination**: Maria Montessori faced many obstacles in her life, such as being one of the first women doctors in Italy and dealing with skepticism about her educational ideas. Instead of giving up, she stayed focused and worked hard to prove that her methods were effective. This shows that true leaders keep pushing forward, even when things get tough.
- **Child-Centered Empowerment**: Montessori believed in placing the needs of children at the center of education. She encouraged independence and helped kids take charge of their own learning. In leadership, this means supporting team members and allowing them to take responsibility for their work. When people feel trusted and empowered, they are more motivated to do their best.
- **Visionary Leadership and Adaptability**: Montessori had a clear goal of changing education for the better, which guided her throughout her career. When she faced challenges, like having to leave Europe during World War II, she adapted her methods to fit new situations, like teaching in India. This highlights the importance of being flexible and open-minded as a leader while also having a strong vision to inspire others.
- **Collaboration and Lifelong Learning**: Montessori recognized that she couldn't achieve her goals alone. She built strong relationships with supporters and mentors who helped her along the way. Additionally, she was always eager to learn and improve

her teaching methods. This teaches us that good leaders work well with others and never stop seeking knowledge, which helps everyone grow together.

Coaching Leaders for Mental Agility: Story No 35

Empathetic Leaders Mindset

> **"Leaders who fail to listen will eventually be surrounded by people who have nothing to say."**
>
> **– Andy Stanley**

Arne Sorenson, the former CEO of Marriott International, was known for his leadership style that combined empathy, strong communication, and a focus on the bigger picture of humanity.

Arne Sorenson's empathetic leadership style offers valuable lessons for creating a thriving workplace. His approach starts with embracing transparency. He understood that being open and honest with employees, especially during tough times, builds trust. When leaders communicate clearly and share their vulnerabilities, they establish credibility and a sense of unity within their teams.

Prioritizing employee welfare was another cornerstone of Sorenson's leadership. He believed that investing in the well-being of employees directly contributes to their engagement and productivity. By providing support through benefits, career development opportunities, and fostering a positive work environment, leaders demonstrate their empathy and commitment to the team.

Sorenson also excelled at building personal connections. He knew that personal recognition and appreciation significantly impact how valued employees feel. Simple gestures, like handwritten notes of thanks, can lift morale and strengthen loyalty. Such small acts show employees that they are seen and appreciated for their contributions.

Championing diversity and inclusion was essential to Sorenson's vision for a successful workplace. He recognized that promoting a diverse and inclusive environment fosters innovation and mutual respect. Leaders should actively support initiatives that embrace diversity, ensuring everyone has equitable opportunities to thrive.

Additionally, Sorenson engaged in corporate responsibility, recognizing the importance of giving back to the community and addressing social and environmental challenges. By championing corporate responsibility initiatives, leaders can enhance their company's reputation while positively influencing employee engagement and public perception.

In essence, Arne Sorenson's empathetic leadership serves as an inspiring example of how leaders can create an environment where trust, support, and respect flourish, ultimately leading to a more engaged and productive workforce.

Key Takeaways from Arne Sorenson's Leadership:

- **Transparent Communication**: Build trust through honesty and openness.
- **Employee Welfare**: Show commitment to the well-being and development of your team.
- **Personal Connection**: Foster a sense of belonging through personal recognition and appreciation.
- **Diversity and Inclusion**: Support initiatives that create a fair and inclusive workplace.
- **Corporate Responsibility**: Engage in activities that benefit communities and promote sustainability.

Arne Sorenson's leadership at Marriott International exemplifies how empathy and compassion can drive both business success and positive organizational culture. His legacy provides valuable insights for leaders aiming to lead with empathy and make a meaningful impact on their employees and communities.

Cheryl Bachelder, the former CEO of Popeyes Louisiana Kitchen, is renowned for her empathetic and servant leadership style. Her approach to leadership transformed the company and its culture, leading to significant business success.

Cheryl Bachelder's empathic leadership style offers valuable insights for anyone looking to create a more supportive and effective workplace. She believed in adopting a servant leadership approach, where the focus is on serving others first. By prioritizing the needs of employees and stakeholders, she fostered a collaborative environment where trust could flourish. This mindset not only strengthened relationships but also drove better business outcomes.

Bachelder knew that actively listening to her team was essential. She took the time to genuinely hear their thoughts and challenges, which allowed her to understand their perspectives better. This deep listening not only informed her decision-making but also motivated her team, making them feel valued and engaged.

Investing in the development of her employees was another key aspect of her leadership. Bachelder recognized that when individuals grow, the organization benefits as a whole. By providing training, mentorship, and opportunities for career advancement, she helped cultivate a skilled and committed workforce that was ready to take on challenges.

Creating a clear and compelling purpose was central to Bachelder's leadership philosophy. She understood that when employees grasped and believed in the company's mission, they felt a sense of belonging and were more motivated to work towards achieving its goals. This shared purpose united the team and inspired them to put in their best efforts.

Bachelder also emphasized the importance of fostering transparency and open communication. She believed that transparent communication builds trust and ensures everyone is aligned with the company's vision and objectives. By encouraging open dialogue, she invited diverse perspectives, which led to better problem-solving and sparked innovation.

In essence, Cheryl Bachelder's empathic leadership shines as a guiding example of how prioritizing others, listening actively, investing in growth, creating a clear purpose, and fostering open communication can create a thriving workplace where everyone feels empowered and engaged.

Key Takeaways from Cheryl Bachelder's Leadership:

- **Servant Leadership**: Focus on serving and empowering others.
- **Active Listening**: Engage with stakeholders to understand and address their needs.
- **Employee Development**: Invest in the growth and skills of your team.
- **Purpose-Driven Culture**: Align actions with a clear and motivating purpose.
- **Transparent Communication**: Build trust through openness and honesty.

Cheryl Bachelder's leadership at Popeyes Louisiana Kitchen is a testament to the power of empathy and servant leadership in driving both cultural and business success. Her approach provides valuable insights for leaders aiming to create a positive and impactful organizational environment.

Tony Hsieh, the former CEO of Zappos, is remembered as a leader who put empathy and employee happiness at the forefront of his vision. His approach centered around fostering a positive and empowering work culture where everyone could thrive. Hsieh believed that a strong company culture was vital. He worked to create an environment filled with vibrant values that resonated deeply with his employees, making them feel a strong sense of belonging and purpose. By living and articulating these core values, he connected with his team, encouraging engagement and commitment.

He understood the importance of empowering his employees. Hsieh encouraged them to take ownership of their work, granting them the autonomy to make decisions. This trust not only enhanced job satisfaction but also sparked innovation, as employees felt respected and accountable for their contributions.

Hsieh placed a high priority on the well-being of his team, recognizing that their happiness, both at work and in their personal lives, was essential. He implemented programs that focused on physical health, mental well-being, and personal development, creating a supportive atmosphere where employees felt cared for. This commitment to their overall well-being contributed to a motivated and productive workforce.

Communication was another key pillar of Hsieh's leadership. He believed in fostering open and honest dialogue within the company. By creating channels for feedback and being approachable, he built trust among his team. Employees knew their perspectives were valued and respected, which further enhanced their connection to the organization.

But Hsieh's empathy didn't stop within the walls of Zappos. He extended this caring approach to customers as well. By truly understanding and addressing the needs of customers, he helped Zappos build lasting relationships and achieve high levels of satisfaction and loyalty.

Through these practices, Tony Hsieh showed that empathetic leadership is not just about caring for employees; it's about creating a sustainable and thriving business. His legacy at Zappos stands as a powerful example of how empathy and success can go hand in hand, inspiring future leaders to prioritize connection and compassion in their own workplaces.

Empathic leadership exercises are essential to developing the skills necessary to effectively lead with compassion and understanding.

1. Exercise for Transparent Communication

David, a team leader at a busy marketing agency, noticed that his team wasn't communicating well, which was affecting their mood and productivity. Many employees were afraid to speak up about problems, so issues were going unresolved. To fix this, David decided to start a monthly "Open Forum," where anyone could freely ask questions and share their thoughts.

The first forum was set for a Thursday afternoon. David was both excited and nervous about how his team would respond. He invited everyone to come prepared to share their ideas. When the day arrived, David welcomed the team into a relaxed meeting room with snacks and drinks, hoping to create a comfortable space. He began by sharing the company's recent wins and challenges. He even spoke openly about a project that hadn't gone well and how they were working to fix it.

As David talked, he noticed some employees exchanging glances, so he paused and encouraged them to speak up. He reassured them that no question was too small and that they were all in it together. Slowly, people started raising their hands. Sarah, a graphic designer, asked how budget cuts would affect their future work. David answered her honestly, explaining how they planned to keep delivering quality work despite the tighter budget.

Another employee, Tom, expressed his concerns about the heavy workload and the stress it was causing. David listened carefully and acknowledged the problem. He didn't have an immediate fix but promised to talk to the management team about redistributing some tasks.

As the meeting went on, more employees began sharing their thoughts, and the mood shifted from nervous to engaged. People were relieved to finally be heard. David took notes on all the issues raised and promised to follow up on them.

By the end of the forum, the atmosphere in the room had noticeably improved. Employees left feeling valued and connected, understanding more about the company's goals and their place in it. The Open Forum not only encouraged transparency but also strengthened the team's bond. From then on, the forum became a regular part of their work culture, helping the team face challenges together and celebrate their successes as a united group.

2. Exercise for Prioritizing Employee Welfare

At a growing tech startup, Sophie, the team leader, started noticing subtle signs of burnout among her staff. Employees seemed less engaged, and productivity was slipping. While they were hitting their targets, there was a visible strain. Sophie realized that the fast-paced environment was taking a toll on her team, and it was time to do something about it.

Determined to prioritize her team's well-being over just their performance metrics, Sophie decided to implement regular "Well-being

Check-ins." These one-on-one meetings weren't about project deadlines or performance reviews—they were solely focused on how each person was feeling and coping with the demands of work and life.

Sophie scheduled her first check-in with Mark, a software engineer who had recently been working long hours on a major project. Instead of diving into work matters, she asked, "Mark, how are you feeling lately? How's the balance between work and your personal life?"

Surprised by the question, Mark hesitated, but then opened up. He admitted he had been feeling overwhelmed, juggling his work responsibilities while caring for his aging parents at home. Sophie listened carefully, nodding in understanding. She didn't try to jump in with solutions right away. Instead, she let Mark express everything on his mind.

Once Mark finished, Sophie asked, "Is there anything I can do to make things easier for you? Maybe adjust your hours or bring in more support for the project?" Mark was relieved that Sophie cared enough to ask and appreciated her offer for flexibility.

Sophie didn't just stop there. After their conversation, she followed up with him in the weeks to come, checking in on how the adjusted schedule was working and making sure he still felt supported. She extended this same approach to the rest of her team, scheduling regular check-ins and creating an open space for her employees to share their concerns.

As a result, her team began to feel more valued and cared for. With flexible working hours, mental health resources, and an empathetic ear always available, the staff's overall well-being improved. Productivity and morale soared—not because of pressure, but because the employees felt understood and supported in a meaningful way. The company flourished as a direct result of prioritizing its people over simply pushing for results.

3. Exercise for Building Personal Connections

One afternoon, Rachel, a team leader at a growing tech startup, sat at her desk, reflecting on how to better connect with her team. The fast-paced environment often made it hard to acknowledge individual contributions, and she worried that her team members were beginning to feel unappreciated. She wanted to find a simple yet meaningful way to make them feel valued and remind them that their hard work didn't go unnoticed.

An idea came to her: handwritten notes. In a world dominated by emails and instant messages, she realized that a personalized, handwritten message might leave a lasting impact.

The next day, Rachel began writing notes to her team. Each note was thoughtful and specific, acknowledging individual achievements. For Alex, her top coder, she highlighted the extra hours he had put in to solve a major bug before a product launch. For Sarah, a marketing lead, Rachel thanked her for the creativity that brought the latest campaign to life. She expressed genuine gratitude and encouraged each of them to keep striving for excellence.

Rather than leaving the notes on their desks, Rachel chose to deliver each one personally, taking a few moments to chat and show her appreciation face-to-face. The team's response was immediate. They smiled as they read her words, some even keeping the notes pinned to their workspace as a reminder that their efforts mattered.

Over the following weeks, Rachel noticed a shift in the atmosphere. The team seemed more connected, motivated, and engaged, not just with their work but with each other. The simple gesture of a handwritten note had created a sense of belonging, reminding everyone that they were part of something meaningful.

4. Exercise for Championing Diversity and Inclusion

At a medium-sized marketing company, Jessica, the HR leader, noticed that although the company valued having a diverse workforce, employees were not always comfortable talking about diversity and inclusion. While the workplace seemed friendly, she realized some people felt left out, and important views were missing.

To make the environment more open and inclusive, Jessica started an initiative called "Diversity Dialogues." The goal was simple: hold regular meetings where employees could come together to share their experiences and have meaningful talks about diversity and inclusion.

For the first meeting, she invited Malik, a successful entrepreneur from a minority background, as a guest speaker. Malik shared his story, discussing the challenges he faced and how embracing diversity helped him succeed. His story struck a chord with the employees and led to heartfelt conversations.

After Malik spoke, Jessica encouraged everyone to share their own experiences. At first, people were shy and unsure if they could speak freely. But when Priya shared her feelings of being overlooked in meetings, others started to join in. They talked about topics like unconscious bias and how cultural differences affected teamwork. Jessica made sure the environment was supportive and reminded everyone that it was a safe space to express their thoughts.

The feedback from the first meeting was very positive. Employees appreciated having a place to speak openly and felt more connected to each other. Jessica emphasized that these sessions were not just for talking—they were also for making real changes. She took the feedback and worked with the leadership team to address specific issues, such as improving mentorship programs for underrepresented employees and making hiring practices more inclusive.

Over time, "Diversity Dialogues" became a regular part of the company's culture. The sessions helped create a sense of belonging and respect, turning the firm into a truly inclusive workplace. Employees felt heard, and their ideas led to real improvements that strengthened the company from within.

5. Exercise for Engaging in Corporate Responsibility

The lesson of engaging in corporate responsibility emphasizes the importance of giving back to the community. To achieve this, organizing community service projects or volunteer opportunities for your team on a quarterly basis can be highly effective. Employees are encouraged to suggest causes or organizations they feel passionate about, fostering a sense of ownership and enthusiasm for the projects.

The company can demonstrate its commitment by allocating work hours for participation, showing employees that community involvement is valued at an organizational level. After each event, a debrief session allows team members to reflect on their experiences, share personal insights, and discuss the positive impact they've made on the community. This process not only encourages social responsibility but also fosters teamwork and personal growth within the company.

By integrating these exercises into leadership practices, organizations can build a culture of giving while strengthening team bonds and aligning employees with a shared mission beyond business goals.

To effectively integrate these exercises into your leadership practice, consider the following steps:

- Commit to Regular Practice: Schedule these exercises regularly to ensure they become a part of your leadership routine.
- Lead by Example: Participate actively in all exercises to demonstrate your commitment to empathic leadership.
- Seek Feedback: Continuously seek feedback from your team on the effectiveness of these exercises and adjust them as needed.
- Reflect and Improve: Reflect on the outcomes of these exercises and strive to improve your empathic leadership skills continually.

By incorporating these exercises, leaders can develop and enhance their empathic leadership abilities, fostering a more supportive, inclusive, and productive work environment.

Here are the key messages from the text, simplified into four points:

- **Transparent Communication:** Leaders should be open and honest with their teams, especially during difficult times. This builds trust and creates a united work environment.
- **Prioritize Employee Well-being:** Investing in employees' well-being through support programs and a positive work atmosphere leads to greater engagement and productivity.

- **Build Personal Connections:** Simple gestures, like handwritten notes of appreciation, can make employees feel valued and strengthen their loyalty to the company.
- **Champion Diversity and Inclusion:** Supporting diverse voices and fostering an inclusive workplace encourages innovation and mutual respect, ensuring everyone has a fair chance to succeed.

Coaching Leaders for Mental Agility: Story No 36

How Alan Mullally's Leadership Drove a Historic Turnaround

> **"I'm not afraid to fail. I'm afraid of not trying."**
>
> **- Alan Mulally**

Alan Mulally's leadership at Ford during the 2006-2009 financial crisis is considered a masterclass in crisis management and corporate turnaround. When he became CEO in 2006, Ford was struggling financially, losing market share, and on the verge of bankruptcy.

In 2006, Ford found itself facing severe financial challenges, having posted a staggering loss of $12.6 billion, making it one of the most difficult years in the company's long history.

This financial crisis was a symptom of deeper problems within the company. Ford's product line had become overly complex, leading to inefficiencies in both manufacturing and decision-making. The company struggled to streamline its operations, which slowed its ability to respond to market changes.

Internally, Ford faced significant cultural issues. Transparency and collaboration were lacking, with different departments working in silos, isolated from one another. This lack of cohesion further hindered the company's ability to act quickly and efficiently.

The situation became even more dire in 2008 when the global financial crisis hit, causing car sales to plummet across the industry. As Ford was trying to get back on track, its competitors, General Motors, and Chrysler, declared bankruptcy. While Ford avoided this fate, the economic downturn added immense pressure, making recovery even more challenging.

Mulally's Strategic Actions:

Alan Mulally's transformation of Ford Motor Company reads like a riveting tale of vision, risk-taking, and bold leadership. When Mulally stepped in as CEO during one of Ford's darkest hours, he saw an organization fractured by regional divisions, inefficiencies, and a struggling product line. His vision for "One Ford" wasn't just a slogan; it was a call to unify Ford's global operations under a shared purpose. He dismantled regional silos, urging teams to collaborate across borders. By reducing the number of platforms and focusing on a few globally viable vehicles, Mulally streamlined production and cut costs, transforming Ford's product line into a model of efficiency and relevance.

One of his most daring moves came when he mortgaged nearly every asset Ford owned, including its iconic blue oval logo. This audacious decision raised $23.6 billion, giving Ford the cash reserves it needed to weather the coming financial storm. When the 2008 crisis devastated the auto industry, Ford stood tall, avoiding the government bailout that entangled its competitors. This independence bolstered Ford's reputation and gave the company a decisive edge.

Mulally's foresight extended to understanding the shifting needs of consumers. He pivoted Ford's focus toward fuel-efficient vehicles like the Ford Fusion and Ford Focus, anticipating the growing demand for greener cars. His push for innovation didn't stop at fuel efficiency—he championed advancements in technology and manufacturing that laid the groundwork for Ford's foray into hybrid and electric vehicles.

But perhaps Mulally's most lasting impact came from the culture he cultivated at Ford. His leadership radiated transparency and teamwork. Weekly "Business Plan Review" meetings became a cornerstone of his strategy, forcing executives to confront challenges openly and work together toward solutions. Initially, resistance was palpable—Ford's culture had long rewarded silence over honesty. Yet, Mulally's unwavering commitment to openness slowly broke down barriers, fostering a new sense of accountability and collaboration.

Even in the face of financial turbulence, Mulally didn't alienate Ford's workforce. Instead, he partnered with the United Auto Workers union, negotiating cost reductions without resorting to mass layoffs. His collaborative approach not only preserved jobs but also strengthened Ford's relationship with its employees during a time of immense uncertainty.

Under Mulally's leadership, Ford didn't just survive—it thrived. His story is a masterclass in vision, courage, and the power of bringing people together to achieve extraordinary results.

Outcomes:

- **Financial Recovery**: Under Mulally's leadership, Ford returned to profitability in 2009, posting a $2.7 billion profit after years of losses.
- **Avoiding Bankruptcy**: Ford was the only major U.S. automaker to avoid bankruptcy and government bailouts during the 2008-2009 financial crisis.
- **Rebuilding the Brand**: Ford's ability to avoid bankruptcy while maintaining product quality and innovation helped rebuild consumer confidence. The company's reputation improved significantly, particularly as it was seen as more self-reliant than competitors like GM and Chrysler.

Legacy:

Mulally's leadership is widely credited with saving Ford from collapse and positioning the company for long-term success. His focus on efficiency, teamwork, and strategic foresight transformed Ford into a more resilient and innovative company. His success at Ford is often cited as a prime example of crisis leadership, particularly in industries facing massive disruption.

Ford's performance during and after the crisis proved that with strong leadership, even a legacy company with deep-rooted issues can adapt and thrive in challenging circumstances.

The story of Alan Mulally's leadership at Ford offers key lessons about leadership and the resilience mindset, especially during times of crisis:

1. Visionary Leadership

Mulally's "One Ford" vision provided a clear, unified goal that focused on collaboration and efficiency across global operations. Strong leaders must articulate a clear and compelling vision that unites teams and gives them direction.

Having a long-term, consistent vision helps leaders stay focused and prevents them from being overwhelmed by short-term crises. It also gives employees a sense of purpose.

2. Decisiveness in Crisis

One of Mulally's boldest decisions was mortgaging Ford's assets to raise capital before the financial crisis. This action was risky but crucial for the company's survival. Leaders must be willing to make tough decisions in uncertain times, even if those decisions carry risk.

Resilient leaders have the courage to take calculated risks when necessary, knowing that proactive action is often better than waiting for the situation to worsen.

3. Transparency and Accountability

Mulally's regular "Business Plan Review" meetings fostered transparency and open communication within Ford. He made it clear that identifying and solving problems was more important than avoiding mistakes.

Open communication builds trust, which is essential for resilient teams. Leaders who encourage transparency can adapt to challenges more effectively because they know what's truly going on in their organization.

4. Collaboration and Empowerment

Mulally worked closely with the United Auto Workers (UAW) and executives to ensure cooperation. He believed in empowering people across the organization to contribute to the solution.

Resilient leaders understand the importance of collaboration. They create environments where employees are empowered to contribute ideas and solutions, which strengthens the entire organization's capacity to weather difficulties.

5. Focus on the Future

Mulally's strategic shift toward fuel-efficient vehicles and innovation prepared Ford for long-term success, showing that leadership in a crisis isn't just about surviving but also positioning the company for future growth.

Resilient leaders maintain a forward-looking perspective. They don't just focus on getting through the immediate crisis; they plan for the future and invest in innovation that can lead to long-term sustainability.

6. Adaptability

The shift from a traditional, hierarchical structure to a collaborative, leaner organization required adaptability. Mulally's ability to pivot Ford's operations to focus on efficiency and innovation exemplifies the need for flexibility.

Resilient leaders remain adaptable in the face of change. They know that rigid thinking can prevent growth and survival during crises, so they encourage adaptability within their teams.

7. Leading by Example

Mulally modeled the behavior he wanted to see by being transparent, approachable, and results-driven. His commitment to the "One Ford" plan showed that he was fully invested in the company's success.

Resilient leaders lead by example, showing others how to respond to adversity through their actions. This behavior fosters resilience within the team, creating a culture that can bounce back from setbacks.

> **"It's not about what you're going to do. It's about what you're going to make happen."**
>
> **- Alan Mulally**

From Alan Mulally's leadership at Ford, we learn that resilient leaders:

- **Maintain a clear vision and long-term focus.**
- **Are decisive and willing to take risks.**

- **Foster a culture of transparency and accountability.**
- **Encourage collaboration and adaptability.**
- **Focus not just on survival but on future growth and innovation.**

These qualities enable leaders and organizations to not only survive crises but emerge stronger, more unified, and better positioned for future success.

Coaching Leaders for Mental Agility: Story No 37

From Rubble to Riches: The Rise of a Post-War Powerhouse

> **"Our history has taught us that from the depths of despair, we can rise again with creativity and innovation."**
>
> **- Masayoshi Son (CEO of SoftBank):**

Japan's post-war economic miracle:

In the heart of Japan, a remarkable transformation took place in the automotive and technology industries, marking the rise of several iconic companies. Toyota Motor Corporation began its journey as a modest operation, but through sheer determination and innovative thinking, it grew into one of the largest automakers in the world. This evolution was driven by the Toyota Production System (TPS), a groundbreaking approach that emphasized efficiency, quality, and a relentless commitment to continuous improvement. Toyota's influence reshaped the automotive industry, showcasing Japan's industrial strength on a global scale.

Similarly, Sony Corporation emerged from the ashes of World War II, founded by the visionary duo Akio Morita and Masaru Ibuka. Starting with humble beginnings, they crafted transistor radios that quickly gained popularity. As the years unfolded, Sony expanded its horizons, introducing a diverse range of products, from televisions to audio equipment. The company's crowning achievements came with the launch of the Walkman and PlayStation gaming consoles, which revolutionized how people interacted with music and games. Sony's dedication to innovation and uncompromising quality solidified its position as a powerhouse in consumer electronics.

In the automotive realm, Honda Motor Co., Ltd. tells a similar story of resilience and growth. Founded by Soichiro Honda in the aftermath of World War II, Honda began its journey producing motorized bicycles. However, with a keen focus on engineering excellence, fuel efficiency, and reliability, Honda quickly transitioned into motorcycles and automobiles. Its success in Japan soon extended to international markets, where Honda became synonymous with quality and performance.

Meanwhile, Nintendo Co., Ltd. started its life as a playing card company in the late 19th century. Over the decades, it transformed into a giant in the video game industry. The release of the Nintendo Entertainment System (NES) in the 1980s marked a turning point, bringing beloved franchises like Super Mario and The Legend of Zelda into homes around the world. Nintendo's innovative approach to game design and its ability to create unforgettable characters not only reshaped the gaming landscape but also made it a household name.

Lastly, Panasonic Corporation, originally known as Matsushita Electric Industrial Co., Ltd., has stood the test of time as a leading manufacturer of consumer electronics and home appliances. With a steadfast focus on quality and customer satisfaction, Panasonic built a strong reputation for reliability across its extensive product lines. The company's commitment to innovation has allowed it to thrive in an ever-changing market, ensuring its legacy continues.

These stories of perseverance, creativity, and innovation showcase the incredible journey of Japanese companies that not only transformed their industries but also inspired countless others around the world. Through their commitment to excellence, they remind us that with vision and determination, remarkable achievements are possible.

These success stories highlight Japan's ability to innovate, adapt, and excel in various industries, setting a high standard for global competition and contributing to the country's economic growth and prosperity.

After World War II, Japanese leaders faced numerous challenges in their efforts to rebuild and industrialize the economy.

Some of the key challenges included:

In the wake of World War II, Japan faced a daunting landscape marked by devastation and the urgent need for reconstruction. Much of the country's industrial infrastructure lay in ruins, with factories, transportation networks, and urban centers shattered by conflict. The task of rebuilding this vital infrastructure loomed large, demanding an immense commitment of time, resources, and meticulous planning.

As Japan embarked on this monumental challenge, it grappled with economic instability. The immediate post-war period was characterized by soaring inflation and a scarcity of essential goods, leaving the populace anxious and uncertain. Japanese leaders recognized the necessity of implementing effective policies to stabilize the economy, restore public confidence, and set the stage for long-term growth and recovery.

During this turbulent time, Japan was under the occupation of Allied forces, which introduced another layer of complexity. The country was undergoing a process of demilitarization and democratization, overseen by the occupying powers. Japanese leaders faced the difficult task of navigating the reconstruction of their nation while adhering to the conditions imposed by their occupiers. It was a delicate balancing act, requiring resilience and adaptability.

Japan's lack of natural resources presented a significant hurdle in its reconstruction efforts. With limited access to essential raw materials such as oil, coal, and iron ore, leaders were forced to think creatively. They explored alternative strategies for economic development, focusing on import substitution, resource conservation, and improving efficiency. This resourcefulness became a hallmark of Japan's recovery.

Additionally, the war had inflicted profound social dislocation on the country. Labor shortages became a pressing concern as many workers were lost during the conflict or were unable to return to civilian life. Japanese leaders understood the importance of addressing these shortages and providing support to displaced workers. They recognized that a stable and productive workforce was essential for the nation's revitalization.

As Japan sought to rebuild, its recovery was closely linked to re-establishing connections with the global economy. Leaders understood that international trade and foreign investment were vital for growth. Navigating complex international relations, they worked diligently to negotiate trade agreements and rebuild diplomatic ties. This engagement with the world marked a significant step in Japan's journey toward economic integration and prosperity.

Through determination, innovation, and a commitment to rebuilding, Japan gradually transformed itself from the ashes of war into a thriving nation, showcasing the power of resilience in the face of adversity.

Despite these challenges, Japanese leaders demonstrated resilience, innovation, and determination in rebuilding the economy and laying the foundation for Japan's remarkable post-war economic miracle.

Their efforts paved the way for Japan to emerge as one of the world's leading industrial powers in the decades that followed.

The year is 1945. Japan lies in ruins, its cities ravaged by war. Yet, amidst the smoke and ash, a flicker of determination ignites. A nation, battered but not broken, vows to rise from the ashes. This is the story of Japan's miraculous economic ascent, a testament to the power of resilience, vision, and unwavering spirit.

Our story begins with the ***unyielding spirit*** *of the Japanese people. Fueled by a deep sense of national pride and a yearning for a brighter future, they rallied behind a common goal – to rebuild their shattered nation. This wasn't just about bricks and mortar; it was about reclaiming their place on the world stage.*

Kaizen*, a philosophy ingrained in the Japanese psyche, became their guiding light. It meant* ***unceasing improvement****, a relentless pursuit of perfection in every aspect of life. From factory floors to boardrooms, the mantra of "better today than yesterday" echoed. Every worker, every leader, became an architect of progress, meticulously refining processes and pushing the boundaries of innovation.*

But vision is the fuel that propels ambition. Japanese leaders, with a keen eye on the horizon, charted a course for long-term growth. Instead of quick fixes, they invested heavily in the nation's ***future****. Infrastructure projects* *crisscrossed the landscape, classrooms bustled with eager learners, and research labs hummed with the promise of technological breakthroughs. This farsighted approach laid the foundation for decades of prosperity.*

Gone were the days of rigid hierarchies. A new leadership style emerged, one that championed ***collaboration and consensus****. Decisions weren't dictated from above; they were forged through open communication and a shared sense of purpose. This fostered a spirit of teamwork, where creativity and innovation could flourish.*

Japan also understood the importance of ***putting the customer first****. Companies became laser-focused on exceeding expectations, building a reputation for exceptional quality and unwavering commitment to customer satisfaction. This customer-centric approach became a cornerstone of their success in global markets.*

The world watched in awe as Japan transformed itself. Their ***willingness to adapt*** *was remarkable. They embraced new technologies, readily adjusting to the ever-evolving economic landscape. This adaptability allowed them to seize opportunities in emerging industries, leaving competitors scrambling to catch up.*

The Japanese work ethic is legendary. A ***deep respect for hard work*** *and dedication permeates their society. Long hours were seen not as a burden, but as a badge of honor, a contribution to the collective good. This unwavering* ***commitment to excellence*** *fueled Japan's rise as a leader in manufacturing, technology, and various other sectors.*

Japan's post-war economic miracle is more than just statistics and soaring GDP. It's a story of a nation's unwavering spirit, a testament to the power of vision, collaboration, and a relentless pursuit of excellence. Even today, the lessons learned from this extraordinary period continue to shape Japan's journey as a global leader.

Here are some key leadership traits we can learn from Japan's post-war economic rise:

In the aftermath of World War II, Japan faced the daunting challenge of rebuilding itself from the ground up. The leaders of this resilient nation understood that to achieve lasting success, they needed a long-term vision. Rather than chasing quick profits, they directed their efforts toward strategic planning that would create a solid foundation for the future. Investments in infrastructure, education, and technology became their priorities, allowing Japan to rise from the ashes and forge a path toward sustained economic growth.

As these leaders worked together, they embraced a style of collaborative leadership that fostered teamwork and open communication. They didn't just make decisions in isolation; they encouraged the voices of their employees, inviting everyone to contribute. This approach cultivated a sense of ownership among the workforce, inspiring them to engage fully in their roles. The result was an environment where productivity flourished, and innovative ideas thrived.

A relentless commitment to quality and efficiency became a hallmark of Japanese industry. Leaders instilled a culture of continuous improvement known as *kaizen*. This wasn't just a motto; it was a way of life. Employees at every level took pride in their work, constantly seeking ways to enhance processes and ensure that every product met the highest standards. This dedication to excellence not only distinguished Japanese goods on the global stage but also set new benchmarks for quality.

In a world of rapid change, Japanese leaders demonstrated remarkable adaptability. They recognized that staying ahead required embracing new technologies and being open to innovation. By supporting research and development initiatives, they equipped companies with the tools necessary to respond to evolving market demands. This willingness to change allowed Japanese businesses to stay on the cutting edge, often leading the way in technological advancements.

Understanding that human capital is invaluable, Japan's leaders made substantial investments in education and training. They built programs designed to cultivate a skilled workforce, ensuring that employees had the knowledge and capabilities needed to drive innovation and contribute to the nation's growth. This commitment to developing talent created a thriving pool of workers who were eager to advance both personally and professionally.

The partnership between the government and the private sector was another critical element of Japan's success story. The government took on a guiding role, offering financial support and infrastructure development, while businesses implemented the strategies that would propel the economy forward. This cooperation between public and private entities allowed for swift progress, turning ambitious plans into reality.

At the heart of this transformation was a focus on trust and social harmony. Leaders understood the power of fostering a supportive and stable work environment. They encouraged a culture of shared purpose and collective responsibility, making employees feel valued and connected to the broader mission of their organizations. This sense of unity not only enhanced productivity but also contributed to a more positive workplace atmosphere.

However, the road to success wasn't without its challenges. The intense dedication to work sometimes led to long hours and an expectation of loyalty that could overshadow individual well-being. While building consensus was beneficial for team cohesion, it occasionally slowed down decision-making processes, hindering the ability to respond swiftly in a fast-paced market.

By examining the leadership traits that powered Japan's post-war economic miracle, we uncover essential lessons for leaders everywhere. The importance of strategic vision, collaboration, a commitment to quality, and a readiness to adapt and innovate shines through as guiding principles. Yet, it is equally crucial to strike a balance—prioritizing a healthy work-life balance and nurturing individual creativity is essential for long-term success.

As we reflect on Japan's remarkable journey, we find inspiration and valuable insights for leaders across various contexts, illuminating a path toward sustainable growth and a flourishing workforce.

"Japan's post-war economic miracle was a combination of disciplined labor, innovative technology, and an unwavering commitment to education."

- Robert F. Engle (Economist):

Here are the top four messages drawn from the text about Japan's post-war economic miracle:

- **Resilience and Vision**: Japan's leaders exhibited remarkable resilience in the face of immense challenges after World War II. They prioritized long-term planning over immediate gains, focusing on rebuilding infrastructure, education, and technology. This visionary approach laid the groundwork for Japan's sustained economic growth and transformation into a global industrial power.
- **Collaborative Leadership**: The leadership style in Japan emphasized collaboration and consensus-building. By fostering open communication and teamwork, leaders created a sense of ownership among employees. This inclusive approach not only boosted morale but also drove innovation and productivity across various industries.
- **Commitment to Quality and Continuous Improvement**: Japanese companies adopted a culture of *kaizen*, which means continuous improvement. This commitment to quality and efficiency became a hallmark of their industries, allowing companies like Toyota and Sony to set new standards for excellence and outperform global competitors.
- **Adaptability and Human Capital Development**: The ability to adapt to changing market conditions was crucial for Japan's economic success. Leaders invested significantly in education and training, recognizing that a skilled workforce was vital for innovation. This focus on human capital development ensured that employees were well-equipped to meet evolving challenges and seize new opportunities in the global market.

These messages highlight the key factors behind Japan's remarkable recovery and ongoing success, offering valuable lessons for leaders aiming for sustainable growth in any context.

Part 6

Leadership Pillar-6(Enablement)

Summary

This chapter highlights the remarkable journeys of influential leaders and organizations, illustrating the power of resilience, collaboration, and a commitment to continuous improvement.

Dr. Maria Montessori exemplifies resilience and determination as she navigated the challenges of being a pioneering woman doctor in Italy. Her unwavering focus on child-centered education emphasized the importance of empowering individuals to take charge of their learning, a concept that mirrors effective leadership. Montessori's visionary approach and adaptability, especially during tumultuous times like World War II, showcase the need for leaders to remain flexible while pursuing their goals. Furthermore, her belief in collaboration and lifelong learning underscores that true leadership involves building strong relationships and fostering growth among team members.

Similarly, Alan Mulally's leadership at Ford emphasizes the significance of maintaining a clear vision and fostering a culture of transparency and collaboration. By prioritizing employee well-being and encouraging diverse perspectives, he created a united and innovative work environment that not only survived challenges but thrived in the long run.

The resilience of Japan's post-war leaders serves as a powerful reminder of the importance of long-term planning and adaptability. Their commitment to rebuilding infrastructure and investing in human capital enabled Japan to emerge as a global industrial power. The culture of continuous improvement, or *kaizen*, became a hallmark of their industries, emphasizing quality and efficiency as keys to success.

Together, these stories illustrate essential leadership qualities: resilience, vision, collaboration, a commitment to quality, and a focus on developing human capital. They serve as valuable lessons for current and future leaders, highlighting the importance of empowering others, adapting to change, and striving for excellence in every endeavor.

Skill	Action Steps	Follow-Up
1. Delegation and Trust	- Clearly define tasks and expectations. - Assign tasks to team members based on strengths. - Provide autonomy for decision-making.	- Regularly check if tasks are completed with quality. - Seek feedback on delegation style.
2. Empowerment and Resource Allocation	- Ensure all team members have access to tools and resources. - Grant authority to make decisions in their roles.	- Review resource usage and effectiveness. - Measure decision-making success and areas for improvement.
3. Professional Development and Mentorship	- Identify growth areas for each team member. - Organize regular coaching and training sessions. - Support career aspirations with a clear plan.	- Conduct quarterly career progression reviews. - Track completed training and development outcomes.
4. Feedback and Recognition	- Provide timely, specific, and constructive feedback. - Recognize and reward team contributions.	- Assess improvement based on feedback given. - Monitor team morale and motivation through surveys or conversations.
5. Innovation and Creativity	- Encourage brainstorming sessions and idea-sharing. - Support calculated risk-taking and experimentation.	- Track the implementation of innovative ideas. - Reflect on lessons learned from successes and failures.

Here's a structured 6-month plan for someone working on improving their **Enablement Leadership Skills**. The program focuses on gradual, measurable progress.

Daily Program:

1. **Delegation Practice**: Give at least one task or responsibility to a team member that they can own.
    - **Action**: Allow them to make decisions.
    - **Measurement**: Track how often tasks are delegated and if team members are empowered to make decisions.

2. **Supportive Conversations**: Start or end your day with a check-in with a team member about their challenges and needs.
    - **Action**: Offer advice but refrain from taking over.
    - **Measurement**: Reflect on whether you offered solutions or enabled independent action.
3. **Skill Recognition**: Identify one team member's strengths each day and encourage them to further develop that skill.
    - **Action**: Give verbal acknowledgment or send a supportive message.
    - **Measurement**: Track recognition and whether employees have taken up the challenges to develop further.

Weekly Program:

1. **Leadership Training**: Dedicate time each week to develop leadership skills around enablement—read a book, watch a webinar, or attend a coaching session.
    - **Action**: Implement one new leadership strategy.
    - **Measurement**: Weekly self-assessment on how the new strategy impacted your team's performance.
2. **Provide Growth Opportunities**: Identify one team member each week who needs to learn something new and support them in taking on a development project or learning opportunity.
    - **Action**: Facilitate the opportunity.
    - **Measurement**: Track who took on the growth opportunities and whether they succeeded.
3. **Feedback and Reflection**: Meet with a peer or mentor to discuss progress on enabling your team.
    - **Action**: Implement any feedback and adjust your strategies.
    - **Measurement**: Record feedback and the actions taken to improve.

Monthly Program:

1. **Team Autonomy Review**: Reflect on the level of autonomy your team members have and how well they've responded to increased responsibility.
   - **Action**: Empower teams to take on more complex tasks.
   - **Measurement**: Evaluate the performance and feedback on how well they managed increased responsibility.
2. **Personal Development Plan (PDP)**: Create a personalized development plan for each team member with a focus on skills they want to learn or improve.
   - **Action**: Have a conversation about their career goals and develop a roadmap.
   - **Measurement**: Track the progress of each team member's development.
3. **Enablement Leadership Review**: At the end of each month, reflect on how well you have enabled your team to succeed. Ask for feedback and assess your actions.
   - **Action**: Review your progress and areas for improvement.
   - **Measurement**: Reflect on feedback received, actions taken, and improvements observed.

Action and Result Measurement:

- **Daily Actions**: Track delegation and feedback sessions. Measure empowerment by the quality of decisions and independence shown by the team.
- **Weekly Actions**: Monitor the integration of leadership strategies and the progress of growth opportunities provided.
- **Monthly Actions**: Assess team autonomy and personal development plans through feedback and individual achievements.

This structured plan should enable a leader to take practical steps toward improving enablement leadership skills, gradually seeing improvement over a 6-month period.

Here are some key coaching questions derived from the themes and lessons in the text:

Questions for Reflection and Growth

Resilience and Determination:

- Can you share a time when you faced a significant obstacle? How did you overcome it, and what did you learn from the experience?
  1. What strategies do you employ to maintain focus on long-term goals during challenging times?
- **Child-Centered Empowerment (or Team Empowerment):**
  1. How do you currently empower your team members to take ownership of their work?
  2. In what ways can you encourage independence and initiative among those you lead?
- **Visionary Leadership and Adaptability:**
  1. What is your vision for the future, and how does it guide your decisions today?
  2. How do you adapt your leadership style to respond to changing circumstances or unexpected challenges?
- **Collaboration and Lifelong Learning:**
  1. Who are the key individuals or mentors in your professional network, and how do they support your growth?
  2. What steps can you take to foster a culture of collaboration and open communication within your team?

- **Commitment to Quality and Continuous Improvement:**
  1. What processes do you have in place for seeking feedback and implementing improvements in your work or organization?
  2. How do you ensure that quality remains a priority in your projects and initiatives?
- **Adaptability and Human Capital Development:**
  1. How are you investing in your own professional development and that of your team members?
  2. What skills or knowledge areas do you believe are essential for your team to succeed in the future?
- **Building Trust and Social Harmony:**
  1. How do you cultivate trust and a sense of community within your team?
  2. In what ways can you enhance employee well-being and create a positive work environment?

Concluding Reflection:

- **What one action can you take this week to embody the leadership qualities discussed in the chapter?**

This question can help facilitate deeper reflection and dialogue, encouraging individuals to connect their personal experiences with the principles outlined in the text.

Part-7

Leadership Pillar-7(Effectiveness)

Transformative Leadership: Making a Lasting Impact

- **Impact of Leadership Behavior on Organizations**
- **The Hospitality Legend: How Horst Schulze Redefined Luxury**
- **Ken Kutaragi: The Tinkerer Who Became a Gaming Titan**
- **The Grand Design and the Human Psyche: Leadership Lessons from the Pyramids**
- **Are you on the journey towards self-actualization?**

In the realm of leadership, the most enduring influence comes from those who harness innovation to inspire change and foster a sense of purpose. **Transformative Leadership** embodies this essence, demonstrating how leaders can leave an indelible mark not only within their organizations but also across entire industries and communities. This section delves into the multifaceted nature of effective leadership, illustrating how specific behaviors and strategies can create ripples of positive change.

As we explore the profound impact of leadership behavior on organizations, we reflect on how the choices leaders make resonate deeply within their teams, shaping culture and driving performance. Consider Horst Schulze, whose visionary approach revolutionized the hospitality industry by prioritizing exceptional service and redefining luxury, illustrating that the heart of leadership lies in understanding and elevating the human experience.

Similarly, Ken Kutaragi's journey from a tinkerer to a titan in the gaming world showcases the power of relentless innovation and risk-taking. His ability to foresee market trends and consumer needs transformed not only his company but also the entire gaming landscape, proving that effective leaders possess the foresight to envision new possibilities.

Moreover, as we draw lessons from the grand designs of ancient leaders and their insights into human behavior, we uncover timeless principles that continue to resonate in today's leadership practices. Each story in this chapter serves as a testament to the fact that impactful leadership is not just about achieving results—it's about creating an environment where innovation thrives, individuals feel empowered, and the potential for greatness is unlocked.

Through these narratives, readers will be inspired to reflect on their own leadership journeys, considering how they can cultivate transformative practices that leave a lasting impact in their own spheres of influence. The stories of these extraordinary leaders illuminate the path toward meaningful change, reminding us that true effectiveness in leadership goes beyond mere management; it's about crafting a legacy that inspires future generations.

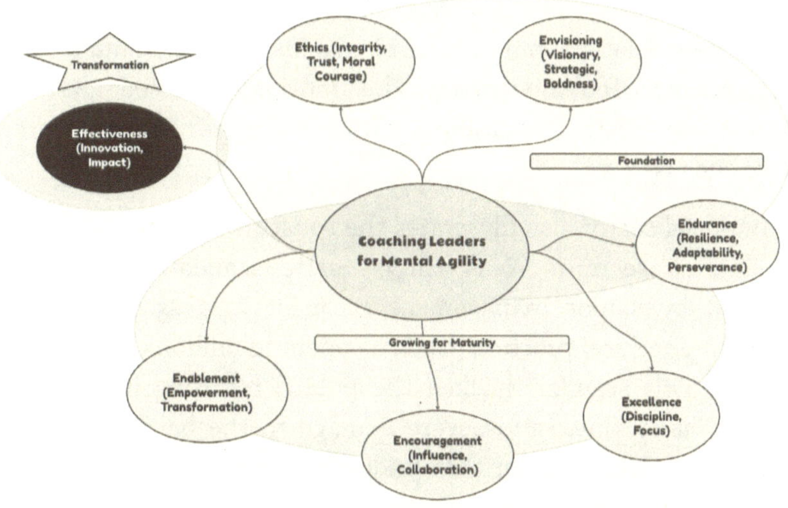

Coaching Leaders for Mental Agility: Story No 38

Impact of leadership behavior on organizations

> **"If your actions inspire others to dream more, learn more, do more, and become more, you are a leader."**
>
> **- John Quincy Adams**

Leadership behavior profoundly shapes the culture and success of organizations across various industries.

Take Uber, for example. Under the leadership of former CEO Travis Kalanick, the company faced serious challenges due to a toxic work environment. Employees reported aggressive behavior and harassment, describing a "bro" culture that fostered dissatisfaction. This negative atmosphere drew public attention, leading to investigations and significant leadership changes. In response, Uber embarked on a company-wide effort to transform its culture, showing how leadership can directly impact employee morale and company reputation.

In the entertainment industry, the case of Harvey Weinstein had a far-reaching effect on workplace dynamics. Once a powerful Hollywood producer, Weinstein faced numerous allegations of sexual harassment and assault. Investigative reports unveiled his abusive behavior toward employees, actors, and other professionals in the industry. The fallout from these revelations not only tarnished his reputation but also ignited the global #MeToo movement. This movement raised awareness of sexual misconduct, prompting significant changes in how workplaces handle such issues.

The financial sector also illustrates the consequences of poor leadership behavior, as seen in Wells Fargo's sales scandal. Employees were pressured by senior management to meet aggressive sales targets, leading to unethical practices, such as opening millions of unauthorized accounts. This scandal shocked the public, resulting in congressional hearings, hefty fines, and severe damage to the bank's reputation. It served as a stark reminder that leadership decisions can lead to a toxic work environment with far-reaching repercussions.

Amazon's work environment has come under scrutiny as well. Reports have surfaced about the harsh conditions in its warehouses and fulfillment centers, where employees face intense productivity quotas and constant surveillance. Concerns over inadequate working conditions and worker rights have prompted criticism and calls for the company to improve employee welfare. The situation highlights how leadership priorities can directly affect the well-being of workers.

In the automotive industry, Volkswagen's emissions scandal serves as another cautionary tale. The company was found to have installed software in diesel engines to cheat emissions tests. This choice, driven by leadership's desire to maintain market competitiveness and regulatory compliance, led to severe financial penalties and legal troubles. More importantly, it damaged Volkswagen's reputation as a reliable automotive manufacturer, showing how leadership decisions can have lasting impacts on a company's integrity and trustworthiness.

In each of these cases, the actions and behaviors of leaders significantly influenced their organizations. From fostering toxic environments to igniting movements for change, leadership has the power to shape not only company culture but also the broader landscape of industries.

Here are some key leadership lessons we can learn from these scandals in the Tech, Entertainment, Financial, Retail, and Automotive industries:

The importance of creating an ethical culture in a company cannot be overstated. When leaders prioritize ethical behavior, respect for employees, and accountability, they set a strong example for everyone in the organization. This tone from the top is essential for fostering a positive environment where everyone feels valued.

To truly empower employees, it's vital to create a safe space where they can speak up about their concerns without fearing punishment. When employees know they can voice their thoughts freely, it helps identify problems early on, preventing minor issues from turning into major crises.

Moreover, focusing on long-term sustainability is crucial. When companies prioritize quick profits through aggressive sales tactics, data manipulation, or ignoring ethical issues, they risk severe consequences that can harm the entire organization. Leaders must think carefully about how their decisions impact the company's culture and reputation.

The choices leaders make resonate deeply within their organizations. Each decision can shape how employees feel about their work and the company itself. Leaders need to weigh the potential outcomes of their actions, always prioritizing ethical conduct over short-term gains.

When issues do arise, it's essential for leaders to respond swiftly and transparently. By being open about the problems, taking responsibility, and implementing corrective actions, they can rebuild trust with their employees and demonstrate accountability.

Every crisis is an opportunity to learn and grow. Companies should view these challenging moments as chances to review their internal practices, identify weaknesses, and make changes to prevent similar situations in the future.

It's important to remember that the pressure to meet targets or compete should never compromise ethical behavior or employee well-being. Leaders must be aware of the dynamics within their organizations and actively work to eliminate any toxic environments.

Building trust with employees and encouraging open communication is the foundation of a healthy and successful organization. When leaders create a culture where everyone feels safe to speak up, they foster an environment of collaboration and shared success.

These stories highlight the downfalls of poor leadership and its impact on companies and entire industries.

Overall Leadership Learnings:

- Leaders set the tone. Their behavior and decisions have a profound impact on the entire organization.
- Prioritizing short-term gains over long-term sustainability through unethical practices can have devastating consequences.
- Fostering a culture of ethics, transparency, and employee well-being is essential for building trust and a successful organization.

- Leaders need to be accountable for their actions and create a safe space for employees to voice concerns without fear of retaliation.

By understanding these leadership failures, companies can strive to create positive work environments that promote ethical conduct, employee well-being, and long-term success.

When we understand how leadership behavior impacts organizations, we can identify several key areas where mindset improvements can be beneficial:

A leader with a fixed mindset believes that their abilities are set in stone. In contrast, a leader with a growth mindset is always eager to learn and improve. This kind of leader adapts their style based on the needs of the organization and its people. By being open to feedback and trying new approaches, they navigate challenges more effectively and seize opportunities for growth.

Instead of focusing solely on short-term wins, a leader with a long-term perspective prioritizes the future success of the organization. They make decisions that consider the health and sustainability of the company, which helps create a stable environment for everyone involved.

When it comes to problem-solving, a leader who thinks in systems understands how different parts of the organization connect. They see the bigger picture and make decisions that positively impact various aspects of the company. This holistic approach leads to better outcomes for the entire organization.

Empathy is another crucial quality. A leader who focuses only on tasks and deadlines often overlooks the needs and feelings of their employees. However, a leader who demonstrates empathy fosters understanding and prioritizes employee well-being. This compassionate approach builds trust and loyalty, resulting in a more engaged and productive workforce.

Transparency and accountability are essential in leadership. A leader who operates in secrecy and avoids responsibility creates distrust. In contrast, a leader who communicates openly and takes ownership of their decisions strengthens the organization's reputation and builds trust with employees and stakeholders.

Humility plays a vital role as well. A leader who believes they have all the answers often resists feedback, limiting their growth. But a humble leader welcomes diverse perspectives and values input from others. This openness helps them identify areas for improvement and strengthens relationships within the team.

Leaders who focus on learning and development are always on the lookout for ways to grow. They attend leadership programs and actively seek opportunities to enhance their skills. This commitment to lifelong learning keeps them current with industry trends and inspires their teams to pursue their own growth.

Encouraging innovation and calculated risk-taking is also important. A leader who shies away from risks limits creativity. On the other hand, a leader who fosters an environment where experimentation is encouraged can develop innovative solutions and uncover new opportunities. This spirit of innovation gives the organization a competitive edge.

Building trust and psychological safety is crucial for a thriving workplace. A leader who creates a culture of fear and micromanagement stifles creativity. However, a leader who fosters trust allows employees to take risks and share their ideas without fear of retribution. This safe environment leads to collaboration and creativity, driving success for the organization.

Awareness of unconscious bias is another important aspect of leadership. A leader who is unaware of their own biases may make decisions that hinder diversity and inclusion. In contrast, a leader who actively works to understand and address these biases promotes fairness and creates a more inclusive workplace.

Embracing diversity of thought is also essential. A leader who surrounds themselves with "yes men" discourages dissenting opinions, which can stifle innovation. However, a leader who values diverse perspectives encourages healthy debate and harnesses the collective intelligence of their team. This approach leads to creative solutions and better decision-making.

A leader who understands the importance of work-life balance prioritizes employee well-being. Instead of focusing solely on productivity, they promote flexible work arrangements and mental health initiatives. This focus on well-being results in higher employee engagement, lower turnover, and a more positive company culture.

Imagine a leader who sees their position as one of power and control, believing that their authority alone will drive success. This leader often makes decisions from a distance, focusing on maintaining control rather than connecting with their team.

Now, picture a different kind of leader. This leader embodies a servant leadership style, placing the needs and growth of their employees at the forefront. They understand that their success is tied to the success of their team members. By offering support, guidance, and resources, this leader empowers employees to reach their full potential.

The benefits of this approach are remarkable. In an environment shaped by servant leadership, trust flourishes. Employees feel valued and heard, leading to a strong sense of collaboration. They take ownership of their work, feeling motivated to contribute to the team's goals. As a result, the workforce becomes more engaged and productive, creating a positive atmosphere where everyone thrives.

Through the lens of servant leadership, this inspiring leader transforms not only their team but also the overall workplace culture. Their commitment to empowering others cultivates a shared sense of purpose, demonstrating that true leadership is about lifting others up and nurturing their growth.

Imagine a leader whose only goal is to make money and please shareholders, paying little attention to the environment or society. This leader sees profit as the sole measure of success, often ignoring the negative effects their decisions have on the planet and the people who inhabit it.

Now picture a different kind of leader. This leader understands that true success goes beyond just numbers on a balance sheet. They actively think about how their business can be a force for good, incorporating sustainability and social responsibility into their strategy. This leader seeks to create a positive impact, recognizing that a thriving business can also contribute to a healthier world.

The benefits of leading with a focus on sustainability are immense. By prioritizing environmental and social considerations, this leader attracts consumers who care about the planet and want to support ethical businesses. Employees, too, are drawn to organizations that share their values, creating a motivated and dedicated workforce. Additionally, this approach enhances the brand's reputation, making it stand out in a crowded marketplace.

In choosing to lead with purpose, this visionary leader not only contributes to a better future but also demonstrates that business can be a powerful tool for positive change. Their journey shows us that when leaders take responsibility for the world around them, they inspire others to do the same, creating a ripple effect that benefits everyone.

Leaders can move beyond short-term gains and create a sustainable future for their organization and the world around them. Their commitment to creating a positive impact will inspire not just employees but also stakeholders and the broader community.

> **"Leadership is not about being in charge. It's about taking care of those in your charge."**
>
> **- Simon Sinek**

Key Message:

- **Leaders Shape the Workplace**: Leaders have a big influence on how people feel at work. If leaders are positive and ethical, employees will feel valued and happy. But if leaders are harsh or unethical, it can make the workplace toxic and hurt the company's reputation, like in the examples of Uber and Wells Fargo.
- **Honesty and Ethics Matter**: Being honest and doing the right thing are important for long-term success. Leaders who make bad decisions, like cheating or ignoring problems, can cause big damage to the company, as seen with Wells Fargo and Volkswagen.

- **Empowerment and Responsibility Are Key**: Good leaders listen to employees and make sure they feel safe speaking up. They also take responsibility for their mistakes and fix problems quickly, which helps build trust and create a stronger company.

These points highlight that leadership isn't just about making decisions—it's about creating a good culture, being ethical, and taking care of employees.

Coaching Leaders for Mental Agility: Story No 39

The Hospitality Legend: How Horst Schulze Redefined Luxury

> **"Excellence wins. When you focus on excellence, you win."**
>
> **- Horst Schulze**

Horst Schulze isn't just a name in hospitality; it's synonymous with exceptional service and unforgettable experiences. Co-founding the Ritz-Carlton Hotel Group, Schulze revolutionized luxury by focusing on what truly matters – **the human touch**.

Here's why his story is a must-read for anyone in the business of creating magic for their guests:

1. From Opulence to Experience: Redefining Luxury

Luxury used to be about gold-plated everything. Schulze dared to be different. He understood that true luxury lies in exceeding expectations at every turn. **Exceptional service became the cornerstone of the Ritz-Carlton experience**, ensuring every guest felt valued and cared for. This shift in focus had a ripple effect, inspiring other brands to up their service game, ultimately benefiting the entire industry.

2. "Ladies and Gentlemen Serving Ladies and Gentlemen": A Service Revolution

Respect wasn't just for guests at the Ritz-Carlton. Schulze introduced the now-famous **"Ladies and Gentlemen serving Ladies and Gentlemen"** philosophy. This wasn't just a fancy slogan; it fostered a culture of mutual respect and professionalism. Employees felt valued, leading to higher morale and a genuine desire to deliver exceptional service. Guests, in turn, felt pampered and appreciated. It was a win-win for everyone.

3. Building a Culture of Excellence: The Gold Standard

The Ritz-Carlton wasn't just a collection of hotels; it was a family with shared values. Schulze believed in **hiring the right people** who embodied those values and then **investing in their growth**. The company's renowned Gold Standards – a set of service principles – became a benchmark in the industry. This focus on a strong, values-driven culture showed how a united team could achieve phenomenal success.

4. Empowering Employees: Unleashing Innovation

Schulze wasn't a fan of micromanagement. He **trusted his employees** to take ownership of their roles and make decisions that would enhance the guest experience. Imagine a concierge empowered to solve a guest's travel dilemma or a chef given the freedom to create a personalized birthday dessert – that's the power of empowerment. This approach not only boosted employee satisfaction but also led to **innovative solutions** that delighted guests.

5. The Neverending Pursuit of Perfection: Continuous Improvement

Settling for good enough wasn't an option at the Ritz-Carlton. Schulze fostered a culture of **continuous improvement**. Processes were constantly reviewed and refined, ensuring that the brand remained at the forefront of the industry. This commitment to excellence ensured that guests kept coming back for more, knowing they would always experience the best.

6. Leading with Vision: A Beacon for Others

Schulze wasn't just a leader; he was a visionary. He had a clear picture of what the Ritz-Carlton brand represented and passionately communicated that vision to his team. His **leadership style** – characterized by vision, clarity, and inspiration – played a significant role in the brand's global expansion and success. His story is a reminder that a clear vision, effectively communicated, can unite a team, and propel them towards achieving great things.

7. Success Beyond Service: The Bottom Line

Exceptional service wasn't just about making guests feel good; it was also a smart business move. Under Schulze's leadership, the Ritz-Carlton didn't just achieve legendary service standards, it also achieved **outstanding financial performance**. The brand became synonymous with luxury, attracting loyal customers willing to pay a premium for exceptional experiences. This proves that a focus on quality and service can lead to both happy customers and a healthy bottom line.

Horst Schulze's legacy is a testament to the power of exceptional service, empowered employees, and a strong organizational culture.

The Battles Behind the Butlers: Challenges Horst Schulze Conquered to Build a Hospitality Empire

Horst Schulze, the name synonymous with luxury service, didn't have a smooth ride to the top. Building the Ritz-Carlton brand was a constant battle against skepticism, inconsistency, and the ever-changing hospitality landscape. Here are some of the warzones he navigated:

Imagine attempting to reshape an entire industry. For Schulze, it wasn't about the typical symbols of wealth, like gold-plated fixtures. His goal was to create memorable, personalized experiences for every guest. Critics wondered if it was possible to maintain such high standards. His answer? The philosophy of "Ladies and Gentlemen serving Ladies and Gentlemen." This wasn't just a motto—it was a cultural shift. It required deep training and a change in mindset, but it became the foundation of the Ritz-Carlton experience.

At every step, Schulze faced skepticism, especially from employees, competitors, and investors. They doubted his vision's sustainability. But instead of backing down, he led by example, instilling rigorous training and relentless quality control. Over time, belief in his vision grew stronger, brick by brick.

As the Ritz-Carlton expanded, maintaining consistent service across multiple locations became a challenge. Whether in bustling cities or serene beach resorts, every hotel needed to deliver the same top-tier service. To ensure this, Schulze introduced the Ritz-Carlton Gold Standards—a set of guiding principles that ensured uniform excellence. These weren't just rules; they were a living framework, reinforced by continuous training and communication.

Then came the financial crunch of an economic downturn. The luxury hospitality industry felt the pinch, but Schulze saw it as an opportunity. He focused on keeping guests loyal by continuing to deliver exceptional service, even while managing costs. His belief was simple: outstanding service would keep guests coming back, even in tough times, and it worked.

As new technologies emerged and guest expectations evolved, there was pressure to modernize the Ritz-Carlton experience without losing its essence. Schulze embraced innovation that aligned with the brand's values. He championed technologies that enhanced the guest experience while preserving the personal touch, allowing the Ritz-Carlton to stay relevant and competitive.

Building a culture of service excellence wasn't easy. Every employee, from top management to front-line staff, had to embody the Ritz-Carlton spirit. Schulze knew the key to this was hiring the right people and investing in them. A meticulous hiring process ensured the right fit, and continuous training empowered employees to uphold the brand's high standards.

Finally, as Ritz-Carlton expanded globally, the challenge was to respect local cultures while maintaining a consistent brand identity. Each new location brought its own set of unique challenges. Schulze's approach was to balance the integrity of the Ritz-Carlton brand with a deep respect for local customs. By conducting thorough market research and collaborating with local stakeholders, he ensured the brand resonated with guests worldwide.

Horst Schulze's journey is a testament to his leadership, vision, and unwavering commitment to service excellence. He conquered numerous challenges, proving that with persistence, a strong culture, and a clear vision, even the most ambitious dreams can become reality.

The Ritz-Carlton Revolution: How Horst Schulze Redefined Hospitality Leadership

Forget stuffy suits and impersonal service. Horst Schulze, the visionary co-founder of the Ritz-Carlton, ushered in a new era of hospitality leadership. His focus wasn't on chandeliers and caviar; it was on creating unforgettable experiences for guests, and he did it by building a world-class team through a leadership style that continues to inspire leaders across industries.

From Service to Service Excellence: A Lesson in Priorities

Luxury hotels used to be about opulence, but Schulze saw an opportunity to redefine the concept. He placed **exceptional service** at the heart of the Ritz-Carlton experience. Imagine anticipating a guest's needs before they even arise, or empowering employees to resolve any issue on the spot. This shift in focus became the industry standard, raising the bar for hospitality experiences everywhere.

Empowering Employees: Unleashing the Magic Makers

Schulze wasn't a fan of micromanagement. He believed in **empowering his employees**, the true magic makers behind the scenes. His now-famous **"Ladies and Gentlemen serving Ladies and Gentlemen"** philosophy wasn't just a slogan; it fostered a culture of mutual respect and professionalism. Employees felt valued, leading to higher morale and a genuine desire to go the extra mile for guests.

Building a Culture of Gold: The Power of Shared Values

The Ritz-Carlton wasn't just a collection of hotels; it was a family with a shared mission. Schulze **invested in his people**, hiring those who embodied the company's core values and then provided ongoing training and development. The **Gold Standards**, a set of service principles, became a benchmark for excellence in the industry. This focus on a strong, values-driven culture showed how a united team could achieve phenomenal success.

Continuous Improvement: The Neverending Pursuit of Perfection

Settling for "good enough" wasn't an option at the Ritz-Carlton. Schulze instilled a culture of **continuous improvement**. Processes were constantly reviewed and refined, ensuring that the brand remained at the forefront of hospitality. This commitment to excellence ensured that guests kept coming back for more, knowing they would always experience the best.

Leading with Vision: Inspiring a Legacy

Schulze wasn't just a leader; he was a visionary. He had a clear picture of what the Ritz-Carlton brand represented and passionately communicated that vision to his team. His **leadership style** – characterized by vision, clarity, and empowerment – played a significant role in the brand's global expansion and success. His story is a reminder that a clear vision, effectively communicated, can unite a team, and propel them towards achieving great things.

Beyond Service: The Business Case for Empowerment

Exceptional service wasn't just about making guests feel good; it was also a smart business move. Under Schulze's leadership, the Ritz-Carlton didn't just achieve legendary service standards, it also achieved **outstanding financial performance**. The brand became synonymous with luxury, attracting loyal customers willing to pay a premium for exceptional experiences. This proves that a focus on quality and service can lead to both happy customers and a healthy bottom line.

The Leadership Lessons of Horst Schulze: A Blueprint for Success

Horst Schulze's legacy is a masterclass in leadership. He showed the world the power of **service excellence, empowered employees, and a strong organizational culture**.

His story continues to inspire leaders across various industries, reminding them that the key to success lies in creating a customer-centric experience that values and respects both employees and guests.

By incorporating these lessons into your own leadership style, you can create a team that thrives on making a difference, leaving a lasting impression on everyone they encounter.

> **"People want to be proud of what they are doing. They want to be proud of where they work."**
>
> **- Horst Schulze**

Here are the top three takeaways from the piece about Horst Schulze and his leadership at the Ritz-Carlton:

- **Redefining Luxury: From Opulence to Experience:** Schulze revolutionized the concept of luxury by moving away from extravagant material displays and focusing on creating exceptional, personalized guest experiences. His belief that true luxury comes from exceeding expectations had a lasting impact on the entire hospitality industry.
- **"Ladies and Gentlemen Serving Ladies and Gentlemen": A Service Revolution:** Schulze's philosophy introduced a culture of mutual respect between employees and guests. This approach empowered employees and fostered professionalism, ensuring that they felt valued, which translated into exceptional service for guests.
- **Building a Culture of Excellence:** Schulze was committed to creating a values-driven organizational culture. He hired employees who shared Ritz-Carlton's core values and invested heavily in their growth. This focus on a united team, built around service excellence, became the foundation of the brand's success.

These lessons demonstrate the power of vision, leadership, and culture in building a world-class organization.

Coaching Leaders for Mental Agility: Story No 40

Ken Kutaragi: The Tinkerer Who Became a Gaming Titan

> **"The moment you give up is the moment you let someone else win."**
>
> **- Ken Kutaragi**

Ken Kutaragi isn't your typical corporate leader.

He's an engineer at heart, a tinkerer with a boundless passion for technology and a mischievous glint in his eye.

This is the story of the man who, against all odds, revolutionized the gaming industry with his brainchild – the PlayStation.

From Printing Press to Playgrounds:

Born in Tokyo in 1950, Kutaragi wasn't destined for the world of electronics. He grew up surrounded by the whirring machines of his family's printing press, learning about mechanics and the satisfaction of building things with his own hands. This love for tinkering translated into a passion for electronics, and he pursued a degree in electrical engineering.

A Young Visionary at Sony:

Fresh out of college, Kutaragi joined Sony, a company then known for its high-fidelity audio equipment. While the world saw him as a promising engineer, Kutaragi harbored a secret dream – video games. He wasn't just a player; he saw the immense potential for this new form of entertainment.

In the late 1980s, when gaming was still a niche market dominated by Nintendo, Kutaragi spearheaded the development of the SPC700 sound chip for the Super Famicom. This was his first foray into the gaming world, a stepping stone towards his future endeavors.

The Birth of a Legend: The PlayStation Project

Kutaragi's true calling came with the PlayStation. He envisioned a console unlike any other – one with powerful 3D graphics, a user-friendly interface, and a focus on developer accessibility. His vision, however, wasn't met with immediate support. Sony executives viewed gaming with skepticism.

Undeterred, Kutaragi, with the tenacity of a bulldog, lobbied relentlessly for his project, often working on it in secret. He assembled a team of passionate engineers, designers, and marketers, a ragtag group united by their love for games.

Innovation and Persistence: Overcoming Challenges

The path to the PlayStation wasn't paved with rose petals. Technical hurdles loomed large. Developing a console that could outperform the competition required pushing the boundaries of technology.

Kutaragi and his team had to innovate, finding creative solutions to challenges in areas like 3D rendering and user interface design. Their biggest gamble? Embracing CD-ROM technology, a relatively new format at the time. This decision proved to be a masterstroke, allowing for richer and more complex games compared to the limitations of cartridges.

From Underdog to King: The Legacy of PlayStation

When the PlayStation finally launched in 1994, it was a game changer. With its superior hardware and a growing library of exciting games, it quickly captured the hearts of gamers worldwide.

The PlayStation wasn't just a commercial success; it redefined the gaming industry, setting new standards for design and performance. It ushered in the era of 3D gaming experiences and broadened the gaming audience, attracting a wider demographic than ever before.

Beyond the PlayStation: A Life of Innovation

Kutaragi's story doesn't end with the PlayStation. He continued to lead the charge at Sony, overseeing the development of the PlayStation 2, PlayStation 3, and PlayStation Portable. He was a visionary leader who wasn't afraid to take risks and challenge the status quo. He retired from Sony in 2007, leaving behind a legacy that continues to inspire gamers and innovators alike.

Ken Kutaragi's story is a testament to the power of passion, persistence, and a little bit of rebellion.

He's a reminder that even the most ambitious dreams can become reality with unwavering belief, a willingness to challenge the norm, and a team of passionate individuals by your side.

Ken Kutaragi stood at the forefront of a gaming revolution, driven by a passion that burned brightly within him. His unwavering love for gaming didn't just fuel his own ambitions; it ignited a fire in his team, inspiring them to share his enthusiasm and work tirelessly toward a common vision for the PlayStation. Each challenge that arose only strengthened his resolve, and his passion became the lifeblood of their collective journey.

While many doubted the gaming industry's potential, Kutaragi looked beyond the immediate skepticism and saw a future brimming with possibilities. His ability to believe in something unseen set him apart as a visionary leader. This unique perspective allowed him to see beyond the obstacles, envisioning a world where gaming could captivate millions.

Kutaragi's path was fraught with challenges, including internal resistance and daunting technical hurdles. Yet, he met each obstacle with relentless determination. His persistence was not merely a personal trait; it was a powerful reminder to those around him that true leadership often means refusing to back down in the face of adversity.

Understanding that no great vision can be achieved alone, Kutaragi built a dream team of talented individuals who brought diverse skills to the table. He nurtured collaboration among them, fostering an environment where their shared passion for gaming could flourish. This collective spirit became a cornerstone of the PlayStation's success, as each member contributed to the realization of their dream.

Taking calculated risks was part of Kutaragi's strategy. When he decided to incorporate CD-ROM technology into the PlayStation, it was a bold move that many viewed as a gamble. However, he recognized that innovation often requires stepping into the unknown, and this decision ultimately paid off, propelling the console to new heights.

Kutaragi never shied away from challenging the status quo. He confronted established giants in the gaming industry, driven by his vision for a more powerful and developer-friendly console. His willingness to push boundaries opened up new avenues for what was possible in gaming, inspiring others to think differently.

Leading by example, Kutaragi's passion for technology and gaming was infectious. His enthusiasm and dedication became a constant source of motivation for his team, propelling them forward even during tough times. He demonstrated that true leadership is about embodying the values and excitement that one hopes to instill in others.

In a rapidly evolving industry, Kutaragi understood the importance of adaptability. His openness to embracing new technologies, such as CD-

ROMs, ensured that the PlayStation stayed ahead of the curve, always ready to meet the changing needs of gamers.

Kutaragi celebrated the successes of the PlayStation, but he also acknowledged the projects that didn't perform as well. A wise leader learns from both triumphs and failures, and he used these experiences to grow and refine his vision further. This reflective mindset fostered resilience and a commitment to continuous improvement within his team.

Today, Ken Kutaragi's legacy in the gaming industry shines brightly. His impact is undeniable, inspiring future generations of innovators and leaders. His journey serves as a powerful reminder that passion, persistence, collaboration, and courage to take risks can transform dreams into reality, leaving an indelible mark on the world.

By incorporating these lessons into your own leadership style, you can create a more passionate, collaborative, and innovative environment for your team, paving the way for success in your own endeavors.

Ken Kutaragi's journey with the PlayStation was anything but smooth sailing. **Here are some of the key challenges he faced and how his mental stamina shone through:**

At Sony, Ken Kutaragi faced significant challenges as he pursued his dream of creating a revolutionary gaming console. The first hurdle came from internal resistance. Many executives within Sony viewed gaming as a risky venture, a territory they were hesitant to explore. Despite their skepticism, Kutaragi refused to back down. He passionately advocated for his vision, often working on the project in secret. Armed with data and competitor analysis, he slowly began to win over the doubters around him. His infectious enthusiasm for gaming gradually chipped away at their resistance, showing them that this venture could change the landscape of entertainment.

The next challenge was technological hurdles. Kutaragi aimed to develop a console that would deliver superior 3D graphics and an easy-to-use interface, all while being friendly to developers. This required a leap into uncharted territory. Undeterred, Kutaragi and his team tackled these challenges head-on. They explored unconventional solutions, collaborating with engineers and embracing new technologies, like CD-ROMs, to push the boundaries of what was technically possible. Their relentless efforts laid the groundwork for a groundbreaking console.

Kutaragi faced tough competition in the gaming market. Sony was new and up against big players like Nintendo and Sega. Knowing this, Kutaragi worked hard to create a console that was different from the rest. He focused on making the hardware better and aimed to attract game developers by keeping the price competitive. This smart strategy allowed the PlayStation to find its own special place in a busy market.

Kutaragi faced the challenge of building a strong, diverse team of engineers, designers, and marketers. He fostered a collaborative environment that encouraged creativity and kept everyone motivated and focused on their shared goals, even during tough times.

Amid these challenges, Kutaragi also navigated uncertainties, particularly regarding the gamble of using CD-ROM technology. At the time, CD-ROMs were relatively new and unproven in the gaming world. However, Kutaragi recognized the potential advantages they offered, such as larger game sizes and richer experiences for players. With conviction, he decided to take this calculated risk, and it ultimately became a major factor in the PlayStation's success.

Through determination, innovation, and unwavering belief in his vision, Kutaragi transformed challenges into stepping stones, leaving an indelible mark on the gaming industry. His journey inspires others to embrace their passions and persevere through obstacles, proving that great achievements often come from facing the unknown head-on.

Ken Kutaragi's remarkable journey in revolutionizing the gaming industry provides several key lessons in leadership that can inspire anyone striving for success. Here are five essential messages:

- **Passion Fuels Innovation**: Kutaragi's unwavering passion for gaming ignited not just his vision for the PlayStation but also inspired his team to rally behind a shared dream. This fervor serves as a reminder that a leader's enthusiasm can be contagious, driving a collective pursuit of innovation and excellence.

- **Persistence in the Face of Adversity**: When confronted with skepticism and resistance, Kutaragi never wavered. His relentless determination to advocate for his vision, even in secret, illustrates how persistence is crucial for overcoming challenges. True leadership often means standing firm against doubt and continuing to push forward.

- **Embrace Collaboration**: Understanding that no great vision is achieved alone, Kutaragi built a diverse team of talented individuals. By fostering a collaborative environment, he enabled creativity to flourish and kept the team focused on their common goals. This highlights the importance of surrounding oneself with skilled people and working together toward a unified vision.

- **Take Calculated Risks**: Kutaragi's decision to embrace CD-ROM technology was a significant gamble that paid off, proving that innovation requires stepping into the unknown. This reflects the reality that leaders must be willing to take risks, understanding that breakthroughs often come from daring to challenge the status quo.

- **Learn from Both Success and Failure**: Kutaragi recognized the value of celebrating achievements while also reflecting on setbacks. His ability to learn from both successes and failures cultivated resilience within his team and emphasized the importance of continuous improvement. This mindset fosters a culture of growth, encouraging leaders and their teams to adapt and evolve.

Ken Kutaragi's story not only showcases his pioneering spirit but also serves as a profound reminder of the attributes that define effective leadership. His journey encourages aspiring leaders to pursue their passions, remain resilient in adversity, collaborate with others, embrace risks, and learn from every experience.

> **"I wanted to prove that even an engineer could revolutionize the world."**
>
> **- Ken Kutaragi**

Here are three key messages inspired by Ken Kutaragi's journey:

- **Pursue Your Passion Relentlessly**: Kutaragi's unwavering love for gaming and technology drove him to create the PlayStation, illustrating that passion can lead to groundbreaking innovations. His story encourages aspiring leaders to embrace their passions wholeheartedly, as this fervor can inspire and rally others around a common goal.

- **Embrace Challenges as Opportunities**: Throughout his career, Kutaragi faced skepticism and significant technical obstacles. Instead of backing down, he viewed these challenges as opportunities to innovate and improve. This mindset of resilience teaches us that setbacks can be valuable learning experiences that pave the way for future success.

- **Collaboration Fuels Innovation**: Kutaragi built a diverse team of engineers, designers, and marketers, fostering an environment of collaboration. By valuing each team member's unique skills, he cultivated creativity and shared ownership of the vision. This underscores the importance of teamwork in achieving ambitious goals and driving innovation.

These messages resonate with the principles of effective leadership and can inspire anyone looking to make a meaningful impact in their field. For more insights on Kutaragi's contributions and leadership style, you can explore articles from sources like *The Verge* and *Forbes*.

Coaching Leaders for Mental Agility: Story No 41

The Grand Design and the Human Psyche: Leadership Lessons from the Pyramids

> **"Success is peace of mind which is a direct result of self-satisfaction in knowing you made the effort to become the best of which you are capable."**
>
> **- John Wooden**

The towering pyramids of Egypt stand as testaments not just to engineering marvel but also to the complex psychology of leadership.

Imagine the **Pharaoh** at the helm, a figure who wielded immense power and responsibility.

Their success hinged on a unique blend of leadership qualities, each with deep roots in human psychology.

The Pharaoh stood as a beacon of unity and purpose, a leader who inspired thousands to rally behind a grand vision: the construction of a monument that would stand the test of time. With a charismatic presence, the Pharaoh painted a picture of what could be achieved, igniting passion and motivation in the hearts of the vast workforce. This powerful vision aligned perfectly with the principles of transformational leadership, where inspiring change and motivating others becomes the driving force behind monumental achievements.

Creating a pyramid was no simple task; it required a diverse array of talents. Skilled artisans, tireless laborers, and capable overseers all came together, forming a dynamic team that thrived under the Pharaoh's guidance. Understanding the unique strengths of each individual was crucial, as the Pharaoh adeptly harnessed the potential within this workforce. This approach mirrored the concepts of situational leadership, where the leader adjusts their style to suit the needs of their followers and the challenges they face.

The pyramid's workforce was not merely a collection of individuals but a complex tapestry of social relationships and hierarchies. Skilled laborers found camaraderie among their peers, often identifying more with fellow workers than with the overseers who managed them. As the ultimate authority figure, the Pharaoh skillfully navigated this intricate social landscape, maintaining order and fostering cooperation among all involved. This awareness of social dynamics reflected the essence of social identity theory, emphasizing the importance of understanding group affiliations and loyalties.

Amidst the immense weight of expectation, the Pharaoh bore the responsibility of delivering this monumental project while ensuring that the workforce remained motivated and unified. This challenge illuminated the vital role of emotional intelligence in effective leadership. The Pharaoh needed to empathize with the workers' struggles, providing inspiration during tough times and cultivating a sense of purpose that transcended individual hardships. By connecting on an emotional level, the Pharaoh could uplift the spirits of the laborers, reminding them that their collective effort would lead to something greater than themselves.

In this way, the Pharaoh's leadership journey showcases how vision, understanding, social navigation, and emotional intelligence can inspire others to achieve extraordinary feats. Through their actions, the Pharaoh not only aimed to construct a grand pyramid but also sought to weave a legacy of unity and resilience that would echo through the ages.

The story of pyramid construction isn't just about engineering; it's a captivating illustration of how leadership and psychology intertwine.

By understanding the human aspects of leading such a vast undertaking, we gain valuable insights into the multifaceted nature of effective leadership, even in the face of immense challenges.

We can glean some interesting insights into potential psychological aspects of leadership from their construction:

The Pharaoh stood before the vast expanse of workers, embodying the essence of transformational leadership. With a vision that reached beyond his own lifetime, he rallied thousands to join in a monumental effort, the construction of a great pyramid. The Pharaoh understood the power of a shared dream and inspired purpose, igniting a fire within each laborer and craftsman. They felt a sense of belonging to something larger than themselves, a cause that would resonate through the ages.

Managing such a diverse workforce was no simple task. The Pharaoh recognized that each group, whether artisans, laborers, or overseers, required a different approach. He adapted his leadership style to suit their varying skills and needs, embodying the principles of situational leadership. By adjusting his methods, he ensured that each worker felt valued and understood, fostering a spirit of cooperation and dedication among all.

As the pyramid rose from the ground, the workforce began to form social bonds, identifying with one another through shared experiences. The Pharaoh navigated these intricate social dynamics, understanding the importance of group identity. By acknowledging the unique roles and relationships within the workforce, he maintained order and harmony, creating an environment where collaboration flourished.

Yet, the journey was not without its challenges. The work was arduous, and the physical demands took a toll on the laborers. The Pharaoh understood the importance of empathy in this situation. He walked among his workers, listening to their concerns, and recognizing their struggles. By demonstrating genuine care and compassion, he lifted their spirits, ensuring that morale remained high throughout the long construction process. This emotional intelligence became a cornerstone of his leadership, allowing him to connect deeply with those who toiled under the sun.

While the Pharaoh's story is a source of inspiration, it is also essential to approach it with a sense of awareness. The historical context limits our understanding of the specific leadership styles employed, and it is crucial to acknowledge the human cost of such monumental projects. While we can draw valuable lessons about leadership from this narrative, we must also recognize the complexities and ethical considerations that come with it, ensuring that we learn from the past without glorifying potentially exploitative practices.

In this way, the Pharaoh's leadership journey serves as a powerful reminder of the impact one can have by inspiring others, adapting to their needs, and fostering an environment of empathy and understanding. Through his actions, he not only built a magnificent structure but also created a legacy of unity and resilience that would echo through history.

Here are some additional areas for psychological exploration:

- **The Psychology of Obedience:** What motivated workers to follow potentially dangerous or demanding orders?
- **The Power of Ritual and Symbolism:** Did the Pharaoh use rituals or symbolic actions to motivate and unify the workforce?
- **The Role of Religion:** Religion likely played a significant role in Egyptian society. How did the Pharaoh leverage religious beliefs to inspire workers and legitimize their authority?

Here are some questions a Pharaoh might have asked to drive the pyramid work as a leader, categorized by their focus:

Motivation and Efficiency:

- **"How can we incentivize skilled laborers to relocate and dedicate themselves to this long-term project?"** (Attracting and retaining talent)
- **"Are there ways to improve the efficiency of transporting these massive stones? Can we develop new tools or techniques?"** (Streamlining processes)
- **"How can we ensure the workers are adequately fed, housed, and cared for to maintain morale and productivity?"** (Employee well-being)

Quality and Planning:

- **"Have the architects meticulously planned the alignment and structural integrity of the pyramid for generations to come?"** (Long-term vision and planning)
- **"What quality control measures can we implement to ensure the stonework is precise and flawless?"** (Maintaining high standards)

- **"Are there alternative materials or construction techniques we can consider to improve the pyramid's durability or aesthetics?"** (Openness to innovation)

Logistics and Organization:

- **"How can we effectively manage such a large workforce, ensuring clear communication and task delegation across different skill levels?"** (Effective communication and delegation)
- **"What logistical challenges might arise during different seasons, and how can we prepare for them?"** (Anticipating and mitigating risks)
- **"Can we establish a reward system that recognizes and incentivizes outstanding contributions from workers across the project?"** (Motivation through recognition)

Maintaining Order and Authority:

- **"How can we prevent discontent or dissent among the workers while maintaining a clear hierarchy and respect for authority?"** (Balancing order and morale)
- **"Are there ways to promote a sense of purpose and shared accomplishment among the workforce, fostering unity and dedication to the project?"** (Building a sense of community)
- **"How can we effectively address potential conflicts that may arise between different groups of workers or officials?"** (Conflict resolution)

Here are some key messages drawn from the exploration of leadership as illustrated by the Pharaoh during the construction of the pyramids:

- **Transformational Leadership**: The Pharaoh exemplified transformational leadership by inspiring a collective vision among thousands of workers. This type of leadership is marked by the ability to motivate and ignite passion, fostering a sense of belonging to something greater than oneself, which can lead to extraordinary achievements.

- **Situational Leadership**: The Pharaoh adapted his leadership style to accommodate the diverse needs of the workforce, recognizing that different groups—artisans, laborers, and overseers—required distinct approaches. This flexibility in leadership mirrors the principles of situational leadership, where understanding and responding to the context and needs of followers is crucial.

- **Emotional Intelligence**: The importance of emotional intelligence was paramount in the Pharaoh's leadership. By empathizing with the workers' struggles and providing support, the Pharaoh maintained high morale, ensuring the workforce remained motivated throughout the challenging construction process. This connection on an emotional level is vital for effective leadership.

- **Navigating Social Dynamics**: The Pharaoh understood the complex social relationships among the workers, fostering camaraderie and cooperation. His ability to navigate these dynamics and maintain order highlights the significance of social identity and group affiliations in leadership.

- **Legacy and Responsibility**: The Pharaoh's leadership journey was not solely about building a physical monument; it was also about weaving a legacy of unity and resilience. This dual focus underscores the responsibility leaders have to inspire their teams while being aware of the broader implications of their actions.

- **Learning from History**: While the story of pyramid construction is inspiring, it is essential to approach it critically, recognizing the complexities and ethical considerations involved. Leaders today can learn from both the successes and challenges of historical figures, ensuring that they build inclusive and respectful environments.

These insights illustrate how the psychology of leadership, coupled with a strong vision and understanding of human dynamics, can lead to monumental successes, both in ancient and modern contexts.

Coaching Leaders for Mental Agility: Story No 42

Are you on the journey towards self-actualization?

> **"To be yourself in a world that is constantly trying to make you something else is the greatest accomplishment."**
>
> **- Ralph Waldo Emerson**

1. Martin Luther King Jr.: (Self-Actualization through Social Justice)

Dr. Martin Luther King Jr. dedicated his life to achieving racial equality in the United States. He tirelessly worked to champion nonviolent resistance, using his voice and leadership to advocate for social change. Despite facing threats and even imprisonment, he remained steadfast in his mission, inspiring countless others to join him in the fight for justice.

King was not motivated by personal gain or the desire for power. Instead, he acted from a deep moral conviction, driven by the vision of a more just world for all. His commitment to this cause resonated with many, encouraging them to stand up for what was right.

His approach to dismantling racial segregation showcased his creativity and problem-solving skills. King organized nonviolent protests, including marches and boycotts, which were innovative ways to draw attention to the injustices of segregation. Through these peaceful demonstrations, he demonstrated that change could come from unity and courage rather than violence.

Dr. King's legacy continues to inspire people to strive for equality and justice, reminding them that fulfilling one's potential can lead to profound societal change.

2. Nelson Mandela: (Self-Actualization through Forgiveness and Reconciliation)

Nelson Mandela faced immense challenges during his life, spending 27 years in prison for his fight against apartheid. Despite the long years behind bars, he never lost sight of his dream for a united South Africa. When he finally emerged from prison, he did so with a spirit of forgiveness and a commitment to reconciliation, determined to heal a divided nation.

His time in prison didn't weaken him; instead, it made him stronger. The hardships he endured only deepened his resolve to create a better future for all South Africans. He transformed his suffering into a source of strength and inspiration, showing others that it is possible to overcome even the toughest obstacles.

Mandela's leadership was instrumental in guiding South Africa through its transition to a multiracial democracy. His dedication to forgiveness and understanding helped to bridge divides and foster a sense of unity among people who had long been at odds. His legacy continues to inspire individuals around the world, reminding them that perseverance and compassion can lead to profound change.

3. Marie Curie: (Self-Actualization through Scientific Discovery)

Marie Curie was a passionate scientist who dedicated her life to research, driven by an insatiable thirst for knowledge rather than personal gain. In a time when society expected women to stay away from science, she bravely pursued groundbreaking work in radioactivity, paving the way for future generations of female scientists.

Her journey was marked by a commitment to continuous learning. Curie never stopped seeking knowledge, always eager to explore and expand the boundaries of scientific understanding. She devoted herself to her work, not just for accolades but to uncover the mysteries of the universe.

Curie's remarkable discoveries about radioactivity had a profound impact on humanity. Her research led to significant advancements in medicine and technology, changing the way we understand the world around us. Through her dedication and perseverance, she not only transformed the scientific community but also contributed to the well-being of countless lives, leaving a legacy that continues to inspire people everywhere.

4. Leonardo da Vinci: (Self-Actualization through Multifaceted Creativity)

Leonardo da Vinci was a true Renaissance man who never allowed himself to be confined to just one field. His genius shone through as he painted stunning masterpieces, sculpted incredible works of art, invented groundbreaking machines, studied the human body, and designed innovative engineering projects. His wide-ranging interests and talents showed a relentless curiosity that drove him to explore every possible avenue of knowledge.

Da Vinci's quest for mastery was evident in everything he pursued. He constantly pushed the boundaries of art and science, experimenting with new techniques and ideas that changed the way people viewed the world. Whether he was perfecting the art of painting or exploring the intricacies of human anatomy, his innovative spirit was always at the forefront.

Even centuries after his death, da Vinci's legacy continues to inspire countless artists, scientists, and inventors. His work resonates with those who seek to blend creativity and intellect, reminding everyone that the pursuit of knowledge knows no limits. His life story encourages us all to explore our potential and to never stop questioning, learning, and innovating.

These are just a few examples. Leaders who demonstrate self-actualization often share these characteristics:

- **Strong Moral Compass:** They are driven by a desire to make a positive impact on the world.
- **Lifelong Learning:** They are constantly seeking new knowledge and experiences.
- **Creativity and Problem-Solving:** They approach challenges with innovative solutions.
- **Resilience and Perseverance:** They are undeterred by setbacks and remain committed to their goals.

Here are some things you can do to assess your self-actualization state and work towards improvement:

Characteristics of a Self-Actualized Person:

Self-actualized individuals are fueled by a deep desire for growth and knowledge. They focus on making a positive impact on the world rather than seeking recognition or status. Their motivation comes from within, guiding them to explore their potential and contribute to something greater than themselves.

These individuals have a strong sense of self-acceptance. They are comfortable with who they are and embrace their flaws. This acceptance extends to others, as they appreciate people for their authentic selves, understanding that everyone has imperfections.

Creativity flows through their veins as they constantly search for new ideas and solutions. When faced with challenges, they approach them with an open mind, ready to take risks and think outside the box. This willingness to experiment often leads to innovative solutions and fresh perspectives.

Living in the moment, they savor the beauty and wonder of life's experiences. Rather than dwelling on the past or worrying about the future, they immerse themselves in the present, appreciating every little detail around them.

Their strong moral compass guides their actions and decisions. They strive to lead meaningful lives that align with their values, making choices that reflect their ethics. This commitment to living authentically inspires others to do the same.

With a thirst for knowledge, they embrace lifelong learning. Their curiosity drives them to seek new experiences and insights, both personally and professionally. This constant pursuit of understanding keeps their minds sharp and their spirits high.

Independence is vital to them. They make their own choices based on internal values, standing firm against external pressures. This autonomy empowers them to live life on their terms, reinforcing their sense of self.

At times, they experience moments of intense joy and fulfillment, often referred to as "peak experiences." In these moments, they feel a profound connection to the world around them, leaving them inspired and energized to continue their journey of growth and contribution.

Self-Assessment:

To embark on a journey of self-discovery, one must first reflect on what truly matters in life. Imagine sitting quietly, pen in hand, as you contemplate your values and goals. What ignites your passion? Are your current aspirations in harmony with what you believe in? Engaging in open conversations with trusted friends or mentors can further illuminate these important questions, helping you to navigate your inner landscape.

Next, consider your mindset about growth. Do you view challenges as stepping stones for personal improvement? A growth mindset is key to realizing your full potential. By exploring articles or taking online quizzes, you can gain a deeper understanding of how you perceive your ability to learn and evolve throughout your life. This awareness empowers you to embrace obstacles as opportunities rather than setbacks.

Identifying your strengths and weaknesses is another vital step in this journey. Each person possesses a unique blend of skills and talents, and recognizing your strengths can lead you to activities that bring fulfillment and joy. At the same time, acknowledging areas where you struggle opens the door to growth. Taking personality or skills assessments can provide valuable insights, guiding you toward a clearer understanding of your capabilities.

As you reflect on your values, assess your mindset, and identify your strengths, you will lay the groundwork for a more meaningful and inspired life. This journey of self-exploration is not just about achieving goals; it's about becoming the best version of yourself and making a positive impact on the world around you.

Strategies for Improvement:

To embark on a journey of personal growth, one must embrace the idea of stepping outside familiar boundaries. Imagine a person eager to learn new skills and explore different hobbies. They might sign up for a class that piques their interest or attend workshops where they can interact with others who share their passions. They dive into books that spark curiosity, feeding their thirst for knowledge and igniting a sense of adventure.

Setting meaningful goals is another vital part of this journey. Rather than chasing empty achievements, they focus on goals that resonate with their core values and enrich their sense of purpose. These aspirations can span personal endeavors, professional ambitions, or even efforts to help others. By crafting goals that are specific, measurable, achievable, relevant, and time-bound, they have a clearer path toward success.

Challenges often loom ahead, but instead of shrinking away, they learn to embrace them. Each obstacle becomes a chance to grow, prompting a shift in perspective. Adopting a problem-solving mindset, they approach difficulties with optimism, ready to learn and adapt along the way.

Creativity plays a significant role in their life as well. Engaging in artistic pursuits allows them to express their unique voice. Whether it's writing stories, painting vivid landscapes, or playing a musical instrument, these creative outlets offer joy and fulfillment. They might even start a blog to share their thoughts or volunteer for a cause close to their heart, finding ways to make a difference in their community.

Gratitude becomes a daily practice, shaping their outlook on life. By reflecting on the positive moments and appreciating the little things, they cultivate a sense of well-being. They might keep a gratitude journal or take time each day to acknowledge the kindness of others, deepening their connection to the world around them.

Lastly, prioritizing self-care is essential for nurturing their potential. Understanding that burnout hinders progress, they commit to getting enough sleep, eating nutritious foods, and engaging in relaxing activities. By taking care of themselves, they create the space and energy needed to pursue their dreams fully.

In this immersive journey of growth and exploration, they discover not only who they are but who they can become. Each step taken opens new doors, filling their life with purpose and inspiration.

There are several reasons why people might struggle to reach the self-actualization stage in Maslow's hierarchy of needs:

In the quest for self-actualization, many people face significant barriers that can keep them from realizing their full potential. Imagine a person struggling to find enough food or pay for a safe place to live. Their daily life is consumed by worries about meeting these basic needs, leaving little energy for personal growth or self-discovery. Each month, as they fret over rent, the thought of pursuing dreams feels like a distant luxury, overshadowed by the immediate demands of survival.

When love and belonging needs are unmet, this journey becomes even more challenging. Picture someone who feels isolated and alone, lacking the supportive relationships that often motivate growth. Humans thrive on connection, and without a community or close friendships, it can be tough to find the encouragement needed to move forward.

Internally, fear can become a formidable obstacle. The anxiety of failing or being rejected can paralyze even the most ambitious individuals. They might hesitate to take risks or try new things that are crucial for their personal development. Alongside this fear often lies negative self-talk. Thoughts like "I'm not good enough" echo in their minds, drowning out any hope of pursuing their dreams. Without a clear understanding of their own values, strengths, and weaknesses, they may feel lost, unsure of what self-actualization even means for them.

External pressures add another layer of complexity. Society often imposes expectations regarding career paths, wealth, and appearance. These pressures can create a chasm between what is traditionally deemed successful and what genuinely fulfills an individual. Additionally, limited access to education, healthcare, or opportunities can hinder personal development, making it harder to cultivate talents and pursue passions. In dire circumstances, such as living amidst war, famine, or poverty, the focus shifts even more toward mere survival, rendering the idea of self-actualization nearly unattainable.

It's essential to remember that self-actualization is a journey, not a fixed destination. Along the way, setbacks and challenges are inevitable, shaping the experience. Each person's path is unique, with different sources of fulfillment guiding them. Even if someone doesn't reach the pinnacle of self-actualization, they can still lead a meaningful and fulfilling life, rich with purpose and joy.

Here are some tips for overcoming these obstacles:

- **Focus on fulfilling your basic needs first.**
- **Build strong and supportive relationships.**
- **Challenge negative self-talk and limiting beliefs.**
- **Practice self-awareness and identify your values and goals.**
- **Don't be afraid to take risks and step outside your comfort zone.**
- **Seek out resources and opportunities that can help you develop your talents.**
- **Surround yourself with positive and inspiring people.**

By working on these aspects and addressing the challenges that hold you back, you can move closer to achieving self-actualization and living a more fulfilling life.

Here's a simplified overview of five inspiring figures who show what self-actualization looks like through their lives and achievements:

- **Martin Luther King Jr.**: He fought for equal rights for African Americans and promoted peaceful protests. King believed in justice and worked hard to make the world fairer. His efforts show how personal goals can help create big changes in society.
- **Nelson Mandela**: Mandela spent 27 years in prison for opposing apartheid in South Africa but emerged with a focus on forgiveness. He worked to unite his country and promote equality. His story teaches us that overcoming hardship can lead to important social changes.
- **Marie Curie**: Curie was a dedicated scientist who made groundbreaking discoveries about radioactivity. She faced

challenges as a woman in science but pursued her passion for learning. Her work greatly advanced medicine and technology, showing that curiosity and determination can lead to great achievements.

- **Leonardo da Vinci**: Known as a Renaissance man, da Vinci excelled in many fields like art, science, and engineering. His endless curiosity and creativity pushed him to explore various interests. His life encourages us to keep learning and trying new things.
- **Helen Keller**: Despite being deaf and blind, Keller became an influential writer and speaker. She worked hard to advocate for people with disabilities and showed that overcoming personal struggles can lead to helping others. Her determination inspires many to strive for their dreams.

Part 7

Leadership Pillar-7(Effectiveness)

Summary

In the world of leadership, the impact of a leader's approach can shape the atmosphere of an entire workplace. Picture a team where the leader radiates positivity and ethics; employees thrive, feeling valued and content. They collaborate seamlessly, inspired by the integrity and encouragement from above. However, when leaders adopt a harsh or unethical stance, the environment can quickly turn toxic, like what happened at Uber and Wells Fargo. Employees become disengaged and demoralized, leading to a decline in morale and productivity.

Honesty and ethics play a vital role in long-term success. Consider leaders who make poor choices, perhaps by cheating or overlooking serious issues. Their decisions can lead to significant harm, as seen in the cases of Wells Fargo and Volkswagen. These examples serve as cautionary tales, highlighting how integrity must guide every action.

Empowerment and responsibility form the foundation of effective leadership. Good leaders foster an open dialogue, ensuring employees feel safe and encouraged to voice their opinions. They don't shy away from their mistakes; instead, they own up to them and act swiftly to resolve any problems. This approach builds trust and strengthens the organization. Leadership, then, becomes more than just decision-making; it transforms into a commitment to nurturing a positive culture, acting ethically, and prioritizing employee well-being.

Horst Schulze, during his tenure at the Ritz-Carlton, exemplified this principle of leadership. He didn't just redefine luxury; he revolutionized it. Schulze shifted the focus from lavish material displays to crafting personalized and unforgettable guest experiences. His belief that true luxury lies in exceeding expectations left an indelible mark on the hospitality industry, inspiring others to rethink what it means to offer exceptional service.

In his philosophy, Schulze coined the phrase, "Ladies and gentlemen serving ladies and gentlemen." This mantra created a culture of mutual respect between employees and guests. When staff members felt valued and empowered, they delivered outstanding service, enhancing the overall guest experience. Schulze's commitment to a values-driven organizational culture was evident in his hiring practices; he sought out individuals who shared the Ritz-Carlton's core values and invested in their growth. This commitment to building a united team around service excellence laid the groundwork for the brand's enduring success.

Similarly, Ken Kutaragi's journey in the gaming world exemplifies the power of passion and resilience. His unwavering love for gaming and technology fueled the creation of the PlayStation, proving that following one's passion can lead to groundbreaking innovations. Kutaragi faced skepticism and significant technical hurdles throughout his career. Instead of retreating in the face of adversity, he embraced these challenges as opportunities to innovate. His story serves as a reminder that setbacks often provide valuable lessons that can pave the way for future success.

Kutaragi also understood the importance of collaboration. He built a diverse team of engineers, designers, and marketers, fostering an environment where creativity flourished. By valuing each team member's unique skills, he cultivated a sense of shared ownership in their ambitious vision. This collaborative spirit underscored the vital role of teamwork in achieving goals and driving innovation.

The lessons drawn from the Pharaoh during the construction of the pyramids highlight the essence of transformational leadership. The Pharaoh inspired a collective vision among thousands of workers, igniting their passion and motivating them to contribute to something greater than themselves. He understood the diverse needs of his workforce, adapting his leadership style to accommodate artisans, laborers, and overseers. This flexibility exemplified situational leadership, where understanding and responding to the needs of followers is crucial.

Emotional intelligence also played a critical role in the Pharaoh's leadership. By empathizing with the workers' struggles and offering support, he maintained high morale, ensuring that the workforce remained motivated despite the demanding nature of their tasks. His ability to navigate the complex social dynamics among the workers fostered camaraderie and cooperation, underscoring the importance of social identity in effective leadership.

The Pharaoh's journey was not merely about erecting a physical monument; it was about creating a legacy of unity and resilience. This dual focus highlights the responsibility leaders have to inspire their teams while considering the broader implications of their actions. While the story of pyramid construction is inspiring, it is essential to approach it with a critical lens, recognizing the complexities and ethical considerations involved. Today's leaders can learn from both the triumphs and challenges of historical figures, ensuring that they create inclusive and respectful environments.

Looking at inspiring figures throughout history reveals what self-actualization truly means. Martin Luther King Jr. fought tirelessly for equal rights for African Americans, advocating for peaceful protests and justice. His dedication to fairness shows how personal ambitions can drive significant societal change. Nelson Mandela, after spending 27 years in prison for his opposition to apartheid, emerged with a commitment to forgiveness and unity. His story teaches us that overcoming personal hardship can inspire important social transformations.

Marie Curie's groundbreaking work in radioactivity illustrates the power of perseverance. As a woman in a male-dominated field, she faced numerous challenges but pursued her passion for science relentlessly. Her discoveries advanced both medicine and technology, proving that curiosity and determination can yield remarkable achievements.

Leonardo da Vinci, known as a true Renaissance man, excelled in various fields such as art, science, and engineering. His insatiable curiosity pushed him to explore different interests, inspiring us to keep learning and experimenting with new ideas. Helen Keller, despite her deafness and blindness, became an influential writer and advocate for people with disabilities. Her journey reveals that overcoming personal struggles can empower one to uplift others, encouraging many to pursue their dreams despite the odds.

These narratives illustrate the profound impact of leadership, passion, and resilience, serving as powerful reminders that anyone can make a meaningful difference in their field.

Skill	Key Actions	Follow-Up Steps
Strategic Vision	- Define long-term organizational goals. - Develop actionable plans aligned with the mission. - Conduct risk assessments for future challenges.	- Regularly review and adjust strategic goals. - Monitor progress with KPIs. - Schedule periodic vision alignment sessions with stakeholders.
Decision-Making	- Use data-driven approaches to make informed decisions. - Evaluate risks and benefits for major decisions. - Establish a clear decision-making framework.	- Maintain a decision journal for reflection and improvement. - Solicit feedback on key decisions. - Conduct post-decision reviews to assess outcomes.
Communication and Collaboration	- Foster open communication within the team. - Practice active listening and empathy. - Schedule regular team check-ins and updates.	- Measure team alignment through surveys or feedback sessions. - Address communication gaps promptly. - Celebrate team milestones and foster ongoing collaboration.
Problem-Solving and Innovation	- Implement structured problem-solving techniques (e.g., root cause analysis). - Encourage brainstorming sessions for innovative ideas. - Pilot creative solutions to challenges.	- Track the outcomes of implemented solutions. - Host periodic innovation reviews to refine processes. - Reward contributions that drive meaningful change.
Team Empowerment and Development	- Delegate responsibilities effectively. - Provide regular, constructive feedback. - Invest in training and professional growth opportunities for team members.	- Monitor team performance through individual development plans (IDPs). - Schedule one-on-one coaching sessions. - Recognize and reward individual and team accomplishments.

Here's a **6-month development plan** for an individual aiming to improve their **Effectiveness** leadership skills:

Daily Actions:

1. **Set Clear Priorities**: Every morning, identify the 3 most impactful tasks for the day.
   - **Measurement**: At the end of the day, review what was achieved.
2. **Focus on Outcome, Not Just Activity**: Avoid "busy work." Ask yourself, "How will this contribute to the long-term success of the team/organization?"

- **Measurement**: Track completed tasks that directly contribute to key organizational goals.

3. **End-of-Day Reflection**: Reflect on what worked and what didn't. Ask, "Did my actions move us closer to our vision?"

- **Measurement**: Keep a daily journal of actions and their outcomes.

Weekly Actions:

1. **Review and Align with Long-Term Goals**: Every week, revisit your long-term objectives. Adjust strategies if necessary.

- **Measurement**: Track progress on long-term projects using a visual tracker or dashboard.

2. **Engage Team for Feedback**: Ask your team for feedback on what you could do to be more impactful in your leadership.

- **Measurement**: Document suggestions and implement one per week.

3. **Problem-Solving Sessions**: Every week, focus on solving a challenge that aligns with strategic goals.

- **Measurement**: Document challenges solved and the impact they had on team productivity or project timelines.

Monthly Actions:

1. **Review Effectiveness**: At the end of each month, evaluate the impact of your actions on long-term goals.

- **Measurement**: Conduct a self-assessment and seek feedback from your team and managers on your effectiveness.

2. **Mentorship or Coaching**: Seek advice from a mentor or coach who can help you sharpen your effectiveness.

- **Measurement**: Apply one new piece of advice or strategy each month.

3. **Adjust Strategy for Improvement**: If you're not seeing measurable results, tweak your approach to how you're working toward your goals.
    - **Measurement**: Compare the results to previous months and adjust accordingly.

Final Result Measurement:

- **Effectiveness Scorecard**: Create a scorecard with KPIs aligned to your objectives (e.g., team performance, achievement of project milestones, customer satisfaction, and long-term goal completion).
- **Self-Review**: At the end of each week, evaluate if you're hitting your impact targets.

By the end of the 6-month plan, a person will ideally be making more informed decisions, with measurable impact and clarity on their leadership effectiveness.

Here are some key coaching questions inspired by the themes and lessons from the text:

Leadership and Workplace Culture

1. **Influence of Leadership**: How do you believe your leadership style influences the morale and productivity of your team?
2. **Creating a Positive Environment**: What specific actions can you take to foster a positive and ethical workplace culture?
3. **Handling Mistakes**: How do you currently respond to mistakes made by yourself or your team? What could you change to build more trust?
4. **Employee Empowerment**: How do you encourage open communication among your team members, and what might you do to improve this?

Learning from Leaders

5. **Lessons from Horst Schulze**: What aspects of Schulze's approach to redefining luxury and service can you apply to your own work or organization?
6. **Respect in Service**: How can you create a culture of mutual respect within your team or organization?
7. **Values-Driven Culture**: What core values do you want to instill in your team, and how can you promote those values in everyday actions?

Passion and Resilience

8. **Pursuing Passion**: What is your passion, and how can you integrate it more fully into your work?
9. **View on Challenges**: Can you think of a recent challenge you faced? How did you respond, and what opportunities for growth did it present?
10. **Team Collaboration**: How can you promote collaboration among your team to enhance creativity and innovation?

Historical Lessons

11. **Transformational Leadership**: In what ways can you inspire a collective vision among your team, similar to the Pharaoh's example?
12. **Adapting Leadership Style**: How do you adapt your leadership approach to meet the diverse needs of your team members?
13. **Emotional Intelligence**: How do you connect with your team on an emotional level, and how does this affect morale and motivation?

Legacy and Responsibility

14. **Building a Legacy**: What kind of legacy do you want to leave in your organization, and what steps can you take to begin building that today?

15. **Ethical Considerations**: How do you ensure that your decisions consider the broader implications for your team and the organization?

Self-Actualization and Role Models

16. **Inspirational Figures**: Who inspires you, and what lessons can you learn from their experiences to apply to your own journey?
17. **Personal Goals and Social Change**: How can your personal goals align with creating positive changes in your community or organization?
18. **Overcoming Struggles**: Reflect on a personal struggle you've faced. How did overcoming this struggle shape your perspective on leadership and resilience?

These questions encourage self-reflection and help individuals consider their leadership styles, personal goals, and the impact they can make in their environments.

Concluding Reflection:

- **What one action can you take this week to embody the leadership qualities discussed in the chapter?**

This question can help facilitate deeper reflection and dialogue, encouraging individuals to connect their personal experiences with the principles outlined in the text.

Conclusion

The interconnected attributes of the 7E Leadership Framework—Ethics, Envisioning, Endurance, Excellence, Encouragement, Enablement, and Effectiveness—form a robust foundation for mental agility in leaders.

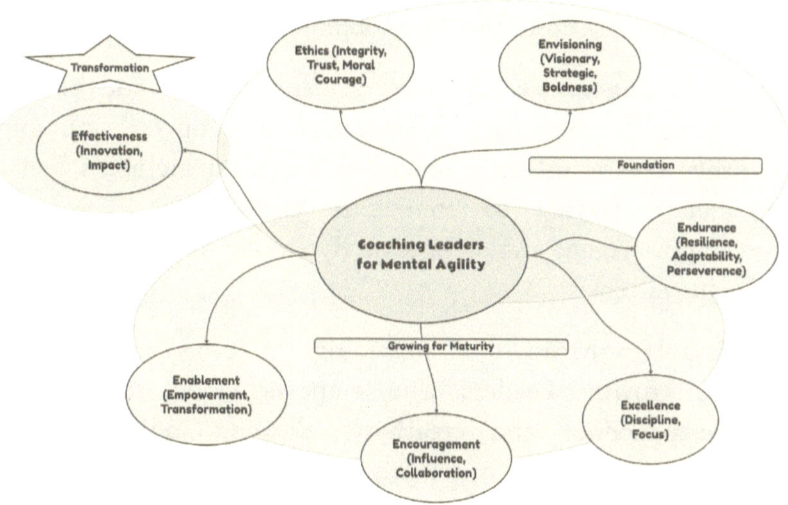

This synergy enhances a leader's ability to navigate complexities, adapt to change, and drive meaningful impact.

1. **Ethics** provides a solid base of integrity and trust. When leaders are grounded in moral principles, they foster a culture of accountability

and transparency. This ethical foundation not only builds trust within their teams but also equips leaders with the moral courage to make tough decisions, particularly in times of crisis.

2. **Envisioning** injects direction into leadership. By crafting a clear and strategic vision, leaders can inspire their teams and guide them toward common goals. This visionary approach encourages leaders to think critically and anticipate future challenges, enhancing their mental agility.

3. **Endurance** speaks to a leader's resilience, adaptability, and perseverance. In the face of setbacks, mentally agile leaders leverage their endurance to pivot strategies and stay focused on long-term objectives. They view challenges as opportunities for growth, maintaining their motivation and that of their teams.

4. **Excellence** emphasizes discipline and focus, critical for sustained progress. A mentally agile leader balances daily tasks with overarching goals, consistently seeking improvement and innovation. Their commitment to excellence drives teams to excel and embrace continuous development.

5. **Encouragement** empowers leaders to unite and inspire their teams. By fostering collaboration and open communication, they create an environment where team members feel valued and motivated to contribute their ideas. This collective empowerment enhances team dynamics and fosters a culture of innovation.

6. **Enablement** involves providing the tools and opportunities for growth. Leaders who empower their teams encourage independence and creativity, allowing individuals to take ownership of their roles. This fosters a sense of responsibility and cultivates an adaptable workforce ready to tackle challenges.

7. **Effectiveness** ensures that all leadership actions create positive, lasting impacts. Leaders with mental agility focus on long-term success rather than short-term gains. They measure their effectiveness not only by immediate outcomes but also by the

transformational effects their actions have on their organization and community.

By weaving these attributes together, leaders enhance their mental agility, enabling them to respond proactively to challenges, inspire others, and create sustainable change. This interconnectedness ultimately leads to a more resilient, innovative, and effective leadership style, positioning leaders to thrive in dynamic environments.

Leadership Mental Agility Coaching questions for each of the 7E Leadership Framework areas:

1. Ethics (Integrity and Trust)

1. How do you ensure your decisions align with your core values and ethical standards?
2. What strategies do you use to promote transparency within your team?
3. How do you handle situations where you must make tough decisions that could be unpopular but morally correct?
4. What role does integrity play in your leadership style, especially during crises?
5. How do you build a culture of accountability and responsibility in your organization?
6. Can you think of a time when acting ethically conflicted with immediate business goals? How did you manage it?
7. How do you encourage ethical behavior among your team members?
8. What measures do you have in place to ensure that integrity is maintained in all levels of your organization?
9. How do you respond when a team member's actions are inconsistent with the organization's ethical standards?
10. How do you balance personal moral values with organizational objectives when making decisions?

2. Envisioning (Strategic Vision)

1. How clearly have you communicated your vision to your team? How do you know they understand it?
2. What steps do you take to ensure your vision is adaptable to changing circumstances?
3. How do you encourage your team to align their individual goals with the broader vision?
4. What challenges do you foresee in achieving your long-term vision, and how do you plan to address them?
5. How do you inspire others to not just accept but embrace your vision?
6. What tools or processes do you use to anticipate future trends or challenges in your industry?
7. How do you adjust your vision when faced with unforeseen obstacles?
8. What role does critical thinking play in your approach to envisioning the future?
9. How do you integrate short-term wins into the bigger picture of your long-term vision?
10. How often do you reflect on and refine your vision to stay relevant in a changing environment?

3. Endurance (Resilience and Perseverance)

1. How do you maintain your motivation and focus during challenging times?
2. Can you share an example of a major setback you've faced and how you bounced back from it?
3. How do you foster resilience and perseverance within your team?
4. What strategies do you use to adapt when your original plan doesn't go as expected?

5. How do you balance persistence with the need to pivot when circumstances change?
6. How do you stay focused on long-term goals when faced with short-term difficulties?
7. How do you maintain team morale and motivation during prolonged periods of uncertainty?
8. What techniques do you use to help your team view challenges as opportunities for growth?
9. How do you measure progress and success when your goals require long-term endurance?
10. How do you manage stress and maintain your mental agility during crises?

4. Excellence (Discipline and Focus)

1. How do you stay disciplined and focused on your long-term goals while managing daily tasks?
2. What processes do you put in place to ensure that your team strives for continuous improvement?
3. How do you maintain a culture of high performance without causing burnout?
4. How do you encourage your team to prioritize excellence in everything they do?
5. What strategies do you use to measure progress toward achieving excellence in your work?
6. How do you balance innovation and risk-taking with maintaining a standard of excellence?
7. What habits have you developed to maintain your focus on both immediate tasks and broader objectives?
8. How do you ensure that excellence in execution doesn't stifle creativity within your team?

9. What is your approach to giving constructive feedback to ensure continuous development?
10. How do you lead by example when it comes to maintaining discipline and pursuing excellence?

5. Encouragement (Inspiration and Empowerment)

1. How do you foster a sense of collaboration and teamwork among your team members?
2. What specific actions do you take to show your team that you value their input and ideas?
3. How do you encourage open communication and ensure everyone feels heard?
4. How do you build an environment where team members feel empowered to take initiative?
5. How do you keep your team motivated, especially during times of stress or uncertainty?
6. How do you recognize and celebrate the strengths and achievements of individual team members?
7. How do you inspire creativity and innovation within your team?
8. What steps do you take to create a supportive and inclusive culture within your organization?
9. How do you encourage team members to embrace challenges and see them as growth opportunities?
10. How do you manage conflicts in a way that encourages learning and strengthens relationships?

6. Enablement (Providing Tools and Opportunities)

1. How do you identify and provide the resources your team needs to succeed?
2. How do you encourage independent thinking and problem-solving within your team?

3. How do you support your team members' personal and professional development?
4. What opportunities do you create to help your team grow and take on more responsibility?
5. How do you ensure your team has the right tools and training to tackle challenges?
6. How do you foster a culture of learning and adaptability within your team?
7. How do you create an environment where team members feel comfortable taking ownership of their work?
8. How do you delegate responsibilities in a way that empowers rather than overwhelms your team?
9. How do you encourage your team to take calculated risks and learn from failure?
10. How do you enable your team to be proactive in identifying and solving problems?

7. Effectiveness (Positive and Lasting Impact)

1. How do you measure the long-term impact of your leadership decisions?
2. How do you ensure that your leadership actions align with the broader goals of your organization?
3. What steps do you take to make sure your team's efforts create lasting value?
4. How do you prioritize actions that lead to sustainable success rather than short-term gains?
5. How do you evaluate the effectiveness of your leadership style and adjust it when necessary?
6. What methods do you use to track the transformational impact of your leadership on your team and organization?

7. How do you ensure that your leadership decisions positively affect your team, organization, and community?
8. How do you create a legacy of positive change within your organization?
9. How do you balance achieving immediate results with building long-term success?
10. How do you inspire your team to focus on creating lasting impact in their work?

Here are actionable insights that correspond to each of the coaching questions from the **7E Leadership Mental Agility Framework**:

1. Ethics (Integrity and Trust)

1. **Action**: Regularly reflect on your core values. Before making decisions, ask yourself: *Is this choice aligned with my values?*
2. **Action**: Implement open communication channels like regular team check-ins to ensure transparency.
3. **Action**: Be willing to stand by morally correct decisions even when they may not be popular. It will reinforce your credibility over time.
4. **Action**: During a crisis, model ethical behavior. Your actions will set the tone for the entire organization.
5. **Action**: Develop a culture of accountability by setting clear expectations and giving constructive feedback.
6. **Action**: When faced with ethical dilemmas, pause, and weigh the long-term consequences of each decision.
7. **Action**: Lead by example. Reward team members who demonstrate ethical behavior to encourage the same from others.
8. **Action**: Set up processes like audits or regular reviews to monitor and maintain ethical standards.
9. **Action**: Address unethical behavior immediately. Explain how it affects the team and provide a clear plan for improvement.

10. **Action**: Create a decision-making framework that weighs both ethical considerations and organizational goals.

2. **Envisioning (Strategic Vision)**

    1. **Action**: Use clear language when communicating your vision. Repeat it often and link it to team goals to ensure understanding.
    2. **Action**: Stay flexible. Regularly assess your vision and adjust as market or organizational conditions evolve.
    3. **Action**: Conduct vision-alignment workshops where team members can discuss their roles in achieving the long-term goal.
    4. **Action**: Identify potential challenges and prepare proactive solutions or adjustments to your strategy.
    5. **Action**: Share personal stories or examples that illustrate your vision. This will make it more relatable and inspiring.
    6. **Action**: Use tools like SWOT analysis or market research to stay ahead of future trends and position your team accordingly.
    7. **Action**: When obstacles arise, involve the team in discussions about adjusting strategies without losing sight of the ultimate vision.
    8. **Action**: Regularly challenge yourself and the team to think critically and question assumptions that could hinder progress.
    9. **Action**: Break the vision into smaller, achievable milestones that contribute to the long-term objective, and celebrate progress.
    10. **Action**: Set aside time to review your vision and ask yourself whether it's still relevant or if it needs fine-tuning.

3. **Endurance (Resilience and Perseverance)**

    - **Action**: Set small, attainable goals that keep you motivated during challenging periods, and celebrate small wins.
    - **Action**: Reflect on a past setback where you bounced back. Break down what worked and how you can apply that resilience in the future.

- **Action**: Organize team-building activities that foster resilience and provide a sense of collective strength during challenges.
- **Action**: Practice flexibility by encouraging brainstorming sessions when a plan doesn't go as expected.
- **Action**: Periodically review long-term goals and assess whether a shift in strategy is required to stay on course.
- **Action**: Develop mental endurance by setting both long- and short-term goals, focusing on maintaining progress through adversity.
- **Action**: Provide regular motivation through positive reinforcement, especially during tough times, to maintain team morale.
- **Action**: Shift the perspective on challenges by reframing them as opportunities for team growth and skill development.
- **Action**: Use progress-tracking tools to monitor milestones and ensure that you're moving steadily toward your goals.
- **Action**: Practice mindfulness or stress-relief exercises to maintain mental balance and agility during crisis situations.

4. Excellence (Discipline and Focus)

- **Action**: Create a daily task list and align it with your broader goals. Prioritize tasks that contribute most to long-term success.
- **Action**: Encourage a culture of continuous learning. Allocate time and resources for team training or workshops.
- **Action**: Monitor team workloads and encourage regular breaks to prevent burnout while maintaining high performance.
- **Action**: Hold regular check-ins to ensure each team member understands their role in achieving overall excellence.
- **Action**: Develop performance metrics that focus on improvement, rather than just outcomes, to foster a growth mindset.
- **Action**: Balance innovation with risk assessment by introducing small, controlled experiments that can lead to bigger improvements.

- **Action**: Set up time-blocking strategies for yourself and the team to maintain focus on priority tasks without distractions.
- **Action**: Allow room for creative thinking by providing the freedom to experiment within the boundaries of excellence.
- **Action**: Implement 360-degree feedback where team members can provide input on areas for improvement.
- **Action**: Model disciplined behavior by consistently following through on commitments, demonstrating the value of persistence.

5. **Encouragement (Inspiration and Empowerment)**

- **Action**: Initiate team activities that promote collaboration, like workshops or brainstorming sessions, to build stronger connections.
- **Action**: During meetings, actively solicit input from every team member, showing them their ideas are valued.
- **Action**: Schedule regular one-on-one sessions to ensure team members feel heard and supported.
- **Action**: Delegate meaningful tasks that align with individual team members' strengths and career goals to boost confidence.
- **Action**: Recognize both small and large contributions regularly, either through verbal praise or formal recognition programs.
- **Action**: Organize brainstorming sessions where team members feel comfortable expressing their creative ideas without fear of judgment.
- **Action**: Share inspirational stories of overcoming challenges, showing how setbacks can lead to innovation and success.
- **Action**: Create a culture of inclusivity by encouraging diverse perspectives and ideas, reinforcing the value of each team member.
- **Action**: Create opportunities for team members to take on new challenges, encouraging them to stretch beyond their comfort zones.
- **Action**: Mediate conflicts with a growth mindset by framing disagreements as learning opportunities for all involved.

6. **Enablement (Providing Tools and Opportunities)**

    - **Action**: Conduct regular needs assessments to identify the tools or resources your team requires to perform at their best.
    - **Action**: Empower your team by giving them the authority to make decisions in their areas of expertise, fostering independence.
    - **Action**: Create a personal development plan for each team member, providing training opportunities and career growth paths.
    - **Action**: Offer leadership development programs to encourage team members to take on more responsibility and leadership roles.
    - **Action**: Assess whether your team has the latest tools and technology to meet current challenges efficiently and effectively.
    - **Action**: Encourage a culture of self-learning by providing access to online courses, books, or seminars.
    - **Action**: Empower team members by giving them autonomy in how they achieve goals, as long as they stay aligned with the bigger picture.
    - **Action**: Practice delegating key tasks to capable team members, while offering guidance, when necessary, to build confidence.
    - **Action**: Reward creative problem-solving and create an environment where team members feel safe to experiment with new ideas.
    - **Action**: Hold regular review meetings where team members present their solutions to challenges, reinforcing the sense of ownership.

7. **Effectiveness (Positive and Lasting Impact)**

    - **Action**: Use a combination of short-term KPIs and long-term metrics to measure the impact of your leadership decisions.
    - **Action**: Regularly assess whether the team's activities are moving the organization closer to its overall goals, making adjustments as needed.
    - **Action**: Encourage team members to share success stories of how their work has contributed to lasting outcomes.

- **Action**: Focus on initiatives that deliver sustainable value, even if they don't produce immediate gains.
- **Action**: Ask for regular feedback from your team and stakeholders to ensure your leadership remains aligned with the organization's needs.
- **Action**: Implement long-term projects that leave a positive impact on the organization and the community.
- **Action**: Lead by example by taking part in activities that benefit both the organization and the broader community.
- **Action**: Set a goal of leaving a legacy—whether in improved processes, culture, or team dynamics—within your organization.
- **Action**: Develop leadership programs that ensure continuity and long-term success for your organization beyond immediate results.
- **Action**: Encourage your team to think beyond short-term results by focusing on building a lasting legacy through their work.

Each of these actionable steps encourages reflection and change, helping leaders and teams move toward growth and success while embodying the principles of the 7E framework.

To measure leadership agility based on the **7E Leadership Framework**, individuals can assess their progress through quantifiable metrics aligned with each of the seven attributes. This approach allows leaders to track their effectiveness, make data-driven improvements, and ensure they are cultivating the right behaviors to navigate challenges, inspire their teams, and drive long-term success. Below is a breakdown of how leaders can measure their **leadership agility** with examples, actions, and specific metrics:

1. Ethics (Trust and Integrity)

Key Metric: Trust and Integrity Index

- **Metric:** Percentage of employees who trust their leader's decisions and view their leadership as transparent and ethical.
- **Data Source:** Employee engagement surveys, trust scorecards.

- **Action to Improve:** Improve transparency in decision-making by holding regular "open forum" meetings to discuss ethical dilemmas and decision-making processes.
- **Example of Improvement:** If 70% of employees currently trust leadership, set a target of 85% by increasing transparency in communications and providing concrete examples of ethical decision-making.
- **Measurement Example:** Track feedback through anonymous surveys and compare year-over-year improvements.

2. Envisioning (Vision and Strategy)

Key Metric: Vision Alignment Score

- **Metric:** Percentage of team members who can clearly articulate the leader's vision and how their work contributes to it.
- **Data Source:** Employee feedback, performance appraisals, strategic alignment audits.
- **Action to Improve:** Schedule monthly meetings to communicate the vision, reinforce the connection between daily work and long-term strategy, and involve employees in strategic planning.
- **Example of Improvement:** If the vision alignment score is 60%, aim to increase it to 80% by ensuring clear communication through town halls, team meetings, and regular updates.
- **Measurement Example:** Conduct quarterly pulse surveys and strategic audits to track alignment and adapt the communication approach.

3. Endurance (Resilience and Adaptability)

Key Metric: Resilience Score

- **Metric:** Number of successful adaptations or pivots after setbacks or crises.
- **Data Source:** Post-project analysis, crisis management reports, feedback from teams.

- **Action to Improve:** Provide training in crisis management and resilience, focusing on the importance of adaptive leadership and maintaining a positive mindset after failures.
- **Example of Improvement:** If resilience is currently demonstrated 50% of the time after setbacks, target a 70% success rate by enhancing crisis response plans and offering team support.
- **Measurement Example:** Track the number of crises and how quickly leadership teams recover, documenting the lessons learned and any long-term changes.

4. Excellence (Focus and Discipline)

Key Metric: Innovation Rate

- **Metric:** Number of new initiatives, products, or improvements successfully implemented.
- **Data Source:** Project tracking tools, innovation reports, product development documentation.
- **Action to Improve:** Encourage creative thinking and risk-taking by fostering a culture where experimentation is valued. Implement structured processes for feedback and iterative improvement.
- **Example of Improvement:** If 10% of projects are deemed innovative, aim to increase that to 15% by setting clear innovation goals and rewarding creativity.
- **Measurement Example:** Track the number of new product launches or process improvements quarterly, reviewing their success rates and any customer feedback.

5. Encouragement (Inspiring and Uniting Teams)

Key Metric: Employee Empowerment Index

- **Metric:** Percentage of employees who feel empowered to make decisions and contribute ideas.
- **Data Source:** Employee surveys, feedback platforms, team performance reviews.

- **Action to Improve:** Implement recognition programs, give employees ownership over key initiatives, and hold open forums to encourage idea sharing.
- **Example of Improvement:** If only 50% of employees report feeling empowered, aim for 70% by introducing a formal recognition program and increasing opportunities for team leadership.
- **Measurement Example:** Track participation in leadership programs and measure the percentage of decisions made by employees versus top-down directives.

6. Enablement (Providing Growth Opportunities)

Key Metric: Employee Development Index

- **Metric:** Percentage of employees who report having access to professional development opportunities.
- **Data Source:** Employee feedback surveys, mentoring program participation, training completion rates.
- **Action to Improve:** Increase the availability of learning opportunities by introducing mentorship programs, online training, and clear career development paths.
- **Example of Improvement:** If 40% of employees feel supported in their development, set a target of 60% by expanding career development resources and aligning learning initiatives with organizational goals.
- **Measurement Example:** Monitor participation in professional development programs and gather feedback from employees on how these opportunities have impacted their performance.

7. Effectiveness (Long-Term Impact)

Key Metric: Long-Term Impact Score

- **Metric:** Percentage of leadership initiatives that result in sustainable, long-term outcomes, such as employee retention, improved customer satisfaction, or financial performance.

- **Data Source:** Post-mortem project reviews, employee retention rates, long-term strategic reviews.
- **Action to Improve:** Shift focus to long-term planning by implementing strategies that foster sustainable growth and continuous improvement, while also tracking the long-term impact of leadership decisions.
- **Example of Improvement:** If 60% of leadership initiatives have a lasting impact, aim for 75% by making decisions that focus on long-term outcomes, such as employee well-being, continuous learning, and innovation.
- **Measurement Example:** Evaluate leadership decisions at the 1, 3, and 5-year marks to assess their long-term effects and compare these outcomes to the original goals.

Actionable Framework for Measuring Leadership Agility:

1. **Establish Baseline Metrics**: Determine where you stand for each of the 7E attributes, using surveys, feedback, and historical performance data.
2. **Review and Track Progress Regularly**: Set quarterly or biannual check-ins to review progress. Update your approach based on feedback and observed changes.
3. **Use Feedback Loops**: Gather input from direct reports, peers, and self-assessments to measure the perceived success of leadership behaviors and attribute areas.
4. **Set Clear Improvement Targets**: Based on baseline data, define realistic goals, such as improving trust by 15% or innovation rates by 10%.
5. **Monitor Long-Term Outcomes**: Track the lasting effects of leadership decisions, ensuring that improvements lead to sustained success over time.

By quantifying leadership agility using these metrics, leaders can see their growth, recognize where adjustments are needed, and continue refining their approach for maximum impact. Regularly assessing these key areas ensures leaders stay aligned with their goals and foster an environment that promotes long-term organizational success.

Let us look into several real time examples and how **7E leadership Framework** helped them to become great at Leadership.

In times of challenge, true leaders don't just manage—they inspire. Mahatma Gandhi, through his remarkable leadership journey, wasn't just leading a nation; he was coaching an entire generation in the art of courage, resilience, and unwavering ethical commitment. His story is one of personal endurance, steadfast principles, and, perhaps most importantly, a deep and abiding faith in the power of people. Gandhi's leadership became a living lesson in seven core principles: **Ethics, Envisioning, Endurance, Excellence, Encouragement, Enablement,** and **Effectiveness**.

Imagine this: a frail man, dressed simply, no wealth or weaponry in hand, standing before vast crowds under a blazing sun. He speaks softly, yet his words ignite fire in hearts across the country. Through his unshakable belief in non-violence and truth, Gandhi asked people to look inward and reflect on their own strengths and values. For Gandhi, these values weren't abstract ideas; they were living guides that he carried into every speech, every protest, and every fast he undertook.

1. Ethics: Coaching a Nation with Integrity

To Gandhi, ethics meant truth in every action. He coached others by example, holding himself to the highest standards. "My life is my message," he often said, demonstrating that integrity is not negotiable. When faced with British aggression, he maintained a dignified resistance, modeling an unbreakable moral code. In this way, Gandhi's leadership served as a coaching lesson for millions, teaching them that to be a true leader, one must have an unshakable foundation in ethics.

Imagine yourself in his shoes, facing the might of the British Empire with nothing but the truth on your side. Would you have that courage? Gandhi's story asks readers to consider their own ethical backbone, inspiring us to think about how we might strengthen it, especially when tested.

2. Envisioning: A Vision that Unites

Gandhi's vision went far beyond independence—it was about unity, self-reliance, and dignity for all, irrespective of caste, class, or religion. He believed that freedom was hollow if it didn't also mean social equality. As a coach, he invited his people to think bigger, to embrace a future where everyone had a voice. Gandhi's vision wasn't something he imposed; he nurtured it in others, helping each person become a torchbearer of the vision.

In his quiet way, he would challenge each follower: "How do you envision freedom? How do you see your role in our nation?" This simple but profound question stirred millions to imagine their place in an independent India, making the vision theirs to own and work toward.

3. Endurance: Teaching Resilience by Example

Gandhi's endurance in the face of adversity became a coaching lesson in resilience. Despite frequent imprisonments, physical hardships, and near-constant threats, he remained unwavering. Each march, each fast, each quiet day in jail taught his followers that strength comes from within, and that true resilience is a commitment to a cause greater than oneself.

As a coach, Gandhi didn't just say, "Be strong"—he lived it. Think of the Salt March, a grueling 240-mile trek to the sea to protest the British salt tax. Gandhi endured this journey to show others that resilience means pushing forward, even when the path is uncertain and painful. His quiet strength called on others to find that inner well of endurance in their own lives.

4. Excellence: The Relentless Pursuit of Improvement

Gandhi's pursuit of excellence wasn't just about political strategy; it was a commitment to personal growth and discipline. He encouraged his followers to focus on self-improvement, believing that a disciplined life was essential to meaningful progress. His days were meticulously organized, filled with prayer, work, and learning.

In his coaching, Gandhi would often ask: "How are you improving yourself today?" He urged his followers to continually refine themselves, not for personal glory but to be of better service to others. He set the example by constantly honing his own strengths, showing that leadership requires a lifetime commitment to excellence.

5. Encouragement: The Power of Belief in Others

Gandhi deeply believed in the potential of every individual. He encouraged his followers, not by telling them what to do, but by believing in their power to act. His words were a source of encouragement, urging people to rise above fear and uncertainty. He inspired millions to find courage within, even when faced with violence and oppression.

"Be the change you wish to see in the world," he would tell them, instilling in each person a sense of agency. Gandhi's leadership was a lesson in empowerment; his belief in others made them believe in themselves. Imagine hearing those words from him—how would they make you feel? For many, it was the fuel that kept them going when times grew dark.

6. Enablement: Empowering a Nation to Stand on Its Own

Gandhi didn't seek to be a hero; he sought to make heroes of ordinary people. He taught self-reliance, encouraging Indians to spin their own cloth and make their own salt as acts of defiance. This wasn't just symbolic; it was a tangible way of giving power back to the people.

Through his coaching, Gandhi taught his people that they didn't need to rely on a foreign power or even on him as a single leader. He enabled each person to see their role in the freedom struggle, creating a movement that was powerful, widespread, and self-sustaining.

7. Effectiveness: Turning Vision into Action

Despite his peaceful approach, Gandhi was remarkably effective in achieving his goals. His protests, boycotts, and strategic non-violent actions were meticulously planned and executed. As a coach, he showed that effectiveness lies in being both visionary and pragmatic. His movements didn't just make noise—they achieved results.

Gandhi's story teaches us that real effectiveness comes from aligning our actions with our values and our vision. He led with purpose, creating a legacy of practical wisdom for those who would follow. For him, leadership was about more than speeches—it was about results, rooted in compassion and clarity.

The Legacy: A Call to Reflect and Act

Gandhi's life is a coaching lesson for leaders, managers, and individuals seeking to make an impact. His principles encourage us to ask tough questions of ourselves:

- Are our actions aligned with our ethics?
- How strong is our vision, and are we inspiring others to share it?
- Do we model resilience, and are we committed to continual self-improvement?
- Are we empowering those around us, encouraging them to find their strength?

As we reflect on these questions, we see how Gandhi's approach to leadership wasn't just about words—it was about inspiring others to rise above limitations, embrace their potential, and shape the world around them. For Gandhi, leadership was an invitation, and his life remains a powerful testament to what's possible when we lead with heart, integrity, and vision.

From Air Mattresses to a Global Movement: How Brian Chesky's Vision Built Airbnb

In 2008, Brian Chesky stood at a crossroads with his friends Joe Gebbia and Nathan Blecharczyk.

Struggling to pay rent in their San Francisco apartment, they devised a creative plan: why not offer a spot to sleep for attendees of an upcoming design conference?

They placed air mattresses in their living room and called it "Air Bed and Breakfast," offering something affordable and personal for guests looking to avoid expensive hotels.

This simple solution soon became Airbnb, a platform where people could share their homes with travelers around the world.

Yet, getting Airbnb off the ground was anything but easy. Investors initially turned them away, doubting the idea of people sleeping in strangers' homes.

Chesky and his co-founders had to find another way to fund their dream. Instead of giving up, they decided to sell something unusual: cereal.

In 2008, during the presidential election, they created limited-edition boxes of "Obama O's" and "Cap'n McCain" cereal.

This unexpected product sold well, raising $30,000 that they put directly back into Airbnb. It was a bold move, demonstrating Chesky's determination and ability to think creatively under pressure.

Chesky knew that convincing people to stay in others' homes required a deep sense of trust. Travelers needed reassurance, and so did hosts. Chesky and his team worked hard to make Airbnb a safe and trustworthy community.

They introduced identity verification, guest reviews, and a generous host guarantee for property damage. With each added measure, Airbnb's reputation grew, turning wary customers into loyal users who felt safe embracing this new way of travel.

As Airbnb gained popularity, Chesky's leadership faced an unexpected test—the COVID-19 pandemic. Almost overnight, travel plummeted, and with it, Airbnb's revenue. Tough decisions followed, including the painful choice to lay off a quarter of the workforce.

Chesky focused on Airbnb's core mission of "belonging anywhere" and kept his attention on the safety of hosts and travelers.

He pivoted the company's offerings toward local travel and long-term stays, positioning Airbnb to adapt to a world with new restrictions. Under Chesky's guidance, Airbnb not only survived the pandemic but found new ways to thrive.

Chesky's vision for Airbnb went beyond lodging; he wanted it to foster genuine connection. He emphasized belonging, not just booking. From this foundation, Airbnb created "Airbnb Experiences," letting travelers connect with hosts through curated experiences that celebrated local cultures. Even as the company scaled, Chesky held tight to his vision of making the world feel a little closer.

With resilience and a clear long-term view, Chesky led Airbnb through regulatory challenges, economic downturns, and public scrutiny, eventually taking the company public in 2020. His approach kept Airbnb from being just another travel company—it became a resilient, transformative force in the industry.

Central to Chesky's success was his people-first leadership style. Hosts, he believed, were the heart of Airbnb. He made it a priority to equip them with tools and resources, building a community of empowered hosts rather than a simple marketplace. Chesky's dedication to empowering his team and his hosts created a culture of partnership and trust.

As a leader, Chesky embraced empathy, accountability, and integrity, always treating his team, hosts, and guests with respect. His leadership built a culture where accountability and compassion drove decisions, which not only strengthened Airbnb's brand but deeply resonated with millions of users worldwide.

Under Chesky's vision, Airbnb grew from a small experiment into a global community, fundamentally changing how people travel and connect. It wasn't just a new business model—it was a new way of seeing the world, all led by a man who believed in sharing and belonging.

Chesky's leadership approach to the 7E Leadership Model

1. Ethics

Chesky's actions, especially his emphasis on transparency and creating a culture of trust, align closely with the ethics principle. For example, he worked directly with hosts and guests, even staying in properties himself, to understand and address concerns. This transparency in understanding customer pain points built trust within the Airbnb community and reinforced Airbnb's values.

2. Envisioning

Chesky had a clear vision to "create a world where anyone can belong anywhere," which went beyond simple travel accommodations. His commitment to this vision inspired his team to rally around the idea of belonging and community, unifying them under a shared goal. This vision also guided strategic choices, even in moments of uncertainty, which kept the company aligned with long-term growth.

3. Endurance

During Airbnb's early days, Chesky showed remarkable resilience, pivoting strategies, and staying focused through financial struggles and investor rejection. His creativity in selling branded cereals to fund the company exemplifies his endurance and ability to view challenges as opportunities, inspiring his team to persevere and grow together.

4. Excellence

Chesky's Approach: Chesky's dedication to customer experience reflects his pursuit of excellence. By focusing on improving Airbnb's platform to ensure safety and transparency, Chesky not only created a better user experience but also drove the team to strive for higher standards in service. His disciplined focus on refining Airbnb's mission and vision helped the team achieve a world-class product.

5. Encouragement

Chesky fostered an inclusive, collaborative environment by hiring people who aligned with Airbnb's core values and encouraging open communication. His leadership style emphasized team empowerment, which helped Airbnb attract talent who were motivated and aligned with its mission. Chesky's actions to understand different perspectives also inspired a strong sense of unity and purpose among employees.

6. Enablement

Chesky enabled his team by providing them with the freedom to make decisions that would benefit Airbnb's growth. By actively seeking mentorship himself and encouraging a learning culture, Chesky supported an environment where creativity and independence flourished. His empowerment of team members cultivated an adaptable workforce ready to innovate in a dynamic environment.

7. Effectiveness

Rather than seeking immediate profits, Chesky focused on building Airbnb into a platform that prioritized trust and long-term value. His commitment to creating a lasting brand demonstrated a keen focus on effectiveness. Chesky's decisions around trust-building and customer-centric improvements showed a commitment to Airbnb's long-term success and the broader impact on community-building in the travel industry.

Through these 7E leadership skills, Chesky's approach shaped Airbnb into a resilient, customer-focused, and visionary organization that transformed the travel industry by focusing on a balance of ethics, endurance, and effectiveness.

Angela Merkel exhibited each of the **7E Leadership attributes** during her tenure as Germany's Chancellor:

1. Ethics: Building Trust and Integrity

Angela Merkel's leadership was deeply rooted in **ethics**, which provided a solid foundation of integrity and trust. Merkel was known for her honesty, humility, and transparency. She earned the respect of her people and leaders worldwide by consistently adhering to moral principles, even in difficult situations. A significant example of her ethical leadership was during the **European debt crisis** in 2008–2009, when Merkel stood firm on Germany's commitments to fiscal responsibility while also working to ensure the survival of the Eurozone. Her clear, honest communication and focus on maintaining fairness and accountability in negotiations built trust across Europe. She also made a controversial but morally driven decision to welcome over **1 million refugees** in 2015, saying, "We can do this," reflecting her ethical stance on humanitarian responsibility.

2. Envisioning: Crafting a Strategic Vision

Merkel had a clear vision for Germany's place in Europe and the world. Her long-term focus on European unity shaped much of her foreign policy. She was a staunch advocate for a **strong, united Europe**, understanding that Germany's future prosperity was tied to the stability and success of the European Union. Merkel's vision extended to global challenges as well, particularly in areas like **climate change** and **renewable energy**, where she pushed Germany to be a global leader in sustainability through policies like the **Energiewende**, the transition from fossil fuels to renewable energy. Merkel's vision for Germany was not only about economic strength but also about social responsibility, stability, and leadership on the global stage.

3. Endurance: Demonstrating Resilience and Perseverance

Merkel's leadership was defined by her resilience and endurance, particularly in navigating crises. From the **2008 financial crisis** to the **European refugee crisis** and the **COVID-19 pandemic**, Merkel remained calm, steady, and adaptable. She faced criticism and opposition, but her persistence helped Germany navigate through economic turmoil, social tensions, and global health challenges. Merkel's ability to remain focused on the long-term and make difficult decisions under pressure was key to her leadership success. Her resilience also shone in her personal life — she was one of the few women leading a major global economy, and as a former physicist from East Germany, she shattered many glass ceilings in a male-dominated political world.

4. Excellence: Striving for Discipline and Focus

Merkel was known for her meticulous attention to detail and her disciplined approach to governance. She was deliberate in decision-making, often focusing on gathering all relevant information before committing to a course of action. Merkel's disciplined leadership style allowed her to maintain **Germany's economic stability** during volatile times. Her commitment to **fiscal discipline** helped Germany recover quickly from the 2008 financial crisis, avoiding the deep recessions that plagued other European nations. Merkel's focus on excellence also extended to international diplomacy, where her patience and thoughtful negotiation skills earned her respect on the world stage. Her leadership was grounded in competence and careful, measured actions, ensuring that Germany remained a reliable partner in the European Union and globally.

5. Encouragement: Empowering and Inspiring Teams

Merkel had a unique way of empowering those around her by fostering a culture of collaboration. While her leadership style was often described as reserved, she encouraged open communication and valued diverse perspectives. Merkel's ability to **inspire and unite** her team came from her willingness to listen and her calm, consensus-building approach. This was particularly evident during the European Union negotiations, where she often played the role of mediator, encouraging cooperation among member states. She believed in **teamwork and collective decision-making**, allowing her ministers and advisors to contribute meaningfully to Germany's progress. Merkel's encouragement also extended to her support for the European project, fostering an environment where nations could come together to solve common problems despite differing views.

6. Enablement: Providing Tools for Growth and Success

Merkel enabled growth and progress through her policies on innovation, education, and technology. She was a strong advocate for **research and development**, ensuring that Germany stayed at the forefront of **technological advancement** and **manufacturing excellence**. Merkel also championed **renewable energy**, pushing Germany to become a global leader in green technologies. Her commitment to enabling growth was evident in her support for **STEM education** and job creation, ensuring that future generations had the skills necessary to thrive in a rapidly changing world. By providing her people with the tools and opportunities for success, Merkel cultivated a resilient workforce capable of tackling both present and future challenges.

7. Effectiveness: Delivering Long-Term Impact

Throughout her 16 years in office, Merkel's leadership was marked by her focus on **long-term effectiveness** rather than short-term gains. She consistently took a pragmatic approach to challenges, prioritizing decisions that would benefit both Germany and Europe in the long run. One clear example of this was her leadership during the European debt crisis, where she pushed for austerity measures and reforms that, while unpopular at the time, ultimately helped stabilize the Eurozone and ensure its survival. Merkel's effectiveness extended beyond economics

— her **foreign policy** was geared toward **peace and diplomacy**, particularly in navigating relationships with major global powers like the U.S., Russia, and China. Her decisions had lasting impacts, both in Germany's prosperity and in its role as a **stabilizing force in Europe**.

Angela Merkel's leadership is a remarkable example of how the **7E Leadership attributes** can be applied to achieve meaningful, sustainable success. Her ethics built trust, her vision guided Germany through challenges, her resilience allowed her to endure crises, her discipline ensured excellence, her encouragement inspired her team and nation, her enablement fostered growth, and her effectiveness delivered long-term, positive impacts. Merkel's legacy is one of stability, pragmatism, and strength, proving that ethical and mentally agile leadership can drive profound change, both within a nation and across the world.

As we conclude this exploration of **mental agility** and its crucial role in leadership, it's clear that mental agility is not just a skill—it's a mindset, a way of being. The 7E Leadership Framework has illuminated the path toward becoming a more agile, adaptable, and effective leader, empowering you to navigate the complexities of the modern world.

Each of the **7Es** provides a unique lens through which leaders can strengthen their decision-making, foster collaboration, and inspire their teams:

1. **Ethics** provides a rock-solid foundation of integrity and trust. It ensures that every decision made, whether in calm or in crisis, is grounded in a sense of moral responsibility. By aligning your actions with your core values, you inspire trust, build respect, and create a culture of accountability within your team.

2. **Envisioning** gives you the foresight to look beyond the immediate and plan for a dynamic future. As a leader, you must continually anticipate challenges and opportunities ahead, adapting your strategy and maintaining clarity of purpose. A clear vision fuels motivation and guides teams toward long-term success.

3. **Endurance** speaks to resilience—the ability to keep going when the road gets tough. Leadership requires perseverance, especially during difficult times. By embracing setbacks as growth opportunities, you'll be able to push through adversity, inspire your team's stamina, and lead by example in times of uncertainty.

4. **Excellence** calls you to maintain a high standard of performance. Mental agility is not about reacting in the moment alone—it's about being disciplined and focused, continuously striving for improvement. As a leader, your commitment to excellence sets the tone for your entire organization, inspiring others to follow your lead.

5. **Encouragement** allows you to motivate and empower your team. Creating an environment of support and open communication leads to a culture of innovation, where new ideas are nurtured, and everyone feels valued. A mentally agile leader knows that true strength lies in collaboration and shared vision.

6. **Enablement** fosters growth and independence in others. A leader who enables their team gives them the tools, resources, and autonomy to excel. You'll be able to create a team that is adaptable, resourceful, and empowered to make decisions and take action on their own.

7. **Effectiveness** ensures that every action has a lasting, positive impact. Mental agility isn't just about responding quickly; it's about ensuring that your decisions contribute to the long-term success and sustainability of your organization. You lead not only by achieving immediate results but by creating a legacy of transformation.

The mental stamina of **Napoleon Bonaparte** and **Alexander the Great** was pivotal to their legendary leadership, enabling them to overcome extraordinary challenges, inspire loyalty, and achieve monumental feats. Both leaders exhibited unique mental traits that set them apart, yet their approaches reflected their distinct historical and cultural contexts.

Mapping the **7E Leadership Framework** to the traits of Napoleon Bonaparte and Alexander the Great reveals significant alignment, with both leaders embodying aspects of these leadership principles. Here's a detailed comparison:

7E Leadership Element	Alexander the Great	Napoleon Bonaparte	Comparison
1. Ethics	Maintained loyalty through trust and camaraderie; integrated cultures to build moral authority.	Inspired trust but sometimes overstepped ethical boundaries for ambition.	Both exhibited trust-building, but Alexander leaned more toward ethical unity.
2. Envisioning	Crafted a bold vision of a unified, multicultural empire.	Pursued a vision of European dominance through reforms and conquests.	Both leaders demonstrated visionary thinking, but Napoleon's focus was narrower.

7E Leadership Element	Alexander the Great	Napoleon Bonaparte	Comparison
3. Endurance	Endured long campaigns, adapting strategies to diverse challenges.	Showed resilience, particularly during exile and military setbacks.	Both exhibited perseverance, though Napoleon faced more self-inflicted adversity.
4. Excellence	Maintained focus through disciplined planning and execution of campaigns.	Applied rigorous discipline to reforms and military innovations.	Both excelled in maintaining focus, with similar attention to strategic discipline.
5. Encouragement	Inspired troops with charisma and a sense of shared purpose.	Motivated followers but sometimes alienated allies through authoritarianism.	Alexander excelled in fostering loyalty, while Napoleon's encouragement waned at times.
6. Enablement	Empowered generals and spread Greek culture as a transformative force.	Centralized power but also initiated transformative legal and social reforms.	Alexander leaned toward empowerment; Napoleon focused on transformation via central control.

7E Leadership Element	Alexander the Great	Napoleon Bonaparte	Comparison
7. Effectiveness	Left a lasting cultural legacy through Hellenism.	Created enduring legal frameworks like the Napoleonic Code.	Both created impactful legacies, with Alexander emphasizing cultural innovation and Napoleon focusing on governance.

Similarities Between the Traits and 7E Framework:

- **Visionary Leadership (Envisioning)**

  Both leaders exemplified bold, strategic, and visionary thinking, aligning closely with the Envisioning element.

- **Resilience (Endurance)**

  Their ability to persevere through challenges and adapt to dynamic circumstances highlights their strong alignment with Endurance.

- **Focus on Legacy (Effectiveness)**

  Both leaders' actions resulted in lasting impacts, from cultural integration to systemic reforms, reflecting Effectiveness.

- **Influence and Empowerment (Encouragement and Enablement)**

  Alexander empowered and inspired through inclusivity, while Napoleon motivated through decisive reforms and governance.

Key Differences:

- **Ethics**: Alexander's efforts to integrate cultures demonstrated a more inclusive ethical approach, while Napoleon's occasional authoritarianism and missteps, such as his Russian campaign, suggest a weaker alignment with ethics.

- **Enablement**: Alexander excelled in distributing authority and empowering generals, while Napoleon centralized power, relying more on his own control.

The **7E Leadership Framework** and the traits of Napoleon and Alexander significantly overlap, illustrating timeless leadership principles. Both leaders displayed traits that resonate strongly with **Envisioning, Endurance, Excellence, Encouragement, and Effectiveness**. The differences mainly arise in **Ethics** and **Enablement**, where their distinct contexts and leadership styles shaped divergent approaches. These insights emphasize that while historical leaders operated in unique environments, the core of effective leadership remains remarkably consistent.

Coaching Conversation:

Coach: Hi **Alex**, today we'll explore how the 7E Leadership Framework can strengthen your mental agility and leadership effectiveness. Let's start by identifying a current challenge you're facing as a leader.

Alex: I'm struggling with leading my team through a major transformation. Balancing stakeholder demands, team morale, and progress feels like juggling too many balls.

Ethics: Aligning Values to Build Trust

Coach: Let's begin with **ethics**. In tough situations like this, how do you ensure your decisions align with your values and build trust?

Alex: I try to remain honest, but sometimes I feel pressured to overpromise just to satisfy stakeholders.

Coach: Let's try this approach: When stakeholders demand unrealistic timelines, instead of agreeing outright, propose phased milestones. For example, say, *"To deliver with quality, we suggest focusing on feature A by this date, followed by feature B. This ensures sustained value for all parties."* Does this approach resonate with your values?

Alex: Yes, it feels more honest and achievable.

Envisioning: Defining a Clear Path Forward

Coach: Moving to **Envisioning**, how well have you communicated the transformation's purpose and roadmap to your team?

Alex: I think I've shared it, but they might not fully grasp the bigger picture.

Coach: Try using a visual metaphor. For example: *"Imagine we're building a bridge. Each milestone is a section that connects us to the other side. By completing each section, we ensure safety and stability."* Use a visual timeline in your next meeting to anchor this metaphor.

Alex: That's a great idea! It will simplify the process for the team.

Endurance: Demonstrating Resilience

Coach: Let's talk about **Endurance**—your ability to navigate setbacks. What recent example tested your resilience?

Alex: When a major deliverable failed due to unforeseen dependencies, the team was demoralized.

Coach: Resilience is about transforming setbacks into opportunities. For example, gather the team and say: *"This didn't go as planned, but here's what we learned. Let's regroup and tackle it differently by trying X and Y."* This shows them that obstacles are part of the journey, not the end of it.

Alex: I can do that. It's about reframing failure as learning.

Encouragement: Motivating and Uniting the Team

Coach: How do you encourage your team during tough times?

Alex: I try to stay positive, but I'm not sure it's enough.

Coach: Let's add actionable encouragement. For example, after a milestone, send a message like: *"Shoutout to Alex for their innovative idea that moved us forward!"* Recognize small wins publicly. This builds morale and teamwork.

Alex: I like that. It's easy to do and can have a big impact.

Enablement: Empowering Ownership

Coach: Let's move to **Enablement**—how do you empower your team to take ownership?

Alex: I tend to step in too much when they're struggling.

Coach: Try this instead: When a challenge arises, ask, *"What solutions do you think would work here?"* Let them brainstorm first, then guide. For example, if a project is delayed, involve them in creating a recovery plan.

Alex: That makes sense. I need to give them more room to grow.

Excellence: Striving for Quality

Coach: Excellence is about driving quality. How do you balance high standards with realistic timelines?

Alex: That's tricky. I sometimes feel I have to compromise one for the other.

Coach: Focus on "quick wins" that align with excellence. For example, introduce a weekly review: *"Let's dedicate 30 minutes to assess progress and ensure quality before we move to the next stage."* This creates a habit of excellence without overwhelming the team.

Alex: I'll start incorporating weekly reviews.

Effectiveness: Measuring Impact

Coach: Lastly, let's talk about **Effectiveness**. How do you measure the impact of your leadership?

Alex: I focus on project delivery, but I'm not sure it reflects leadership effectiveness.

Coach: Broaden your metrics. For example, track team engagement, feedback scores, and how often your team proposes new ideas. This reflects how inspired and supported they feel under your leadership.

Alex: That's insightful. I'll start collecting feedback regularly.

Closing the Conversation

Coach: You've identified great actions today: anchoring your vision with visuals, celebrating small wins, empowering ownership, and setting metrics for effectiveness. Which one will you prioritize first?

Alex: I'll start with encouraging and empowering the team—it feels like the foundation for everything else.

Coach: Excellent choice! Let's follow up in a month to see how these strategies are working. Remember, great leadership is about steady growth, not perfection.

Alex: Thank you! I feel more confident already.

7E Leadership Attribute	Famous Leadership Quote	Action to Take
Ethics (Trust and Integrity)	"In matters of conscience, the law of the majority has no place." – Mahatma Gandhi	Foster transparency in decision-making and lead with integrity, even in tough situations. When facing ethical dilemmas, take a stand that reflects your values.
	"I am not a saint, unless you think of a saint as a sinner who keeps on trying." – Nelson Mandela	Lead by example with humility and moral courage. Be transparent about mistakes, but continuously strive to improve.
Envisioning (Vision and Strategy)	"The best way to predict the future is to create it." – Peter Drucker	Articulate a clear and inspiring vision that motivates the team. Engage team members in the process of vision creation and align day-to-day actions with long-term goals.
	"A leader is a dealer in hope." – Napoleon Bonaparte	Keep the team inspired and focused on a hopeful and shared vision. Cultivate optimism even during uncertain times.
Endurance (Resilience and Adaptability)	"It does not matter how slowly you go as long as you do not stop." – Confucius	Stay focused on long-term objectives and maintain persistence through setbacks. Train the team in resilience techniques and encourage a growth mindset.
	"Success is not final; failure is not fatal: It is the courage to continue that counts." – Winston Churchill	Demonstrate resilience by staying calm under pressure and showing how failure can be an opportunity for learning and growth.
Excellence (Focus and Discipline)	"We are what we repeatedly do. Excellence, then, is not an act, but a habit." – Aristotle	Set high standards for yourself and your team, consistently striving for improvement. Encourage continual learning and reward excellence.
	"Do not wait for leaders; do it alone, person to person." – Mother Teresa	Encourage personal accountability for excellence. Foster a culture where every individual is motivated to achieve the highest standards independently.
Encouragement (Inspiring and Uniting Teams)	"You don't have to be a genius; you just have to be someone who inspires people." – Steve Jobs	Inspire and uplift your team through communication, support, and recognition. Celebrate achievements and make team members feel valued.
	"The function of leadership is to produce more leaders, not more followers." – Ralph Nader	Focus on empowering others by providing opportunities for leadership within the team. Develop mentorship and coaching initiatives that inspire others to lead.
Enablement (Providing Growth Opportunities)	"A good leader leads the people from within them." – Lao Tzu	Enable the team by providing opportunities for professional development, autonomy, and ownership over their work. Empower individuals to make decisions and take responsibility.
	"Leadership is unlocking people's potential to become better." – Bill Bradley	Provide mentorship and coaching to help individuals realize and maximize their potential. Offer regular learning and development opportunities to foster personal growth.
Effectiveness (Long-Term Impact)	"Leadership is not about being in charge. It's about taking care of those in your charge." – Simon Sinek	Focus on creating a sustainable, positive impact. Measure success not only by immediate results but by the long-term transformation your leadership brings.
	"We are what we repeatedly do. Excellence, then, is not an act, but a habit." – Aristotle	Drive continuous improvement across all areas of the organization. Establish systems that lead to ongoing success and consistently evaluate the long-term impact of decisions made.

Final Thoughts: Unlocking Your Leadership Potential

In the timeless wisdom of the **Upanishads**, leadership transcends the boundaries of mere skill or technique; it emerges as a profound spiritual journey. This journey calls on individuals to dive deeply into the essence of self-awareness, exploring the inner realms of their consciousness to unearth clarity, purpose, and strength. True leadership, as described in these ancient texts, is rooted in moral integrity—an unwavering commitment to what is right, fair, and just. It is not about wielding power for personal gain but about harnessing one's abilities in service to a higher, collective purpose.

The Upanishads envision a leader as someone who is in harmony with both themselves and the world around them. This harmony begins with an internal awakening, where self-awareness becomes the compass that guides every decision and action. The leader's journey is akin to a sculptor carefully carving a masterpiece, chipping away ego, selfishness, and doubt, to reveal a vision that uplifts and inspires others. Leadership, in this context, is not just about managing people or achieving targets; it is about becoming a light that guides others to discover their own potential and purpose.

The 7E Leadership Framework beautifully mirrors these ancient teachings, offering a modern lens through which these eternal principles can be practiced and understood. Each of the seven elements provides a stepping stone for leaders to transform not only themselves but also the teams and organizations they serve. Ethics becomes the foundation, envisioning gives direction, endurance fosters resilience, and excellence ensures continuous improvement. Encouragement and enablement empower teams, while effectiveness ensures that every action resonates with a lasting, positive impact.

By embracing these principles, leaders step into their role as custodians of collective well-being, living the Upanishadic ideal of *Vasudhaiva Kutumbakam*, the world as one family. This ideal teaches that no action is isolated, no success singular; every decision ripples outward, influencing the lives of many. A leader who embodies this philosophy becomes not just a figure of authority but a force for unity, compassion, and growth.

This transformative vision of leadership invites readers to see beyond conventional metrics of success. It inspires them to view leadership as a journey of connection—connecting with one's higher self, with the people they lead, and with the greater purpose that binds humanity together. It is in this interconnectedness, this sacred alignment of self and service, that the true essence of leadership is found. And it is through frameworks like the 7E that the wisdom of the Upanishads can be brought alive, guiding today's leaders to inspire, uplift, and unite in their pursuit of a better world.

As you reflect on the lessons shared in this book, remember that **mental agility** is not an inherent trait—it's a skill that can be nurtured and developed with intention and practice. The **7E Leadership Framework** provides a roadmap, but the true work lies in your commitment to adopting these principles daily.

Start by evaluating where you currently stand in each of the seven areas. Which aspects of your leadership require more focus? Where can you grow to become more adaptable, innovative, and resilient?

The world is changing faster than ever before. The challenges you face are unprecedented, but so are the opportunities to lead with purpose, drive, and vision. With the tools provided by the **7E Leadership Framework**, you have the power to rise above uncertainty and lead your team through even the most challenging times.

The journey to mastering mental agility begins today. Take the first step and lead with agility, resilience, and a commitment to excellence. Your leadership, shaped by the 7Es, will not only help you thrive in a volatile world but will inspire others to do the same.

Take the first step towards enhancing your mental agility. Evaluate your leadership approach using the 7Es and choose one area to focus on today. Tomorrow, your leadership will be more agile, more adaptable, and more impactful. Let's embark on this journey together—one step at a time.

|| In the storm of change, mental agility is your anchor ||

Notes

- "Long Walk to Freedom" by Nelson Mandela (Published by Macmillan)
- "The White Rose: Munich, 1942" by Inge Scholl (Published by University of Wisconsin Press)
- "Joan of Arc: A History" by Helen Castor (Published by HarperCollins)
- "Harriet Tubman: The Road to Freedom" by Catherine Clinton (Published by Little, Brown, and Company)
- "Corruption: Why It Happens and How to Stop It" by Robert I. Rotberg (Published by Princeton University Press)
- "The Tata Group: From Torchbearers to Trailblazers" by Harish B. Kumar (Published by HarperCollins India)
- "Mao: The Unknown Story" by Jung Chang and Jon Halliday (Published by Knopf)
- "Iacocca: An Autobiography" by Lee Iacocca (Published by Bantam)
- "Made in America: My Story" by Sam Walton (Published by Doubleday)

- “Hit Refresh” by Satya Nadella (Published by Harper Business)
- “Lee Iacocca: The Man Who Saved Ford” by Richard J. Tofel (Published by HarperCollins)
- “Direct from Dell: Strategies That Revolutionized an Industry” by Michael Dell (Published by HarperBusiness)
- “The Last Lion: Winston Spencer Churchill” by William Manchester (Published by Little, Brown, and Company)
- “Reinventing Organizations” by Frederic Laloux (Published by Nelson Parker)
- “Leading” by Sir Alex Ferguson (Published by Penguin Press)
- “Where You Are Is Not Who You Are” by Ursula Burns (Published by HarperCollins Leadership)
- “The Man Who Knew Infinity” by Robert Kanigel (Published by Scribner)
- “Churchill: A Life” by Martin Gilbert (Published by Holt Paperbacks)
- “Dare to Lead” by Brené Brown (Published by Random House)
- “Leadership Lessons from the Peacekeepers” by Various Authors (Published by Routledge)
- “The 5 AM Club” by Robin Sharma (Published by HarperCollins)
- “The Art of War” by Sun Tzu (Published by Cambridge University Press)
- “Good to Great: Why Some Companies Make the Leap... and Others Don’t” by Jim Collins (Published by HarperBusiness)
- “Neutron Jack: A Biography of Jack Welch” by Robert Slater (Published by HarperBusiness)
- “Thirteen Days: A Memoir of the Cuban Missile Crisis” by Robert F. Kennedy (Published by W. W. Norton & Company)
- “Influence: The Psychology of Persuasion” by Robert Cialdini (Published by Harper Business)

- "The Leadership Challenge" by James Kouzes and Barry Posner (Published by Wiley)
- "Crucial Conversations: Tools for Talking When Stakes Are High" by Kerry Patterson (Published by McGraw-Hill)
- "Leaders Eat Last: Why Some Teams Pull Together and Others Don't" by Simon Sinek (Published by Portfolio)
- "How to Win Friends and Influence People" by Dale Carnegie (Published by Simon & Schuster)
- "The Empathic Civilization" by Jeremy Rifkin (Published by TarcherPerigee)
- "American Icon: Alan Mulally and the Fight to Save Ford Motor Company" by Bryce G. Hoffman (Published by Crown Business)
- "The Transformational Leader" by John P. Kotter (Published by Free Press)
- "The Power of Habit" by Charles Duhigg (Published by Random House)
- "The Servant: A Simple Story About the True Essence of Leadership" by James C. Hunter (Published by Crown Business)
- "Leadership and Self-Deception: Getting Out of the Box" by The Arbinger Institute (Published by Berrett-Koehler Publishers)
- "Mindset: The New Psychology of Success" by Carol S. Dweck (Published by Ballantine Books)
- "The Lean Startup: How Today's Entrepreneurs Use Continuous Innovation to Create Radically Successful Businesses" by Eric Ries (Published by Crown Business)
- "Dare to Lead: Brave Work. Tough Conversations. Whole Hearts." by Brené Brown (Published by Random House)
- "Agile Leadership Toolkit: How to Create an Agile Business in a Digital Age" by Peter Koning (Published by CreateSpace Independent Publishing Platform)

- "Leadership Agility: Five Levels of Mastery for Anticipating and Initiating Change" by Bill Joiner and Stephen Josephs (Published by Jossey-Bass)
- "The Innovator's Dilemma: When New Technologies Cause Great Firms to Fail" by Clayton M. Christensen (Published by Harvard Business Review Press)
- "Radical Candor: Be a Kick-Ass Boss Without Losing Your Humanity" by Kim Scott (Published by St. Martin's Press)
- "The 5 Levels of Leadership: Proven Steps to Maximize Your Potential" by John C. Maxwell (Published by Center Street)
- "Resilient: How to Grow an Unshakable Core of Calm, Strength, and Happiness" by Rick Hanson (Published by Harmony Books)
- "Leaders Eat Last: Why Some Teams Pull Together and Others Don't" by Simon Sinek (Published by Portfolio)

www.ingramcontent.com/pod-product-compliance
Lightning Source LLC
LaVergne TN
LVHW091246150826
845673LV00006B/1333

* 9 7 9 8 8 9 6 7 3 6 2 2 6 *